Intellectual Property and Human Rights

CIER

Centre for Intellectual Property Law

IN ASSOCIATION WITH CIER – CENTRE FOR INTELLECTUAL PROPERTY LAW

Series editors: *Members of the staff of the Centre for Intellectual Property Law (CIER), Molengraaff Institute for Private Law, Utrecht University, The Netherlands*

The CIER series is dedicated to the publication of research outcomes stemming from the CIER.

Intellectual Property and Human Rights

A Paradox

Edited by
Willem Grosheide

Prof. Dr. F, Centre for Intellectual Property Law (CIER), Utrecht University, The Netherlands

Edward Elgar
Cheltenham, UK • Northampton, MA, USA

Published by
Edward Elgar Publishing Limited
The Lypiatts
15 Lansdown Road
Cheltenham
Glos GL50 2JA
UK

Edward Elgar Publishing, Inc.
William Pratt House
9 Dewey Court
Northampton
Massachusetts 01060
USA

A catalogue record for this book
is available from the British Library

Library of Congress Control Number: 2009933407

Mixed Sources
Product group from well-managed forests and other controlled sources
www.fsc.org Cert no. SA-COC-1565
© 1996 Forest Stewardship Council

ISBN 978 1 84844 447 8

Typeset by Cambrian Typesetters, Camberley, Surrey
Printed and bound by MPG Books Group, UK

Contents

Copyright Law and Patent Law: to its Enforcement – Differing Views

Contributors

Martin J. Adelman is Theodore and James Pedas Family Professor of Intellectual Property and Technology Law; Co-Director of the Intellectual Property Law Program; Co-Director of the Dean Dinwoodey Center for Intellectual Property Studies, George Washington University Law School.

Lucky Belder is Associate-Professor of Intellectual Property Law at the Centre for Intellectual Property Law (CIER), Molengraaff Institute for Private Law, Utrecht University.

Jan Brinkhof is Professor of Patent Law at the Centre for Intellectual Property Law (CIER), Molengraaff Institute for Private Law, Utrecht University and attorney at law with Brinkhof, Amsterdam.

Abbe E.L. Brown is Lecturer at the School of Law, University of Edinburgh and Associate AHRC Research Centre for Studies in Intellectual Property and Technology Law.

Madeleine de Cock Buning is Professor of Copyright and Media & Communications Law at the Centre for Intellectual Property Law (CIER), Molengraaff Institute for Private Law, Utrecht University and is appointed by the Crown to the board of the Supervisory Authority to the Media (CvdM).

Rochelle Cooper Dreyfuss is Pauline Newman Professor of Law and Director of the Engelberg Center on Innovation Law and Policy, New York University, New York, USA.

Cees Flinterman is Honorary Professor of Human Rights at Utrecht University and member of the United Nations Committee on the Elimination of Discrimination against Women (CEDAW).

Wendy J. Gordon is the Philip S. Beck Professor of Law at the Boston University School of Law in the USA.

Willem Grosheide is Professor of Intellectual Property Law at the Centre for Intellectual Property Law (CIER), Molengraaff Institute for Private Law, Utrecht University and attorney at law with Van Doorne, Amsterdam.

Jerzy Koopman is a PhD-student at the Centre for Intellectual Property Law (CIER), Molengraaff Institute for Private Law, Utrecht University.

Duncan Matthews is a member of the Centre for Commercial Law Studies, Queen Mary University of London. He has held academic positions as a lecturer in law at the University of Warwick and as a research fellow at the ESRC Centre for the Study of Globalisation and Regionalisation, also at the University of Warwick.

Charles R. McManis is Thomas and Karole Green Professor of Law, Director of the Intellectual Property and Technology Law Program and Co-Director of the Center for Law, Innovation & Economic Growth at Washington University, St. Louis, USA.

Joost Smiers is Professor (em.) of Political Science of the Arts, Research Fellow in the Research Group Arts & Economics at the Utrecht School of the Arts, the Netherlands, and formerly visiting professor at the Department of World Arts and Cultures, UCLA, Los Angeles.

Geertrui Van Overwalle is Professor of IP Law at the University of Tilburg in the Netherlands and at the Universiteit Leuven, the Universiteit Brussel and the Université Liège, in Belgium.

Charlotte Waelde is Professor at the School of Law, University of Edinburgh and Co-Director AHRC Research Centre for Studies in Intellectual Property and Technology Law.

Preface

This volume is the first in what from now onwards will be the CIER series, containing some of the results emanating from research carried out by researchers belonging to the Centre for Intellectual Property Law, Molengraaff Institute for Private Law, Utrecht University or working regularly or incidentally in co-operation with the CIER in the field of intellectual property law and related law.

This present collection of chapters on the relation between intellectual property law and human rights law presents the outcome of a conference held in 2006 to celebrate the 20th anniversary of the centre.

Willem Grosheide
The Editor

PART I

Setting the stage: the law and its trends

1. General introduction

Willem Grosheide*

1. INTELLECTUAL PROPERTY RIGHTS AND HUMAN RIGHTS: RELATED ORIGIN AND DEVELOPMENT[1]

It may be said that intellectual property law and human rights law share a related origin. Both stem from Western European societal developments starting in the nineteenth, if not already in the eighteenth century.[2] The indicated societal developments were of three kinds. The first was the rapid industrialization and economic growth that affected countries unevenly and that was underpinned to a large extent by scientific, technological and cultural innovations. The second was a growing divide between the countries affected by

* Willem Grosheide is Professor of Intellectual Property Law at the Centre for Intellectual Property Law (CIER), Molengraaff Institute for Private Law, Utrecht University and attorney at law with Van Doorne, Amsterdam.

1 In what follows I use *intellectual property law* as a generic term referring to the legal system with regard to intellectual property rights, being rights with regard to the commercial and non-commercial use of information.

Until far into the twentieth century it was customary to refer in this respect to industrial and intellectual property rights. *Industrial* was used to cover trade-related areas like patent law, designs law and trademark law; *intellectual* was used to refer to culture-related copyrights. Particularly since the conclusion of the WIPO Treaty in 1967 it is conventional to use the term *intellectual property* to refer to both industrial and intellectual property rights. Note that this terminology is broader than the one used in Article 1(2) TRIPS A. Taking into account that *information* is a rather diffuse term, having different meanings depending on the relevant context, it is used here as a generic term for the subject-matter of intellectual property rights. Comp. ITU, World Summit on the Information Society, Geneva 2003-Tunis 2005, Document WSIS-03/Geneva/DOC/5-E 12 December 2003 in combination with ITU, Declaration of Principles, Document WSIS-03/Geneva/DOC/4-E 12 December 2003. Comp. Drahos (1999), p. 1.

2 See Grosheide (1986) and Ishay (2004), pp. 8; 107–16; Sellars (2002), pp. vii–ix. To some both human rights and the public interest were already used to justify early intellectual property law systems; see UN, Committee on Economic, Social and Cultural Rights, Protection of Intellectual Property Under the TRIPS Agreement, Doc. 29/11/2000, E/C.12/2000/18; idem, Human Rights and Intellectual Property, Doc. E/C. 12/2001/15.

these trends, and those that were left outside these developments. The third was a sustained expansion of international commerce that was promoted by economically dominant countries.[3]

That which indeed may be called modern intellectual property law was shaped not earlier than the second half of the nineteenth century is illustrated and evidenced by the Paris Convention (PC) of 1883 on industrial property law and the Berne Convention (BC) of 1886 on copyright law.[4] It is equally true that the second half of that age saw the breakthrough of various forms of social emancipation – general support for self-determination without any distinction as to race or sex, as well as the broad promotion of social, economic and political rights for everyone – legally speaking laying the fundamentals of modern human rights law.[5]

---

[3] Comp. Dutfield and Suthersanen (2008), p. 6. In this respect it is noteworthy that the expansion of trade relates not only to commerce in ipr-protected products and services but also (and today even increasingly so) to commerce in the iprs themselves (either by transfer or by licence).

[4] See Grosheide (1986); Firth (1997); Dutfield and Suthersanen (2008). It is of note that at this early moment in the history of modern intellectual property law for different reasons not all leading industrial countries of the time immediately joined either union: for example, the USA did not join the PC until 1887, Germany not until 1903; the Netherlands did not join the BC until 1912, the USA not until 1989.

[5] The indicated societal developments were driven by a combination of the dominant ideological and political considerations at that time. Most of the outcomes can be largely ascribed to the socialist movements of the time. See Ishay (2004), p. 155:

> If socialists were responsible for the first emulation of a supranational authority to resist either the aggressive politics of states or their colonial enterprises, their position also represented the first historical assertion that all humans, regardless of wealth, gender, race, or age, were entitled to both political and social rights. In this respect, they broadened the narrow definition of universalism they inherited from the Enlightenment, articulating a broad commitment to enhance simultaneously, rather than selectively, the rights of slaves, children, women, homosexuals, and Jews.

See also (with a focus on copyright law) Grosheide (2008), pp. 410–11:

> (…) two interconnected phenomena would interfere with this steady process in the last quarter of the 20th Century:
> 1. the changed relationship between the industrialized and the non industrialized world,
> 2. the changes in *the hidden* code of the industrialized world, in particular the evolution from the industrial era into the information era. (…) The following new societal and paradigmatic components of the hidden code will prove to be determinative: the development of technology, the expansion of the possibilities to communicate, the creation of the welfare state and the related increase in cultural participation, the dominance of ideological utilitarianism, short-term compromise politics and an instrumental approach to the law.

In addition, not only do intellectual property law and human rights law have a related origin, but the same can be said of their development, particularly during the twentieth century, as can be illustrated by the legislative history of the Universal Declaration of Human Rights (UDHR) of 1948 and that of the TRIPS Agreement of 1994 (TRIPS A).[6] All this despite the fact that, dogmatically speaking, intellectual property law, by addressing primarily private parties, is of a private law character, while human rights law, addressing primarily states, is of a public law nature.

It appears, however, that in spite of the fact that the two domains of law are both rooted in the indicated societal developments, from their beginning and over the years they have evolved largely separately, from being not interrelated at all into a rather problematic relationship.[7]

Two opposing views have been proposed in this respect. The first view maintains that intellectual property law and human rights law are in fundamental conflict since the legal protection of individually held intellectual property rights is considered to be incompatible with communally-based human rights. In that, so to speak, hierarchical perspective, human rights are seen as legal instruments to limit and restrict the execution and enforcement of intellectual property rights. In other words: human rights are perceived as a countervailing force against intellectual property rights. Strategically, this view is often used during international trade negotiations in order to weaken the position of the developed world. In order to overcome the consequential tension between the two, it is suggested in this first view that human rights should always prevail over intellectual property rights.

The second view holds that intellectual property law and human rights law are compatible since they pursue the same aim. In this, so to speak, equal footing view, intellectual property rights are in fact embodied in the human rights system. In other words: human rights law is seen as the fundament of intellectual property law. This view requires, on the one hand, a definition to be given to the appropriate scope of protection for private monopoly power to create and invent and, on the other, at the same time ensuring adequate access to intellectual products for the public at large. However, at the same time it follows from the compatibility of intellectual property rights and human rights that a balance should be struck between protection and access. How to do that is a real challenge.[8]

---

6 See generally on the UDHR Sellars (2002) and Ishay (2004); on the TRIPS A see Blakeney (1997), Gervais (2003) and Correa (2007).

7 See Helfer (2003), questioning whether the relationship between both domains reflects a *conflict or a coexistence*. Comp. Cullet (2007).

8 Comp. Helfer (2003), pp. 48–9. A different approach to these conflicting views is taken by Yu (2007b) (instead of inquiring whether human rights and intellectual

As will be discussed in the following sections of this general introduction, taking account of the indicated situation in the light of these two opposing views, any attempt at trying to reconcile the one view with the other raises many questions. In trying to come to terms with these questions, I will follow the approach that is generally taken in the various contributions bundled in this book, focusing on those questions that consider the status of intellectual property rights as human rights.[9] It suffices in these introductory remarks to mention only some of these questions. Are human rights universal or culturally defined? Do any legal consequences follow from the fact that dogmatically (at least from a civil law perspective) intellectual property law belongs to the domain of private law and human rights law to that of public law? Are all intellectual property rights, seen from a human rights perspective, of the same ranking? Construing intellectual property rights as human rights implies construing them as absolute rights – is executing any of these absolute rights acceptable even if it is at the expense of society at large? Can human rights such as intellectual property rights be held by corporate identities? How should a proper balance be found between the protection of intellectual property rights and access to intellectual products protected by them? Is the debate about the human rights qualification of intellectual property rights equally relevant for the developed world and the developing world?

---

property rights conflict or coexist with each other, it is important to identify the human rights attributes of intellectual property rights and to distinguish them from the non-human rights aspects of intellectual property protection) to which I will return in Section 3.

[9] As a consequence I will not principally discuss the tension or even the conflict that may arise between human rights and intellectual property rights, offering such interesting questions as whether human rights can block the execution of intellectual property rights or whether it is possible to legally force an owner of an intellectual property right to actually execute its right. See for an example of the first situation the Dutch *Scientology* case; Court of Appeal of The Hague, Case No. 99/1040, Chamber M C – 5, Mediaforum 200310, pp. 337–42 (no copyright infringement by the defendant who published copyright-protected documents without the permission and against the will of the copyright owner based upon the human right of freedom of speech, that is, the right to be informed), and for an example of the second situation the British *Ashdown v Telegraph Group Ltd* case; [2001] EWCA Civ 1142, [2001] 3 WLR 1368 (human rights arguments served the purpose of making it possible for a third party to use works that were kept secret by the copyright owner and as a consequence were not already lawfully disseminated to the public), see Karnell (2004) and Yu (2007a). Another, again copyright-related, example can be found in the application of human rights law as a weapon against globalisation, that is, the Americanization of cultures, see Porsdam (2007). See for an alternative perspective Grosheide (2008) (copyright law is not the appropriate legal instrument to promote cultural diversity and to protect cultural identity). For a view from the perspective of patent law see Prove/Kothari (2000) (the TRIPS A has raised serious human rights concerns such as the restriction of access to patented pharmaceuticals for citizens of developing countries).

In order to come to terms with these and other related questions, this general introduction will proceed in the following order. Section 2, offering a brief account of the status of intellectual property rights in the actual international regulation of human rights law as well as of the status of human rights in the actual international regulation of intellectual property law, will be followed by Section 3 in which these international regulations will be analysed in the light of their appreciation and estimation in the legal literature. It follows from this order of things that there will occasionally be some overlap between Sections 2 and 3. The general introduction ends with some concluding observations in Section 4. As a whole, this general introduction may be read as a guide to the different views exposed in the contributions that have been collected in this book.

2. THE RELATIONSHIP BETWEEN INTELLECTUAL PROPERTY RIGHTS AND HUMAN RIGHTS IN THE ACTUAL INTERNATIONAL REGULATIONS

Taking account of the relationship between intellectual property rights and human rights can best be done by placing intellectual property law in the context of its recent history. Following the generally accepted main view, the protection of modern intellectual property rights at an international level can roughly be divided into three periods: the territorial period, the international period, and the global period.[10]

The territorial period is dominated by national law, that is, the principle of territoriality: intellectual property rights do not extend beyond the national territory where the rights have been granted in the first place. This period runs from the end of the eighteenth century and during the greater half of the nineteenth century. It is marked by bilateralism, that is, the conclusion of bilateral agreements between national states. This bilateralism was important in as far as it contributed to the recognition that an international framework for the regulation of intellectual property law had to be developed.[11] The international period is characterised by a growing interest in cooperation between national states in the domain of intellectual property law. This period in fact saw the introduction of the required international framework with the establishment of

---

10 Comp. Drahos (1999), pp. 1–13.

11 See Sherman and Bentley (1999); Bentley and Sherman (2004). What is here called *bilateralism* is sometimes called *unilateralism* referring to the fact that it is the legal regime of a particular nation state which counts. See also Okediji (2003–2004), suggesting that the actual need for intellectual property law policies may lead to a swing of the pendulum back to bilateralism.

the PC and the BC. The global period that is still running today can be marked by the constant efforts made to transform the existing international framework for intellectual property law into a real form of harmonised interstate regulation that would fit the growing international commercial interdependency of the developed world.[12] Sticking to the territoriality principle and maintaining the possibility of binding their signatories led to all sorts of reservations by the member states, so that the international harmonization of intellectual property law under the PC and the BC did not progress very quickly. In that last perspective it is of note that the corridor from the international period to the global period saw, next to various revisions of the PC and the BC, a proliferation of international intellectual property regimes leading to harmonisation in specific areas.[13]

What becomes clear from this brief overview of its historical development is that modern intellectual property law was introduced primarily out of economic considerations. Indeed, intellectual property law was mostly made for doing business. By its very nature it is mainly policy-driven, time and place-bound trade law. This is not contradicted by the fact that also cultural

---

12 It is of note that, as rightly stated by Dutfield and Suthersanen (2008), p. 22,

> (t)he histories of these agreements make evident that despite the fact that in each case their bringing into being had much to do with the activism of IP owners and legal practitioners, neither their direct nor underlying purposes were the same. The Paris Convention was about helping inventors and trade mark and industrial design owners to get wider geographical protection, but cannot really be seen as a means to bind the catcher-uppers to standards of the leaders with respect to substantive IP law.(…) Much the same can be said to apply to the Berne Convention, which again was primarily a response to the strong commercial interests of copyright owners in securing protection in foreign markets. However, over time the Berne Convention came to differ markedly from the Paris Convention in that it increasingly dealt with more substantial rules (…). A second reason why the Berne Convention represents a much more cohesive international architecture of rules is that copyright interests are very ably presented not only by the publishing and entertainment industries, but also by collecting societies.

13 Examples of these regimes are the Madrid Agreement 1891 (trademarks), the Madrid Agreement 1891 (indication of source), the Hague Agreement 1925 (designs), the Rome Convention 1961 (performing rights), the International Convention for the Protection of New Varieties of Plants 1961, 1991 (plant varieties), the Patent Co-operation Treaty 1970 (patents), the Integrated Circuits Treaty 1989 (semiconductor chips). These changes were accompanied by the spread of new forms of international organization: the United International Bureaux for the Protection of Intellectual Property (BIRPI) 1893, the World Intellectual Property Organization (WIPO) 1967, becoming a specialized agency of the UN in 1974. See Bogsch (1992), pp. 7–8.

objectives have always been part of intellectual property law.[14] This equally holds true for industrial property law and copyright law, bearing in mind that since their encoding in the BC in 1928, copyright law also, and next to economic rights, grants so-called moral rights to right owners which underlines the cultural objectives of the latter. As will be seen later, this moral rights aspect plays an important role in the discussion on the relationship between copyright law and human rights law.

It seems that recently the primary economic character of intellectual property law has been underlined by the TRIPS A. This is at present the most prominent international legal instrument aiming, as far as possible, to overcome the still existing lack of substantive law harmonization in the global period, set in the key of law enforcement. For that reason, somewhat more attention will now be paid to the TRIPS A.[15]

---

14 See in this respect the WIPO Copyright Treaty (WCT 1996), in its Preamble recognizing 'the need to introduce new international rules and clarify the interpretation of certain existing rules in order to provide adequate solutions to the questions raised by new economic, social, cultural and technological developments'. Comp. Dinwoody in Gervais (2007), pp. 113–14, formulating his conclusion as follows:

> The international intellectual property system has always been driven, to some extent, by trade concerns. However, the recent incorporation of intellectual property within the apparatus of the World Trade Organization, along with other social and economic developments, has caused the rapid evolution of the international intellectual property system. The contours of that system are now quite different than when the system first took shape in the late nineteenth century. Yet, appreciating the important role of trade institutions in changing the intellectual property system should not distract commentators from other developments that are now effecting the creation of international intellectual property norms equally. In particular, private ordering activities have the capacity to regulate extensive international activity, and to do so without full public scrutiny.

See also Drahos (1999).

15 See generally on TRIPS A, Blakeney (1997), Gervais (2003), Correa (2007). The TRIPS A of 1994 entered into force in 1995.The TRIPS A has been characterized by its designers as a prerequisite for the worldwide stimulation of innovation and creativity, and as a consequence thereof as an essential legal instrument for human progress. I share the view of Dutfield and Suthersanen (2008), p. 7, that '(i)t is unlikely that history or economic analyses can prove beyond doubt that having an IP system is better than not having one, or vice versa'. See already in the same sense Plant (1934). However, as observed by Gervais, p. 47, the TRIPS A being 'the strongest normative vector in setting intellectual property policy (…) and it (*being*) unlikely that TRIPS norms will be diluted in the Doha Round, it would seem to be pragmatically justified to take TRIPS as a given quantity in the policy equation'. I do not discuss in this context the latest development (at the end of 2007) in this respect: the Anti-Counterfeiting Trade Agreement (ACTA), a multilateral intellectual property trade

What, then, really induced the developed world to set off on the making of the TRIPS A? In order to answer this question, it is of note that from the 1960s onwards gradually the awareness spread in the developed world that intellectual property rights regimes had to cope with at least two major changes, one of a technological, the other of an economic nature. All this whereas, as already indicated, and seen from an international perspective, the global period became dominated by growing interstate commercial interdependency. This state of affairs instigated the desire to come to a more elaborate international legal instrument with regard to the granting and the protection of intellectual property law.

The technological change mainly followed from the progressive development of computer technology, offering new products bearing their properties on their face and simultaneously available everywhere and for everyone. In reaction to this change, already from the 1980s onwards in the developed world concerns were voiced by policymakers and academics that producers in competing countries, alongside consumers, could copy the new technologies too easily because of their vulnerable nature. Therefore, those concerned asked for a new approach towards the extensive free-riding which, following from the then liberal view of foreign trade, was tolerated in the international period, but which was felt to be increasingly counterproductive. With regard to the legal consequences, this led to a governmental and scholarly appraisal of these new technological products as being possibly protectable subject-matter and, related to that, the creation of new hybrid semi-intellectual property rights like that in software and chips.

The economic change can be labelled as a swing towards neo-liberalism, characterized by privatization, deregulation and the elimination of the concept of public good, sublimized in the supremacy of the market rule.[16] Interestingly, however, it appeared that this swing towards neo-liberalism

---

agreement aiming at creating new global standards for intellectual property rights enforcement, proposed and spearheaded by the US, the EU, Japan and Switzerland. Neither do I discuss in this contribution that the TRIPS A, as rightly stated by Drahos (1999), pp. 12–13, '(…) is but one part of a much deeper phenomenon in which intellectual property is playing a crucial role – the regulatory globalization of the norms of contract and property' and that 'intellectual property norms are also becoming a part of the emerging *lex cybertoria* – the trade norms of cyberspace'. Idem, I consider it beyond the focus of this contribution to go into the actual relationship between the two main institutional players in the international arena of intellectual property law: the World Intellectual Property Organisation (WIPO) and the World Trade Organisation (WTO). Their relationship has basically been established by their Cooperation Agreement which came into force on 1 January 1996. The relationship between WIPO and WTO has recently been at issue during the WIPO-WTO Colloquium for Teachers on Intellectual Property 30 June–10 July 2008; see the WIPO and WTO websites.

16 See Maskus and Reichman (2004).

fitted very well into the indicated turn towards the granting of new intellectual property rights, as advocated by policymakers and academics. Obviously, the granting of new intellectual property rights leads to more protection and in that sense it is the opposite of providing for more access. Besides, such a development may have – and in this case did have – as a side-effect an increase in claims for stronger protection of intellectual property rights over the whole range. So the situation that resulted therefrom may be called rather ambiguous. For, on the one hand, neo-liberalism promotes free access, but, on the other, it creates new intellectual property rights favouring overall protectionism.[17] And, indeed, what happened was the gradual revision of trade law to strengthen the protection of owners of intellectual property rights, not only in relation to the new subject-matter but over the whole range.[18] With respect to international trade it now became a matter of urgency to break away from the old unilateralism, guided by national policies and practices, towards a real multilateralism as the dominant method of dealing with matters of intellectual property law. All this was also lobbied by a group of big US-based internationally operating companies and supported by their counterparts in the EU, Japan and Switzerland.[19]

The TRIPS A which finally resulted from all of this is undoubtedly primarily instigated by economic reasons. This state of affairs is also reflected in the early commentaries from both the developed and the developing world. Both sides emphasized that negotiating the treaty required concessions to be made and that, as a consequence, seen from their respective perspectives, no optimal result was attained. But their evaluation of that result was quite opposite. The developed world being satisfied overall, the developing world generally feeling economically trapped by the developed world. It is interesting, however,

---

[17] Comp. Maskus and Reichman (2004), p. 2: 'We find it ironic that, as tariffs, quotas, and often formal barriers to trade are dismantled, there has been a strong push to re-regulate World technology markets.'

[18] See Braithwaite and Drahos (2000); Sell (2003); Merlin-Bennett (2004); Hveem (2007).

[19] It suffices here to observe that in the words of Musungu and Dutfield (2003), p. 10:

> (t)he permissive nature of the rules under the WIPO regime and the lack of an enforcement mechanism is what led key industry players in the USA, in particular, to conclude that the organisation had failed to secure for them the appropriate levels of intellectual property protection around the world and to argue for a shift to the General Agreement on Tariffs and Trade (GATT). In the 1980s, the strategy of the USA and its major industries was therefore aimed at shifting the intellectual property regulatory focus from WIPO to the GATT which would permit the use of trade remedies to enforce intellectual property standards.

that some ten years later in retrospect things appear to be evaluated somewhat differently.[20]

Of course, this firstly follows from the fact that legal instruments, once introduced, tend – so to say – to develop a life of their own. So, it may well be that provisions that at first seemed to have a clear meaning need interpretation with the course of time. A good example in this context is the interpretation of Articles 7 and 8 TRIPS A that was requested by the TRIPS Council in 2001 in order to define the relationship between intellectual property rights and access to essential medicines.[21] A later evaluation that differs from a previous one may, secondly, very well follow from unexpected effects which a legal instrument appears to have. A good example here seems to be the reported qualification of the TRIPS A as a failure by Bruce Lehman, who headed the United States Patent and Trademark Office (USPTO) during its negotiations and who initially called its outcome a victory. A failure, he calls it in retrospect, because in his view the treaty opened US markets to overseas manufactured goods and destroyed the US manufacturing industry.[22] In the meantime similar dissatisfaction concerning the TRIPS A had already led the developed world to impose the so-called bilateral TRIPS-plus agreements on the developing world.[23]

But not only from the perspective of the developed world have second thoughts been formulated with regard to the success of the TRIPS A, the same is somewhat surprisingly true from the perspective of the developing world. For it appears that a feeling of being economically trapped (and not taking account of the occasionally imposed TRIPS-plus standards) is countered by the often proved unexpected beneficial outcomes of the policy flexibilities that have been introduced in the TRIPS A with an eye on the interests of the developing world.[24]

---

[20] See the reports on the TRIPS Agreement ten years on, International Conference on the 10th Anniversary of the WTO TRIPS Agreement, Brussels, 24 June 2004 at which Lamy (2004) observed that most panellists agreed that, by and large, the balance struck in TRIPS was correct. See for a more nuanced view Musungu and Dutfield (2003) and Maskus and Reichman (2004).

[21] See Gathii (2002).

[22] See the reports on the conference 'The Politics and Ideology of Intellectual Property', 20–21 March 2006, Brussels, http://.www.tacd.org/events/intellectual property/media-coverage.htm and http://www.ip-watch.org/weblog/index.php? p=249.

[23] Deplored by most panellists at the anniversary conference mentioned in footnote 20, considering it unfair that developing countries were sometimes put under pressure to adopt substantive TRIPS-plus standards that are not adapted to their level of development. At present the indicated discontent in the developed world seems to be the driving force behind the proposed Anti Couterfeiting Trade Agreement, http://jamie.com/2008/06/02/the-proposed-anti-counterfeiting-trade-agreement-acta-global-policy-implications/.

[24] See Kamperman Sanders in Gervais (2007), p. 170, stating that:

It is here that a shift to the human rights perspective of intellectual property law becomes apparent. Interestingly, although the reported dissatisfaction with the TRIPS A is still about economics and fits well in Lamy's characterization of the TRIPS A as a good economics framework, this feeling appears to coincide with recent voices that can be heard to the effect that economics are no longer the only or even the primary driving force behind intellectual property law.[25] Of particular interest in this respect is the question whether the qualification of intellectual property rights as private rights, that is as a subcategory of property rights generally, means anything at all. A related but different question is what other relation may exist between the two categories of rights. In answering both questions, it seems appropriate to investigate whether any of the existing international legal instruments on intellectual property law as well as human rights law sheds any light on them. In Section 3 I will come back to these questions in order to see what legal doctrine has to offer in this respect.

To start with the PC and the BC: these conventions are silent on human rights. This is understandable in retrospect, since at the time of the establishment of these treaties human rights were not an issue. However, later adaptations do not refer to them either, which raises the question whether those concerned with keeping the international intellectual property law system up to date ever thought of relying on human rights law for that aim.[26] For a positive answer to that question reference can be made to at least one document: the Solemn Declaration of the BC member states in 1986 asserting that copyright

> (t)he flexibilities of the TRIPS Agreement can be used to allow WTO members to develop at their own pace. (…) This is supported by the economic progress in developing countries like India, China and Brazil. Effective enforcement and the establishment of minimum IPR standards form the conditions for including developing economies in the global marketplace.

Comp. also Lamy (2004), stating that 'the essential conditions to get the balance right lies in the possibility to exploit the key flexibilities in TRIPS' and that 'flexibility should not be taken away through the backdoor' (of TRIPS-plus agreements). See also Hveem (2007).

25 Lamy (2004). This coincidence is reflected in the UN High Commissioner for Human Rights and the World Health Organisation's (WHO) strong objections to the TRIPS-plus agreements on human rights grounds. See the Report of the High Commissioner, The Impact of the Agreement on Trade-Related Aspects of Intellectual Property Rights on Human Rights, ESCOR Sub. Comm. on the Promotion and Protection of Human rights, 52nd Sess., Provisional Agenda Item 4 at 5, UN Doc. E/CN.4/Sub.2/2001/13 (2001); WHO, WHO Policy Perspectives on Medicines, WHO No. 3, Mar. 2001 at 5.

26 With the exception of moral rights in copyright law, I did not find much on the reason why later adaptations do not refer to human rights in the literature. For the moment I will leave it at that and the observation that the reason why requires further study. See Ricketson and Ginsburg (2006).

is based on human rights and justice and that authors, as creators of beauty, entertainment and learning, deserve that their rights in their creations be recognized and effectively protected both in their country and in all other countries of the world.[27] But a solemn declaration was all that the BC community committed itself to. In fact, an investigation over the years into human rights references in the catalogue of international intellectual property law instruments leads directly to the TRIPS A. It appears, then, that also in this treaty no provision *expressis verbis* refers to either any human rights law instrument or to any human right in particular. But references to human rights (law) could be said to be found in the Preamble, if one is prepared to accept intellectual property rights being a (sub-)category of property rights generally. If so, then in the Preamble the 'whereas' that recognizes intellectual property rights as private rights may be mentioned here. From that it would follow that intellectual property rights fall under the protection of property as laid down in Article 27 Universal Declaration of Human Rights and Article 1 First Protocol to the European Convention for the Protection of Human Rights and Fundamental Freedoms 1952 (First Protocol ECHR). But even these references to the right to property provide only for a small human rights basis, since no other key international human rights instruments refer to the right to property.[28]

---

[27] Comp. Peifer (2008), p. 685:

> The natural law approach in our time has been elaborated to become a human rights approach. We are no longer discussing whether national law has to accept authors' rights as something pre-existing to the State. States are moving toward a system of human rights whose protection is granted on the basis of international understanding.

Of course, it may be argued that the inclusion of moral rights in Article 6bis BC in 1928 is an indication of human rights thinking in the BC community. Comp. Rigamonti (2006); Grosheide (2009).

[28] Comp. van der Vyver (1996), p. 468:

> The absence of any reference to the right of (private) ownership in the key human rights covenants sponsored by the United Nations Organization and which are taken to constitute the bill of rights of the international community of states – i.e. the International Covenant on Economic, Social and Cultural Rights, 1966 – except for a provision in the later document prohibiting discrimination against children on the basis of property or birth, is therefore particularly conspicuous.

See also Singh (2000), reporting on the unanimously adopted resolution on intellectual property rights and human rights by the UN Sub-Commission for the Protection and Promotion of Human Rights E/CN.4/Sub.2/2000/L.20 (TRIPS regime at odds with human rights law).

So, instead of referring to the right to property, sometimes another reference is made: that to Article 15.1 (a) (b) (c) International Covenant on Economic, Social and Cultural Rights (ICESCR) establishing everyone's right to take part in cultural life (a), to enjoy the benefits of scientific progress and its applications (b) and to the protection of the moral and material interests resulting from any scientific, literary or artistic production of which he is the author (c) as a human right. This provision was indeed presented in 2000 as a basis for a human rights qualification of intellectual property rights by the UN Committee on Economic, Social and Cultural Rights (CESCR).[29] It is well understood that this provision should be read in the light of the drafting history of Article 27 UHDR which, according to some, already reflects a human rights approach to intellectual property rights.[30] However, following Chapman the drafting history underscores four points: the relatively weak claims of intellectual property as a human right, the interrelationship of the three provisions of Article 15, human rights considerations imposed conditions on how to protect intellectual property rights, and the lack of a conceptual foundation for the interpretation of intellectual property rights as human rights.[31]

Studying Article 15 ICESCR more in particular the following can be said. The rights granted under a and b were said to converge with the objectives which are contained in the WTO Agreement to which the TRIPS A is an annex, as well as with Article 7 TRIPS A which put emphasis on the public interest rationale of intellectual property law protection.[32] As to Article 15.1(c) the CESCR argued that the TRIPS Agreement, including the pre-existing IP conventions incorporated into it, also seeks to give effect at the multilateral level to Article 15.1(c) of the ICESCR. The approach taken in 2000 started a long process of reflection within the CESCR for the time being ending in 2005

---

29 See in this respect the Report of the High Commissioner, The Impact of the Agreement on Trade-Related Aspects of Intellectual Property Rights on Human Rights, E/CN.4Sub.2/2001?13 dated 27 June 2001.

30 See, among others, Morsink (1999), Chapman (2001), also pointing to Article 13 American Declaration on the Rights and Duties of Man 1948 which refers to the protection of moral and material interests as regards inventions as well as literary, scientific or artistic works.

31 Chapman (2001), p. 13.

32 This is done in the document mentioned in footnote 2. Article 7 TRIPS A states that:

> the protection and enforcement of intellectual property rights should contribute to the promotion of technological innovation and to the transfer and dissemination of technology, to the mutual advantage of producers and users of technological knowledge and in a manner conducive to social and economic welfare, and to a balance of rights and obligations.

with its General Comment No. 17 on Article 15.1(c) in particular.[33] Although the General Comment does not directly refer to TRIPS A, it is here worth quoting its paragraph I, Introduction and Basic Premises sub. 2 in the light of the statements of the 2000 document: 'In contrast to human rights, intellectual property rights are generally of a temporary nature, and can be revoked, licensed or assigned to someone else. While under most intellectual property systems, intellectual property rights, often with the exception of moral rights, may be allocated, limited in time and scope, traded, amended and even forfeited, human rights are timeless expressions of fundamental entitlements of the human person. Whereas the human right to benefit from the protection of the moral and material interests resulting from one's scientific, literary and artistic productions safeguards the personal link between authors and their creations and between peoples, communities, or other groups and their collective cultural heritage, as well as their basic material interests which are necessary to enable authors to enjoy an adequate standard of living, intellectual property regimes primarily protect business and corporate interests and investments. Moreover, the scope of protection of the moral and material interests of the author provided for by Article 15.1(c), does not necessarily coincide with what is referred to as intellectual property rights under national legislation or international agreements.' In addition, sub. 3 opens as follows: 'It is therefore important not to equate intellectual property rights with the human right recognized in Article 15.1(c)'. Previously in sub. b it was stated that their human rights character distinguishes the entitlements of Article 15.1(c) and other human rights from most legal entitlements recognized in intellectual property systems.[34]

Against this background it is somewhat confusing that the General Comment's terminology, although clearly in line with the terminology of Article 15, closely relates to what may be called ipr-speak. This terminology is for instance used in paragraph 9, defining what is to be considered as any scientific, literary or artistic production within the meaning of Article 15.1(c). But when it comes to interpreting the meaning of the phrase 'benefit from the

[33] CESCR, General Comment No. 17 (2005) – The right of everyone to benefit from the protection of the moral and material interests resulting from any scientific, literary or artistic production of which he or she is the author (article 15, paragraph 1 (c)), of the Covenant, Doc. E/C.12/GC/17, 12 January 2006, prepared by rapporteur Eibe Riedel in his Draft General Comment No. 18 (2004). The General Comment was issued with a view to assisting member states' implementation of the Covenant and the fulfilment of their reporting obligations.

[34] See note 32, above. See on the Committee's reasoning Anderson and Wager (2006); Policy Brief 3 (2006). It is beyond the focus of this contribution to go into the details of the clarifications by the CESCR with respect to implementing the ICESCR. See also Cullet (2007).

protection' in this respect, paragraph 10 holds that the protection under Article 15.1(c) need not necessarily reflect the level and means of protection found in present copyright, patent or other intellectual property regimes (...).[35] Further, it is of note that whereas the CESCR qualified intellectual property rights as human rights in 2000, it did not take into account the fact that the TRIPS A recognizes that intellectual property rights are private rights, and that the General Comment takes their private law character as a basic premise. Then it is worth considering that the General Comment consequently stresses in many instances the obligation of member states to implement Article 15.1(c) in their domestic laws. This makes clear that the ICESCR is not directly applicable in national law. It follows from the foregoing that in the CESCR's estimation of the relationship between intellectual property law and human rights law as articulated in the ICESCR, particularly its Article 15.1, this relationship is of a public law character and has a twofold aim. First, it is up to the member states to implement the ICESCR in their domestic laws. Secondly, it is up to the owners of intellectual property rights to exercise these rights in conformity with these implemented human rights. The reported finding comes as a surprise in the light of the 2000 resolution adopted by the United Nations Sub-Commission on the Promotion and Protection of Human Rights, noting that actual or potential conflicts exist between the implementation of the TRIPS A and the realization of economic, social and cultural rights. The resolution affirms that the right to the protection of the moral and material interests resulting from any scientific, literary or artistic production of which one is the author is a human right, subject to limitations in the public interest. Reminding all governments of the primacy of human rights obligations over economic policies, it declares that since the implementation of the TRIPS Agreement does not adequately reflect the fundamental nature and indivisibility of all human rights, including the right of everyone to enjoy the benefits of scientific progress and its applications, the right to health, the right to food, and the right to self-determination, there are apparent conflicts between the intellectual property rights regime embodied in the TRIPS Agreement, on the one hand, and international human rights law, on the other. [36]

---

[35] This confusing terminology may well be the reason why Helfer (2004) in my mind seems to acknowledge intellectual property rights as human rights despite the clear rejection of that categorisation in paragraph 3 of the General Comment. See in this respect also Section 3. Comp. idem Beiter (2008), pp. 717–20.

[36] Sub-Commission on the Promotion and Protection of Human Rights, Intellectual Property Rights and Human Rights, Fifty-second Session, Agenda item 4, E/CN.4/Sub.2/2000/7, adopted on 17 August 2000 2000/21. This resolution is supported by Chapman (2001) but is contradicted by Anderson and Wager (2006) (among other things stating that the TRIPS A represents an effort to provide an essential constitutional framework for the regulation of international markets) – see more on

In addition, it seems appropriate to say something more about the state of affairs concerning human rights in both the Council of Europe (CE) and the European Union (EU). As far as the CE's Convention for the Protection of Human Rights and Fundamental Freedoms (ECHR) and the First Protocol (FP) thereto are concerned, they are silent on intellectual property. As rightly stated by Cullet it is apparent that no in-depth analysis of the place of intellectual property protection in the context of the Convention has been undertaken. This is, for instance, indicated by the fact that the Commission and the Court have simply assumed that existing intellectual property rights constitute the property rights over science, technology, and culture (which need to be protected in the context of the Convention) without considering the impacts that this has over the realization of other human rights.[37] And whereas the European Commission of Human Rights (ECHR) has on many occasions analyzed Article 1 FP with regard to a person's peaceful enjoyment of his possessions, there are only a few decisions dealing with intellectual property law.[38] A similar approach can be found in the decisions of the European Court of Human Rights (ECrtHR). Mention should be made here of the recent *Anheuser-Busch v Portugal* case.[39] This case concerned the concept of possessions, equated with property rights, in the first part of Article 1 Protocol No. 1, as applied with respect to a trademark application. According to the ECrtHR such an application, being recognized under Portuguese law as a set of property rights, is indeed a possession in the sense of the Protocol, even though such application could be revoked under the applicable law. However, this decision seems to be incorrect in at least one respect by recognizing a corporation (not an individual) as the owner of a human right.[40] With respect to the EU mention can be made of the recently adopted Charter of Fundamental Rights (ChFR). Article 17(2) ChFR specifically provides that intellectual

---

that particularly in Section 3. See also WIPO Publication No. 762 (E), Intellectual Property and Human Rights, outcome of a seminar on intellectual property and human rights held by the WIPO and the UN Sub-Commission for the Promotion and Protection of Human Rights in 1998.

37 Cullet (2007), p. 410.

38 See for example, ECHR, App. No. 12633/87, 60 (*Smith Kline and French Laboratories v The Netherlands*), Dep. & Rep. 77, 79 (1990), recognizing a patent right as a property right in the sense of the ECHR.

39 See for example, ECrtHR 11 January 2007, www.iept.nl (IEPT20070111) in the case of *Anheuser-Busch v Portugal (Budweiser)*, considering, among other things, that a legitimate expectation of obtaining an asset may qualify as a possession in the sense of Article 1 FP, that this article applies to intellectual property as such, and that a trademark application is in fact a possession (in this case a set of proprietary rights recognized under Portuguese law, even though they could be revoked under certain conditions).

40 See in the same sense Helfer (2008), to which I will return in Section 3.

property shall be protected.[41] However, as is again correctly stated by Cullet, the Charter falls short of introducing a human right to intellectual property rights because it is addressed to institutions of the European Union rather than right holders.[42]

Finally, and for the sake of good order, mention should be made of the fact that worldwide the constitutional or related legislations of many countries (often in conjunction with guaranteeing the freedom of and participation in cultural life) pay attention to acknowledging and securing the promotion and protection of creativity and innovation in various ways, for example by stating that the expression of intellectual, artistic, scientific and communication activities is free, without any censorship or licence (Article 5 (IX) of the Constitution of Brazil), or the right to ownership of creative and intellectual property is protected by law (Article 43 of the Constitution of Slovakia).[43] However, all these provisions grant human rights status to the indicated cultural expressions with regard to the vertical relations between state governments and their citizens, not with regard to the horizontal relations between citizens. But it is equally true that for example, in the European context, national courts under the circumstances, also in cases of intellectual property law, have applied the ECHR horizontally.[44]

From the foregoing the following findings can be inferred.

Taking account of the actual governing international human rights instruments no specific mention is made of intellectual property rights per se, albeit that some of them refer to objectives and objects of protection which concur with the objectives and objects covered by intellectual property law proper. But even if it may be true that, seen in this perspective, intellectual property rights, being considered as private rights fall within the scope of human rights protection, in order to judge the legal consequences thereof the following should be taken into consideration.

First, human rights law belongs to the legal category of public law. In that capacity it concerns primarily the so-called vertical relations between states

---

41 Charter of Fundamental Rights of the European Union, 2000 J.O. (C 364) 12.

42 Cullet (2007), p. 411. Reference could also be made in this respect to the Preamble to the Information Society Directive (Directive on the Harmonisation of Certain Aspects of Copyright and Related Rights in the Information Society, 2001/29 EC, para. 3) providing that '(t)he proposed harmonisation will help to implement the four freedoms of the internal market and relates to compliance with the fundamental principles of law, and especially of property, including intellectual property, and freedom of expression and the public interest'.

43 See for other examples Article 34 of the Czech Charter of Fundamental Rights; Article 42(2) of the Portuguese Constitution; Article 44(1) of the Russian Constitution; Chap. 2, Sec. 19 of the Swedish Constitution.

44 See on this Geiger (2006) sub. II (A)(b).

and citizens, and not (and if so, only indirectly) the so-called horizontal mutual relations between citizens.[45] With regard to international instruments of human rights law *mutatis mutandis* the same is true: they address primarily affiliated states, not the citizens of these states. This state of affairs is important, since most of the questions concerning the applicability of human rights in relation to intellectual property rights are raised with regard to horizontal relations. It is of note in this respect that since the second half of the twentieth century, which saw the spread of international human rights instruments, it has been increasingly advocated that these instruments not only charge contracting states with duties of care to ensure the adequate protection of, for example, material and immaterial property, but that these instruments, if not explicitly then implicitly, express the view that, even in the absence of existing domestic law, individuals are given a direct claim against government authorities so as to grant them (and against fellow citizens to ensure respect for) a right to create. Secondly, by their very nature human rights are generally considered to be universal, that is, they exist independently of their implementation in positive law.[46] However, it seems to be also accepted in legal doctrine and legal practice that two categories of human rights should be distinguished: fundamental human rights (for example, the prohibition of slavery) and non-fundamental human rights (for example, the right to property). The endorsed view in this respect depends on whether one follows a positivist or a naturalist approach.[47] This distinction is not without consequence, since

---

[45] Mention should be made here of a recent tendency labelled as the *constitutionalisation of private law*, present particularly in German law, according to which human rights should indeed also reign in horizontal relations. See Barkhuijsen and Lindenbergh (2006). See for an application of this doctrine to intellectual property law Geiger (2004).

[46] See World Conference on Human Rights, Vienna 1993 (human rights are universal, indivisible, interdependent and interrelated), available at http://www.unhchr.ch/huridocda/huridoca.nsf/(Symbol)/A.CONF.157.23.EN.

[47] Falk (1992), p. 44:

> The positivists consider the content of human rights to be determined by the texts agreed upon by states and embodied in valid treaties, or determined by obligatory state practice attaining the status of binding international custom. The naturalists, on the other hand, regard the content of human rights as principally based upon immutable values that endow standards and norms with a universal validity.

It goes without saying that the whole concept of human rights taken either way is a fruit of Western thinking which does not concur in every respect with non-Western thinking. See for an Asian view the Report of the Regional Meeting for Asia of the World Conference on Human Rights, UN Doc. A/Conf.157/PC/59 (7 April 1993), available at http://www.unhchr.ch/html/menu5/wcbangk.htm. However, it is beyond the scope of this introduction to deal with that aspect; see on that Human Rights in Cross-Cultural Perspectives from which source Falk's essay is taken.

it adds to the generally agreed margin of appreciation which states have when applying internationally consolidated human rights law, the possibility of state interference with respect to non-fundamental human rights.[48] Thirdly, human rights are addressed to individuals, not to corporate entities.

These findings can be represented, from a dogmatic point of view, in the scheme hereunder:

Human Rights Characteristics	*Intellectual Property Rights Characteristics*
• public law	• private law
• ex persona	• ex lege
• universal	• territorial
• individual rights	• individual rights + corporate rights
• immaterial interests	• material interests (but moral rights may be involved)
• unlimited term	• limited term (but sometimes renewable)
• not-assignable	• assignable
• non-exploitable	• exploitable

3. THE RELATIONSHIP BETWEEN INTELLECTUAL PROPERTY RIGHTS AND HUMAN RIGHTS IN THE LEGAL LITERATURE

The aim of this Section is to offer a bird's-eye account of the actual positions taken in legal writing with regard to the debated human rights status of intellectual property rights. In doing so, I will generally distinguish some authors who take a more positive and some authors who take a more negative view in this respect. It will not come as a surprise that the positions taken concur with those represented by the various contributors to this book.[49] It seems appropriate to

---

48 Schermers (1988). See for a different view Geiger (2006) and Flinterman (in this book) (stating that all human rights are of the same ranking). See for an analysis of the debate in terms of the distinction between *first generation human rights* (that is, civil and political rights) and *second generation human rights* (that is, economic, social, and cultural rights) Yu (2007a), p. 1074.

49 The brief nature of the account relates to both the presented survey itself as well as to the literature which has been taken into account, the latter since this literature over the last 25 years or so has become rather abundant. However, it is claimed that the referenced legal writings provide a fair insight into the pros and cons of the debate.

start this account by giving some attention to works that approach the relationship at issue from a structural point of view.

In his article on the origin and development of the universality of intellectual property rights Drahos takes as a general point of reference that today's legal theory accepts that the existence (and exercise) of some rights presupposes the existence of other rights, some of which are foundational in securing the feasibility of claiming other types of rights. According to Drahos property law as it developed in the course of time into a human right, has that indicated presupposed function and as a consequence has become foundational for today's information society, vesting a secure non-arbitrary property right environment. In Drahos' view the rights created through the enactment of intellectual property laws fit well in that property right environment and can be called instrumental rights, '(i)deally', he writes, 'under conditions of democratic sovereignty, such rights should serve the interests and needs that citizens identify through the language of human rights as being fundamental. On this view, human rights would guide the development of intellectual property rights; intellectual property rights would be pressed into service on behalf of human rights.'[50] However, as Drahos explains, the history of intellectual property does not square with this ideal. It has as much to do with powerful elites using such privileges to obtain economic rents for themselves as it has to do with parliaments working on behalf of citizens to design rights that maximize social welfare.[51] All this leads Drahos to the following conclusion: 'Viewing intellectual property through the prism of human rights discourse will encourage us to think about ways in which the property mechanism might be reshaped to include interests and needs that it currently does not.'[52]

In conclusion, it may be said that, according to Drahos, whatever their legal nature may be, intellectual property rights are instrumental in promoting and protecting human rights, for which aim they need to be implemented into domestic law.

Also instrumental is the approach taken by Okediji, who reaches the following conclusion in her study on the limits of development strategies at the intersection of intellectual property and human rights: 'I conclude that human rights can be used instrumentally to deflect the moral appeal of certain affirmative rights of intellectual property holders, e.g. by justifying compulsory licenses for public health, or requiring national exceptions to copyright laws in the interests of freedom of expression.'[53] According to Okediji:

---

50 Drahos (1999). See in the same sense Suthersanen (2007), pp. 52–3.
51 Drahos (1999).
52 Drahos (1999).
53 Okediji (2007), p. 359.

> (g)iven the strong justification for the free trade ideal as the improvement of national welfare through open access by non-citizens into local-markets, notwithstanding adverse effects on local industries, mandatory intellectual property regulation embedded in the multilateral trade system and human rights appear to have much more in common, at least structurally in the global context, than ever before.

Earlier the author expressed her view that in this respect the TRIPS A, with its mandatory provisions and the requirement of oversight by an international dispute settlement system, has brought the international economic system much closer to the conceptual foundations and assumptions of the human rights framework.[54]

Interestingly, when Okediji speaks of instrumentality it is with regard to human rights in their acknowledged function of tempering the execution of intellectual property rights. The reference that is made to the TRIPS A may be interpreted as pointing to the supposedly built-in checks and balances in that treaty with an eye to general interest issues such as those addressed by human rights law.

Dinwoodie has pointed in this respect to lawmaking stemming from what he calls private ordering activities. He mentions the following two examples, both of which are taken from the domain of copyright law: online contracts and digital rights management. According to Dinwoodie, it is no longer only state law that shapes the system of intellectual property law, but private initiatives do so as well.[55] What Dinwoodie's analysis illustrates is that apparently private practice can go, and in fact does go, beyond at least non-mandatory intellectual property law in order to serve the needs of today's information society. It underlines that under the TRIPS A – see its Preamble – intellectual property law is still part of private law and, as a consequence, is a tool for ordering private relations. However, in that same function intellectual property law is subordinate to international and national public law, such as human rights law and competition law.[56]

If this instrumental view may be characterized as a middle position concerning the relationship between intellectual property law and human rights law, the following authors can be seen as the representatives of a more outspoken position. These positions all concentrate on the interpretation of Article 27 UHDR and Article 15.1(c) ICESCR.

It is argued by Chapman in a series of articles that Article 27(2) and Article 15.1 recognize the intellectual property claims of authors and inventors, linking them to the right to participate in cultural life and to the enjoyment of the

---

54 Okediji (2007), p. 358.
55 Dinwoodie (2007), pp. 100–113.
56 Dinwoodie (2007), pp. 113–14.

benefits of scientific progress. In her analysis of the impact of these international human rights instruments, the participating States are under an obligation to develop intellectual property rights regimes that have an explicit human rights orientation. Executing this obligation is not without consequences since a human rights approach differs from a narrowly economic interpretation of intellectual property rights in various respects, for example implying respect for the material as well as the immaterial (moral) interests of authors and inventors, acknowledging that the author or inventor can be an individual as well as a group or community, and contributing to the promotion of cultural diversity. In that perspective it becomes clear that intellectual property rights are not first and foremost economic commodities, but have an intrinsic value as an expression of human dignity and creativity. Recognizing intellectual property rights as human rights raises the crucial question of how to balance these rights with other human rights.[57] In Chapman's view any understanding of intellectual property rights as human rights is lacking in the WTO and as a consequence thereof in the TRIPS A.[58]

Again in a series of articles Helfer and Yu have taken similar positions to that taken by Chapman.

Placing the relationship between intellectual property law and human rights law in a historic context, Helfer observes that it was the human rights community that first took notice of intellectual property law. Two events, Helfer states, caused intellectual property to be placed on the agenda for human rights lawmaking. The first was an emphasis on the neglected rights of indigenous peoples. The second was the consequence of linking of intellectual property and trade through the TRIPS A.[59] Taking account of the two opposing views with regard to the respective domains of law, as already indicated in Section 1: a conflict approach and a co-existence approach, Helfer states that the tension between them is not likely to be resolved at any time soon.[60] On the contrary, since in his view this tension is likely to have at least the following four distinct consequences for the international legal system: an increased incentive to develop soft law human rights norms (a), a paradigm shift granting to users a status conceptually equal to that of owners and producers of intellectual property (b), the articulation of the 'maximum standards' of intel-

---

[57] Chapman (1998), (2001), (2002), underlining that prior to the coming into existence of the UDHR in 1948 ip claims, cultural life or scientific development was not considered to be covered by human rights law. See for a view that closely concurs with that of Chapman, Riedel (2004).

[58] See for another view Anderson and Wager (2006) (the promotion by the WTO of well-functioning (inter)national markets is a necessary and inevitable consequence of concern with human rights).

[59] Helfer (2003), p. 51.

[60] Helfer (2003), p. 57.

lectual property protection (c), an articulation which will depend on how human rights norms are received in established intellectual property lawmaking venues such as the WIPO and the WTO (d).[61] From this Helfer concludes as follows: 'Although the debates within the WTO and WIPO will surely be contentious, trade and intellectual property negotiators should embrace rather than resist opening up these organizations to human rights influences. Allowing greater opportunities for airing a human rights perspective on intellectual property issues will strengthen the legitimacy of these organizations and promote the integration of an increasingly dense thicket of legal rules governing the same broad subject matter.'[62] In a later publication Helfer offers to that aim a – what he calls – human rights framework for intellectual property.[63] Such a framework in his view can be built upon the human rights approach of intellectual property rights which in his reading is taken in the CESCR's General Comment No. 17, analysed in Section 2. According to Helfer such a framework should encompass a rule of equality between domestic and foreign owners of intellectual products '(…) including many additional prohibited grounds of discrimination and mandating equal access to legal remedies for infringement, including access for "disadvantaged and marginalized groups" '.[64] Introducing such a framework in Helfer's view would have as its most striking consequence that it would substantially diminish the ability of States to restrictively regulate intellectual property rights.[65] It is of note that by pointing at the aspect of the legitimacy of the involved NGOs, Helfer brings a new element into the debate.

Like Helfer's studies, Yu's recent comments have as their primary aim to introduce a human rights framework for intellectual property rights. Particularly his response to – as he puts it – ten common questions about intellectual property and human rights is worth mentioning in this respect. In his response Yu also takes as his starting point the juxtaposition of the two views on the relationship between intellectual property law and human rights law. To the extent that human rights and intellectual property rights serve similar goals, he writes, the development of a human rights framework can only be beneficial, because it will promote and reinforce the underlying goals of these

61 Helfer (2003), pp. 57–61.
62 Helfer (2003), p. 61.
63 Helfer (2006–07).
64 Helfer (2006–07), p. 15.
65 Helfer (2006–07), p. 16. In Helfer (2008) it is argued that according to his reading a similar approach to intellectual property rights as is presented in General Comment No. 17 can be found in the decisions of the ECrtHR (it thus seems plausible that the ECHR has an understanding of intellectual property's place in the European human rights system, even if it has not thus far articulated a theory to justify this placing).

two sets of rights. To the extent that human rights and intellectual property rights are in conflict, however, the framework is urgent and necessary. The fact that there are limited or no conflicts in other areas does not mean that the existing conflicts are unimportant. Moreover, as intellectual property rights continue to expand, the expanded rights are likely to pose conflicts in other unforeseen areas.[66] According to Yu conflicts can possibly be avoided by taking a non-uniform view of intellectual property rights. In doing so, first, one should accept that not all intellectual property rights can be considered as human rights. For example, trademarks, works made for hire, employee inventions, neighbouring rights, and database rights should not be acknowledged as human rights. The same is true for intellectual property rights held by corporate identities.[67] Secondly, one should make a distinction between – what Yu calls – the human rights attributes and the non-human rights attributes of intellectual property rights. Indeed, an emphasis on the human rights attributes of intellectual property rights is likely to further strengthen intellectual property rights, especially in civil law countries (because of their protection of moral rights, FWG):

> (…) The development of a human rights framework for intellectual property therefore may result in what I have described elsewhere as the undesirable 'human rights ratchet' of intellectual property protection. Such a development would exacerbate the already severe imbalance in the existing intellectual property system and would ultimately backfire on those who seek to use the human rights forum to enrich the public domain and to set maximum limits of intellectual property protection.[68]

He adds, however, that since the existing international human rights instruments have recognized only certain attributes of existing intellectual property rights as human rights, there will not be much of a problem if we clearly delineate which attributes of intellectual property rights would qualify as human rights.[69] In Yu's view it is further quite feasible that also indigenous peoples will benefit from a human rights approach to intellectual property rights since the right to protection of interests in intellectual creations (by the international human rights instruments, FWG) is not as biased against non-Western countries and traditional communities as some might have thought.[70]

---

66 Yu (2007b), p. 720.
67 Yu (2007b), pp. 727–8; 730.
68 Yu (2007b), pp. 738–73, particularly pointing to the concerns of public interest advocates. Comp. for a non-uniform approach to copyright law Grosheide (1986) (promoting a tailor-made copyright law).
69 Yu (2007b), p. 740.
70 Yu (2007b), p. 751.

It appears that Yu brings in particular the following two important aspects into the debate: the human rights status of intellectual property rights (not all of them should be given this status); and the distinction between the human rights and non-human rights attributes of those intellectual property rights that in principle are given a human rights status.

Again a somewhat different approach has been offered by Geiger. His suggestion is to apply the recently developed, particularly in Europe, theory of the constitutionalisation of private law in this respect. Referring to the signs of an over-accentuation of the economic aspect which can be found in actual intellectual property law, he argues that 'constitutionalizing' intellectual property could represent an effective tool to check these tendencies of overprotection and to help this field of law recover the legitimacy that it seems to have lost.[71] According to Geiger such an approach is without problems since fundamental rights and human rights '(…) offer a synthesis of the bases of natural law and utilitarianism and represent the values from which intellectual property law developed'.[72] In his reading Articles 8 (privacy) and 10 (freedom of expression) of the UCHR as well as Article 1 (property) of the First Protocol should be interpreted as constituting a fair balance between the interests of right owners and society at large, based upon the foundation of natural law by acknowledging an exploitation right and a 'droit moral' for the creator; '(…) the utilitarian foundation, because this acknowledgment has the promotion of intellectual variety and the spreading of culture and science throughout society as goal'. In sum, according to Geiger fundamental rights would serve not only as a guideline for the application of IP law, but also for a reorganisation of IP law in the future.[73]

Seen in that perspective, the constitutionalization of intellectual property rights means that in as far as national legislation does not already protect intellectual property rights on the constitutional level, the courts should nonetheless interpret intellectual property laws in the light of fundamental rights.

So it appears that in Geiger's view it is not so much the intrinsic human rights character of intellectual property rights themselves that leads to a balanced framework as well as the evaluation of these rights in the light of constitutional values.

Finally, with regard to the positive view of the human rights quality of intellectual property rights, it is worth mentioning Gibson. Departing from the view that intellectual property law is a tool rather than an end to be valued in

---

71 Geiger (2006), p. 372. See on constitutionalisation Cherednychenko, Ch. 4 (2007).

72 Geiger (2006), p. 382.

73 Geiger (2006), p. 385.

itself, she raises the point that intellectual property law is about the right to benefit. Taking account of the fact that General Comment No. 17 identifies the right to benefit as a human right, she arrives at the following conclusion with regard to the status of intellectual property law. 'Since the right to benefit', she writes, 'is identified through the intellectual property system, (t)herefore, any "right to benefit" will be administered by the intellectual property system. Thus, although the General Comment establishes that intellectual property rights are not human rights, nevertheless, by the very fact that the intellectual property system has been established as the primary means by which to access this "benefit", intellectual property rights are in effect aligned with human rights.'[74]

The accent which Gibson lays on the right to benefit is intriguing in the light of the material and immaterial interests which intellectual property law is said to protect as well as with an eye on benefit sharing which is promoted by those who oppose the expansion of intellectual property law with regard to, among other things, the objects of protection, the prerogatives of right owners and the term of protection.

For a more nuanced or even negative consideration of the human rights status of intellectual property rights, the following authors can be mentioned: Drahos, Ostergard, Cullet – a nuanced view; Deazley and Ranjan – a negative view.

Drahos, as already mentioned, takes a sceptical view particularly because of what he indicates as the intrinsic legal-systematic properties of human rights law on the one hand, and intellectual property law on the other. Intellectual property rights, he writes, are universally recognized but that does not make them universal human rights, since they depend on a legislative declaration, are for a limited period of time, do not belong to all human beings, and not all intellectual property rights protect the personal interests of their originators.[75]

Ostergard starts his analysis of the question whether intellectual property is a universal human right with the following assumption. 'Given the ever-widening acceptance of a right to protection of intellectual property (IP), one might assume that there is at least implicitly an equally broad and agreed upon ration-ale or justification for this right.'[76] According to Ostergard, that rationale or justification can indeed be found in Article 27 UDHR. However, despite this recognition as a human right, the UN's position on intellectual property rights and its duty to carry out agreements promoting universal IP protection are incompatible with other important goals, particularly the

---

74 Gibson (2007), pp. 2–3.
75 Drahos (1999).
76 Ostergard (1999), p. 156.

promotion of human physical well-being.[77] Arguing that today's intellectual property law system should be reconsidered with regard to the relationship between the developed world and the developing world, in view of the interest of the industrialized countries in improving the living conditions of the latter with an eye on both expanding their potential markets for intellectual goods and the duty to bring aid to those countries, Ostergard ascertains that '(i)n fact, what is called into question is the position that IP is a guaranteed universal human right (…)'.[78] This leads Ostergard to conclude that the indicated position of the UN could be detrimental to the developing nations. By promoting stronger protection of all IP, the developing nations will be placed at a more severe disadvantage, both in developing policies to sustain economic growth and in the increasingly competitive global markets.[79] As a consequence thereof Ostergard proposes that it should be accepted that some human rights may take priority over other human rights, in this case the right to physical well-being over intellectual property rights.

So, quintessential for Ostergard's argument is the hierarchy of human rights which he promotes.

In many ways Cullet's considerations concur with those of Drahos and Ostergard. His starting point is that although in the light of their separate development the actual link between intellectual property rights and human rights is still tenuous, this does not imply that there is no connection between human rights and intellectual contributions.[80] This connection is particularly seen in Article 15.1(c) CESCR which is said to recognize intellectual contributions in general without making any special reference to one or the other category of existing intellectual property rights.[81] Cullet stresses, however, that the link between the two categories of law has been discussed almost exclusively in human rights forums, intellectual property rights instruments having never directly addressed the impacts on the realization of human rights.[82] Having also taken account of other regional and national human rights instruments with regard to intellectual property rights (such as the EU Charter of Fundamental Rights), Cullet concludes that there remains uncertainty concerning the place of intellectual contributions in a human rights framework for at least three reasons:

> First, while it can be argued that the material interests of authors have nothing to do

77 Ostergard (1999), p. 175.
78 Ostergard (1999), p. 175.
79 Ostergard (1999), p. 177.
80 Cullet (2007), p. 406.
81 Cullet (2007), p. 409.
82 Cullet (2007), pp. 414; 429.

> with a human rights framework. (…) Second, conceptual and practical debates concerning the place of intellectual contributions in a human rights context have usually failed to take into account the multi-dimensional aspects of a provision like Article 15(1) of the Covenant. (…) Third, the material and moral interests of holders of intellectual property rights such as patent holders are more than adequately covered by intellectual property laws and treaties in place.[83]

In line with Ostergard's concerns is what Cullet presents in his final appreciation of the actual realization of human rights in the context of the execution of intellectual property rights, particularly in the developing world since the establishment of the TRIPS A. Cullet indicates two main challenges here.

> First, the increasingly visible impacts of certain types of intellectual property rights on the realization of human rights needs to be addressed by ensuring that measures are taken to protect everyone who is likely to be negatively affected by strengthened intellectual property rights standards. Second, the broader question of the place of science and technology in a human rights framework needs to be further considered.(…) A human rights perspective on knowledge contributions that is not bound by intellectual property rights treaties and laws constitutes a basis to rethink the position of bodies of knowledge, which cannot be protected at present.[84]

It is ominous that Cullet does not expect much in this respect from either the WIPO or WTO. These two institutions neither have any specific mandate to consider human rights issues nor do they show any definite inclination to address human rights implications of the legal regimes they put forward.[85]

Three points of Cullet's view may be underlined: the fact that the recognition of intellectual property rights as human rights may have counter-productive effects, the suggestion to develop new systems of law in order to protect knowledge and technology, and the lack of trust in the WIPO and WTO as the vehicles for building a human rights framework for the execution of intellectual property rights.

Although taken from the same perspectives as that of the previous authors, an even more negative view is offered by Ranjan. Construing intellectual property rights (IPR) as human rights, he argues, implies construing the right to enjoy monopoly right and rent as a human right even if it is at the expense of society at large. This goes against the very basis of Article 15.1 that talks of striking a balance. Moreover, there is the dominant view that IPR and human

---

83 Cullet (2007), p. 412.

84 Cullet (2007), p. 430.

85 Cullet (2007), p. 419, referring to what is called the limited human rights-related Panel discussion organised by the WIPO and the Office of the UN High Commissioner for Human Rights 1998, available at http://www.wipo.int/tk/en/hr/paneldiscussion.

rights are incompatible, that is, that there is a conflict between IPR and human rights as the former gets in the way of countries enforcing the latter.[86]

So, what Ranjan fears is the ratchet effect of recognizing intellectual property rights as human rights.

The most radical stance in my view in this respect is taken by Deazley when referring to the EU Charter of Fundamental Rights and English case law like the *Ashdown* decision. What is being suggested here, he writes with regard to copyright law, is that the conceit and language of intellectual property as a natural property right has provided one of the key foundations for the rampant expansionism which is the story of copyright law throughout the twentieth and into the twenty-first century.[87]Articulating the position of the user Deazley ends his appreciation as follows:

> Both historical and theoretical analyses suggest that the logical manner in which to discuss intellectual property is not that the user (or the state on behalf of the user) should have to articulate, defend and pay for every action which encroaches upon the author's property, but rather that the author or owner (or the state on behalf of the same) should have to articulate and defend every monopoly use of the intangible good which encroaches upon the public's freedom to engage with that intangible good.[88]

The reported reading of the referenced reflections in legal writing on the relationship between intellectual property rights and human rights leads me to the following conclusions.

First, both the protagonists and the sceptics of linking these two domains of law (in vertical as well as horizontal relations), share the view that this cannot be done without reshaping the existing (international and national) intellectual property law because of the apparent tensions between the two in the light of their respective political justifications and their legal dogmatics (that is, the subject and object of protection). Secondly, the governmental intervention which is needed in this respect – again a shared view – should focus upon an instrumental approach, aimed at introducing what is called a human rights framework for the execution of intellectual property rights. However, instrumentality is proposed in two different ways. On the one hand, it is said that human rights law should be instrumental with regard to the execution (that is, the restriction) of intellectual property rights; on the other hand, it is said that intellectual property law should be instrumental with regard to the implementation of human rights. The first approach may be indentified as giving horizontal effect to human rights the second approach seems to require an internalization

86 Ranjan (2007), p. 6.
87 Deazley (2006), p. 152.
88 Deazley (2006), p. 160.

of human rights into substantive intellectual property law. Next to governmental intervention, attention is required for the possibilities of private ordering. This may be the more interesting in view of the fact that at the same time doubts have been uttered with regard to what can be expected from the WIPO and WTO as mediators in this respect. Thirdly, of interest is the proposal to apply what is called a human rights hierarchy in order to avoid certain negative consequences of giving intellectual property rights a human rights status. Particularly interesting in this light is the suggestion to take a non-uniform approach to intellectual property rights when introducing such a human rights framework, distinguishing between intellectual property rights that either do or do not qualify as human rights. By doing so, it is said, also some of the negative effects (for example, stressing the human rights quality of intellectual property rights stands in the way of access to patented medicines) can be overcome. But at the same time granting a human rights quality to intellectual property rights under the circumstances may contribute to the protection of cultural expressions. It is even suggested that supporting the developing world in increasing its economic abilities is equally economically beneficial for the developed world. However, doubts about the possibility of overcoming just that rachet of uplevelling intellectual property rights to human rights in the relationship between the developed and the developing world appears to be one of the reasons why some object to that approach. Even the intermediate postion of the UN is questioned here. An even more restrictive view is taken by those who argue that given the way actual substantive intellectual property law is shaped, a proper account has already been given to whatever human rights-like aspect may be required in the execution of intellectual property rights.

As already indicated at the beginning of this section, the above *tour d'horizon* of the legal literature with regard to intellectual property rights in their relation to human rights concurs in many ways with the contributions that are bundled in this book. Even the rather extreme absolutist view taken by Smiers in his contribution to this book comes close to the position taken by Deazley. Further, it appears that both the positive and the negative approach towards linking intellectual property rights and human rights are represented in this book. It is of interest in this respect that particularly those authors writing on patent law (Brinkhof, Cooper-Dreyfuss, Gordon) tend to reject linking patent law with human rights law. However, this is on different grounds such as patent law being based upon a justification other than that of human rights law. This is with the notable exception of Van Overwalle, however, who together with most of those writing on copyright law (Matthews, Waelde and Brown) underline the interface between intellectual property law and human rights law.

4. CONCLUDING OBSERVATIONS

With reference to the findings of Section 2 and the conclusions of Section 3 this final section can be rather brief.

Indeed, as has been seen in Section 2, no mention or even reference to human rights is made in any binding international legal instrument (for example PC, BC, TRIPS A or WCT). The same is true for national legislation on intellectual property law. And although it may be argued that some international human rights instruments do deal with intellectual property rights (such as the UCHR, ICESCR, ECHR, EU Charter, Culture Convention), this involvement is mostly – and with the exception of Article 17(2) EUCH – written in an indirect way, thereby obliging the contributing states to promote and protect the creative and innovative output of their citizens. Case law handed down by any international or national court reflects the same position. If in the international arena any action is taken at all, it is by the UN and UNESCO, not by the WIPO or WTO.

What seems to be most striking in this respect, however, is that one has witnessed in the last ten to fifteen years an emerging real debate on the relationship between intellectual property law and human rights law which is taking place between the respective epistic communities of either domain of law. This is particularly true with regard to the application of human rights law with respect to the execution of intellectual property rights. But it equally concerns the human rights status of intellectual property rights which is the focus of this introduction. Mention is made in that respect of building a human rights framework for (the execution of) intellectual property rights. Obviously and taking into consideration the different characteristics of intellectual property rights and human rights, this cannot be done without quite fundamentally reshaping intellectual property law as it stands today, which requires interference by the WIPO and/or the WTO, if not cooperation with UNESCO. Less drastic than fundamentally reshaping intellectual property law is of course expanding the way in which human rights law may be applied horizontally, that is, with regard to the execution of intellectual property rights between private parties. Doing this may well contribute to vesting a proper and adequate balance between the two domains of law if it would be allowed, on the one hand, to distinguish between fundamental and non-fundamental human rights, and, on the other, not giving a human rights status to all intellectual property rights.

BIBLIOGRAPHY

Anderson, Robert D. and Hannu Wager (2006), 'Human Rights, Development, and the WTO: The Cases of Intellectual Property and Competition Policy', *Journal of International Economic Law*, Volume 9, Number 3, pp. 707–47.

Barkhuijsen, Tom and Siewert Lindenbergh (2006), *Constitutionalisation of Private Law* (The Netherlands, Brill).

Beiter, Klaus D. (2008), 'The Right to Property and the Protection of Interests in Intellectual Property – A Human Rights Perspective of the Europen Court of Human Rights' Decision in *Anheuser Busch Inc. v Portugal*', IIC Vol. 39 2008/6, p. 714 et al.

Bentley, Lionel and Brad Sherman (2004), *Intellectual Property* (Oxford University Press).

Blakeney, Michael (1997), *Trade Related Aspects Of Intellectual Property Rights: A Concise Guide to the TRIPS Agreement* (Sweet & Maxwell).

Bogsch, A. (1992), *Brief History of the First 25 Years of the World Intellectual Property Organization* (Geneva: WIPO).

Boyle, James (2004), A Manifesto on WIPO and the Future of Intellectual Property, *Duke Law & Technology Review* 9 August 2004.

Chapman, Audrey R., 'A Human Rights Perspective on Intellectual Property, Scientific Progress, and Access to the Benefits of Science', http://www.wipo.int/tk/en/hr/paneldiscussion/papers/chapman-summary.html.

Chapman, Audrey R. (2001), 'Approaching Intellectual Property as a Human Right: Obligations related to Article 15 (I)(c)', *Copyright Bulletin* Vol. XXXV, 2001 No 3.

Chapman, Audrey R. (2002), 'The Human Rights Implications of Intellectual Property Protection', *Journal of International Economic Law* 5(4), pp. 861–82.

Coombe, Rosemary J. (2005), 'Communication and Culture: The Politics of Intellectual Property, Human Rights and Development – Revised Syllabus', http://www.yorku. ca/coombe/courses/6308.

Cornides, Jacob (2004), 'Human Rights and Intellectual Property: Conflict or Convergence?' 7, *J. World Intell. Prop.* 135.

Correa, Carlos (2007), *Trade Related Aspects of Intellectual Property Rights: A Commentary on the TRIPS Agreement* (Oxford University Press).

Cullet, Philippe (2004), *Human Rights and Intellectual Property Rights: Need for a New Perspective* (International Environmental Law Research Centre).

Deazley, Ronan (2006), *Rethinking Copyright – History, Theory, Language* (Edward Elgar Publishing).

Dinwoodie, Graeme B. and Rochelle C. Dreyfuss (2004), 'TRIPS and the Dynamics of Intellectal Property Lawmaking', 36 *Case W Res J Int'L* 95, p. 121.

Drahos, Peter (1999), *The Universality of Intellectual Property Rights: Origins and Development* (WIPO Publications No. 762 (E)).

Dutfield, Graham and Uma Suthersanen (2008), *Global Intellectual Property Law* (Edward Elgar Publishing).

Falk, Richard (1992), 'Cultural Foundations for the International Protection of Human Rights', in Abdullahi Ahmed An-Naim (ed.), *Human Rights in Cross-Cultural Perspectives: A Quest for Consensus* (University of Pennsylvania Press).

Firth, A. (ed.) (1997), *The Prehistory and Development of Intellectual Property Systems*, Perspectives on Intellectual Property Series, Volume 1 (Sweet & Maxwell/Queen Mary).

Gathii, James Thuo (2002), 'The Legal Status of the Doha Declaration on TRIPS and Public Health under the Vienna Convention on the Law of Treaties', *Harvard Journal of Law & Technology*, Volume 15, Number 2, Spring 2002, p. 292.

Geiger, Christophe (2006), '"Constitutionalizing" Intellectual Property Law? The Influence of Fundamental Rights on Intellectual Property in the European Union', 37 *Int'l Rev. Intell. Prop. & Competition L.* 371.

Geiger, Christophe (2008), 'The Constitutional Dimension of Intellectual Property

Law', in Paul Torremans (ed.), *Intellectual Property and Human Rights* (Kluwer Law International), pp. 101–31.
Gervais, Daniel (ed.) (2007), *Intellectual Property, Trade and Development* (Oxford University Press).
Gervais, Daniel (2007), 'TRIPS and Development', in Gervais (2007), pp. 3–59.
Gervais, Daniel (2005), 'Traditional Knowledge and Intellectual Property: A TRIPS-Compatible Approach', *Mich St LR* 137.
Gervais, Daniel J. (2003), *The TRIPS Agreement: Drafting History and Analysis* (Sweet & Maxwell).
Grosheide, F. Willem (2008), *Cultural Diversity and Copyright Law – Between Good Intentions and Better Functioning*, ALAI.
Grosheide, Willem (2008), 'Moral Rights', in Estelle Derclaye (ed.), *Research Handbook On The Future Of EU Copyright* (Edward Elgar Publishing), pp. 242–66.
Helfer, Laurence R. (2003), 'Human Rights and Intellectual Property: Conflict or Coexistence?', 5 *Minn LP R* 47; idem, *Netherlands Quarterly of Human Rights* 2004, Vol. 22/2, pp. 167–79.
Helfer, Laurence R. (2008), 'Redesigning the European Court of Human Rights: Embeddedness as a Deep Structural Principle of the European Human Rights Regime', *The European Journal of International Law* Vol. 19 No. 1, pp. 125–59.
Helfer, Laurence R. (2008), 'The New Innnovation Frontier? Intellectual Property and the European Court of Human Rights', *Harvard International Law Journal* Winter 2008, Volume 49, Number 1–52.
Hveem, Helge (2007), *Knowledge, Intellectual Property Rights and Equity. The WTO's TRIPS Agreement and EU Policy*, Garnet Policy Paper August 2007.
Ishay, Micheline (2004), *The History of Human Rights* (University of California Press).
Karnell, Gunnar W.C. (2004), 'Copyright Protection under Human Rights Control – In Particular of Works Not Dissiminated to the Public', *BNA International* Volume 4, Number 9.
Lamy, Paul (2004), 'Conclusions, formulated at the end of the International Conference on the 10th Anniversary of the WTO TRIPS Agreement – *The TRIPS agreement 10 years on*', Brussels 24 June 2004; trade.ec.europa.eu/doclib/ html/119347.htm.
Maskus, Keith E. and Jerome H. Reichman (2004), 'The Globalization of Private Knowledge Goods and the Privatization of Global Public Goods', *Journal of International Economic Law*, Volume 7, Issue 2, June 2004, pp. 279–320.
Mokyr, J. (1990), *The Lever of Riches: Technological Creativity and Economic Progress* (Oxford University Press).
Morsink, Johannes (1999), *The Universal Declaration of Human Rights: Origins, Drafting and Intent* (University Press Pennsylvania).
Okediji, Ruth L. (2004), 'Back to Bilateralism? Pendulum Swings in Intellectual Property Protection', 2003–2004 1 *Univ. Ottawa L & Tech J* 125, http://www.uoltj.ca/articles/vol.1.1-2/2003-2004.1.1-2.uoltj.Okediji.125-147.pdf.
Ostergard, Robert L. (1999), 'Intellectual Property: A Universal Human Right?', *Human Rights Quarterly* 21.1.1999, pp. 156–78.
Petersmann, Ernst-Ulrich (2001), 'Time for Integrating Human Rights into the Law of Worldwide Organizations', *Jean Monnet Working Paper of New York University School of Law*, http://www.jeanmonnetprogram.org/papers/01/012301.html.
Peifer, Karl-Nicolaus (2008), 'The Return of the Commons – Copyright History as a Helpful Source?', *IIC* Vol. 39 2008/6, p. 679 et al.
Plant, Arnold (1974), 'The economic Aspects of Copyright in Books, *Economica*, New Series Volume 1 Issue 2, May 1934, pp. 167–195, http://www.compilerpress.atfreeweb.com/Anno%20Plant%20Copyright.htm.

Porsdam, Helle (2007), 'On European Narratives of Human Rights and Their Possible Implications for Copyright', in F. Macmillan, *New Directions in Copyright Law*, Volume 6 (Edward Elgar Publishing).
Ricketson, Sam (2002), 'Intellectual Property and Human Rights', in Stephen Bottomley and David Kinley (eds.), *Common Law and Human Rights* (Ashgate Dartmouth).
Ricketson, S. and J. Ginsburg (2006), *International Copyright and Neighbouring Rights: The Berne Convention and Beyond (Volume I and II*) (Oxford University Press).
Rigamonti, Cyrill P. (2006), 'Deconstructing Moral Rights', *Harvard International Law Journal*, Volume 47, Number 2, pp. 353–412.
Schermers, H.G. (1990), 'The European Communities Bound by Fundamental Human Rights', 27 *CML Rev* 1990, pp. 249–58.
Sellars, Kirsten (2002), *The Rise and Rise of Human Rights* (Sutton Publishing).
Sherman, Brad and Lionel Bentley (1999), *The Making of Modern Intellectual Property Law* (Cambridge University Press).
Suthersanen, Uma (2007), 'Some Initial Thoughts on Copyright, Human Rights and Market Freedom', in Guido Westkamp (ed.), *Emerging Issues in Intellectual Property* (Edward Elgar Publishing), pp. 35–53.
UN (2001a), Sub-Commission for the Promotion and Protection of Human Rights – Resolutions E/C.12/2001/15 dd 26-11-2001.
UN (2001b), Report High Commissioner UN E/C N.4/Sub 2/2001/13 dd 27-6-2001.
UN ESCOR (2004), Comm. On Econ., Soc. & Cult. Rts, 33rd Sess., 10, UN Doc. E/C.12/2004/SR.51.
van der Vyver, J.D. (1996), 'Property in International Human Rights Law', in G.E. van Maanen and A.J. van der Walt, *Property Law on the Threshold of the 21st Century* (Metro), p. 451.
WIPO (2000), *Intellectual Property Needs and Expectations of Traditional Knowledge Holders [1998–1999]*, Report on Fact-finding Missions on Intellectual Property and Traditional Knowledge (WIPO).
WIPO (1999), Publication No. 762 (E) *Intellectual Property and Human Rights* (WIPO).
Yu, Peter K. (2007a), 'Reconceptualizing Intellectual Property Interests in a Human Rights Framework', *UC Davis Law Review*, Volume 40, Number 3, pp. 1039–149.
Yu, Peter K. (2007b), 'Ten Common Questions About Intellectual Property and Human Rights', *Georgia State University Law Review*, Volume 23, Number 4, pp. 709–53.

2. Human rights law status report

Cees Flinterman*

1. INTRODUCTION

The theme of this chapter is human rights in a divided world. For a long period in the history of international law and international relations human rights were seen as falling almost exclusively within the scope of the sovereign powers of each and every state; the consequence thereof was that states did not have the right to intervene in situations of gross violations of human rights in other states: the principle of non-intervention. How much the world has changed! Over the past 60 years a new strong branch of international law has developed focusing on the protection and promotion of human rights. This is reflected inter alia in a mushrooming of academic human rights centers, in specific masters' programmes in the field of human rights and maybe most importantly, in a huge number of national and international human rights non-governmental organizations (NGOs).

In this chapter I will focus on the process of universalisation of human rights in which the United Nations (UN) has played a preponderant role. I will then discuss the important issue of the indivisibility of all human rights. The next issue will be a survey of the establishment of a wide variety of monitoring mechanisms aimed at holding states accountable both at international and regional level. The final issue discussed is the growing relevance of human rights in the programs and policies of the UN itself and of various specialized agencies and other UN entities.

2. UNIVERSALIZATION OF HUMAN RIGHTS

With hindsight it can be argued that the establishment of the UN in 1945 heralded a new era in the field of international relations and international law.

* Cees Flinterman is Honorary Professor of Human Rights at Utrecht University (The Netherlands) and member of the United Nations Committee on the Elimination of Discrimination Against Women (CEDAW).

For the first time ever a world-wide organization was created which had as one of its purposes the promotion of respect for human rights and fundamental freedoms for all, without distinction as to race, sex, language or religion; see the preamble and Article 1(3) of the UN Charter.

The UN Charter only relates to human rights in general terms. In the Universal Declaration of Human Rights, adopted by the UN General Assembly on 10 December 1948, a detailed catalogue of human rights was presented. Since the Universal Declaration was only, from a legal point of view, a recommendation, 18 years later the UN General Assembly adopted (in 1966) the text of two international human rights treaties, the International Covenant on Economic, Social and Cultural Rights (ICESCR) and the International Covenant on Civil and Political Rights (ICCPR); these two Covenants have in the meantime been ratified by more than 150 states around the world. Together with the Universal Declaration, the Covenants are considered the International Bill of Rights.

The International Bill of Rights has become the foundation for a large and strong building of binding and non-binding international human rights norms covering virtually all areas of government policies. But not only at the international, but also at the regional level spectacular developments have taken place: regional systems of protection and promotion of human rights have been created in Europe, thereafter in the Americas, and in the 1980s in Africa. The regional system created in Europe in 1950 within the framework of the Council of Europe, now covers all European states, from Ireland to the Russian Federation. Here it is of interest to note that all regional human rights treaties refer explicitly in their preambles to the International Bill of Rights as a whole or to the Universal Declaration of Human Rights in particular.

This general overview of the development of international and regional human rights law has had two important, related consequences. The first is that it is now justified to consider, in the light of state practice and *opinio iuris*, the Universal Declaration of Human Rights as part and parcel of customary international law, which means that the Universal Declaration contains a set of human rights which impose obligations even on those states that have not (yet) ratified international human rights treaties. Secondly, the question of whether human rights can be truly regarded as universal should be answered unequivocally in an affirmative way. This was already done in 1993 at the end of the Second World Conference on Human Rights which stated in its Final Declaration and Programme of Action that '(t)he universality of all human rights is beyond question'. It should be added, however, that the World Conference also emphasized that in the interpretation and application of human rights the historical, cultural and religious situation of each country should be taken into account, thereby providing a certain margin of discretion for each state. At the same time this entails that 'universality' of human rights should not be confused with uniformity in their interpretation and application.

3. INDIVISIBILITY OF HUMAN RIGHTS

The Universal Declaration of Human Rights is based on a comprehensive, holistic approach to human rights. It comprises both a list of civil and political rights and of economic, social and cultural rights thus reflecting the Four Freedoms speech of the American President Roosevelt in 1941 in which he stated that a future world order should be based on the freedom of speech, the freedom of religion, the freedom from fear and the freedom from want. It is noteworthy that the Universal Declaration already explicitly refers in Article 27 paragraph 1 to the right of every person to participate in the cultural life of his community, to enjoy the arts and to share in scientific advancement and its benefits; in Article 27 paragraph 2 it is provided that everyone has the right to the protection of the moral and material interests resulting from any scientific, literary or artistic production of which he is the author.

It proved to be impossible to maintain the comprehensive, holistic approach to human rights after 1948 due to the emerging Cold War. The result was, as indicated above, that the UN General Assembly adopted two covenants. The idea behind that was that civil and political rights are essentially negative in nature: they oblige states to refrain from any interference in the freedoms and rights of the individual and can, therefore, easily be regarded as justiciable. Economic, social and cultural rights on the other hand are essentially positive in nature: they require active government involvement. This category of rights is, so the argument goes, dependent on the economic situation in a particular country and can, therefore, not be regarded as justiciable. For the above reasons, the two Covenants provided for different monitoring procedures: in the field of civil and political rights a state reporting procedure was established, and optionally, a state complaint procedure and an individual communication procedure, whereas in the field of economic, social and cultural rights only a state reporting procedure was accepted.

It was only in 1993, at the Second World Conference on Human Rights, that the interdependent, interrelated and indivisible nature of all human rights was once again reaffirmed. In practice it has not yet led to the introduction of individual complaint procedures in the field of economic, social and cultural rights at the international and regional level. It has already been indicated above that the International Covenant on Economic, Social and Cultural Rights does not provide for such a procedure; neither do economic, social and cultural rights fall within the scope of the European and Inter-American Courts of Human

Rights. So far only the African Court on Human and Peoples' Rights may consider individual complaints about violations of economic, social and cultural rights but this Court has yet to become operational.

The rediscovery and reaffirmation of the indivisibility of all human rights has, however, had important consequences for the interpretation and application of human rights. Most important in this respect is that a more nuanced approach to human rights has emerged which is based on the notion that no sharp distinction can be made between civil and political rights on the one hand and economic, social and cultural rights on the other. It is recognized that *all* human rights carry three types of obligations. The first obligation is the obligation to respect, which is the obligation on the part of the state not to interfere with the right or freedom of the individual. Secondly, the obligation to protect, which is the state obligation to adopt legislation, policies, programmes, and so on, which are aimed at the protection of the individual not only against public authorities, but also against private actors, such as individuals, organizations and corporations. It is clear that this obligation throws a new light on the issue of the private/public dichotomy in the field of human rights: human rights were long seen as merely relevant in relations between the state and the individual, but it is presently accepted that state obligations flowing from human rights do not only have a significance in relations between the state and the individual, but also in relations between individuals and in the private sphere in general.

The obligation to fulfill is the third type of state obligation following from human rights. It refers to the obligations of the state to help create the conditions under which the full realization of human rights is possible. The prohibition of torture for example requires states not only to see to it that their officials (do not) engage in acts of torture, but also to train their officials in proper investigation and interrogation procedures and to engage in general in human rights education and information.

4. MONITORING OF HUMAN RIGHTS

4.1 Introduction

The Universal Declaration of Human Rights heralded a new era in the field of public international law. Never before had human rights been formulated at international level. It is, therefore, no surprise that in the first 20 years after the Second World War the emphasis of the United Nations was on the elaboration of normative standards, culminating in the adoption of the two Covenants of 1966.

It was only after 1966 that there was a shift towards the creation of appropriate monitoring or supervisory procedures at UN level. The process of further developing substantive human rights norms, of course, continued, but it was realized that without adequate supervision substantive human rights norms could easily remain empty shells, hollow words or mere illusions.

Two separate but related developments took place: first, political monitoring by the UN political human rights organs; and second, (quasi-)legal monitoring by the committees composed of independent experts which were created under the various human rights conventions adopted by the UN General Assembly – the so-called treaty bodies.

4.2 Political Procedures

I will first focus on the political monitoring procedures developed by the UN Commission of Human Rights. This Commission, established in 1946 by the UN Economic and Social Council, was composed of government representatives; in 2006 it was replaced, on the basis of a UN General Assembly Resolution, by the Human Rights Council, which is also composed of representatives of the governments of the Member States of the UN. The Council has 47 members, whereas the Commission on Human Rights had 53 members in the last years of its existence. The new Human Rights Council has, for the time being, taken over the supervisory monitoring instruments which had been developed over the years by the Commission on Human Rights.

Two such instruments may be distinguished: first, the Council may decide to appoint a Special Rapporteur for a state in which serious, systematic violations of human rights are occurring. Such Special Rapporteurs, the so-called country rapporteurs, have been appointed, since 1967, for an impressive number of states. The mandate of such Special Rapporteurs, independent experts appointed by the Chair of the Council, is to closely monitor the human rights developments in the country concerned. Given the fact that for the appointment of a country rapporteur there is a need for a majority vote in the Council, it is clear that the establishment of such a rapporteur is highly political in nature. Some countries with serious human rights violations records have escaped scrutiny by the Council. It is for that reason that the Commission initiated a second supervisory instrument, the so-called thematic rapporteur.

The mandate of the thematic rapporteur is not related to a particular country, but to a particular theme, a particular issue, of human rights violations wherever they take place in the world. In 1981 the Commission first used this instrument by creating a Working Group of Individual Experts on the issue of enforced disappearances. In the following years, a large network of thematic rapporteurs – mostly individual experts, sometimes working groups of individual experts – has been created, first in particular in the field of civil and political rights (for example, prohibition of torture, extra-judicial executions, the independence of the judiciary, and the freedom of expression) but in later years also in the field of economic, social and cultural rights, such as the right to food, health and education and issues of extreme poverty.

Presently there are about ten country rapporteurs and more than 30 thematic rapporteurs; all of them undertake studies and may take action in concrete situations where such action is deemed appropriate; they all report on an annual basis to the Human Rights Council and in some cases also to the General Assembly and/or the Security Council. It is clear that at least in theory, country rapporteus and in particular thematic rapporteurs constitute an effective instrument to hold states politically accountable at the international level for their respect for human rights.

4.3 (Quasi-)legal Procedures

The two Covenants of 1966 and the five other major binding international human rights treaties – the Convention on the Elimination of All Forms of Racial Discrimination (CERD, 1965), the Convention on the Elimination of All Forms of Discrimination Against Women (CEDAW, 1979), the Convention against Torture and Other Cruel, Inhuman or Degrading Treatment or Punishment (CAT, 1984), the Convention on the Rights of the Child (CRC, 1989) and the Convention on the Rights of Migrant Workers and Their Families (CMW, 1991) – provide for so-called (quasi-)legal supervisory procedures in which independent expert committees, treaty bodies, play an important role. Recently – in 2006 – two new international human rights treaties have been added to the this list: the Convention on the Rights of Disabled Persons and the Convention on Enforced Disappearances. Both of them also provide for the establishment of independent expert committees, but they are, of course, not yet operating as treaty bodies.

All UN human rights treaties oblige states parties thereto to report to such a treaty body at regular intervals. An initial report is due one year after the treaty has entered into force for the state concerned; periodic reports have to be submitted every two, three or four years depending on the provisions of the specific treaty. Such state reports form the basis for a dialogue between the state party and the treaty body; the members of the treaty body may, in this questioning of the state party's delegation, also make use of information provided for by NGOs and by relevant international governmental organizations and entities, such as UNESCO, ILO, WHO, UNIFEM and UNDP. Mostly such dialogues which are held in public meetings, take a full UN-day, which is approximately $5\frac{1}{2}$ hours. The treaty body thereafter meets in private in order to discuss the concerns it has regarding the state it has examined and to prepare a list of specific recommendations which after adoption as concluding comments or observations will be sent to the government of the state party concerned.

The state reporting procedure has developed over the years into a highly relevant instrument through which the progress (or lack thereof) a state party has made in fulfilling its obligations under a human rights treaty can be assessed. The information provided by the state party in its report, together with the quite often very informative NGO-reports and the concluding comments or observations of the treaty body give a fair picture of the human rights situation (in particular fields) in the country concerned; especially important is that the dialogue with the state party is carried out in a largely non-political context by members of a treaty body who are experts in the fields covered by a specific international human rights treaty.

The state reporting procedure is, as has been indicated above, common to all UN human rights treaties. That is not the case for the three other quasi-legal supervisory procedures which have been created in the framework of human rights treaties. The individual complaint procedure, by which an individual person or group of persons may hold a state accountable for a violation of his or her rights, has only been created in the context of four human rights treaties (ICCPR, CERD, CEDAW, and CAT), and this procedure is always optional in nature; the consequence is that the number of states that have accepted this procedure is considerably less than the number of states that have ratified UN human rights treaties themselves.

Individual complaint procedures are potentially highly relevant, but it is clear that these procedures also have important weaknesses. Complaints may only be submitted to relevant treaty bodies after all local remedies have, in principle, been exhausted. Another problem is that, even if a state has accepted an individual complaint procedure, such a procedure is hardly known (among the legal profession) in the state concerned. Also problematic is that a decision (view) of a treaty body on the merits of an individual complaint is non-binding in nature; for that reason, an individual who is seeking redress at the international level may prefer to submit his or her case to a regional human rights court, such as the European Court of Human Rights, if that option is available to him or her. Despite these shortcomings there is a growing case law of treaty bodies – especially of the Human Rights Committee under the International Covenant on Civil and Political Rights, but gradually also of other relevant treaty bodies – in which the generally formulated human rights in various treaties have been given further substance. The case law of these treaty bodies is easily accessible through the website of both the Office of the UN High Commissioner for Human Rights in Geneva and the Netherlands Institute of Human Rights (SIM) of Utrecht University.

Finally, two other quasi-legal procedures should be briefly mentioned here: the state-complaint procedure and the independent investigation procedure. The former procedure is contained in a number of human rights treaties (ICCPR, CERD, and CAT); its significance is, however, limited since it has never been used. States prefer the political arena to hold other states accountable rather than getting entangled in quasi-legal procedures which may for a long time have a negative impact on the relations between the complaining and the accused state.

The independent investigation procedure is only provided for in the framework of two human rights treaties (CAT and CEDAW); the treaty bodies under these two treaties have a mandate, if specifically accepted by a state party, to initiate, on the basis of reliable information, an independent investigation in cases of gross or systematic violations of human rights falling within the scope of the treaty. This investigation procedure is confidential, but the final report and its recommendations are made public.

4.4 General Recommendations

On the basis of their experiences in the examination of state reports and, where appropriate, in the examination of individual complaints and in the framework of the independent investigation procedures, treaty bodies prepare and adopt so-called general recommendations. In such recommendations treaty bodies give, sometimes detailed, interpretations of (substantive) provisions of the treaty, thereby clarifying the scope of the obligations of state parties. For a proper understanding of the meaning of the provisions of a human rights treaty, it is, therefore, highly important to check whether a general recommendation has been adopted. General recommendations can be easily accessed through the websites of the UN and of the Netherlands Institute of Human Rights (SIM).

4.5 Regional Human Rights Courts

It is fitting to say a few words about the establishment of regional systems of protection and promotion of human rights. The first such system was created in 1950 with the adoption of the European Convention on Human Rights and Fundamental Freedoms by the Council of Europe when it became clear that the elaboration of the Universal Declaration of Human Rights was going to take much more time than anticipated. In 1969 the Organization of American States (OAS) adopted the Inter-American Convention on Human Rights. In 1981 the Organization of African Unity (OAU, now African Union, AU) followed suit by adopting the African Charter on Human Rights and Peoples' Rights. So far, no comprehensive system of protection and promotion of human rights has been established in Asia or sub-regions thereof.

The European, Inter-American and African regional human treaties all provide for a regional human rights court, with the European Court of Human Rights having the longest history followed by the Inter-American Court. The

African Court on Human and Peoples' Rights has yet to begin its work. The mandate of the European Court now covers all European states, including the Russian Federation. The rich case law of the European Court of Human Rights has over the years given a dynamic interpretation to the substantive provisions of the European Convention which is characterized by the Court as a living instrument. An important feature of the European Court is that it can be directly accessed by individuals after, of course, having exhausted all local remedies. Because of that the case load of the European Court has reached dramatic numbers which negatively impact the time-span of the Court's decision-making in individual cases.

The case load of the Inter-American Court is less dramatic but through its case law the Court has certainly had a great impact on the development of international human rights law, not only directly related to the Inter-American Convention as such, but also in general.

5. MAINSTREAMING OF HUMAN RIGHTS

The main purposes of the UN, when the organization was established in 1945, were the maintenance of international peace and security, the promotion of social and economic development and the promotion and protection of human rights. The relationship between these purposes was certainly recognized at the time, but it was only almost 60 years later that the UN Secretary General would underline the closeness and directness of that relationship by stating that there can be no peace and security without development, neither can there be development without peace and security, but both peace and security and development are not possible without human rights. Human rights should give color to all policies of the UN and the organizations belonging to the UN family: the mainstreaming of human rights. The above words of the UN Secretary-General reflect the growing importance of human rights and fundamental freedoms at the UN level. Various specialized agencies of the UN and various UN-entities have adopted a so-called human rights based approach to their policies. Important examples are UNICEF which bases its policies on the International Children's Rights Convention of 1989 which has been ratified by all but two states around the world and UNDP which bases its policies on international human rights obligations of states in general. Other international organizations, such as the World Bank, IMF and WTO, are yet more hesitant to base their policies explicitly on human rights considerations. From an international law point of view, however, both states and international organizations can be held accountable for their contribution to the implementation of human rights and fundamental freedoms recognized by customary international law.

It is interesting to note in this respect that the intimate relationship between peace and security, social and economic development and human rights has also been recognized by private development organizations, such as Oxfam-Novib. It is equally noteworthy that there is a dawning recognition that not only states, but also private corporations, have within their scope of operations certain responsibilities in the field of human rights.

6. FINAL REMARK

The above, admittedly very general survey of the emergence of a new branch of public international law since 1945 makes it clear that the character of public international law has changed drastically. Public international law is not only aimed anymore at serving the interests of sovereign states, but it is also focusing on the relations between states and those staying or living within their territories or territories under their effective control. States can now be held accountable at the regional and international levels, through various political and (quasi-)judicial procedures, for their respect for human rights. It has also been gradually accepted that human rights are not only significant in the relations between individuals and public authorities, but also in relations between individuals and other private actors. These are certainly positive developments. It is, however, clear that the obligation of all Member States of the UN to take joint and separate action to achieve universal respect for, and observance of, human rights and fundamental freedoms for all without distinction as to race, sex, language or religion (Articles 55(c) and 56 UN Charter), is as relevant now, more than 60 years after the establishment of the UN, as it was in 1945.

BIBLIOGRAPHY

Alston, P. and H. Steiner (2008), *International Human Rights in Context, Law, Politics, Morals*, 3rd edn (Oxford: Oxford University Press).

Clapham, A. (2006), *Human Rights Obligations of Non-State Actors, Adacemy of European Law* (New York: European University Institute, Oxford University Press).

Donnely, J. (2005), *Universal Human Rights in Theory and Practice*, 2nd edn (New Delhi: Manas Publications).

Mahoney, K.E. and P. Mahoney (eds) (1993), *Human Rights in the Twenty-first Century, A Global Challenge* (Dordrecht: Nijhoff Publishers).

Martin, F.F, and others (eds) (2006), *International Human Rights and Humanitarian Law: Treaties, Cases, Materials* (Cambridge: Cambridge University Press).

Newman, F. and D. Weissbrodt (1996), *International Human Rights: Law, Policy and Process*, 2nd edn (Cincinnati, Ohio: Anderson Publishing Co.).

Tomuschat, C. (2008), *Human Rights. Between Idealism and Realism*, 2nd edn (Oxford: Oxford University Press).

3. Expansion and convergence in copyright law

Madeleine de Cock Buning[1]

1. INTRODUCTION

This chapter discusses the historical development of copyright law vis-à-vis its human rights context, starting with its roots in the seventeenth century and from thereon providing an overview of the expansion and convergence in this field of law.

The expansion has been greatly accelerated by the influence of electronic information and communication technology during the last few decades. Copyright law has been more significantly influenced by technological developments than patent law and other industrial property rights. Patent law's fundamental objective is to stimulate technology. Important notions such as novelty and inventiveness are neutral to the technique. Unlike patent law, copyright law is not primarily focused on technique. The copyright protection of technology products often results in expansion in the domain of copyright law and the protection of exploitation rights. The introduction of electronic information technology such as semi-conductors, computer programs, electronic databases and network communication provoked numerous legislative initiatives. New objects, exploitation rights and enforcement mechanisms found a place in the domain of intellectual property law. This expansion did not remain without consequences for the freedom of communication, the human right to which it has been detrimental.

This chapter will furthermore discuss another significant development in the field of intellectual property law, a development that is especially relevant for the human rights paradox in intellectual property law. Under the influence of electronic information technology the traditional boundaries between industrial

[1] Professor of Copyright and Media & Communications Law at the Centre for Intellectual Property Law (CIER), Molengraaff Institute for Private Law, Utrecht University, The Netherlands and is appointed by the Crown to the board of the Supervisory Authority to the Media (CvdM). I would like to thank D. van Eek for his profound and helpful preparatory work for this chapter.

property law and copyright law are strained. Principles originating from patent law are brought within the framework of copyright law. This potentially threatens the vulnerable balance between the human right of the freedom of communication, on the one hand, and subjective rights, on the other. With low access to the protection – no formalities are required – substantively strong and long-lasting protection is granted.

2. ORIGINS OF COPYRIGHT LAW

In order to provide a proper context for these developments, the origins of copyright law should be considered.[2] The origins of both copyright and freedom of speech can be partly found in the invention and development of printed texts. As a consequence of this and the fact that people in the sixteenth century were increasingly literate, printed documents and the ideas they contained became widespread.

Printers, publishers and booksellers functioned as intermediaries between the author and his audience. On the one hand, these parties were profiting from the increasing distribution of texts, but, on the other, it resulted in strong competition. Investments in printing and exploitation were substantial. Investors and interested parties put pressure on governments to protect their investments.[3] As a result, printers, publishers and booksellers received certain privileges from local and national governments, such as the privilege to reproduce and sell certain books and writings for a set period of time.[4]

These privileges did not only have their origin in the fact that governments aimed at honest competition. Local and national governments were able to apply censorship before granting privileges and thus to control what was published.[5] Printing thus first gave rise to government privileges that were detrimental to the very nature of the freedom of communication.

A more fundamental and longer-lasting result of mechanical printing was a change of mentality, which was both the start of the fundamental freedoms and

---

2 See for the standard work on the origins of copyright, Grosheide (1986).

3 A pressure group of substantive influence was the British printing craft guild 'The Stationers Company'. In 1577 the King granted this organisation the privilege of printing all printed materials in London; Seignette (1994), p. 13.

4 The first known privilege in Europe was granted by the Venetian Senate in 1469; Darras (1890), mentioned in Ricketson (1987), p. 3. The first privilege in the Netherlands was granted by Karel V in 1516 to a work known as 'Die Cronycke van Hollandt, Zeelandt en Vrieslandt, beginnende van Adamstijd tot de jare 1517', De Beaufort (1909), p. 4.

5 Ricketson (1987), p. 3; Schneiders (1991), p. 28.

the development of a rudimentary form of copyright law.[6] The ability to read and write was no longer a privilege belonging to the upper classes. Large parts of society were being educated and were therefore able to read literature and political pamphlets. Large numbers of pirated editions and other writings were widespread. This enabled the emancipation of the public at large. The revolutions in the eighteenth century further enhanced political freedom.[7] It is in this century that the *Declaration of Rights* (1787) and the *Déclaration des droits de l'homme et du citoyen* (1789) came into effect. The fundamental elements of the freedom of speech were now established. Both the rich and the poor were able to profit from the Industrial Revolution and the Enlightenment. Education was developing, which stimulated the market for books. The suppression of (economic) positions of power, mental self-fulfilment and being able to contain the spread of illegal publications also created a basis for the development of copyright law.[8]

The British *Statute of Queen Anne* (1709) is recognized as being the first Copyright Act. This was the first Act which directly protected authors.[9] In the United States the British copyright law was applicable until the Declaration of Independence was adopted. In 1790 the American Congress developed copyright law founded on the Constitution.[10] In Germany, the system of privileges was prolonged.[11] It would take until 1837 for the first copyright law to be enacted in Prussia.[12] In the province of Holland, the system of privileges was abolished in 1796. Instead, a decree was developed that protected every

---

6 Chaytor (1966), pp. 1–10; Walde (1987), p. 213.

7 Ringer (1977), pp. 117–8.

8 Dommering (1996), p. 211.

9 Boytha (1992), p. 69.

10 Act of 31 May 1790, *I Stat*. 124. Primarily, this Act only protected (post)cards and books. When the need for the protection of engravings and musical compositions increased, the Act was amended (1831). Seignette (1994), p. 16.

11 As a consequence of the existence of more than 100 sovereign states until the second half of the nineteenth century, the necessary condition for the existence of national copyright legislation was lacking.

12 The protection of objects of art and science against imitation and copying for the period of 30 years *post mortem auctoris* was statutorily enacted. The *Gesetz zum Schutz des Eigentums an Werken der Wissenschaft und Kunst gegen Nachdruck und Nachbildung* distinguished itself because of definitions regulated by printing technology, Walde (1987), p. 216. The right to make copies of visual arts was elaborately described by the techniques at that time: 'Vervielfältigung von Zeichnungen oder Gemälden durch kupferstich, Stahlstich, Holzschnitt, Lithography, Farbendruck, Übertragung usw'. Besides this, the national legislation in the field of copyright law, which was established during the unification of Germany, was predominantly influenced by the techniques of the printing press. Reinhart (1987), p. 222.

'original' work.[13] This was a right of copy granted to the publisher. The publication of the administration of the Batavian Republic from 1803 is known to be the first codification of the right to make copies enacted by the decree mentioned above.[14] The first national Dutch regulation dates from 1817 – at the same time as the German Copyright Act – and was focused on the technology of book printing. This Act allowed 'het regt van kopij of van kopiëren door den druk', which means the right to make copies through printing.[15] The Act allowed authors to have exclusive rights to their works for a period of 20 years. It would take until 1881 for this Act to be replaced by a new Act which contained a making available right.[16] In order to harmonize the legislation with the Berne Convention of 1886, the Dutch Copyright Act was enacted.[17] Formal requirements for protection in the 1881 Act were left aside.

3. FURTHER DEVELOPMENT OF THE LAW

3.1 Mechanical and Chemical Recording of Images and Sound in the Twentieth Century

At the end of the nineteenth century and the beginning of the twentieth century copyright was confronted with a new set of objects which arose from the application of information technology. The copyright paradigm was confronted with a list of fundamental questions. Are photographs and films merely reproductions of natural reality or are they objects that can be independently subject to, and therefore protected by, copyright? Around the turn of the twentieth century when photography became well established and economically relevant, it was recognized as an object to be protected by copyright in most countries. With the revision of the Berne Convention in Berlin film was also recognized as copyrightable subject-matter.[18] The United States expanded its

---

13 Decrees of the Assembly of the provincial board of Holland, 6 December 1776 and 6 January 1797, p. 21, mentioned in De Beaufort (1932), p. 6.

14 During the French oppression of the Netherlands French law was applied.

15 Original (Dutch) title of the Act: Wet van den 25 januari 1817, de regten bepalende die in de Nederlanden, ten opzichte van het drukken en uitgeven van letter – en kunstwerken, kunnen worden uitgeoefend, Staatsblad (*Stb.*) 5.

16 Original (Dutch) title of the Act: Wet van 28 juni 1881 tot regeling van het auteursrecht, *Stb.* 124; Wijnstroom & Peremans (1930), p. 30; Du Bois (1981), p. 71.

17 Original (Dutch) title of the act: Auteurswet 1912, houdende nieuwe regeling van het Auteursrecht, *Stb.* 308.

18 De Cock Buning (1998), pp. 92–3 and 124–5; De Beaufort (1909), pp. 244–5; Gotzen (1995), p. 34.

copyright paradigm to include film in 1912.[19] With regard to the recording of sound the question arose whether the registration of music on record had to be considered as a form of reproduction or whether music actually had to be perceived with the human eye, as is the case with written music, before it could be considered to be an act of reproduction.[20] With the improvement in recording techniques, the importance of the trade in mechanical music devices such as pianolas increased and the response was an increased demand for protection by composers. Soon, so-called mechanical rights were recognized and became part of copyright as we know it today.

3.2 Broadcasting of Image and Sound

As the popularity of radio increased, the Berne Convention had to be revised in order to include the exclusive right of radio broadcasting in a new article in 1908.[21] Also the United States assigned rights for radio and television broadcasting around that time.[22] In 1965 in Germany, a specific *Senderecht* was adopted, which determined both *Rundfunk* as well as *Drahtfunk* broadcasting as an act of distribution.[23] Real issues involved the question of what is to be designated as 'secondary making available'. Initially, the introduction of large-scale cable networks gave rise to much discussion.[24] Is the transfer of radio and television broadcasting through a network of cables and satellites at the same time to be included in the right of distribution? It was soon determined under either the law[25] or case law[26] [27] that this was to be considered as

---

19 Act of 24 August 1912, 37 *Stat.* 488, c. 356.

20 Berlin 13 November 1908, Actes 1908, 49–50, Ricketson (1987), p. 259.

21 Art. 11bis(1) under the Berne Convention. In the Netherlands radio broadcasts were indicated as acts of making available to the public and this did not give rise to any problems, Wijnstroom and Peremans (1930), p. 83. The same was true for television broadcasting.

22 Under art. 106.4 United States Copyright Act (USCA).

23 Art. 20 Urheberrechtsgesetz (UrhG); Mom (1990), p. 127.

24 Decades later it was the increasing use of satellites that was the object of discussion.

25 Nimmer § 8.18A and B9.

26 The transfer of radio and television through cable networks is seen as a form of making available to the public, regardless of whether it serves a 'new audience', CAI/Amstelveenarresten. Dutch Supreme Court (HR) 30 October 1981, *Nederlandse Jurisprudentie* (*NJ*) 1982, 470; HR 14 January 1983, *NJ* 1984, 696; HR 25 May 1984, *NJ* 1984, 697; Mom (1990), pp. 24–41.

27 Art. 20 UrhG; Bundesgerichtshof (BGH) 17 November 1980, *Gewerblicher Rechtsschutz und Urheberrecht* (*GRUR*) 1981, p. 412; BGH 4 June 1987, *Zeitschrift für Urheber- und Medienrecht (ZUM)* 1988, p. 35; Mom (1990), pp. 127–36; Fromm and Nordemann (1988), pp. 103–31.

a *separate* act of distribution that needed permission from the right holders of the programmes that are being transferred. The implementation of the European Satellite and Cable Directive confirmed within the European Union that both broadcasting through satellites and simultaneous cable-transfer are exclusive rights.[28]

3.3 Decentralized Reproduction Techniques

Reproduction techniques from the 1970s and 1980s resulted in the decentralization of reproduction. It was now the consumer who copied images, audio and video materials on a large scale.[29] The various legislatures tried to find solutions to this issue and in several countries specific legislation was adopted. To compensate copyright owners for this large-scale copying of audio and video material, levies were imposed on blank information carriers which were designed to retain this kind of material.[30]

4. THE ELECTRONIC ERA

With the increasing scale of electronic information technology during the last few decades of the twentieth century, copyright law was confronted with several new objects of protection and methods of exploitation. Multiple European Directives were adopted and implemented in the Member States to accommodate new objects and methods of exploiting copyrighted materials.

---

[28] Council Directive 93/83/EEC of 27 September 1993 on the coordination of certain rules concerning copyright and rights related to copyright applicable to satellite broadcasting and cable re-transmission. *PbEG* 1993, L 248/15; Hugenholtz (1994), pp. 87–90; Visser (1997), p. 122.

[29] Spoor and Verkade (1993), p. 228; Visser (1997), p. 53.

[30] In Germany, in 1965, a levy was imposed by the Urheberrechtsgesetz on equipment for recording audio and videotapes, Art. 54 UrhG, Ulmer (1980), p. 298. In The Netherlands this was done in the Wet van 30 mei 1990 inzake een vergoeding voor het verveelvoudigen van beeld- of geluidsopnamen voor eigen oefening, studie of gebruik (Act of 30 May 1990 concerning compensation for the multiplying of image and sound recording for private practice, study or use) *Stb.* 305, Art. 16c–16g. In the US a levy was imposed in 1990 on blank information carriers of audio and video material as compensation for losses incurred by the rightful claimants caused by the large-scale (private) copying of audio and video material, Art. 108, Act of October 1976; Goldstein (1994), p. 143. Specific legislation on privately-used video copies was not enacted in the US. The Supreme Court decided that the recording of television shows in order to view them at a later point in time, known as *time shifting*, could be seen as a means of *fair use*, US Supreme Court 17 January 1984, 464 U.S. 417 (*Universal Studios Inc. v Sony Corp. of America*).

On the one hand, *sui generis* legislation was enacted and, on the other, the existing regimes were extended with 'custom-made' regulations, which protected specific information products under specific conditions.[31]

4.1 New Objects of Protection

Semi-conductor chips

The invention of the semi-conductor has been essential for the substantial production of the (personal) computer.[32] Semi-conductor producers pressurized the United States legislator to enact the Semiconductor Chip Protection Act (SCPA) in 1984.[33] This Act provided *sui generis* protection for the topography of the semi-conductor.[34] The European Semi-conductor Directive[35] was adopted many years after the SCPA and is very similar to this Act.[36] An original topography of a semi-conductor[37] is protected for a period of ten years.[38]

This new regime was introduced irrespective of the dominant opinion in legal theory that the existing legislation (for example copyright law, patent law, tort law) was adequate to deal with the imitation of semi-conductors.[39] The need for a specific regime indeed turned out to be dubious, considering the very limited number of registrations of semi-conductors under the new regime. This could very well indicate that there was indeed no need for *sui generis* protection.[40]

---

31 See Grosheide (1986), who introduced the concept of tailor made copyright.

32 De Cock Buning (1998), pp. 133–7.

33 Art. 901–914 U.S. Semiconductor Chip Act.

34 Hugenholtz (1985), pp. 127–34.

35 Council Directive 87/54/EEC of 16 December 1986 on the legal protection of topographies of semi-conductor products. *PbEC* 1987, L 24/36.

36 The European system of protection is founded on an international-political trade base. The SCPA demands material reciprocity.

37 In the Directive this is defined as: A 'series of connected images, somehow recorded, that show the three-dimensional pattern of the layers in a semi-conductor. Every picture shows the pattern or a part of the pattern of a surface of a semi-conductor in a certain stadium of its creational process'.

38 The originality criterion is similar to that of originality in copyright law.

39 Wichers Hoeth (1993), p. 77; In British case law semi-conductor chips were indeed protected by copyright law in 1988.

40 Semi-conductor chips are known for their short cycles of innovation. Besides, the fact that new designs for and innovations in topographies need to be deposited/registered, which enables the competitor to use the know-how, will result in reluctance on the part of certain producers.

Computer software

As a result of the tremendous growth in the computer industry in the last quarter of the twentieth century, the call for the protection of software was increasing.[41] The question arose whether either patent law – with a high threshold and a high level of protection – or copyright law – with a low threshold and a 'low' level of protection – is the most suitable for the protection of software. To clear the way for protection by patent law the requirement that a certain invention needed to be of a technological nature was partially abandoned.[42]

While in legal theory numerous thoughts were aired against the protection of software through copyright law, case law and legislation in most countries were heading in the opposite direction. Several (inter)national legislators enacted laws and acts during the 1980s and 1990s.[43] In the United States the Computer Software Copyright Act became part of copyright law in 1980.[44] Since the implementation of the 1991 European Software Directive the protection of software is regulated in all Member States.[45]

Databases

The protection of databases received full attention at the end of the 1980s. A collection of factual data was until then only protected by copyright law if it

---

41 Kolle (1977), p. 72.

42 According to the case law of the Dutch Supreme Court, only working methods that changed their nature somehow as a result of human influence were subject to protection by patent law. By interpreting the definitions in a different way, software regarded as a working method could be subject to protection by patent law as well, Patent Office (since the Patent Act 1995 was adopted its name was changed into the Netherlands Patent Centre, an agency of the Ministry of Economic Affairs, *MdCB)* 11 May 1987, *BIE* 1987, p. 174. Two years before this judgment, the Dutch Patent Office regarded computers that contained a new and innovative program in the working memory as subjects for patent law protection. Patent Office, 12 September 1985, *BIE* (1985), p. 435; Kaspersen and Oskamp (eds) 1990, pp. 47–59.

43 An interesting example is the fact that France introduced a *sui generis* regulation incorporated in copyright law for computer software. Computer programs were, from that moment onwards, classified as 'applied literature'. Certain moral rights were debarred if they concerned software for computers. Moreover, a shortened protection period of 25 years was introduced. The French implementation of the European Software Act has replaced the 1985 Act. Lucas (1987), pp. 183–262.

44 De Cock Buning (1998), pp. 142–5. Act of 12 December 1980, *PbEC* 1980, L 96/517.

45 Council Directive 91/250/EEC of 14 May 1991 on the legal protection of computer programs, *PbEC* 1991, L 122; De Cock Buning (1998), pp. 169–70. The Directive was transposed into national legislation in 1993 in Germany and in the Netherlands in 1994; Act of 7 June 1993, *Bundesgesetzblatt (BGBl)* 1993 1, p. 910; Act of 7 July 1994, *Stb.* 521.

had a creative order, selection or structure.[46] The true value of databases mainly consists of the collection of complete data and not so much its creative selection or presentation.[47] In addition to this, the arrangement of data in many databases is determined by 'database management software' and not by the human creator of the database. Obviously, this led to questions concerning the ability to protect databases.[48]

Producers of databases pushed for specific protection and were rewarded with a *sui generis* right, the European Database Directive of 1996. Producers were granted protection when they showed substantive investment in the acquisition, the control or the presentation of the database.[49] It is remarkable that the Directive was initially designed for electronic databases; however, the final Directive included paper data collections as well.[50] The Directive provides an extraction right of 15 years, running from the date when the database is produced.[51] The producer is now able to prohibit extraction from or the (re)utilization of his/her database, or a substantial part thereof.[52]

Internationally, the protection of databases was put on the digital agenda of the WIPO, with suggestions for *sui generis* protection of databases, strongly based on the European Directive.[53] As a copyright and neighbouring rights treaty was adopted in December 1996, the Database Treaty has remained on the WIPO shelf since then.[54]

---

46 For example, BGH 7 December 1979, *GRUR* (1980), p. 227; BGH 12 March 1987 *ZUM* 1987, p. 525; HR 4 January 1991, *Computerrecht* (1991), p. 84 m. nt. Hugenholtz, *Intellectueel Eigendom en Reclamerecht (IER)* (1991), p. 96 m. nt. Grosheide, *Informatierecht/AMI* (1991), p. 177 m. nt. Spoor, *AA* (1992), p. 31 m. nt. Cohen Jehoram (van Dale/Romme); US Supreme Court 27 March 1991, 89–1909 (*Feist Publications, Inc. v Rural Telephone Companies, Inc.*).

47 Hugenholtz (1989), pp. 134–6.

48 Hugenholtz (1992b), p. 98; Speyart (1996), pp. 157 and 161.

49 Directive 96/9/EC of the European Parliament and of the Council of 11 March 1996 on the legal protection of databases. *PbEC* 1996, I 77/20. Compare art. 901-914 USCA.

50 Hugenholtz (1996), p. 132.

51 Every substantial change starts with a new period of protection, as can be deduced from art 10.3.

52 The extraction of a database needs to be understood as 'the permanent or temporary transfer of all or a substantial part of the contents of a database to another medium by any means or in any form'. The right to reutilize a database is comparable to the right of making available to the public. It means: 'any form of making available to the public all or a substantial part of the contents of a database by the distribution of copies, by renting, online or through (other) forms of transmission'.

53 Arkenbout (1996), p. 181.

54 WIPO documents CRNR/D/94, CRNR/DC/95 and CRNR/DC/6.

4.2 New Exploitation Rights

Not only have new objects of protection resulted in expansion in the field of intellectual property law, this is also true for new methods of exploitation. As indicted above, at the beginning of the twentieth century the increase in the mechanical recording of music on pianolas and phonograms resulted in a wide range of specific regulations.[55] A new method of exploitation was often explained as being part of the existing, traditional method. If necessary, either the existing law was adjusted, or the exceptions to the right of exploitation were amended. This was further accelerated through digital reproduction techniques.

Right to prevent forms of use of works

The introduction of electronic objects in the domain of copyright law pushed the boundaries of the traditional reproduction right so far that it, at least partly, transformed into a right of utilization.

Computer programs were the first products of electronic information technology that gave rise to questions about copyright status in normal, personal use. Was the temporary recording in the working memory of a computer to be understood as an act of reproduction relevant to copyright law?

The definition of reproduction was considerably extended in the European Software Directive and the European Database Directive.[56] Temporary and – for the use of a computer program – necessary acts of reproduction were defined as relevant acts of reproduction.[57] This was a notable extension to the power of the copyright owner since sole *use* (read, see, listen and to allow listening for private use and so on) never used to belong to its sphere of influence.[58]

In communication through networks information is temporarily stored during the transfer. This inevitable storing raises certain issues, equivalent to the issues relating to the temporary recording of data in the working memory of a personal computer.[59] The broad definition of reproduction first introduced in the Software Directive formed the starting point for the WIPO Copyright

[55] De Cock Buning (1998), pp. 111–3, 117–9 and 121–3.

[56] The right of reutilization in the Database Directive as defined in art. 7.2 (b) is in fact an act of making available to the public and not a right of utilization. Compare Considerans nr. 44.

[57] Under specific circumstances rightful users do not need permission for certain acts of utilization. Compare art. 5.1 Software Directive and art. 6.1 and no. 34 Database Directive.

[58] Hugenholtz (1992a), p. 323; Schelven and Struik (1995), p. 58; Verkade (1997), pp. 191 and 195.

[59] Hugenholtz (1995), pp. 515–6; Visser (1997), p. 45.

Treaty 1996[60] and the European Green Paper 1995.[61] In its turn, the latter formed the basis of the European Directive for copyright and neighbouring rights in the Information Society (2001).[62]

During the negotiations on the WIPO Treaty, it initially appeared that the comprehensive definition of multiplication was about to become the international standard.[63] However, after strong opposition by users' groups these acts of reproduction aiming at the mere use of digitalized works did not become part of the final version of the treaty.[64]

4.3 Limitations

Exemptions for users

Consequently, by extending the definition of multiplication to a right of utilization, certain acts of utilization needed to be permitted once again, in order to make way for the normal utilization of digitised works. The Software Directive does not define the necessary multiplication that is brought about by the rightful acquirer of a piece of work as an infringement of copyright. Also the Database Directive acknowledges such an exemption as does the European Directive for Copyright and Neighbouring law in the Information Society (2001)[65]

Reverse engineering[66]

The Software Directive contains several detailed and technology-related regulations. The provisions on reverse engineering were the result of extending the

[60] WIPO Document CRNR/DC/4, 30 August 1996.

[61] Green Paper on Copyright and Related Rights in the Information Society, Com(95)382 final, pp. 51–2.

[62] 2001/29/EC, Pb. 167/10, art 5.1.

[63] Therefore, *browsing* on the Internet and the showing of text, pictures, moving images and so on without the permission of the rightful claimant would initially be prohibited. De Cock Buning (1997), pp. 20–22.

[64] The Treaty includes an agreed statement concerning *storage*. It reads: 'The reproduction right, as set out in Article 9 of the Berne Convention, and the exceptions permitted thereunder, fully apply in the digital environment, in particular to the use of works in digital form. It is understood that the storage of a protected work in digital form in an electronic medium constitutes a reproduction within the meaning of Article 9 of the Berne Convention.' WIPO Copyright Treaty CRNR/DC/94.

[65] Directive 2001/29/EC of the European Parliament and of the Council of 22 May 2001 on the harmonisation of certain aspects of copyright and related rights in the information society. *PbEC* L 167/10, art 5.1.

[66] Reverse engineering is a term used in computer industry. It means that through the analysis, revision or translation of a certain subject the arrangement of a certain product is uncovered. De Cock Buning (1998), pp. 133–7.

definitions as discussed above. To examine the way a computer program works, several acts of multiplication needed to be carried out. Therefore, the Directive had to define explicitly at what point acts of multiplication were permitted. The Directive includes the precondition that only the rightful owner/acquirer can examine the software.[67]

The earlier semi-conductor legislation contained regulations for reverse engineering as well. According to both the American Semiconductor Chip Protection ACT (SCPA) and the European Chip Directive the rightful claimant to an exclusive right of topography could not prohibit a third party from analysing the semi-conductor, regardless of whether this examination requires the multiplication of the semi-conductor.

4.4 Enforcement Mechanisms

Secondary infringement[68]

To support the enforcement of copyrights on software, the draft text of the Software Directive introduced a form of secondary infringement of copyright.[69] The person who either imported, possessed, or sold an unlawful copy of the program, knowing that it was unlawful, infringed the copyright of the rightful owner. Infringement merely by having an unauthorized copy of a work is very remarkable in copyright law. Therefore, the final Directive was substantially toned down.[70] The selling or possession of an unlawful copy was no longer recognized as an infringement of the exclusive right of the author itself, but it could now result in sanctions as a means of enforcing the copyright.[71]

Technological protection measures

Very relevant in the relationship between copyright law and the freedom of communication is the development with regard to the technological protection of information. As a reaction to uncertainty concerning the effectiveness of copyright protection, a tendency towards the technical protection of copy-

67 De Cock Buning (1993), pp. 129–37; De Cock Buning (1998), pp. 169–70.

68 De Cock Buning (1998), pp. 165–9.

69 Dreier (1991), p. 320.

70 Please note that the Dutch Semi-conductor Chips Act contains a regulation that is similar to the initial regulation regarding secondary infringement for the design of the Directive. It defines both the importation or stocking, and the multiplication and creation of a topography as an exclusive right of the rightful claimant, Art. 5.1 of Act; Original (Dutch) title: Wet van October 1987, *Stb* 484, houdende regelen inzake de bescherming van oorspronkelijke topografiën van halfgeleiderproducten; Compare art. 53.1.a Rijksoctrooiwet (Dutch Patent Act) (ROW).

71 Compare to Art. 28 Dutch Copyright Act 1912.

rightable materials exists.[72] A notable example is the following. An American publisher, Williams & Wilkins, was about to lose a lawsuit in the 1970s against persons copying its medical magazines in libraries on a large scale. The publisher decided to print a substantive part of the magazines on dark grey non-copyable paper.[73] The attorney representing Williams & Wilkins called it *noisy paper:* 'terrific except that it is a little difficult on the eyes'.[74] Technological protection clearly not only has positive sides. For the consumer, technological protection often creates difficulties in using the product. For example, a data file or computer program cannot be copied as a back-up or into archives. Furthermore, every technological protection has a technical answer. In the sensational *Betamax* case Judge Ferguson of the Californian District Court stated on the technological protection of television programmes against private copies:

> As sure as you or I are sitting in this courtroom today, some bright young entrepreneur, unconnected with Sony is going to come up with a device to unjam the jam. And then we have a device to jam the unjamming of the jam and we all end up like jelly.[75]

Within the electronic environment the technological protection of copyrighted materials is further threatened.[76] That is the reason why demands could be heard for legislation that would ensure technical protection.[77] Concerning DAT (digital audiotape) recorders several bills were presented which made it obligatory for producers to create protection systems in DAT recorders. The copies were designed to send a signal to the chip in the recorder that should activate the protection system.[78]

However, the systems proved to be non-selective and protected even material that was not copyright protected. Consequently, the bills were withdrawn. The next technological means of protection was more successful.[79] In 1992 the Audio Home Recording Act was adopted in the US.[80] This made obligatory the installing of the Serial Copyright Managements System (SCMS) in electronic recording equipment. The copying of a copy became completely

---

72 Clark (1996), p. 140.

73 United States Supreme Court 1975, 420 U.S. 376 (*Williams & Wilkins v United States*).

74 Goldstein (1994), p. 92.

75 C.D. Cal. 1979, 480 F. Supp. 429.

76 De Cock Buning (2001), p. 6.

77 Vinje (1996), p. 431; Clark (1996), pp. 139–45.

78 Goldstein (1994), p. 160.

79 Visser (1997), p. 59.

80 Art. 1002(c) USCA.

impossible because of this system.[81] The regulation in the Audio Home Recording Act was very detailed and focused on electronic acts of copying which were not even customary at that time.[82] The American White Paper (1995) on the National Information Infrastructure (NII) contains a recommendation for legal measures concerning technological protection as well.[83] Propositions to revise the Copyright Act that stem from the White Paper contain a regulation on 'anti-circumvention'.[84] The deleting or other form of bypassing the technological protection with the intention of infringing became prohibited. As a result of an American proposal, the protection of databases was regulated as well.[85]

Also the WIPO treaty 1996 contains obligations regarding technological measures. The Member States that signed the Treaty were obliged to come up with legal measures against bypassing the technological protection of the works protected by the Berne Convention. Whoever created or sold systems or decoders with the intention of infringing copyright was acting unlawfully.[86]

> Art. 11: Contracting parties shall provide adequate legal protection and effective legal remedies against the circumvention of effective technological measures that are used by authors in connection with the exercise of their rights under this treaty or the Berne Convention and that restrict acts, in respect of their works, which are not authorized by the authors concerned or permitted by law.[87]

The European Software Directive regulates technological protection as well.[88] Legislators in the Member States were obliged to impose sanctions on persons who act as defined in the following article:

> Art 7.1.c: Any act of putting into circulation, or the possession for commercial purposes of, any means the sole intended purpose of which is to facilitate the un-

---

81 On top of this, a levy was introduced for blank carriers of music and recording equipment.

82 Visser (1997), p. 51.

83 Report of the Working Group on Intellectual Property Rights, 'Intellectual Property and the National Information Infrastructure', Washington D.C., 1995.

84 Digital Era Copyright Enhancement Act 13 November 1997, *House Report (H.R.)* 3048, art. 1201.

85 Proposal of 3 May 1996, *H.R.* 3531, art. 10.

86 This is a highly modified and compromised regulation compared to the original proposal of the WIPO Treaty, WIPO Document, 1996 CRNR/DC/4. It is a compromise between content providers, on the one hand, and consumer electronics and hardware companies in the US, on the other.

87 WIPO Copyright Treaty 20 December 1996, CRNR/DC/94.

88 Compare art. 296 of the British Copyright, Designs and Patents Act 1988 (CDPA). This Act contains regulations on hacking programs which are able to break through the physical barriers of computer software. Bainbridge (1996), p. 47.

> authorized removal or circumvention of any technical device which may have been applied to protect a computer program.[89]

At the European political level other similar regulations were enacted as already announced in the ninth chapter (Technical Systems of Identification and Protection) of the Green Paper on Copyright and Related Rights in the Information Society.[90] In the Information Society Directive the Member States have the following obligations concerning technological measures.[91]

> 6.1. Member States shall provide adequate legal protection against the circumvention of any effective technological measures, which the person concerned carries out in the knowledge, or with reasonable grounds to know, that he or she is pursuing that objective.
> 2. Member States shall provide adequate legal protection against the manufacture, import, distribution, sale, rental, advertisement for sale or rental, or possession for commercial purposes of devices, products or components or the provision of services which (a) are promoted, advertised or marketed for the purpose of circumvention of, or (b) have only a limited commercially significant purpose or use other than to circumvent, or (c) are primarily designed, produced, adapted or performed for the purpose of enabling or facilitating the circumvention of, any effective technological measures.

Noteworthy, especially in the context of this contribution, is the fact that the creation of technological barriers limits access to copyrighted materials and can redetermine the subject and contents of the protection of information producers. Producers and publishers of all kinds of information that are placed on the internet are basically free to determine the threshold of protection themselves. Hence, technological protection creates information monopolies and can therefore substantially limit the freedom of communication.[92] As parties can create contracts in which they combine technological protection with contractual conditions, copyright law exemptions can simply be left aside. Parties are able to evade the limitations of copyright protection. The fourth paragraph of Article 6 tries to remedy this partly by obliging Member States to take measures should right owners block the beneficiary of certain

---

[89] Council Directive of 14 May 1991 on the legal protection of computer programs (91/250/EEC), *PbEC* L. 122/42.

[90] The Committee considered that as soon as an industrial standard is designed and accepted, it should become obligatory to stick to only one specific form of technological protection. *EC COM*(95)382.

[91] Directive 2001/29/EC of the European Parliament and of the Council of 22 May 2001 on the harmonisation of certain aspects of copyright and related rights in the information society. *PbEC* L 167/10.

[92] De Cock Buning (2001), p. 6.

limitations to copyright.[93] However, it does not apply to works made available to the public on agreed contractual terms in such a way that members of the public may access them from a place and at a time individually chosen by them. As a consequence users of those works that are placed online behind technological barriers can in principle be denied of statutory limitations to copyright. Obviously this seriously limits the (receipt of) information.[94]

---

93 6.4. Notwithstanding the legal protection provided for in paragraph 1, in the absence of voluntary measures taken by rightholders, including agreements between rightholders and other parties concerned, Member States shall take appropriate measures to ensure that rightholders make available to the beneficiary of an exception or limitation provided for in national law in accordance with Article 5(2)(a), (2)(c), (2)(d), (2)(e), (3)(a), (3)(b) or (3)(e) the means of benefiting from that exception or limitation, to the extent necessary to benefit from that exception or limitation and where that beneficiary has legal access to the protected work or subject-matter concerned. A Member State may also take such measures in respect of a beneficiary of an exception or limitation provided for in accordance with Article 5(2)(b), unless reproduction for private use has already been made possible by rightholders to the extent necessary to benefit from the exception or limitation concerned and in accordance with the provisions of Article 5(2)(b) and (5), without preventing rightholders from adopting adequate measures regarding the number of reproductions in accordance with these provisions. The technological measures applied voluntarily by rightholders, including those applied in implementation of voluntary agreements, and technological measures applied in implementation of the measures taken by Member States, shall enjoy the legal protection provided for in paragraph 1. The provisions of the first and second subparagraphs shall not apply to works or other subject-matter made available to the public on agreed contractual terms in such a way that members of the public may access them from a place and at a time individually chosen by them. When this Article is applied in the context of Directives 92/100/EEC and 96/9/EC, this paragraph shall apply mutatis mutandis. Directive 2001/29/EC of the European Parliament and of the Council of 22 May 2001 on the harmonisation of certain aspects of copyright and related rights in the information society. *PbEC* L 167/10.

94 The Dutch implementation of the aforementioned articles resulted in a change to the Dutch Copyright Act (articles 29a and 29b DCA), the Dutch Neighbouring Rights Act (articles 19 and 19a DNRA) and the Dutch Database Act (articles 5, 5a and 5b DDA) and prohibited technological measures to bypass protection measures. Aanpassing van de Auteurswet 1912, de Wet op de naburige rechten en de Databankenwet ter uitvoering van richtlijn nr. 2001/29/EG van het Europees Parlement en de Raad van de Europese Unie van 22 mei 2001 betreffende de harmonisatie van bepaalde aspecten van het auteursrecht en de naburige rechten in de informatiemaatschappij. *PbEG* L 167. (Uitvoering richtlijn auteursrecht en naburige rechten in de informatiemaatschappij). *Kamerstukken II* 2001/02, 28 482, nrs. 1-2. De Cock Buning (2005), p. 159.

4.5 Bipolarity and Convergence of Copyright and Patent Law[95]

A development which is very relevant to intellectual property's relationship with the freedom of communication is the convergence of the bipolar copyright and patent law. Since the earliest codifications intellectual property law has acknowledged two different aspects: on the one hand, patent law and, on the other, copyright law. The two tend to converge during the development of intellectual property law. Under the influence of electronic information technology, definitions and principles that were traditionally bound to one of the domains were introduced in the other field of law.

Bipolarity

The introduction of the notion of 'Immaterialgüterrecht' by Josef Kohler sets out the external limits for the field of law which allocates exclusive rights to immaterial objects.[96] On the one side of the intellectual property spectrum one can find copyright law, on the other side patent law. The bipolar structure that exists within the domain of intellectual property law can be extrapolated from the two most important treaties: the treaty of Paris (1883) and the Berne Convention (1886).[97] The Berne Convention contains regulations regarding copyright law, the treaty of Paris contains all fields of industrial property law, except the protection of new varieties of plants by an intellectual property right.[98]

Patent law mainly aims to regulate competition between producers for innovation. It provides a temporary monopoly for important and new inventions.[99] It is mostly focused on exploitation rights.[100] Copyright law acknowledges certain cultural and social purposes. Besides the cultural development of society, the position of the author is of crucial importance. The rightowner has both the exploitation and the moral[101] rights to his work.[102] Also the objects

---

95 The definition of convergence needs to be understood as something other than divergence, as used by Arnbak and Cuilenburg 1990.

96 Kohler (1880), p. 141; Ulmer (1980), p. 11.

97 Both treaties are the responsibility of the WIPO since the revision in Stockholm 1967.

98 Reichman (1992), pp. 325–61.

99 The Explanatory Memorandum to the Dutch Patent Act 1910 shows that the government did not see a priority in rewarding the inventor, but it wanted to use the notion of a reward to stimulate inventions, MvT ROW, *Bijlage Handelingen II* 1904/1905, nr. 197.

100 Teijl and Holzhauer (1991), p. 50; Wichers Hoeth (1993), p. 10.

101 In the Berne Convention formulated in art. 6 bis. This article provides the author with a 'droit de paternité' and a 'droit d'integrité'. In the domain of patent law the personality right is only a right to mention the name of the inventor. For example, the Dutch art. 12A ROW.

102 Exemptions to this regulation can be found in arts 7 and 45a–g of the Dutch Copyright Act 1912.

of copyright law and patent law are different. Copyright protects the original *expression* of an idea. The aim of patent law is to protect the innovative solution to a problem and not, as is the case in copyright law, to protect the *way* this is done.[103]

Another important difference between patent law and copyright law is the permitted use of the object protected.[104] Principally, copyright-protected work may be used in every way. A work of authorship can be read, watched or be listened to. Patent rights grant a monopoly of utilization. Third parties are prohibited from using the invention in any professional way.[105] On the other hand, third parties are able to use freely the ideas and principles of copyright-protected expression. The independent creation of works that are similar to protected works already on the market is permitted in the field of copyright, but is not permitted in the field of patent law.[106] Patent law provides more extensive protection compared to copyright law.

Patent law, similar to most other industrial property rights, provides a shorter protection period than copyright law. The longer the protection period, the more the freedom of information and competition is restricted.[107]

Convergence

During the last few decades the differences between the two areas of intellectual property have become blurred due to the influence of the development of information technology.[108] Both the objects and contents of protection tend to converge.

Mainly due to the application of copyright law to products of electronic information technology, copyright law and patent law converge. Lobbying by software producers has quite successfully achieved the situation where copyright protection has been extended towards patent-like protection.[109] The protection of the mere expression of computer programs leaving the truly valuable programming ideas unprotected was considered inadequate. Lobbying started in order to achieve the most comprehensive way of protection, with the threshold for protection being as low as possible.

Already in American case law from 1986 protection was granted to more than the mere expression of a computer program for the purposes of dentistry.

---

103 The sole solution is not enough to be protected by patent law; it has to be applicable in industry. Algorithms are omitted for this reason. Wichers Hoeth (1993), p. 28.

104 Dorhout Mees (1989), p. 3.

105 Wichers Hoeth (1993), p. 37.

106 Dommering (1990), pp. 105–9.

107 Reichman (1992), p. 331.

108 Grosheide (2006); Hugenholtz (1992a), pp. 319–23; Beier (1991), p. 161.

109 De Cock Buning (1998), pp. 142–5.

Most elements of a computer program designed for dentists are deemed to be protected by copyright law. The sole element that was not recognized as being protected by copyright was the underlying basic concept of organizing a dental practice.[110] Later on, this decision was nuanced and the level of protection by American copyright law was brought back to a more commonly recognized level.[111] This same development can also be found in the American 'look and feel' case law. Producers of software tried to extend the boundaries of copyright protection.[112] On the other side of the intellectual property law spectrum, several principles of patent law (for example, the requirement that the invention is technical and of such technical standards that an average specialist would agree on the high standards) were toned down so as to clear the way for the protection of products and services from information technology.[113]

Concerning exploitation rights, one can also perceive a strong convergence of patent law and copyright law as well. Within copyright law, patent law definitions were introduced in order to provide the determined level of protection. An important example of this development is the widening of the traditional right of reproduction so as to cover the right of utilization as indicated above.[114] The Software Directive grants the use of a computer program exclusively to the legitimate purchaser.[115] The necessary temporary acts of reproduction are regarded as a relevant act of reproduction in the field of copyright law. Because of this 'stretching' of the definition of reproduction a wider range of protection is granted, partly similar to the prohibition of utilization in the field of patent law. The use of an invention is traditionally protected in patent law, but the difference is that patent law exclusively focuses on commercial use, while the above-mentioned copyright law regime focuses on *all* utilization, including general consumer utilization.[116]

---

110 U.S. 3d Cir. 1986, 797 F2d 1222 (*Whelan Associates, Inc. v Jaslow Dental Laboratory, Inc.*).

111 U.S. 2d Cir. 1992, 9693 (*Computer Associates International, Inc. v Altai, Inc.*).

112 'Purely functional items or an arrangement of them for functional purposes are wholly beyond the realm of copyright', N.D. Cal. 1992, 788 F. Supp. 1106 (*Apple Computer, Inc. v Microsoft Corp.*).

113 Meijboom 1990, pp. 47–59; for example, Afdeling van Beroep, 19 January 1983, *Bijblad bij de Industriële Eigendom* (*BIE*) (1983), p. 336 (Tomograafbeschikking Dutch Patent Office, DPO); DPO Afdeling van Beroep 11 May 1987, *BIE* (1987), p. 174 (Streepjes-code-beschikking); US Supreme Court 1981, 450 *U.S.* 175 (*Diamond v Diehr*); BGH *GRUR* (1980), pp. 849–51 (Antiblockiersystem); BGH *Computer und Recht* (1992), p. 600 (Tauchcomputer).

114 De Cock Buning (1998), pp. 50–2; Spoor and Verkade (1993), p. 141; Visser (1997), p. 27; Lucas (1987), pp. 183–262; Reichman (1992), p. 346.

115 De Cock Buning (1998), pp. 50–2.

116 Art. 53.1.a ROW; Wichers Hoeth (1993), p. 40.

Also the regulation of reverse engineering in European copyright protection regimes for software and semi-conductor chips is remarkably similar to the patent law exemption for research. In patent law, acts involving the research of the patented object are permitted.[117] Note that this tendency of convergence is not entirely new and is not always caused by the development of information technology. The protection of models and drafts of industry is of a hybrid character. This kind of intellectual property protection law contains both elements of copyright law and elements of patent law, for example the necessary (for protection purposes) depot.[118] The object of protection contains both an artistic and an industrial element.

5. CONCLUSIONS

In this chapter a characterization has been given of the expansion of and the convergence in intellectual property law, with the focus being on copyright law.

It became apparent that copyright law is particularly sensitive to technological changes because copyright protection is granted to expression and not, contrary to patent law, to content. Manifestations of information on new carriers were brought within the existing categories of copyrightable subject-matter. The development of new methods of expression (film and photography), new methods of multiplication (sound and image recordings and reprography) and new methods of distributing work (broadcasting and cable) laid the foundations for contemporary copyright law in the twentieth century. Besides these analogue information technologies, primarily electronic information technology has had a great influence during the last 30 years on the development of this field of law. Electronic information technologies (semi-conductor chips, computer software programs, electronic databases and network communication) led to a substantial expansion in the domain and content of copyright law. Symptoms of the strong expansion in the domain of intellectual property can be found in the incorporation of new objects as objects of protection, new methods of exploitation as exploitation rights and in the implementation of new mechanisms of enforcement. The introduction of electronic information technology has further substantially increased the quantity and complexity. Most notable in this respect is the inclination to create technological barriers that limit access to copyrighted materials and to redetermine the subject and content of protection. Information which is not

---

117 Wichers Hoeth (1993), p. 40.
118 Reichman (1989), p. 655.

protected by intellectual property law can now be left outside the public domain. Technological protection creates information monopolies and can therefore substantially limit the freedom of communication.[119] When technological protection measures are combined with contractual conditions users can in principle be denied the statutory limitations to copyright thereby limiting the (receipt of) information.

Simultaneously, copyright law has partly moved in the direction of industrial property law. Genuine patent law characterizations such as research exemptions and utilization rights have been adopted in the field of copyright law. With this, the level of protection that was considered to be inadequate was supplemented. This is especially true for those products that have mainly commercial characteristics such as software and databases for which patent and copyright law notions tend to converge. Both the Directives for the protection of software and databases and the Directive for copyright law in the information society extend the right of reproduction to a right of utilization. Copyright traditionally protects the way a work is communicated, and patent law protects the application of information.[120] In order to protect the use of a work for necessary acts of reproduction by copyright law, a patent law-like protection was granted. Moreover, copyright's rights of utilization are even more far-reaching than protection by patent law.[121] Patent protection is restricted to commercial use, since the regime of software and databases is applicable to *all* use, even consumers' use of information.[122] Such legislation can result in a threat to the vulnerable balance between freedom of communication, on the one hand, and subjective rights on the other. A low threshold (no formal claims are required) grants a strong and long-lasting level of protection with respect to content.

BIBLIOGRAPHY

Arkenbout, E.J. (1996), 'Nieuwe internationale regels over auteursrecht en naburige rechten', *Intellectueel Eigendom en Reclamerecht (IER)*, pp. 176–82.

Arnbak, J.C., J.J. van Cuilenburg and E.J. Dommering (eds) (1990), *Verbinding en ontvlechting in de communicatie, een studie naar toekomstig overheidsbeleid voor de openbare elektronische informatievoorziening* (Amsterdam: Otto Cramwinckel).

Bainbridge, D.I. (1996), *Introduction to Computer Law* (London/Hong Kong: Pitman).

de Beaufort, H.L. (1909), *Het auteursrecht in het Nederlandse en het intertnational recht* (diss. Utrecht) (Utrecht: Den Boer).

119 De Cock Buning (2001), p. 6.
120 Hugenholtz (1989), p. 176.
121 Reichman (1992), p. 344.
122 Compare art. 53.1.a ROW; Wichers Hoeth (1993), p. 40.

de Beaufort, H.L. (1932), *Auteursrecht* (Zwolle: W.E.J. Tjeenk Willink).
Beier, F.K. (1991), 'The Future of Intellectual Property in Europe, Thoughts on the Development of Patent, Utility Model and Industrial Design Law', *International Review of Industrial Property and Copyright Law*, pp. 157–77.
du Bois, R.L. (1981), 'Honderd jaren auteursrecht in Nederland', *Auteursrecht/AMR*, pp. 71–2.
Boytha, G. (1992), 'The Justification of the Protection of Authors' Rights as Reflected in their Historical Development', *Revue internationale du droit d'auteur (RIDA)*, 151, p. 69.
Brinkhof, J.J. (1990), 'Over octrooirecht en economie', *Ars Aequi* Rechtseconomie special, pp. 228–36.
Chaytor, H.J. (1966), *From Script to Print* (London: Sidgwick & Jackson).
Clark, C. (1996), 'The answer to the machine is in the machine', in Hugenholtz (ed.), *The Future of Copyright in a Digital Environment* (Boston/Deventer: Kluwer), pp. 81–102.
de Cock Buning, M. (1993), 'Auteursrecht en "reverse engineering", techniek en theorie', *IER* 1993/5, pp. 129–37.
de Cock Buning, M. (1997), 'Recente auteursrecht verdragen met onderhandelingsruimte', *Informatie Professional* 1997/2, pp. 20–2.
de Cock Buning, M. (1998), *Auteursrecht en informatierechnologie* (diss. Amsterdam UvA) (Amsterdam: Otto Cramwinckel).
de Cock Buning, M. (2001), 'Informatieconsument moet stem laten horen', *NRC Handelsblad*, 20 August, p. 6.
Cornish, W.R. (1989), *Intellectual Property: Patents, Copyright, Trade Marks and Allied Rights* (London: Sweet & Maxwell).
Darras, A. (1890), *Rapport sur la deuxième Conférence réunie à Berne par L'Association littéraire et artistique internationale* (Paris).
Dommering, E.J. (1992), 'Reverse Engineering; een softwarepuzzel', *Computerrecht* 1990/3, pp. 105–9.
Dommering, E.J. (1994), 'Het auteursrecht spoelt weg door het elektronisch vergiet, enige gedachten over de naderende crisis van het auteursrecht', *Computerrecht*, pp. 109–13.
Dommering, E.J. (1996), 'Internet: een juridische plaatsbepaling van een nieuw communicatieproces', *Computerrecht* 1996-6, p. 211.
Dorhout Mees, T.J. (1989), *Nederlands handels- en faillissementsrecht II, Industriële eigendom en mededingingsrecht* (Arnhem: Gouda Quint).
Dreier, Th. (1991), 'The Council Directive of 14 May 1991 on the Legal Protection of Computer Programs', *European Intellectual Property Review (EIPR)*, pp. 319–27.
van Engelen, Th.C.J.A. (1994), *Prestatiebescherming en ongeschreven intellectuele eigendomsrechten* (diss. Leiden) (Zwolle: W.E.J. Tjeenk Willink).
Feenstra, J.J. (1996), 'Het Magill-arrest: eendagsvlieg of vogelspin', *informatierecht/AMI* 1996/2, pp. 31–5.
Fromm, F.K. and W. Nordemann (1988), *Urheberrecht* (Stuttgart/Berlin/Cologne/Mainz: Kohlhammer).
Goldstein, P. (1994), *Copyrights' Highway, from Gutenberg to the Celestrial Jukebox* (New York: Hill and Wang).
Gotzen, M.F. (1995), 'From Cinematographic Work to Audiovisual Work, The Evolution of a Nation in the History of the International Texts Concerning Authors' Rights', in *ALAI Audiovisual Works and Literary and Artistic Property*, Paris ALAI, p. 34.

Grosheide, F.W. (1986), *Auteursrecht op maat*, (diss Utrecht) (Deventer: Kluwer).
Grosheide, F.W. (1994), 'Van de Brug af gezien – Kroniek van wetgeving, literatuur en rechtspraak 1993', *Intellectueel Eigendom en Reclamerecht (IER)* 1994/2, pp. 33–7.
Grosheide, F.W. (1995), 'Van de brug af gezien, Kroniek wetgeving, jurisprudentie en literatuur 1994', *IER* 1995/3, pp. 81–4.
Grosheide, F.W. (1999), 'Concurrence of Trademark and Copyright Standards: Some Thoughts – Developments in Dutch Law with reference to American Law', *Fordham University School of Law, Seventh Annual Conference on International Intellectual Property Law & Policy, April 8 & 9 1999*, pp. 1–35.
Grosheide, F.W. (2000), 'Crossing Borders: Convergence in the Field of IPR's', *9th Fordham University School of Law International Intellectual Property Law & Policy, April 19–20 2000*, pp. 1–14.
Grosheide, F.W. (2001a), 'Music Distribution On-line: Ippropriate Legal Framework in Place for Music on Line?', *European Law Conference, (Stockholm 2001)*, pp. 1–29.
Grosheide, F.W. (2001b), 'Database Protection – The European Way, 2001', *Heart of America Intellectual Property Law Conference Washington University School of Law, 2001*, pp. 1–25.
Grosheide, F.W. (2001c), 'Copyright Law from a User's Perspective: Access Rights for Users', *EIPR July 2001*, pp. 321–5.
Grosheide, F.W. (2002), 'Copyright Issues and the Information Society-Dutch perspectives', *Netherlands Reports to the Sixteenth International Congress of Comparative Law, (Brisbane 2002)* (Antwerpen), pp. 211–33.
Grosheide, F.W. and J. J. Brinkhof (2004), 'Intellectual Property 2004, Articles on Crossing Borders between Traditional and Actual', *Molengrafica Series* (Antwerpen: Intersentia), pp. xi–xiv.
Grosheide, F.W. (2006), 'Globalisation, Convergence and Divergence in International Copyright Law: A Question of Expediency or of Right?' in Fiona Macmillan (ed.), *New Directions in Copyright Law, Volume 2* (Cheltenham and Northampton: Edward Elgar Publishing), pp. 37–60.
Hugenholtz, P.B. (1985), 'Juridische bescherming van chips', *Bijblad bij de Industriële Eigendom (BIE)*, pp. 127–34.
Hugenholtz, P.B. (1989), *Auteursrecht op informatie* (diss. Amsterdam) (Deventer: Kluwer).
Hugenholtz, P.B. (1992a), 'Convergence and Divergence in Intellectual Property Law: The Case of the Software Directive', in W.F. Korthals Altes (a.o.) (eds), *Information Law Towards the 21st Century* (Deventer: Kluwer Law and Taxation).
Hugenholtz, P.B. (1992b), 'Het Ontwerp-Richtlijn Databasebescherming: de Europese Commissie lanceert een tweetrapsraket', *Computerrecht* 1992/3, pp. 97–101.
Hugenholtz, P.B. (1994), 'De Europese richtlijn inzake satellietomroep en kabeldoorgifte', *Informatierecht/AMI*, pp. 87–90.
Hugenholtz, P.B. (1995), 'Het auteursrecht, het internet en de informatiesnelweg', *Nederlands Juristenblad (NJB)*, pp. 515–16.
Hugenholtz, P.B. (1996), 'De Databankrichtlijn eindelijk aanvaard: een zeer kritisch commentaar', *Computerrecht* 1996/4, pp. 131–6.
Karnell, G.W.G. (1991), 'The Norduc Cataloque Rule', in E.J. Dommering and P.B. Hugenholtz (eds), *Protecting Works of Fact* (Deventer/Boston: Kluwer Law and Taxation), pp. 67–73.
Kohler, J. (1880), 'Das Autorrecht, eine zivilistische Abhandlung', *Archiv für die civilistische Praxis*.
Kolle, G. (1977), 'Computer Software Protection – Present Situation and Future Prospects', *Copyright*, pp. 70–9.

Koopmans, T. (1983), 'Redactionele kanttekeningen – mini-monopolies', *Rechtsgeleerd Magazijn Themis (RMTh)/4*, pp. 342–4.
Koopmans, T. (1994), 'Intellectuele eigendom, economie en politiek', *Informatierecht/AMI* 1994/6, p. 107.
Laddie, H. (1995), 'Copyright: over-strength, overregulated, over-rated?', *European Intellectual Property Law (EIPR)*, pp. 253–60.
Lucas, A. (1987), *Le droit d'informatique* (Paris: PUF).
Meijboom, A.P. (1990), 'The Question of Software Patentability', in H.W.K. Kaspersen and A. Oskamp (eds), *Amongst Friends in Computers and Law* (Deventer/Boston: Kluwer), pp. 47–59.
Mom, G.J.H.M. (1990), *Kabeltelevisie en auteursrecht* (diss. Amsterdam UvA) (Lelystad: Vermande).
Van Nieuwenhoven Helbach E.A. (1989), *Nederlands Handels – en Faillisementsrecht II, Industriële eigendom en mededingingsrecht* (Arnhem: Gouda Quint).
Nimmer, M.B., 'Nimmer on Copyright' (New York: Matthew Bender) (loose leaf), § 8.18A and B9.
Reichman, J.H. (1989), 'Computer Programs as Applied Scientific Know-How: Implications of Copyright Protection for Commercialized University Research', *Vanderbilt Law Review* 1989/42, pp. 639–723.
Reichman, J.H. (1991), 'Proprietary Rights in the New Landscape of Intellectual Property Law: An Anglo-American Perspective', in ALAI Congrès de la Mer Egée II.
Reichman, J.H. (1992), 'Legal Hybrids between the Patent and Copyright Paradigms' in W.F. Korthals Altes, (a.o.) (eds), *Information Law Towards the 21st century* (Deventer: Kluwer Law and Taxation), pp. 325–61.
Reinhart, B. (1987), 'Vom Einfluss der Technik auf die Entwickelung des subjectiven Urheberrechts', *UFITA*, 106, pp. 219–29.
Ricketson, S. (1987), *The Berne Convention for the Protection of Literary and Artistic Works: 1886–1986* (London and Deventer: Kluwer).
Ringer, B. (1977), 'Two Hundred years of American Copyright Law', in *Two Hundred Years of English and American Patent, Trademark and Copyright Law* (American Bar Association) (Chicago), pp. 117–18.
van Schelven, P.C. and H. Struik (1995), *Softwarerecht. Bescherming en gebruik van programmatuur sedert de Richtlijn Softwarebescherming* (Deventer: Kluwer).
Schneiders, P. (1991), *Van kleitablet tot database, een geschiedenis van de informatievoorziening* (The Hague: NBLC).
Seignette, J.M.B. (1994), *Challenges to the Creator Doctrine* (diss. Amsterdam UvA) (Deventer/Boston: Kluwer).
Speyart, H.M.H. (1966), 'De databank-richtlijn en haar gevolgen voor Nederland (I&II)', *Informatierecht/AMI*, pp. 151–63 and 171–9.
Spoor, J.H. (1990), *De gestage groei van merk, werk en uitvinding* (oratie) (Zwolle: W.E.J. Tjeenk Willink).
Spoor, J.H. and D.W.F. Verkade (1993), *Auteursrecht* (Deventer: Kluwer).
Teijl, R. and R.W. Holzhauer (1991), *De toenemende complexiteit van het intellectuele eigendomsrecht, een economische analyse', Rechtseconomische verkenningen I* (Arnhem: Gouda Quint).
Troller, A. (1983), *Immaterialgüterrecht* (Basel/Frankfurt am Main: Helbing & Lichtenhahn).
Ulmer, E. (1980), *Urheber- und Verlagsrecht* (Berlin/Heidelberg/New York: Springer).
Verkade, D.W.F. (1990), *Intellectuele eigendom, mededinging en informatievrijheid* (oratie) (Deventer: Kluwer).

Verkade, D.W.F. (1997), 'Intellectuele eigendom', in H. Franken, H.W.K. Kaspersen and A.H. de Wild (eds), *Recht en Computer* (Deventer: Kluwer), pp. 178–229.

Vinje, Th. C. (1996), 'A Brave New World of Technological Protection Systems: Will There Still Be Room for Copyright?', *EIPR*, pp. 431–40.

Visser, D.J.G. (1997), *Auteursrecht op toegang, de exploitatierechten van de auteur in het tijdperk van digitale informatie en netwerkcommunicatie* (diss. Leiden) (The Hague: Vuga).

Walde, E. (1987), 'Die Entfaltung des Urheberrechts als Antwort auf technischen Neuwerungen', *Archiv für Urheber-, Film-, Funk-, und Theaterrecht (UFITA)*, 106, pp. 203–17.

Wefers Bettink, H.W. (1997), 'Muziek op Internet:de BUMA-regeling', *Computerrecht* 1997/2, pp. 55–9.

Wichers Hoeth, L. (1993), 'Kort begrip van het recht betreffende het intellectuele eigendomsrecht' (Zwolle: W.E.J. Tjeenk Willink).

Wijnstroom, J.J. and J.L.A. Peremans (1930), *Het Auteursrecht* (Zwolle: W.E.J. Tjeenk Willink).

4. Patents and human rights: where is the paradox?

Rochelle Cooper Dreyfuss*

There is an emerging trend, particularly in international and European circles, to bemoan what is termed the human rights paradox in intellectual property. Thus, it is claimed that intellectual property rights are grounded in fundamental concepts of human dignity and just deserts, in a commitment to accord to creators the benefits of their intellectual efforts. At the same time, however, it is recognized that intellectual property rights protect information, a non-rivalrous good. The paradox is said to arise when one human right is pitted against another, when intellectual property rights are used to restrict access to information that could – at no real cost to the developer – be deployed in ways that satisfy fundamental human needs.[1]

In a sense, it is not difficult to understand why this concern has emerged. At the international level, the Universal Declaration of Human Rights (UDHR) and the International Covenant on Economic, Social, and Cultural

* Pauline Newman Professor of Law and Director of the Engelberg Center on Innovation Law and Policy. This chapter was prepared as a paper for a conference on 'The Human Rights Paradox in Intellectual Property Law' organized by the Centre for Intellectual Property Law (CIER), Molengraaff Institute for Private Law, at Utrecht University. I am grateful to Willem Grosheide and the other Conference organizers and to the Conference participants, who convinced me there was a problem here worth thinking about. I am especially indebted to Geertrui Van Overwalle, who was assigned the task of arguing the contrary view on the ramifications of a patent paradox. I would also like to thank Larry Helfer for his astute comments; my research assistant Jesse Dyer (NYU Law School, Class of 2008), for his careful scholarship; my assistant, Nicole Arzt for her hard work; and the Filomen D'Agostino and Max E. Greenberg Research Fund for supporting the research on this article.

1 See, for example, Helfer, Laurence R. (2007), 'Toward a Human Rights Framework for Intellectual Property', 40 *U.C. Davis L. Rev.*, http://ssrn.com/abstract=891303; Geiger, Christophe (2006), '"Constitutionalising" Intellectual Property Law? The Influence of Fundamental Rights on Intellectual Property in the European Union', 37 *Int'l Rev. of Intell. Prop. & Competition Law* 371; Birnhack, Michael D. (2003), 'Acknowledging the Conflict between Copyright Law and Freedom of Expression under the Human Rights Act', [2003] *Ent. L. Rev*. 24.

Rights (ICESCR) both articulate commitments to the rights of creators;[2] the European Convention on Human Rights (ECHR) can be read in a parallel fashion.[3] At the same time, however, all of these instruments recognize rights that require access to the fruits of creativity.[4] As these commitments become enforceable in courts of law, the stage is set for a clash between the right to control information and the right to use it for such purposes as attaining health and education, participating in cultural activities, engaging in expressive conduct, or freely pursuing intellectual inquiry.

But is there really a paradox here and is it related to patents? My thesis is that the equation of intellectual property rights generally – and patent rights in particular – to human rights is belied by the historical evolution of these rights and negated structurally, by the manner in which claims to intellectual products are recognized in legislative enactments and international instruments. As a theoretical matter, there are clearly dimensions to intellectual property that sound in human rights concerns (rights to protect one's dignity, to be compensated for one's labor, and to enjoy one's property without arbitrary governmental interference). But at least on the patent side, there is little reason to think that the human rights concerns associated with creative labor must be furthered by recognizing a right to full control over the information that creative labor produces.

---

2 Universal Declaration of Human Rights, Dec. 8, 1948, G.A. Res. 217A(III), U.N. Doc. A/810, at 71, art. 27(2) ('Everyone has the right to the protection of the moral and material interests resulting from any scientific, literary or artistic production of which he is the author'); International Covenant on Economic, Social and Cultural Rights, adopted 16 Dec 1966, arts. 15(1)(c), S. Exec. Doc. D, 95-2, at 13, (1997), 993 U.N.T.S. 3, 5 (entered into force 3 January 1976) ('The States Parties to the present Covenant recognize the right of everyone … To benefit from the protection of the moral and material interests resulting from any scientific, literary or artistic production of which he is the author').

3 Convention for the Protection of Human Rights and Fundamental Freedoms, 4 November 1950, 213 U.N.T.S. 221, art. 10(2) (creating an exception to free exercise to protect 'the rights of others', presumably including creators, see, for example, Rindler, Heinz (1997), 'Case Comment – Austria: Copyright – Copyright Infringement Through Publishing A Stock Purchase Agreement in a Newspaper', 19 *Eur. Intell. Prop. Rev.* 170).

4 See, for example, UDHR, arts. 1 (right to dignity); 18 (freedom of thought); 19 (freedom of expression); 25 (right to health); 27(1) (right to 'participate in the cultural life of the community, to enjoy the arts and to share in scientific advancement and its benefits'); ICESCR, Preamble (right to dignity and to 'economic, social and cultural rights, as well as his civil and political rights'); arts. 12 (right to health); 13 (right to an education); 27(1)(a) and (b) (rights to 'take part in cultural life [and] to enjoy the benefits of scientific progress and its applications'); ECHR arts. 9 (freedom of thought); 10 (freedom of expression).

Elevating intellectual property rights to human rights has unfortunate pragmatic consequences. Presumably, human rights can be outweighed only by other human rights. Accordingly, under a human rights approach, the benefit stream flowing from inventive production can be distributed, without a patentee's authorization, only to meet social needs that are likewise classified as fundamental. (Or to put it another way, every incursion on a patent right would need to be justified by showing that it involved an interest that is not only socially desirable, but that can also be categorized as a human right.) Instead of relying on legislatures and courts to wield well-understood tools embedded in existing patent law, ad hoc rights-balancing leads to unpredictable decision-making. The result, ironically, is an environment less conducive to decisions to invest time and money in intellectual efforts. The new – human rights – justification can, in short, thwart the traditional – utilitarian – goal of limiting protection from free riders as a means of encouraging the advancement of knowledge.

This chapter lays out the historical, structural, and economic evidence undermining the equation of patent rights and human rights. It then tries to understand the source of the rhetorical incarnation of patent rights as human rights. It ends with examples of how a utilitarian justification for patent rights is better suited to the task of furthering social welfare. Nothing here is intended to refute the claim that there are social interests that conflict with patent rights, to deny that some of these interests can be characterized as human rights, or to quarrel with the strategy of using human rights justifications to advance social welfare. My focus is limited to the question whether the debate over the balance between the interests of the public and patentees should be structured as a contest among human rights.

1. HISTORY, STRUCTURE, AND ECONOMICS

To an American, the concept of a patent as a human right is particularly hard to grasp. Patent rights are not, like rights in real property, anterior to the constitutional scheme. Rather, it is given to Congress to create them. That Congress has no obligation to do so furnishes some evidence that the Framers of the Constitution did not consider a patent a fundamental right. Indeed, what little is known about the thinking of the founders of the United States points in exactly the opposite direction. In the words of Thomas Jefferson, who as Secretary of State, was the first administrator of the patent system:

> Stable ownership is the gift of social law, and is given late in the progress of society. It would be curious then, if an idea, the fugitive fermentation of an individual brain, could, of natural right, be claimed in exclusive and stable property. If nature

has made any one thing less susceptible than all others of exclusive property, it is the action of the thinking power called an idea, which an individual may exclusively possess as long as he keeps it to himself; but the moment it is divulged, it forces itself into the possession of every one, and the receiver cannot dispossess himself of it. Its peculiar character, too, is that no one possesses the less, because every other possesses the whole of it. He who receives an idea from me, receives instruction himself without lessening mine; as he who lights his taper at mine, receives light without darkening me. That ideas should freely spread from one to another over the globe, for the moral and mutual instruction of man, and improvement of his condition, seems to have been peculiarly and benevolently designed by nature, when she made them, like fire, expansible over all space, without lessening their density in any point, and like the air in which we breathe, move, and have our physical being, incapable of confinement or exclusive appropriation. Inventions then cannot, in nature, be a subject of property. Society may give an exclusive right to the profits arising from them, as an encouragement to men to pursue ideas which may produce utility, but this may or may not be done, according to the will and convenience of the society, without claim or complaint from anybody.[5]

Further evidence is provided by the nature of the authority the Framers actually gave to Congress. Thus, when Congress does choose to create patent rights, its power is highly restricted:

The Congress shall have the power … To promote the Progress of Science and useful Arts, by securing for limited Times to Authors and Inventors the exclusive Right to their respective Writings and Discoveries.[6]

Four features of this grant are especially notable. First is the clear reference to a purely utilitarian purpose – to promote Science (which at the time, meant knowledge) and to encourage the production of useful Arts (that is the products of what we now call science). Secondly, no matter how long the creative work retains its value, the creator can enjoy exclusivity for only 'limited times'. The value that endures belongs to the public. Thirdly, only 'writings'

---

[5] VI Writings of Thomas Jefferson, at 180–81 (Washington ed.), cited in *Graham v John Deere, Co.*, 383 U.S. 1, 9 (1966). See also Dreyfuss, Rochelle Cooper (1992), 'A *Wiseguy*'s Approach to Information Products: Muscling Copyright and Patent into a Unitary Theory of Intellectual Property', *Sup. Ct. Rev.* 195, 231 (arguing that the Framers were skeptical about the need for intellectual property protection but wanted to make sure that Congress could harmonize the disparate intellectual property laws of the various colonies). See also Walterscheid, Edward C. (1999), 'The Use and Abuse of History: The Supreme Court's Interpretation of Thomas Jefferson's Influence on the Patent Law', 39 Idea 195 (citing various Jefferson letters expressing skepticism of the patent system).

[6] U.S. Const. art. I, § 8 [the Copyright and Patent Clause]. A useful comparison can be made to U.S. Const. amend. V, which assumes the right to property, stating that 'No person … shall be deprived of life, liberty or property, without due process of law; nor shall private property be taken for public use without compensation.'

and 'discoveries' are protectable. Ideas, principles of nature, products of nature, and raw facts – no matter how valuable – likewise belong to the public. Finally, while Congress can give creators the right to exclude others, the Constitution does not recognize any affirmative rights of the creator to publish, license, or even use her own work.

The structure of the law Congress enacted under this authority is of a piece with this approach. As required by the Constitution, patents endure for a limited period of time.[7] In many fields, inventions have a long useful life after the patent has expired. (An example particularly relevant to the human rights question is pharmacology, where the entire generic drug industry is based on the value of inventions after patent expiration.)

Similarly, the subject matter of patent protection is circumscribed.[8] 'A scientific concept or mere idea cannot be the subject of a valid patent.'[9] Or as Justice Fortas put it:

> [A] patent is not a hunting license. It is not a reward for the search, but compensation for its successful conclusion. A patent system must be related to the world of commerce rather than to the realm of philosophy.[10]

In other words, a fundamental idea must go into the public domain, even though considerable ingenuity may have been required to formulate it, and even though society may owe a great debt to the originator for articulating it.[11] The patent domain is reserved for end products (applications of fundamental ideas).

---

7 35 U.S.C. § 154-156 (generally, the term is 20 years from application, a term that is much shorter than the copyright term).

8 35 U.S.C. § 101.

9 *Diamond v Diehr*, 450 U.S. 175, 195 (1981). Under the so-called 'mental steps doctrine', earlier law was even more heavily focused on insuring the freedom to engage in mental activity and to exercise judgment, see, for example, *In re Heritage*, 150 F.2d 554, 556 (C.C.P.A.1945) ('purely mental acts are not proper subject matter for protection under the patent statutes').

10 *Brenner v Manson*, 383 U.S. 519,536 (1966).

11 See also *Laboratory Corp. v Metabolite Laboratories, Inc.*, 548 U.S. 124, 126–7 (2006) ('The justification for the principle [excluding laws of nature from patentability] does not lie in any claim that "laws of nature" are obvious, or that their discovery is easy, or that they are not useful. To the contrary, research into such matters may be costly and time-consuming; monetary incentives may matter; and the fruits of those incentives and that research may prove of great benefit to the human race. Rather, the reason for the exclusion is that sometimes too much patent protection can impede rather than "promote the Progress of Science and useful Arts," the constitutional objective of patent and copyright protection.') (Breyer, J, dissenting).

Further, patents are only rights to exclude – and then, only within a specific territory: the US statute provides the patentee with a right of action against anyone who, without authority 'makes, uses, offers to sell, or sells any patented invention, within the United States, or imports [a patented invention] into the United States' during the patent term.[12] Even the right to exclude does not run against the United States government or those utilizing the invention on its behalf.[13]

Patents are constrained in ways that go beyond these constitutionally-mandated limits. The law requires disclosure of the underlying invention.[14] Although there is considerable disagreement on how much research can be conducted using the disclosed information (especially when the experiment also involves use of the invention), it is clear that the informational content is immediately available to all:

> The requirement of disclosure of the details of patented inventions facilitates further knowledge and understanding of what was done by the patentee, and may lead to further technologic advance. The right to conduct research to achieve such knowledge need not, and should not, await expiration of the patent.[15]

Patents are also of limited scope.[16] Sometimes research conducted using a patent's disclosure will infringe the patent, but this is by no means always the case. Often, the technical knowledge contributed by the patentee can be utilized (for free) in other fields, or to make fresh advances in the patentee's own field. (Because patents on genetic materials are generally narrow in scope, there are many examples of non-infringing uses of information in that field.[17])

Relief in patent cases is subject to principles of equity, meaning that especially important social concerns can outweigh the patentee's interest in maximizing its

---

[12] 35 U.S.C. § 271.

[13] 28 U.S.C. § 1498. The government must, however, pay just compensation. See also 35 U.S.C. §§ 181, 183 (right of US government to withhold patent from publication on national security grounds, subject to payment of compensation).

[14] 35 U.S.C. § 112.

[15] *Integra Lifesciences I, Ltd. v Merck KgaA*, 331 F.3d 860, 873 (Fed. Cir 2003) (Newman, J., dissenting in part), vacated and remanded, 545 U.S. 193 (2005).

[16] Cf. *Warner-Jenkinson Co., Inc. v Hilton Davis Chemical Co.*, 520 U.S. 17 (1997) (discussing how far patent rights extend beyond the literal meaning of the claims).

[17] See, for example, *Novo Nordisk v Genentech, Inc.*, 77 F.3d 1364 (Fed. Cir. 1996). See also *Scripps Clinic & Research Found. v Genentech, Inc.*, 927 F.2d 1565 (Fed. Cir. 1991) (sending a noninfringement defense to trial on a reverse doctrine of equivalents theory).

revenue.[18] Patents are also subject to other limits. Some arise from 'inside' patent law – examples include compulsory licensing provisions[19] and priority rules.[20] Other limitations come from 'outside' it, the most significant being antitrust scrutiny.[21]

Nor is the law of the United States unique. In fact, all of the world's patent laws conform to the same basic contours: the inventor is not given plenary rights on a just-deserts theory; rather, rights are shaped by functional considerations.[22] European patent law, for example, is even more narrowly constructed than US law:[23] business methods and software inventions are not patentable (at least, not officially).[24] There are constraints on patenting animals.[25] Even the first to invent can lose the right to patent (and practice) his invention because the priority rule favors the first to file a patent application.[26] There are also more controls over patents coming from 'outside' the intellectual property system: antitrust enforcement is stricter than in the US and the commitment to the free movement of goods further narrows patentees' opportunities to maximize reward through territorial price discrimination.[27] In fact,

---

18 *eBay Inc. v MercExchange, L.L.C.*, 547 U.S. 388, 397 (2006) ('The equitable discretion over injunctions, granted by the Patent Act, is well suited to allow courts to adapt to the rapid technological and legal developments in the patent system.') (Kennedy, J., concurring).

19 The Hatch Waxman Act is an example: it permits generic drug companies to conduct research on patented pharmaceuticals during the patent term, see Drug Price Competition and Patent Term Restoration Act of 1984, 35 U.S.C. § 271(d)–(h). See also Plant Variety Protection Act of 1970, 21 U.S.C. § 2543 (permitting farmers to save seeds from patented plants).

20 Patents are awarded in the United States to the first to invent, 35 U.S.C. § 102(g). In certain technologies, other inventors have limited rights, see 35 U.S.C. § 273; other nations are more generous. However, as Wendy Gordon notes, it is particularly difficult to see how patents can be human rights when it is clear that second – yet independent – inventors do not enjoy these rights, and that patents can, in fact, be used in ways that burden their access to their own creative production (see Wendy J. Gordon, 'Current patent laws cannot claim the backing of human rights', pp. 155–171 of this book).

21 See, for example, *United States v Nat'l Lead Co.*, 332 U.S. 319, 348-50 (1947).

22 See generally, Machlup, Fritz and Edith Penrose (1950), 'The Patent Controversy in the Nineteenth Century', 10 *J. Econ. History* 1.

23 See generally, Dutfield, Graham (2003), *Intellectual Property Rights and the Life Sciences: A Twentieth Century History* (Aldershot: Ashgate).

24 See, for example, European Patent Convention, 5 October 1973, 13 I.L.M. 270, art. 52(2)(c).

25 See, for example, id. art. 52(4).

26 See, for example, id. art. 60(2). Various European nations give first inventors some, but by no means, plenary rights to practice the invention without the patentee's permission.

27 Cf. *Telefis Eireann and Independent Television Publications Ltd v*

there was a period of history in which several European nations flirted with the idea of abolishing patents all together;[28] for many years, there were countries that refused to recognize patents on pharmaceuticals and other therapies.[29]

International patent agreements are consistent with this structure. For example, the TRIPS Agreement safeguards patent rights, but only for a limited term;[30] it envisions national exceptions to patent protection;[31] and permits (some) compulsory licensing.[32] Indeed, in the recent Doha Declaration, TRIPS members agreed to broaden the compulsory licensing possibilities so that one member can manufacture essential medicines to meet the health needs of another.[33] Most important, the objectives of the TRIPS Agreement are cast in utilitarian, rather than human rights, terms; the Agreement also specifies that these rights must be balanced against social welfare concerns. Thus, the Agreement lists its objectives as follows:

> The protection and enforcement of intellectual property rights should contribute to the promotion of technological innovation and to the transfer and dissemination of technology, to the mutual advantage of producers and users of technological knowledge in a manner conducive to social and economic welfare, and to a balance of rights and obligations.[34]

Commission of the European Communities (Magill), 1995 ECR I-743 (Court of Justice 6 April 1995) (joining Cases C-241/91P and C-242/91P); Commission Decision of 24.03.2004 Relating to a Proceeding Under Article 82 of the EC Treaty (Case COMP/C-3/37.792 Microsoft) (21 April 2004) (competition law limits rights of copyright holder to refuse to deal); *Merck & Co., Inc. v Primecrown Ltd* (ECJ Joined Cases C 267-268/95) [1997] 1 CLMR 93; *Centrafarm BV v Sterling Drug Incorporated* [1974] E.C.R. 1147 (Case 15/74) (intra-European exhaustion of patent rights).

28 See Janis, Mark D. (2002), 'Patent System Reform: Patent Abolitionism', 17 *Berkeley Tech. L.J.* 899, 943 (Holland abolished patents for 40 years; France, Germany, and Belgium debated following suit).

29 Drug patents were recognized in Germany in 1967, Italy and France in 1978 (France offered limited pharmaceutical patents in 1966), and Spain in 1986. Boldrin, Michele and David K. Levine, *Against Intellectual Monopoly*, Chapter 9, http://levine.sscnet.ucla.edu/papers/ip.ch.9.m1004.pdf. Germany, France and Spain granted patents on pharmaceutical processes prior to those dates. Id.

30 Agreement on Trade-Related Aspects of Intellectual Property Rights, 15 April 1994, Marrakesh Agreement Establishing the World Trade Organization, Annex 1C, Results of the Uruguay Round vol. 3, 33 I.L.M. 1125 (1994) [hereinafter TRIPS Agreement] and art. 33.

31 Id. art. 27(2) and (3).

32 Id. arts 30 and 31.

33 World Trade Organization, Declaration on the TRIPs Agreement and Public Health of 14 November 2001, WT/MIN(01)/DEC/2, 41 I.L.M. 755 (2002).

34 Id. art. 7.

A moral commitment to inventors, one that recognizes a right to control intellectual production and capture all its benefits is, in short, virtually undetectable in the ways that the world's patent rights are structured. Instead, the perspective is purely utilitarian.[35] In modern terms, it is driven by the notion that there are diminishing returns to patent pay-offs; that there is a point at which increasing the available reward fails to produce a concomitant increase in inventive efforts. Inventors are, therefore, awarded only the amount of protection from free riders that is needed to recoup the costs of discovery – with enough extra to keep inventors at the lab bench, attracting outside investment (clearly, a utilitarian assessment). The rest of the benefit conferred by inventive activity is up for grabs. And, indeed, economists who have studied the innovation system have found that historically, there has been a dramatic shortfall in the appropriability of patented inventions and thus considerable 'spillover' benefits the public has enjoyed for free.[36]

Of course, the interests protected by intellectual property law generally must be unpacked and distinctions kept in mind. There may well be important differences between the intellectual endeavors protected by copyrights and the material protected by patents. It is far easier to see a human rights dimension in the case of the former. After all, expression and personality are intimately intertwined. Because one can learn a great deal about a person from what he has said and how he has said it, protecting expression safeguards human dignity.[37] But it is hard to make that case for a product or process, where value

---

35 In fact, it can be argued that the structure of the law may not even support a *utilitarian* theory because it can fail to fully account for the risks taken by inventors and those who invest in innovation, see, for example, Scherer, F.M. (2001), 'The Innovation Lottery', in *Expanding the Boundaries of Intellectual Property: Innovation Policy for the Knowledge Society 3* (Dreyfuss, Rochelle Cooper, Diane Zimmerman, Harry First (eds) [hereinafter *Expanding the Boundaries*]. Nonetheless, there are structural limits to the benefits that creators can capture, cf., for example, *Feist Publications, Inc. v Rural Telephone Services Co.*, 499 U.S. 340 (1991) (holding that Congress lacks authority under the Copyright and Patent Clause to protect facts).

36 See, for example, Levin, Richard C., Alvin K. Klevorick, Richard R. Nelson, Sidney G. Winter, Richard Gilbert, and Zvi Griliches (1997), 'Appropriating the Returns from Industrial Research and Development', (3) *Brookings Papers on Economic Activity* 783–831.

37 In European law and lore, the connection between copyrights and human rights is even more explicit than it is in the United States because the droit d'auteur system specifically protects such matters as attribution and integrity, see, for example, Kwall, Roberta Rosenthal (1985), 'Copyright and Moral Right: Is an American Marriage Possible?', 38 *Vand. L. Rev.* 1, 5–16. But even there, an argument can be made that the human rights discourse was adopted with economic and utilitarian aims in mind, see Thomas Dreier, in *Expanding the Boundaries*, supra note 35, at 295, 298–303.

resides in functionality and not in the identity of the inventor. There is nothing about a product or a process (or for that matter, a newly discovered principle of nature) that trenches upon the personality of the inventor. For example, we know a great deal about Thomas Edison. But we know it from reading his papers, not from turning on his light bulb.[38] Accordingly, while a case can be made for giving Edison control over his output as an *author*, it is hard to argue that he deserves that protection as an *inventor*.

There is also a difference between protecting creative individuals from involuntary servitude and giving them control over the information that their labor produces. Some inventors may work without monetary compensation (the open source movement in software is one example[39]). For those who require compensation, patent rights are only one alternative. Other methods of assuring payment include lead time advantages, government or private contracts and research grants, contests, bonuses, prizes, tenure, and professorial chairs.[40] Indeed, it can be argued that patent protection is a peculiar choice for a remuneration mechanism, given the lack of any affirmative right to practice or license the patented invention or to require the public to buy it. While there are various reasons to choose patents, the reasons sound in economic and practical considerations, not in human rights.

---

38 See, for example, Hughes, Justin (1988), 'The Philosophy of Intellectual Property', 77 *Geo. L.J.* 287, 339–342 ('We tend not to think of [patents] as manifesting the personality of an individual, but rather as manifesting a raw, almost generic insight', but noting that there is a continuum of personality contributions that does not necessarily correspond to the type of intellectual property involved (for example, contemporary roadmaps, protected by copyright, are almost entirely devoid of personality, but patentable computer software may reflect the programmer's personality based on how he decides to solve a problem)). For information on the Thomas Edison archive, see http://edison.rutgers.edu/.

39 See, for example, Lerner, Josh and Jean Tirole (2004), 'The Economics of Technology Sharing: Open Source and Beyond', Harvard NOM Working Paper No. 04-35 (2004), available at http://ssrn.com/abstract=620904 or DOI: 10.2139/ssrn.620904. Of course, some of these creators want compensation other than money, including attribution and control over downstream products (usually, in the form of making sure the source code used in products that build on their works is also freely available), see, for example, the GNU General Public License, version 2, available at http://www.gnu.org/licenses/gpl.txt. But this control arises from an enforceable – and presumably voluntary – contract, not a general legal obligation. Furthermore, as Hughes suggests, supra note 38, programming may be more similar to works of authorship than to works of inventorship.

40 See, for example, Shavell, Steven and Tanguy Van Ypersele (2001), 'Rewards Versus Intellectual Property Rights', 44 *J.L. & Econ.* 525; Machlup and Penrose, supra note 22, at 19–21. See also Sobel, Dava (1996), *Longitude: The True Story of a Lone Genius Who Solved the Greatest Scientific Problem of His Time*.

Finally, there is a difference between holding a patent and holding the expectation of acquiring a patent. Once a patent is awarded, it should be protected (like other property) against arbitrary and uncompensated governmental interference. In that limited sense, patents are arguably human rights.[41] Similarly, there may be a fundamental right to fair process, to have one's patent applications and claims judged impartially and in accordance with law.[42] But the nature of the award that is available – the details of the protective scheme; the contours of the patent (its duration, scope, and such) – are legislatively determined and can change over time.[43] There is no fundamental right to a particular form of protection – to a patent on a specific product (no matter how ingenious) or to a patent that covers specific uses (no matter how valuable). The legislature is free to use the tools of the patent system (such as term, subject matter, scope, compulsory licenses, right to relief) to allocate excess benefits (those not required to spur optimum production) in any way it sees fit. Human rights concerns should certainly inform that decision, but the legislature could also choose to divert the benefits of inventions to fulfill other social objectives.[44]

2. CONTEMPORARY DEVELOPMENTS

Admittedly, the picture just painted reflects a somewhat outdated view. Patent rights have expanded dramatically, as has the appropriability of the benefits of

---

41 See, for example, *Smith Kline & French Laboratories, Ltd. v the Netherlands*, Application No. 12633/87, 66 Eur. Comm'n H.R. Dec. & Rep. 70, 79 (1990).

42 See, for example, *British American Tobacco Co. Ltd. v the Netherlands*, 331 Eur. Ct. H.R. (ser. A) (1995).

43 Admittedly, there is a grey area where investments made in reliance on a particular scheme of patent protection are frustrated by a change in regime; whether the change amounts to a taking of property is arguably a hard question, but one that is usually answered in the negative, cf, for example, *Ruckelshaus v Monsanto Co.*, 467 U.S. 986 (1984) (right to government protection of a trade secret depends on the law at the time the information is submitted, not when it is created).

44 Thus, in her intervention at the CIER Conference, Geertrui Van Overwalle suggested a variety of concerns that should temper patent rights. Most are well accepted human rights, such as the right to health and human dignity. But some of her suggestions fall into a category where there may be less agreement, such as the right to make informed consent to the use of body material for scientific research or the right to food. Van Overwalle, Geertrui, 'Human rights' limitations in patent law', chapter 12 of this book. On a human rights model of patent law, a decision has to be made whether these concerns are fundamental; from a utilitarian perspective, the legislature can simply choose to alter the law to further these interests once it finds there are sufficient benefits available to encourage the level of innovation the legislature deems optimal.

inventiveness.[45] Thus, although the term of protection has not been explicitly lengthened,[46] the pace of technological change has accelerated. As a result, the term represents a growing proportion of the useful life of patented inventions. Further, the height of the inventive step has been decreasing. This allows inventors to engage in 'evergreening' – modest improvements are patented, producing protection for essentially the same invention for many successive terms.[47]

At the same time, successful challenges to the experimental use defense have made it harder for researchers to use patent disclosures effectively.[48] The subject matter of patents has expanded to include genes, proteins, and other 'upstream' technologies.[49] Finally, the scope of patents has broadened. In part, this is a result of moving patenting upstream, where even a narrow patent can control a wide swath of downstream development. Partly, the expansion is a function of changes in the ways that patent claims are interpreted: doctrines akin to the US doctrine of equivalents are increasingly applied worldwide.[50] In part, enhanced protection can also be attributed to the erosion in the territorial limits on the scope of patent rights: the TRIPS Agreement requires protection in all members of the World Trade Organization (WTO),[51] and the Patent Cooperation Treaty[52] and various regional arrangements (such as the European Patent Convention) make it easier for inventors to acquire foreign rights. As a result, it is harder for potential users of patented technologies to engage in arbitrage – to avoid infringement by locating activities in a place where the inputs they use are in the public domain.[53]

---

45 See Levin, supra note 36.

46 Indeed, for countries like the United States that moved from a term that runs from issuance to one that runs from filing, the effective term may now be shorter for some inventors.

47 Lemley, Mark A. and Kimberly A. Moore (2004), 'Ending Abuse of Patent Continuations', 84 *B.U.L. Rev*. 63, 81–83.

48 See, for example, *Madey v Duke Univ*., 307 F.3d 1343 (Fed. Cir. 2000); Strandburg, Katherine J. (2004), 'What Does the Public Get? Experimental Use and the Patent Bargain', 2004, *Wis. L. Rev*. 81.

49 See, for example, Berman, Helen M. and Rochelle C. Dreyfuss (2006), 'Reflections on the Science and Law of Structural Biology, Genomics, and Drug Development', 53 *UCLA L.Rev*. 871.

50 Takenaka, Toshiko (1998), 'Harmonizing the Japanese Patent System With Its U.S. Counterpart Through Judge-Made Law: Interaction Between Japanese And U.S. Case Law Developments', 7 *Pac. Rim L. & Pol'y* 249, 254–260.

51 TRIPS Agreement, art. 27(1).

52 28 UST 7645 (1979).

53 See Samuelson, Pamela (2004), 'Intellectual Property Arbitrage: How Foreign Rules Can Affect Domestic Protections', 71 *U. Chi. L. Rev*. 223.

Because these developments are contemporaneous with increasing attention to human rights, it is tempting to see a causal connection – to see arguments for expanding patent protection as a move away from a strict utilitarian vision to one that is grounded in the fundamental right of inventors to decide the circumstances under which their intellectual labor is utilized. That is, it could be argued that as sensitivity to human need deepens, as more aspects of human existence are perceived as raising fundamental rights concerns, nations begin to take more seriously their obligations to protect (in the words of the UDHR) every individual's material interests in 'any scientific literary or artistic production of which he is the author'.[54]

It is, however, highly unlikely that human rights law is really influencing the perception of patent law's justifications or that it is responsible for the expansion of patent rights. At the theoretical level, there is a telling difference between the wording of the Universal Declaration of Human Rights and the US Constitution. The former focuses on the 'author'; the latter on 'Authors and Inventors'. But as we just saw, authorship is not the same as inventorship; there may be reasons to give authors control over their output that do not support ceding equivalent control to inventors.

As an empirical matter, the expansion in patent rights can be quite easily and fully explained by forces operating wholly within the technology community.[55] First, technology is changing. Modern technology is 'science intensive' in the sense that many modern discoveries are dual in character: they are fundamental scientific discoveries, but they also have immediate end-use applications.[56] As the line between basic and applied work breaks down, it destroys the dichotomy that the law (and Justice Fortas) relied upon to prevent fundamental work from becoming the subject of exclusive rights. Furthermore, new and highly productive research methodologies are coming

---

54 Universal Declaration of Human Rights, art. 27(2). See generally, Helfer, supra note 1, noting that United Nations Committee on Economic, Social and Cultural rights has begun an 'interpretive foray' into the intellectual property provisions of the ICESCR.

55 See generally, Dinwoodie, Graeme and Rochelle Dreyfuss (2005), 'Preserving the Public Domain of Science in International Law', in Maskus, Keith E. and J.H. Reichman (eds), *International Public Goods and Transfer of Technology under a Globalized Intellectual Property Regime* (Cambridge: Cambridge University Press).

56 See, for example, *Diamond v Chakrabarty*, 447 U.S. 303 (1980); *State St. Bank & Trust Co. v Signature Fin. Group, Inc.*, 149 F.3d 1368 (Fed. Cir. 1998), cert. denied, 119 S. Ct. 851 (1999). See also Narin, Francis and Dominic Olivastro (1992), 'Status Report: Linkage Between Technology and Science', 21 *Res. Pol'y* 237 (using citation measures to demonstrate that the tie between science and technology is becoming closer over time and is more pronounced in drugs, medicine, chemistry, and computing than in fields such as machinery and transportation).

'online'. These tools can represent fundamental advances, but some are also valuable in their own right. Accordingly, there is a demand for patents to spur research into their development. (Examples include computer technologies, which are used in rational drug design.) And because these tools accelerate the pace of research, inventions are more quickly superceded. Since patent length and patent breadth are to some extent interchangeable,[57] increasing the rate of obsolescence increases demand for broad patents.

Secondly, the institutions of science are evolving. Universities are now active participants in the patent system,[58] and that development creates demand for a regime that protects the work that universities do – which is to say, patents on upstream research. Furthermore, research is increasingly conducted in small, highly networked knowledge-intensive firms. These firms put new pressure on the patent system because they use patent rights in novel ways: to facilitate cooperation and as signals of technical and business competence.[59]

Thirdly, globalization generates a demand for harmonized law and the dynamics of harmonization favor expanded protection. It is harder to disappoint those who made specific investments in reliance on exclusive rights than it is to undermine vague expectations that a work will become less expensive. Thus, it is easier to revise the law so that it converges on the law of the most protective nation rather than on the most minimalist regime. (The rounding up of the copyright term in European law is an example.[60])

Fourthly, there is the matter of interest group politics. Groups that are well organized and well funded have a distinct advantage in the legislative arena because they can easily lobby lawmakers, play national interests against each other, and engage in 'regime shifting' – that is, they can shop for the forum that is likely to be the most responsive to their claims.[61] In the context of intellectual property, this means user groups (which are generally highly dispersed and poorly funded) are not as likely as intellectual property owners to influence the

---

57 See, for example, O'Donoghue, Ted, Suzanne Scotchmer and Jacques Thisse (1998), 'Patent Breadth, Patent Life, and the Pace of Technological Progress', 7 *J. of Econ. and Mgmt. Strategy* 1.

58 See, for example, Bayh Dole Act, 35 U.S.C. §§ 200-212 (2000) (permitting universities to own patent rights in federally funded research).

59 See, for example, Long, Clarisa (2002), 'Patent Signals', 69 *U. Chi. L. Rev.* 625; Powell, Walter M., 'Networks of Learning in Biotechnology: Opportunities and Constraints Associated with Relational Contracting in Knowledge-Intensive Fields', in *Expanding the Boundaries*, supra note 35, at 251.

60 Directive 93/98/EEC of 29 October 1993 harmonizing the term of protection of copyright and certain related rights.

61 See Helfer, Laurence R. (2004), 'Regime Shifting: The TRIPS Agreement and New Dynamics of International Intellectual Property Lawmaking', 29 *Yale J. Int'l L.* 1.

content of law and the structure of legal institutions. A US example is the Court of Appeals for the Federal Circuit: establishing that tribunal and vesting it with authority over most patent appeals has, according to many observers, led to a virtual explosion in patent rights.[62] Similarly, at the international level, Susan Sell has demonstrated that a small group of powerful multinational corporations were largely responsible for shifting negotiations over international intellectual property law from the World Intellectual Property Organization (WIPO) to the WTO.[63] Since the WTO controls trade in goods and services, developed countries can now use their large, rich markets to push for an expansion of patent rights worldwide.[64]

These factors are especially potent in combination. International agreements tend to exert a one-way ratchet: nations are obliged to increase protection to the internationally-mandated level, but these agreements do not include rights for users, so they never require a decrease in the level of protection. As a result, the instruments alter the dynamics of domestic lawmaking. Patent holders can enter into domestic legislative deals in which they sacrifice an aspect of protection in exchange for something they want, safe in the knowledge that the 'sacrifice' will be struck down as violating an international agreement, while the benefit will not be subjected to any real scrutiny. A US example, drawn from copyright, is the legislation that prolonged the term and created a new set of rights to play music without authorization. The Supreme Court deferred to Congress's judgment about the lengthened term, but the music provision was invalidated by the WTO.[65]

---

62 See generally, Jaffe, Adam B. and Josh Lerner (2004), *Innovation and its Discontents: How our Broken Patent System is Endangering Innovation and Progress and What to Do About It* (New Jersey: Princeton University Press); Dreyfuss, Rochelle C. (2006), 'Pathological Patenting: The PTO as Cause or Cure', 104 *Mich. L. Rev.* 1559.

63 Sell, Susan K. (2003), *Private Power, Public Law: The Globalization of Intellectual Property Rights* (Cambridge: Cambridge University Press).

64 Bilateral and regional trade-based negotiations can also lead to an expansion of rights, see Kapczynski, Amy, Samantha Chaifetz, Zachary Katz, and Yochai Benkler (2005), 'Addressing Global Health Inequities: An Open Licensing Approach for University Innovations', 20 *Berkeley Tech. L.J.* 1031, 1043 n. 48.

65 *Eldred v Ashcroft*, 537 U.S. 186 (2003) (upholding copyright term); WTO Panel Report on United States–Section 110(5) of the U.S. Copyright Act, WT/DS160/R (15 June 2000) (invalidating music provision). See generally, Dinwoodie, Graeme B. and Rochelle C. Dreyfuss (2004), 'TRIPS and the Dynamics of Intellectual Property Lawmaking', 36 *Case W. Res. J. Int'l L.* 95.

3. THE SOURCE OF THE HUMAN RIGHTS RHETORIC

If rights discourse is insufficient on its own to justify patent rights as a historical or theoretical matter, and there are adequate ways to understand why patent rights are expanding as a practical matter, why then are we beginning to see human rights discussed as a justification for patent law?

One possibility is that the human rights rhetoric is a product of misconception. As intellectual property rights expand, they touch on the lives of people previously unacquainted with patent lore, such as scientists seeking to do research or doctors trying to cure people too poor to afford patented medicines. Those who become activists may be unaware of the history of the patent system. They may erroneously see patent rights as the principal means for assuring payment for intellectual labor or confuse rights in existing patents with inchoate rights to obtain patent protection. To the extent that there is a human rights component to copyright law, they may conflate the respective justifications.[66]

It is not as though this sort of distortion is unknown to the intellectual property community. At the time the TRIPS Agreement was under consideration, similar problems arose. The 'trade hands' who negotiated the General Agreement on Tariffs and Trade took the leading oar in drafting the new WTO agreements, and much of their rhetoric conflated trade and intellectual property policy. They conceptualized the adoption of intellectual property obligations as ending 'protectionism' and increasing trade, even though intellectual property laws are highly 'protectionist' and intellectual property rights raise prices and thus can reduce the global movement of intellectual goods.[67]

In the context of TRIPS, overstating the case for intellectual property protection has had many unfortunate consequences, particularly for developing countries.[68] The human rights trope could be equally catastrophic. Once human rights enter the equation, it is difficult to locate the end to patent prerogatives or to win support for greater public access to patented materials. To be sure, there are balancing techniques and mechanisms allowing international human rights tribunals to defer to local decisions. But these ad hoc

---

66 An example may be the Report of the International Bioethics Committee (IBC) of UNESCO on Ethics, Intellectual Property and Genomics 8, SHS-503/01/CIB-8/2 (10 January 2002), which assumes that 'intellectual property … has a foundation in ethical principles and universal human rights'.

67 See generally Cooper Dreyfuss, Rochelle and Andreas F. Lowenfeld (1997), 'Two Achievements of the Uruguay Round: Putting TRIPS and Dispute Settlement Together', 37 *Va. J. Int'l L.* 275.

68 See, for example, Chon, Margaret (2006), 'Intellectual Property and the Development Divide', 27 *Cardozo L. Rev.* 2821.

determinations do not furnish inventors or the public with predictable protection and they can require the public to compensate for any incursions it makes into a patentee's interests.[69] In contrast, a utilitarian system contains its own limits. For example, at some point, control over research opportunities becomes so tight, progress is chilled and policy makers are forced to reconsider the regime to determine whether it still promotes its core purposes. As a colleague once put it, even if one thought that patent rights *are* hunting licenses, one would advocate limits: hunters do not shoot the females because their survival is crucial to the success of future hunts; by the same token, patents should not create exclusive rights over the fundamental principles and research tools that give birth to future research opportunities.[70] Internal limits are not only easier to identify then a balancing point, the consequence of exceeding a targeted limit is that the excess benefits can be enjoyed by the public free of charge.

Another, even more ominous, reason for the human rights discourse may be that various constituencies have started up a game of 'tit for tat'. That is, the rights rhetoric is most often associated with claims for new sorts of intellectual property. To take the example of bioprospecting, there are demands for rights over plant and animal materials, rights over information discovered from these materials, and rights over the traditional knowledge that led researchers to study these materials in the first place. Thus, the Convention on Biological Diversity[71] begins with a principle of 'fair and equitable sharing of the benefits' associated with biodiversity,[72] but quickly proceeds to a declaration that states have 'the sovereign right to exploit their own resources',[73] an authorization to create incentives and determine access to genetic resources and control technology transfer,[74] and a mandate to respect the 'knowledge, innovations and practices of indigenous and local communities'.[75] Similarly,

---

[69] See, for example, Office of the United Nations High Commissioner for Human Rights. Committee on Economic, Social and Cultural Rights, The Right of Everyone to Benefit from the Protection of the Moral and Material Interests Resulting From any Scientific, Literary or Artistic Production of Which He is the Author (article 15, paragraph 1(c), of the Covenant), General Comment No. 17 (15 November 2005), (E/C.12/2005), 57 http://www.ohchr.org/english/bodies/cescr/docs/gc17.doc ('All *victims* of violations of the rights protected under article 15, paragraph 1 (c), should be entitled to adequate compensation or satisfaction.') (emphasis added).

[70] John Pegram (private communication).

[71] Convention on Biological Diversity, 5 June 1992, 31 ILM 818 (1992).

[72] Id. art. 1.

[73] Id. art. 3.

[74] Id. arts 11, 15, and 16.

[75] Id. art. 8(j).

the Draft UN Declaration on the Rights of Indigenous Peoples[76] recognizes the right of indigenous peoples to 'the full ownership, control and protection of their cultural and intellectual property'.[77]

What appears to be going on is that expanding patent rights have generated a backlash. Nations that lack a strong inventive base resent the obligation to adopt a patent system consistent with the TRIPS Agreement (or more onerous regional or bilateral agreements). Nations that cannot afford the medical treatments their citizens need resent supracompetitive pricing. Nations that lack the capacity to manufacture needed products locally resent the bar on working requirements and the limitations on compulsory licensing that international agreements impose. Nations that have freely given away plants, animals, and local know-how resent the ways in which the information learned from these materials has been commercialized.[78] These nations (and their advisers and advocates) see the development of new rights as a way to even the playing field. They hope that the economic returns these rights can earn will pay for patented technologies. Further, they plan to condition access to their raw products on access to the patented inventions these materials make possible. It would, however, be very difficult to have these rights recognized on a utilitarian theory because the materials over which the rights are asserted are preexisting (and not, as in the patent paradigm, new and inventive). In most cases, any added value (for example, identification of the active ingredient in a plant), is not supplied by the entity claiming the exclusive right. So, instead these nations resort to rights talk:[79] the 'knowledge rich and biologically poor'

[76] See Technical Review of the United Nations Draft Declaration on the Rights of Indigenous Peoples, UN ESCOR Comm'n on Hum. Rts., 46th Sess., Provisional Agenda Item 15, UN Doc. E/CN.4/Sub.2/1994/2/Add.1 (1994) [hereinafter Draft Declaration] (transcribing text of the Draft Declaration). See also Draft United Nations Declaration on the Rights of Indigenous Peoples, Res. 1993/46, Sub-Comm'n Hum. Rts., 35th mtg. (1993) (recounting history of Draft Declaration).

[77] Draft Declaration, supra note 76, art. 29. See generally, Helfer, supra note 61, at 45–51. Regional and national groups have enacted similar instruments, see Safrin, Sabrina (2004), 'Hyperownership in a Time of Biotechnological Promise: The International Conflict to Control the Building Blocks of Life', 98 *Am. J. Int'l L.* 641, 646–58 (2004) (describing rules in the Andean countries, India, and Brazil.)

[78] The intuition that gifts should not be commercialized also explains the popularity of the Creative Commons' Attribution-Noncommercial-Share Alike license, see Elkin-Koren, Niva (2004), 'What Contracts Cannot Do: The Limits of Private Ordering in Facilitating a Creative Commons', 74 *Fordham L. Rev.* 375, 401 n. 87 ('Attribution-Noncommercial-No Derivative licenses were twenty-three percent of all licenses and Attribution-No Derivative licenses were three percent of all version 2.0 and 2.5 licenses').

[79] There is also an environmental/conservation theme in some of the rhetoric, based on fears that local groups will be stripped of their natural resources, or represen-

escape marginalization by laying claim to ownership interests in their information resources.[80]

But this use of human rights is extremely counterproductive. As Sabrina Safrin has shown, the combined effect of recognizing new patent-like protection schemes is (in her words) 'hyperownership': rights to the same information resides in, for example, a patentee, a specific nation, a local authority, a private landowner, and an indigenous group.[81] Each of these 'owners' can exercise veto power and the result can be underutilization of potentially life-saving resources.[82]

More crucially, by framing the issues as a battle among rights holders, this discourse promotes an adversarial perspective, where rights are construed as inuring to one group's benefit over another's, and the system as a whole is viewed as a zero-sum game. Completely obscured are the many substantial areas of common interest. After all, access is a problem for the North *and* for the South. There are poor people who lack the ability to pay for their medicine in *both* developed and developing countries. Fundamental researchers in the North *share* the concerns of the generic drug industries in the South. No one is fully served by a system that depends on the market alone to encourage innovation – there are orphan diseases everywhere. A shift in focus from rights to pragmatics allows nations to find ways to pool their interests and construct a system responsive to technological, institutional, and political developments.

4. UTILITARIAN JUSTIFICATIONS AND SOCIAL WELFARE

It is not as though there is a shortage of interest or ideas for recalibrating the system using existing tools. Arguably, precisely this form of reconsideration is

---

tations that new rights will encourage local groups to preserve the environment. But these arguments are also largely not credible because the value in these materials most often resides in the information contained, not in the materials themselves. Since this information can be reproduced synthetically once it is known, local communities are not likely to lose their resources. Conversely, they are unlikely to benefit from preserving more than sample species.

80 See Coombe, Rosemary J. (1999), 'Culture: Anthropology's Old Vice or International Law's New Virtue?', 93 *Am. Soc'y Int'l L. Proc.* 261, 263, 270; Coombe, Rosemary J. (1998), 'Intellectual Property, Human Rights & Sovereignty: New Dilemmas in International Law Posed by the Recognition of Indigenous Knowledge and the Conservation of Biodiversity', 6 *Ind. J. Global Leg. Stud.* 59, 98.

81 Safrin, supra note 77, at 652–8 (noting the relationship to the more standard anti-commons problem).

82 Safrin recounts examples of negotiations that have collapsed and bioprospecting projects that have been abandoned, see id.

going on right now in the United States. Two studies of the patent system by the National Academies of Sciences suggested that patent rights have now reached the point where they may be chilling further research.[83] Soon after the publication of these studies, Congress began pondering multiple bills to reform the system.[84] Simultaneously, the Supreme Court increased its review of patent cases, examining such calibration tools as the subject matter of protection, the use of patent disclosures, a trial court's power to withhold injunctive relief, the size of the inventive step, and the relationship between patent rights and competition law.[85] The European Commission has similarly announced plans for public hearings on future patent policy.[86] In the international arena, the TRIPS Council was established to monitor implementation.[87] As we saw, the Doha Round has already changed the compulsory licensing rules.[88]

These initiatives are mainly aimed at fixing the conditions of the hunt – at improving the capacity of patent law to encourage innovation. Presumably, however, other social interests can (and, arguably, are) being taken into account. For example, in one recent case, the Supreme Court stressed the judge's power to consider whether 'the public interest would ... be disserved by a permanent injunction', citing with approval a case suggesting that injunctive relief could be denied when health care interests are at stake.[89] Doha's

---

[83] Nat'l Research Council of the Nat'l Acads. (2006), *Reaping the Benefits of Genomic and Proteomic Research: Intellectual Property Rights, Innovation, and Public Health*; Nat'l Research Council of the Nat'l Acads. (2004), *A Patent System for the 21st Century* 93 (Stephen A. Merrill et al. (eds)).

[84] See, for example, Patent Reform Act of 2005, H.R. 2795, 109th Cong., 1st Sess. (2005); United States Patent and Trademark Fee Modernization Act of 2005, H.R. 2791, 109th Cong., 1st Sess. (2005); Patents Depend on Quality Act of 2006, H.R. 5096, 109th Cong., 2nd Sess. (2006).

[85] See, for example, *eBay, Inc. v MercExchange*, L.L.C., 547 U.S. 388 (2006) (injunctive relief); *Illinois Tool Works Inc. v Independent Ink Inc.*, 547 U.S. 28 (2006) (antitrust limits on patent licensing); *Integra Lifesciences I, Ltd. v Merck KgaA*, 545 U.S. 193 (2005) (experimental use defense); *MedImmune, Inc. v Genentech, Inc.*, 549 U.S. 118 (2007); *KSR Intern. Co. v Teleflex Inc.*, 550 U.S. 398 (2007). See also *Laboratory Corp. v Metabolite Laboratories, Inc.*, 548 U.S. 124 (2006) (scope of patentable subject matter); *Bilsky v Kappos*, cert. granted, 129 S.Ct. 2735 (June 1, 2009) (also raising the question of the scope of patentable subject matter).

[86] Directorate General for Internal Market and Services, Consultation and public hearing on future patent policy in Europe (2006), available at http://ec.europa.eu/internal_market/indprop/patent/consultation_en.htm.

[87] TRIPS Ag't, art. 68; The TRIPS Council, http://www.wto.org/english/tratop_e/trips_e/intel6_e.htm.

[88] See supra note 33 (Doha Declaration).

[89] *eBay, Inc. v MercExchange*, L.L.C., 547 U.S. 388, 394 (2006), citing *Roche Products, Inc. v Bolar Pharmaceutical Co.*, 733 F.2d 858 (1984).

reconsideration of the TRIPS was similarly motivated by concern for human health.

It would likewise be possible to restructure the system to account for the increasingly globalized environment in which inventors operate and to capitalize on commonalities between the concerns of North and South. Safrin, for instance, suggests modification of the subject matter requirement to deal with the bioprospecting problem.[90] She uses ESTs, small fragments of genes, as an example. Patent rights in sequenced ESTs are controversial in the North because very little real work is needed to find them, very little is known about what they do even after their genetic sequence is determined, and yet their scope can be quite broad. Banning patents on ESTs would therefore be very welcome to the scientific community in the North. At the same time, the ban would ameliorate concerns in the South over bioprospecting – over commercializing inputs that were made available freely.[91]

Similarly, Yochai Benkler and his co-authors have turned their attention to licensing limitations in an attempt to deal with the increasing tendency of universities to patent work that would, in earlier times, have gone into the public domain. They advocate something they call 'Equitable Access' licensing. Universities could continue to patent, but they would be obliged to require licensees to engage in various public-regarding activities. Thus, licensees could be required to help the South by making product available there at marginal cost (or by sub-licensing parties who wish to make product available), just as universities sometimes help Northern scientists by requiring licensees to permit noncommercial research.[92] Benkler has a somewhat similar proposal for dealing with orphan diseases.[93] In a similar vein, Geertrui Van Overwalle suggests (or might require) universities to engage in 'two tier' or 'dual' licensing, where they would modify their royalty scheme according to the status of the licensee or its intended use. Thus, universities would (be required to) license their technology out cheaply if the use was for humanitarian or developmental purposes, but could charge commercial entities much more.[94]

There are also suggestions for playing with the territoriality aspect of patents. Before her untimely death, Jenny Lanjouw was working on a scheme

---

[90] Safrin, supra note 77, at 673 (suggesting that the law 'take into account the reactions of other countries when deciding as a policy matter whether to expand or restrict patent rights over genetic materials').

[91] Id. at 676.

[92] Kapczynski et al, supra note 64, at 1090–1110.

[93] Id. at 1110–1113.

[94] Van Overwalle, Geertrui (2006), 'Reconciling Patent Policies and University Mission', 13 *Ethical Perspectives* 234, 238.

that would deal with the access problem. She would have required those applying for patents on essential medicines to choose between patent protection in the North or in the South. Her idea was that when the same disease occurred in the North and in the South, the market rewards available in rich countries would encourage the research for cures; there would be no need to charge supracompetitive profits in developing countries. Presumably, when a disease was prevalent only in the South, Southern markets would be needed to spur research, and the patentee would then opt to patent a new pharmaceutical in the South, leaving scientists in the North free to experiment with it.[95]

David Opderbeck would solve the orphan disease problem in a somewhat similar fashion. [96] In his view, these diseases will never be cured by the North because drug companies there are organized around finding 'blockbusters'. Diseases with few sufferers (or, few sufferers rich enough to pay high prices) will not attract these firms' attention. However, Opderbeck notes that some Southern countries are drifting to the 'developed' end of the development spectrum. In these places, there is a pharmaceutical infrastructure – Indian pharmaceutical firms, for example, do considerable work on finding new ways to manufacture generics. But because these firms have not institutionalized the blockbuster model, they are susceptible to incentives to invest in finding treatments for diseases with more modest profit potential.[97] Opderbeck would take advantage of the Doha Declaration and the new opportunities it gives to these generic manufacturers, to create what he calls a new kind of 'research and development culture'. He would make patent protection in lucrative markets contingent on agreeing to conduct research on international orphan diseases. However, a Southern firm that obtains a compulsory license could, instead of paying the 'adequate remuneration' required by the TRIPS Agreement,[98] discharge the Northern patentee's research obligation.[99] In that way, he would move 'the social bargain underlying patent protection … away from insular territoriality toward a more global bargain'.[100]

Opderbeck, Lanjouw, Benkler, Van Overwalle, and Safrin would, in other words, adopt a utilitarian approach to patent protection. But they would construct the global system in a manner that is aligned with worldwide social interests and informed by human rights concerns.

---

95 Lanjouw, Jean O. (2002), 'A New Global Patent Regime for Diseases: U.S. and International Legal Issues', 16 *Harv. J.L. & Tech.* 85.

96 Opderbeck, David W. (2005), 'Patents, Essential Medicines, and the Innovation Game', 58 *Vand. L. Rev.* 501.

97 Id. at 548–9.

98 TRIPS Agreement, art. 31(h).

99 Opderbeck, supra note 96, at 549–50.

100 Id. at 551.

5. CONCLUSION

It is difficult to understand patents as creating a human rights paradox. The premises of patent law are utilitarian and its structure is functional. This is not to say that the current regime works well. Existing laws were developed for technologies new at the time of the Industrial Revolution and for the institutional arrangements prevalent then; these laws have not been updated for the science-intensive world in which we now live. The existing structure is based on a territorial model; international treaties have yet to fully account for the interdependence that globalization has wrought.

But it is hard to see how a rights discourse illuminates decisions on restructuring the patent system. Instead of highlighting concerns that ought to be taken into account, rights talk creates an adversarial climate in which each side ups the ante, further limiting access to important developments and interfering with the proper operation of the system as a whole. Indeed, the real paradox appears to be the following: While the new discourse attempts to help the marginalized, its consequence is double-marginalization – prices go up and output goes down as each right holder seeks to maximize its individual return.[101] A utilitarian perspective allows policy makers to use the ample arsenal of available tools to make law responsive to changes in innovation and to align the system with other social interests, including but not limited to ones that are deemed fundamental.

BIBLIOGRAPHY

Berman, Helen M. and Rochelle C. Dreyfuss (2006), 'Reflections on the Science and Law of Structural Biology, Genomics, and Drug Development', 53 *UCLA L.Rev.* 871.

Birnhack, Michael D. (2003), 'Acknowledging the Conflict between Copyright Law and Freedom of Expression under the Human Rights Act', *Ent. L. Rev*. 24.

Chon, Margaret (2006), 'Intellectual Property and the Development Divide', 27 *Cardozo L. Rev.* 2821.

Coombe, Rosemary J. (1998), 'Intellectual Property, Human Rights & Sovereignty: New Dilemmas in International Law Posed by the Recognition of Indigenous Knowledge and the Conservation of Biodiversity', 6 *Ind. J. Global Leg. Stud.* 59, 98.

Coombe, Rosemary J. (1999), 'Culture: Anthropology's Old Vice or International Law's New Virtue?', 93 *Am. Soc'y Int'l L. Proc.* 261, 263, 270.

[101] See, for example, Lopatka, John E. and William H. Page (2001), 'Monopolization, Innovation, and Consumer Welfare', 69 *Geo. Wash. L. Rev.* 367, 411; Shapiro, Carl, 'Setting Compatibility Standards: Cooperation or Collusion?', in *Expanding the Boundaries*, supra note 35, at 81, 97–101.

Dinwoodie, Graeme B. and Rochelle C. Dreyfuss (2004), 'TRIPS and the Dynamics of Intellectual Property Lawmaking', 36 *Case W. Res. J. Int'l L.* 95.

Dinwoodie, Graeme B. and Rochelle C. Dreyfuss (2005), 'Preserving the Public Domain of Science in International Law', in Keith E. Maskus and J.H. Reichman (eds), *International Public Goods and Transfer of Technology under a Globalized Intellectual Property Regime* (Cambridge: Cambridge University Press).

Dreier, Thomas (2001), in Rochelle Cooper Dreyfuss, Diane Zimmerman, Harry First (eds), *Expanding the Boundaries of Intellectual Property: Innovation Policy for the Knowledge Society* 3, at 295, 298–303.

Dreyfuss, Rochelle Cooper (1992), 'A *Wiseguy*'s Approach to Information Products: Muscling Copyright and Patent into a Unitary Theory of Intellectual Property', *Sup. Ct. Rev.* 195, 231.

Dreyfuss, Rochelle C. (2006), 'Pathological Patenting: The PTO as Cause or Cure', 104 *Mich. L. Rev.* 1559.

Dreyfuss, Rochelle Cooper and Andreas F. Lowenfeld (1997), 'Two Achievements of the Uruguay Round: Putting TRIPS and Dispute Settlement Together', 37 *Va. J. Int'l L.* 275.

Dutfield, Graham (2003), *Intellectual Property Rights and the Life Sciences: A Twentieth Century History* (Aldershot: Ashgate Publishers).

Elkin-Koren, Niva (2004), 'What Contracts Cannot Do: The Limits of Private Ordering in Facilitating a Creative Commons', 74 *Fordham L. Rev.* 375, 401 n. 87.

Geiger, Christophe (2006), '"Constitutionalising" Intellectual Property Law? The Influence of Fundamental Rights on Intellectual Property in the European Union', 37 *Int'l Rev. of Intell. Prop. & Competition Law* 371.

Helfer, Laurence R. (2004), 'Regime Shifting: The TRIPS Agreement and New Dynamics of International Intellectual Property Lawmaking', 29 *Yale J. Int'l L.* 1.

Helfer, Laurence R. (2007), 'Toward a Human Rights Framework for Intellectual Property', 40 *U.C. Davis L. Rev.*, http://ssrn.com/abstract=891303.

Hughes, Justin (1988), 'The Philosophy of Intellectual Property', 77 *Geo. L.J.* 287, 339–42.

Jaffe, Adam B. and Josh Lerner (2004), *Innovation and Its Discontents: How Our Broken Patent System is Endangering Innovation and Progress and What to Do About It* (New Jersey: Princeton University Press).

Janis, Mark D. (2002), 'Patent System Reform: Patent Abolitionism', 17 *Berkeley Tech. L.J.* 899, 943.

Kapczynski, Amy, Samantha Chaifetz, Zachary Katz, and Yochai Benkler (2005), 'Addressing Global Health Inequities: An Open Licensing Approach for University Innovations', 20 *Berkeley Tech. L.J.* 1031, 1043 n. 48.

Kwall, Roberta Rosenthal (1985), 'Copyright and Moral Right: Is an American Marriage Possible?', 38 *Vand. L. Rev.* 1, 5–16.

Lanjouw, Jean O. (2002), 'A New Global Patent Regime for Diseases: U.S. and International Legal Issues', 16 *Harv. J.L. & Tech.* 85.

Lemley, Mark A. and Kimberly A. Moore (2004), 'Ending Abuse of Patent Continuations', 84 *B.U.L. Rev.* 63, 81–3.

Lerner, Josh and Jean Tirole (2004), 'The Economics of Technology Sharing: Open Source and Beyond', Harvard NOM Working Paper No. 04-35, available at http://ssrn.com/abstract=620904 or DOI: 10.2139/ssrn.620904.

Levin, Richard C., Alvin K. Klevorick, Richard R. Nelson, Sidney G. Winter, Richard Gilbert, and Zvi Griliches (1997), 'Appropriating the Returns from industrial Research and Development', (3) *Brookings Papers on Economic Activity* 783–831.

Long, Clarisa (2002), 'Patent Signals', 69 *U. Chi. L. Rev*. 625.

Lopatka, John E. and William H. Page (2001), 'Monopolization, Innovation, and Consumer Welfare', 69 *Geo. Wash. L. Rev.* 367, 411.

Machlup, Fritz and Edith Penrose (1950), 'The Patent Controversy in the Nineteenth Century', 10 *J. Econ. History* 1.

Maskus, K.E. and J.H. Reichman (2005), *International Public Goods and Transfer of Technology Under a Globalized Intellectual Property Regime* (Cambridge: Cambridge University Press).

Narin, Francis and Dominic Olivastro (1992), 'Status Report: Linkage Between Technology and Science', 21 *Res. Pol'y* 237.

O'Donoghue, Ted, Suzanne Scotchmer, and Jacques Thisse (1998), 'Patent Breadth, Patent Life, and the Pace of Technological Progress', 7 *J. of Econ. and Mgmt. Strategy* 1.

Opderbeck, David W. (2005), 'Patents, Essential Medicines, and the Innovation Game', 58 *Vand. L. Rev.* 501.

Van Overwalle, Geertrui (2006), 'Reconciling Patent Policies and University Mission', 13 *Ethical Perspectives* 234, 238.

Powell, Walter M. (2001), 'Networks of Learning in Biotechnology: Opportunities and Constraints Associated with Relational Contracting in Knowledge-Intensive Fields', in Rochelle Cooper Dreyfuss, Diane Zimmerman and Harry First (eds) *Expanding the Boundaries of Intellectual Property: Innovation Policy for the Knowledge Society* 3, at 251.

Rindler, Heinz (1997), 'Case Comment – Austria: Copyright – Copyright Infringement Through Publishing A Stock Purchase Agreement in a Newspaper', 19 *Eur. Intell. Prop. Rev.* 170.

Safrin, Sabrina (2004), 'Hyperownership in a Time of Biotechnological Promise: The International Conflict to Control the Building Blocks of Life', 98 *Am. J. Int'l L.* 641, 646–58.

Samuelson, Pamela (2004), 'Intellectual Property Arbitrage: How Foreign Rules Can Affect Domestic Protections', 71 *U. Chi. L. Rev.* 223.

Scherer, F.M. (2001), 'The Innovation Lottery', in Rochelle Cooper Dreyfuss, Diane Zimmerman and Harry First (eds), *Expanding the Boundaries of Intellectual Property: Innovation Policy for the Knowledge Society* 3.

Sell, Susan K. (2003), *Private Power, Public Law: The Globalization of Intellectual Property Rights* (Cambridge: Cambridge University Press).

Shapiro, Carl (2001), 'Setting Compatibility Standards: Cooperation or Collusion?', in Rochelle Cooper Dreyfuss, Diane Zimmerman and Harry First (eds), *Expanding the Boundaries of Intellectual Property: Innovation Policy for the Knowledge Society* 3 at 81, 97–101.

Shavell, Steven and Tanguy Van Ypersele (2001), 'Rewards Versus Intellectual Property Rights', 44 *J.L. & Econ.* 525.

Sobel, Dava (1995), *Longitude: The True Story of a Lone Genius Who Solved the Greatest Scientific Problem of His Time* (New York: Walker & Co.).

Strandburg, Katherine J. (2004), 'What Does the Public Get? Experimental Use and the Patent Bargain', 2004 *Wis. L. Rev*. 81.

Takenaka, Toshiko (1998), 'Harmonizing the Japanese Patent System With Its U.S. Counterpart Through Judge-Made Law: Interaction Between Japanese And U.S. Case Law Developments', 7 *Pac. Rim L. & Pol'y* 249, 254–60.

Walterscheid, Edward C. (1999), 'The Use and Abuse of History: The Supreme Court's Interpretation of Thomas Jefferson's Influence on the Patent Law', 39 *Idea* 195.

PART II

Intellectual property rights as human rights

5. Introduction

Jerzy Koopman*

1. INTRODUCTION

Intellectual property law regimes have increasingly proliferated during the past decades. One of the results thereof is that they touch upon more and more aspects of human life. It has become obvious that intellectual property law regimes have a profound impact on all sorts of human activity across national, disciplinary and cultural boundaries around the world. Intellectual property increasingly affects cultural, scientific, technological, and commercial exchanges and, thereby, steers and (re)directs courses of action in and among those realms. Whereas economic, cultural, scientific and technological circumstances, preferences and governmental policies may press for such proliferation – may envision positive outcomes thereof – downsides begin to be observed as well. These downsides may vary in kind and in effect, and may be brought about by the workings of different intellectual property regimes as well. They may concern topics as disparate as the deprivation of biological and cultural diversity; the decline of accessibility of information; and a decrease in accessibility of health care products and so forth. Looked at from an overall societal and legal perspective, it may thus not be considered surprising that human rights come into play. At the turn of the millennium, the UN Sub-Commission on Human Rights even held that '[t]here are . . . conflicts between the intellectual property rights regime . . . and international human rights law . . .'[1] Hence, the emergence of a so-called human rights paradox in intellectual property law – the theme of the CIER conference of which this book is one of the tangible, rich outcomes.

Economic policies – and economic instruments that should incorporate them, such as intellectual property law regimes – may lead to a cyclone of societal effects, which may (perhaps necessarily) be the subject of human rights law. Therefore, these policies and instruments should allegedly be

* Jerzy Koopman is a PhD-student at the Centre for Intellectual Property Law (CIER), Molengraaff Institute for Private Law, Utrecht University and works as life science law counsel in Amsterdam.

1 Resolution 2000/7. At: http://www.unhchr.ch/Huridocda/Huridoca.nsf/0/c462b62cf8a07b13c12569700046704e?Opendocument.

approached from those perspectives – and thus human rights law – as well. The paradox central to the CIER conference may relate to a primary, underlying social and governmental paradox that surely supersedes legal interests and complications, but forms the broader context therefor instead. This underlying paradox was accurately pin-pointed by Sonia Gandhi in her 2007 Nexus lecture in Tilburg, the Netherlands: 'Growth without equity tends to destabilize societies, while equity without growth simply cannot be sustained.' The manner in which 'things' are so interrelated – yet at the outset appear contradictory – is necessarily manifested in the human rights paradox in intellectual property law too.

In this Part, the human rights paradox in intellectual property law is made apparent and explored at what may be called its regulatory basis – that is the legislative effect of human rights law on intellectual property law. The central focus thus is whether – and if so, to what extent – human rights law affects the legislative formation of intellectual property law regimes, such as patent law and copyright law, and thereby determines their regulatory make-up and workings.

The legislative effect of human rights law on intellectual property law may be conceived of in both a positive and negative manner. The most initial and fundamental positive effect of human rights law on the legislative formation of intellectual property law may perhaps become apparent from the formation per se. It may be proposed that several human rights pertaining to the individual's social, cultural and economic being, capacity and status may be given legal and practical effect by the provision of proprietary rights, such as copyrights and patent rights. Hence intellectual property rights as human rights themselves. However, the positive influence of human rights law on the formation of intellectual property law regimes could also appear at a later stage of legal formation and then have very specific substantive implications. This may be the case when certain provisions are explicitly incorporated in intellectual property regimes so as to give hands and feet to a certain human right. An example thereof within many copyright laws could arguably be the provisions pertaining to moral rights, which may be related to a host of human rights that hinge on the dignity of human individuals. An example of a positive influence of human rights law on the legislative formation of patent law may be found in compulsory licence provisions that seek to provide a leeway for patents' exclusionary effects for the benefit of healthcare and medicine. Conversely, the negative impact of human rights law on the formation of intellectual property law may be more implicit than the aforementioned examples. The negative impact may lead to restrictions and limitations as to, for example, the object that may be deemed fit to be protected under one or the other intellectual property law regime. The formulation and definition of central notions – such as copyright law's 'work' or patent law's 'invention' – may derive from, among other things, the recognition and effect of human rights. Human rights that demand the recognition of and respect for the individual's proprietary (or other kind of) interest in his or her 'works' or 'inventions' may lead to inherent limitations to what other individuals may subsequently consider their respective 'works' and 'inventions', and which may so be the subject of one or the other intellectual proprietary regime. All of these (rather randomly selected) introductory examples reflect upon the effects of human rights law on the legislative formation of intellectual property law regimes.

The contributions in this Part specifically address, albeit from different pretexts and angles, varying regimes of intellectual property law, and with different goals. This Part so presents a rich diversity in knowledge, explorations and ideas about the topics concerned, and provides the reader with an excellent opportunity to inquire and learn about them.

In Chapter 6, 'Is copyright fit for the 21st century? No!', Joost Smiers approaches some of the issues with regard to copyright law. His firm conclusion that copyright law as it is should be eliminated rests on an exposé of the effects on cultural life and activities of the current legal system. It is argued that the workings of this system severely and negatively affect cultural diversity in its broadest meaning and relevancy, and thus need to be replaced by alternative regulations. This should enhance the flourishing of cultural diversity.

Duncan Matthews' chapter, 'Intellectual property rights, human rights and the right to health' provides analyses of the tensions between intellectual property rights and the human right to health. Intellectual property rights are assessed as human rights themselves and, furthermore, the human right to health is addressed as a possible tool to facilitate access to medicines. Moreover, the implications of the latter right for intellectual property rights are analysed with regard to pharmaceutical product patents, and with a concrete illustrative focus on anti-retroviral medicines and HIV/AIDS in Brazil and South Africa. It is ultimately concluded, among other things, that the human rights discourse may lead to real improvements with regard to the topic at hand. Human rights based approaches may provide leeway for developing countries, if they are able to use these rights to their best advantage. It is finally suggested that developed countries and others should formulate intellectual property law regimes that assist developing countries to do so as well.

In Chapter 8 'On patents and human rights', Jan Brinkhof approaches the topic through close analysis of specific human rights provisions that may relate to the establishment of patent law regimes, as well as by examination of relevant case law. After having addressed the historical legislative context of patent law regimes, certain arguments supporting the view that patent law may be a human right are examined, and a detailed overview is given of human rights provisions that may perhaps bolster those views. Particular attention is given to the First Protocol to the European Convention on Human Rights. Relevant case law of the European Court of Human Rights is analysed in this respect as well. The same applies to the the Charter of Fundamental Rights in Europe. Finally, a holding of the Enlarged Board of Appeal of the European Patent Office as to the meaning of a particularly relevant human right, which may allegedly render a patent right a human right is reiterated and assessed. The author concludes, however, that the human rights provisions that may appear relevant in this respect do not provide sufficient legal basis for the conclusion that patent rights are human rights. It is proposed that patent law should merely be understood as an instrument of economic policy, rather than one of human rights law.

Wendy Gordon's chapter 'Current patent laws cannot claim the backing of human rights' scrutinizes the argument that patent law can be based in human rights from a legal-positivist perspective. Article 15.1(c) of the International Covenant on Economic, Social and Cultural Rights, which requires protection of interests of 'authors' of scientific productions, is particularly addressed. Key is the envisioned nature of 'authorship', which is interrelated to the make-up and workings of, mostly, the US patent regime. It is generally suggested that divergences in the historical formation of said human rights provision and intellectual property law regimes render it unlikely that the latter may be based on the former. Specific patent law requirements and their application appear to support this view. They do not give effect to article 15.1(c) of referenced Covenant. One can for example think of the manner in which rights may (not) be conveyed (e.g. determination of inventorship) or may be forfeited beforehand (e.g. by certain pre-application disclosures). Also the fact that many patentees are corporate assignees, which may principally be deprived of the human right at hand, is emphasized. It is so observed that current patentees may be deprived of said human right, whilst 'authors' that are endowed therewith may be irrelevant for patent law purposes. Ultimately, it is concluded that article 15.1(c) of the Covenant does not support a conception of patent rights as a human right.

It is a pleasure to urge you – the reader – to commence reading the aforementioned chapters. They constructively, congruently and concisely contribute to a highly important, dynamic, timely debate on the complicated interaction between human rights law and intellectual property law. Enjoy!

Copyright law and patent law: to its recognition – differing views

6. Is copyright fit for the 21st century? No!

Joost Smiers*

1. HARD TO IMAGINE

Some serious cracks are surfacing in the system of copyright as we have known it in the Western world for a couple of centuries. The system is substantially more beneficial for cultural conglomerates than for the average artist; a situation that cannot last. Furthermore, it seems inescapable that digitization is undermining the foundations of the copyright system. It must be acknowledged that several authors have recently presented analyses of the untenability of the contemporary system of copyright. Yet, most of their observations only allude to – but do not address – what we deem the most fundamental question of all: if copyright is inherently unjust, what could come in its place to guarantee artists – creative and performing – a fair compensation for their labours, and how can we prevent knowledge and creativity from being privatized (Bettig 1996; Bollier 2003: 119–34; Boyle 1996; Coombe 1998; Drahos 2002, 2002a; Frith 2004; Lessig 2002, 2004; Litman 2001; Perelman 2002; Vaidhyanathan 2003). It is time to move beyond merely criticizing copyright. The pressing question is: which alternative can we offer artists and other cultural entrepreneurs in rich as well as poor countries that benefits *them*, and that brings the increasing privatization of creativity and expertise to a halt? Our goal in this chapter is to develop such an alternative, and to move beyond any notion centred on *private* intellectual *property* rights.

This chapter is an essay. We cannot erase the effect of centuries of Western thought on intellectual property rights with a single stroke of the pen. It is hard to imagine for Western man that a world without copyright could still yield films, theatre productions, novels, music pieces, paintings, and multimedia spectacles; even though people born and living in non-Western cultures find this a lot less hard to believe (Boyle 1996: xiv)!

* Joost Smiers is Honorary Professor of Political Science of the Arts and a Research Fellow in the Research Group Arts & Economics at the Utrecht School of the Arts, the Netherlands.

A first observation must be that the present Western copyright system pays little attention to the average artist, especially those in non-Western societies. The system disproportionately benefits a few famous artists and especially a few major enterprises, but it has little to offer for most creators and performers (Boyle 1996: xiii; Drahos 2002: 15; Kretschmer 1999; Kretschmer and Kawohl 2004: 44; Vaidhyanathan 2003: 5). The copyright system does enable a handful of cultural enterprises to dominate the market, and to withdraw substantive diversity from the public eye (Bettig 1996: 34–42, 103; Boyle 1996: 121–5; Coombe 1998: 144; Drahos 2002: ix–x, 74–84; Litman 2001: 14; McChesney 1999). Copyright has thus become a mechanism for a few cultural conglomerates to control the broad terrain of cultural communication. Something that has been derailed to such a large extent, and that hurts the interests of most artists and the public domain, can no longer be cut back to normal proportions.

For most artists, the profits deriving from copyright do not form much of an incentive to create and perform artistic work, simply because they hardly receive the proceeds. This has been the case in the past, it still is the case in the present, and it holds for almost every culture. From an historical perspective, we may note that the concept of private intellectual property rights has traditionally been absent from most cultures. Yet, there have always been artists who created and performed works (Bettig 1996: 25, 44, 171; Boyle 1996: 38–9). The incentive argument – artists stop their labours if they stop receiving copyright payments – therefore does not hold: 'Copyright today is less about incentives or compensation than it is about control.' (Litman 2001: 80) 'Firms in the creative industries are able to "free-ride" on the willingness of artists to create and the structure of the artists' labour markets, characterised by short term working practices and oversupply, make it hard for artists to appropriate awards.' (Towse 2003: 10) One may add to this observation that:

> value of copyright royalty rates is decided in the market place and it is therefore artists' bargaining power with firms in the creative industries that determines copyright earnings. Artists' bargaining power is, however, considerably weakened by the persistence of excess supply of creative workers to the creative industries . . . As with artists' earnings from other art sources, the individuals' distribution of copyright earnings is highly skewed with a few top stars earning considerable sums but the medium or 'typical' author earning only small amounts from their various rights. (Towse 2003: 11)

For non-Western countries, the Western intellectual property rights system is nothing but a straight-out disaster. Their knowledge and creativity is obfuscated from them, and they have to pay dearly to receive the fruits of these sacrifices in return. This even explains the unfavourable debt position of these countries to some extent (Boyle 1996: 34, 125–30, 141–2; Coombe 1998:

208–47; Correa 2000; Grosheide 2002; von Lewinski 2004; Mitsui 1993; Perelman 2002: 5–7; Rifkin 2000: 229–32, 248–53; Shiva 1997, 2001).

Let's face the reality that *digitization* is axing the roots of the copyright system (Alderman 2001; Lessig 2002; Litman 2001: 89–100, 112–16, 151–70; Motavalli 2002; Rifkin 2000: 218–29; Schiller 2000; Vaidyanathan 2003: 149–84). By abolishing copyright, the process of creative adaptation will once again enjoy every imaginable opportunity. This is all the more interesting in the digital age. After all, digital sampling enables the production of creative works, much like those have always been produced. How? Indeed, by finding inspiration, themes, or certain forms of expression in works previously produced, long ago or yesterday. Digitization enables this lending and borrowing of inspiration, and is helpful as well from another perspective. In the world of copyright there has always existed a bizarre distinction between an idea and the expression: however, in the digital age a work is no longer fixed and separating idea from expression is no longer possible. The artificial distinction and the endless discussions about it have become superfluous.

Another observation, linked to what creative sampling makes possible, is that the philosophical basis of the present system of copyright is founded on a misunderstanding, notably that of the sheer boundless originality of the artist, regardless of whether he or she is a creator or a performer. But let us keep a keen eye on reality. One always builds on the labours of predecessors and contemporaries. Subsequent artists add something to the existing corpus of work, nothing more and nothing less. We may highly respect and admire those additions, but it would be incorrect to provide a creative or performing artist, or his or her producers, with an exclusive, monopolistic claim to something that has largely sprung from knowledge and creativity in the public domain, and that is indebted in important respects to the labours of predecessors (Barthes 1968; Boyle 1996: 42, 53–9).

Of course, we are well aware that an artist receives a copyright for the *addition* he or she makes to what can be found in the public domain of knowledge and creativity. Again, this addition can be very impressive (or banal). But it is quite a stretch to extend to him or her an exclusive, monopolistic property right for that addition, guaranteed until 70 years after his or her death, and which can on top of that be transferred to an individual or corporation that had nothing to do with the creative process in the first place. The credibility of the system really starts to fall apart when we realize that the author and his or her rightful claimants can forbid almost anything that resembles the copying of 'their' work (Coombe 1998: 92–8).

The development of the public domain of creativity and knowledge deserves a reappraisal. Besides, subsequent artists must be enabled to delve into that domain in order to find a supply of artistic materials that they can build on. That road will be closed when artistic materials from the present and past fall into private hands, something that is occurring to an increasing extent under the present system of copyright. This privatization of our past and present cultural heritage is devastating for the further development of our cultural life (Locke in Boyle 1996: 9). In fact, an 'author-centred regime can actually *slow down* scientific progress, *diminish* the opportunities for creativity, and *curtail* the availability of new products' (Boyle 1996: 119; also see: Perelman 2002: 7–9).

For cultural conglomerates, which control the bulk of the property rights worldwide, the possibility to forbid reproduction is exceptionally interesting: it enables them to dominate broad areas of artistic expression in which no contradiction, no counter-melody, no counter-image, in short no dialogic practice is tolerated (Coombe 1998: 42, 46). Yet, we have to realize that 'culture is not embedded in abstract concepts that we internalize, but in the materiality of signs and texts over which we struggle and the imprint of those struggles in consciousness. This ongoing negotiation and struggle over meaning is the essence of dialogic practice. Many interpretations of intellectual property laws squash dialogue by affirming the power of corporate actors to monologically control meaning by appealing to an abstract concept of property. Laws of intellectual property privilege monologic forms against dialogic practice and create significant power differentials between social actors engaged in hegemonic struggle' (Coombe 1998: 86). It is a prerequisite for any democratic society that a surplus of opinionating and emotion-evoking claims can be contradicted (Bettig 1996: 103–6). The broad copyright as we know and have it virtually renders that difficult and sometimes impossible.

2. ALTERNATIVES?

After this summation of the fundamental shortcomings of the copyright system, it may not come as a surprise that we feel the need to investigate alternative ways to protect the public domain of knowledge and creativity, and to assure many artists and other cultural entrepreneurs a fair income for their labours. As stated, this type of investigation only happens too sporadically. Recently a few scholars and policymakers have presented alternatives to the system. But their proposals have many disadvantages and they therefore do not constitute a real alternative to the copyright regime.

The most far-reaching reorientations have been systems like the General Public License and the Creative Commons (Bollier 2003: 27–30, 99–118; Boyle 1996: 132–3; Lessig 2002 and 2004: 282–6). The idea behind this approach is that A's work must be available for use by others, without them being obstructed by prevailing copyright. In turn, the other cannot appropriate the work. Why not? The Creative Commons entails that A supplies some kind of public license for his or her work: go ahead, do with the work as you please, as long as you do not bring the work under a regime of private ownership. The work is thus subjected to a form of 'empty' copyright. This 'hollow' copyright constitutes the most extreme option the author has under the Creative Commons regime. More often, however, the author opts for the choice 'some rights reserved', for example that the usage of a work is restricted to not for profit activities. It is an uncertain form of contract law that will keep lawyers busy. The sympathetic aspect of Creative Commons-like constructions is that it becomes possible, to a certain extent, to withdraw oneself from the copyright jungle. It is of course always laudable to start a new world order on an island, and there is no scepticism in this statement. We hope that more and more artists will renounce the system of copyright that disadvantages them so badly, and begin hollowing it out by embracing the idea of a Creative Commons. Without any doubt this system is helpful for museums and archives that wish to spread their stocks of cultural heritage to the public but also like to avoid it becoming copyrighted or used inappropriately by others.

As long as the system of copyright is still in place, the Creative Commons appears to be a useful solution that may even serve as an exemplar. But there are some strings attached. The Creative Commons does not paint a clear picture of how a diverse set of artists from all over the world, as well as their producers and patrons, might generate an income. But we have to prepare an answer to that question. Most artists will not dare to put the existing copyright regime to rest until they have been offered a clear view of a better alternative – even though the present regime only has smoke and mirrors to offer. That is easily understandable. A second drawback of Creative Commons-like approaches is that they do not fundamentally question and challenge the copyright system. The Creative Commons License suggests that the author wants to exercise some form of control, nonetheless.

Another quite essential objection to the Creative Commons-like approaches is that they involve only those artists who are willing to adhere to this philosophy. Cultural conglomerates, which have the ownership of big chunks of our cultural heritage from past and present, however, will not. This downgrades and limits the sympathetic idea of the Creative Commons. Not free of contradictions is the fact that one of the most outspoken advocates of Creative Commons, Lawrence Lessig, is a strong advocate of the idea that knowledge and creativity can be owned as individual property (Lessig 2004: XIV, XVI, 10, 28, 83). Isn't the title of his 2004 book *Free Culture* a bit misleading? Below we will argue that there is much to say against this private property claim on knowledge and creativity.

A second alternative for copyright is connected to different forms of art created and produced in a collective manner (regardless of whether it concerns more traditional or contemporary works) as is the case in most non-Western countries. In those societies the individual approach of the Western copyright system does not fit the more collective character of creation and performance. If one stays within the paradigm of the private ownership of knowledge and creativity, it is obvious that a concept like *collective* ownership comes to mind. Is it not possible to grant so-called 'traditional' societies a tool that resembles copyright, but is in fact collectively owned? Would this not enable them to protect their artistic expressions from inappropriate use and/or guarantee their artists an income?

The problems involved in effectively introducing a system of collective intellectual ownership rights are abundant. For instance, one may wonder who represents the community and is able to speak on behalf of the community. It is not by definition the case that everybody agrees on how to deal with artistic creations of the past and present. Copyright is about the exploitation of works, but many people in those societies may consider this a blasphemy, or would not like to see their works being used in specific contexts. The appropriation of knowledge and creativity is something that even pinches in the Western world, and it all the more does so in countries where this strange system has never existed, and where artists use each other's works, and so on and so forth, as was the case in the Western world before the introduction of the copyright system. There is, thus, even without considering the position of Western cultural conglomerates, reason to understand why the polite, weak and bleak trials of elaborating a collective intellectual property system have failed thus far.

Is the tweaking of the current system a solution for the problems as we have described them? Several scholars, critical of the present copyright system, propose optimising it. Their contributions vary. Some argue for the re-establishment of the fair use principle, which has suffered enormously over the last decade, or making copyright solely applicable to real authors, creators and performers. Others favour a much shorter period of protection, for instance 14 years. Again, others believe there is no real problem in the European context, because in those countries the collecting societies put aside a portion of the copyright earnings for cultural projects and their distribution scheme favours individual artists in comparison to the Anglo-Saxon copyright system. Unfortunately, it is unthinkable to bring the current system back to normal proportions, because it is not in the interest of the main partners of the system, the cultural conglomerates, to assist in this quest. On the contrary, they have been very eager and highly successful in extending and broadening the copyright system.

Moreover, digitization is greatly impacting the functioning of the system. At what point must a society decide that when almost everybody is participating in an 'illegal' practice – like P2P music or film exchange – it can no longer be considered illegal (Litman 2001)? And even if the European collecting societies have a higher moral ground than those in the Anglo-Saxon world, even then the problem of the individual appropriation of knowledge and creativity, which is the basis of our critique of the system, continues to exist. In the next sections we address this issue more thoroughly.

3. ARTISTS, PRODUCERS AND PATRONS: ENTREPRENEURS

Before presenting our proposal we must observe that artists are inclined to sell their work on the market and – if it all works out – make a living for themselves. Artists have always been merchants and small shopkeepers. They live off an acquisitive audience that wants to admire, enjoy, and buy their produce. To that audience also belong institutional buyers like royalty, churches, maecenases, labour unions, banks, hospitals, and other societal institutions (Hauser 1972). This conclusion, as will be demonstrated further on in this essay, will provide us with something to go by while developing an alternative for copyright.

Artists, as well as their producers and patrons, thus apparently are entrepreneurs. This requires a risk-prone mentality, and it involves competition, under the condition that real competition exists indeed, as much as possible, for many artistic expressions and their artists. The observation that artists, and their producers and patrons are entrepreneurs makes one wonder what the decisive reason is for reducing the entrepreneurial risks of cultural producers, because this is precisely what copyright does. Copyright renders a product exclusive, and provides the entrepreneur with a *de facto* monopoly. This system of institutionally protected gifts is seemingly bizarre in an era in which even cultural conglomerates themselves herald the blessings of free market competition. Major entrepreneurs in cultural sectors bargain for ever-stricter intellectual property rights in the form of extensions and expansions of existing copyright legislation, but this is completely at odds with the so-called rule of the free market! We also observe the exact same phenomenon in the area of patent law and other intellectual property laws such as trademarks, database rights, plant breeder rights and design rights (Drahos 2002; Perelman 2002; Rifkin 1998, 2000; Shiva 1997, 2001; Shulman, 1999).

Before we try our luck by presenting a new system, we must first identify the locus of the impulse to create. That brings us to the following summation, a three-pronged road. One possibility is that a work is being commissioned. The second option is that the artist him- or herself takes the initiative to make an artistic work, possibly in collaboration with multiple, differentially endowed creators and performers. Thirdly, a producer can be a binding factor and bear the responsibility and risk involved in an artistic venture.

In all three cases – the initiative coming from a patron, someone who commissions; from one or several artists themselves; or from a producer – there is a person or an institution that intentionally makes itself responsible and accountable for creating or performing a certain artistic work. To be responsible and accountable not only implies undertaking a broad range of activities to give the artistic project momentum, but also to bear, amongst other things, the financial risks involved. The initiator then becomes an entrepreneur and bears the risk that unavoidably comes with entrepreneurship. In our alternative for copyright it is not the artist who takes centre stage, but the entrepreneur, regardless of whether he or she is an artist, a patron, or a producer.

4. THE SYSTEM WORTH EXPLORING

What are the contours of the system that we find worth exploring? The core of the matter is that we distance ourselves from the present system of copyright, as was probably clear by now. What does that yield? As stated, the protective corral of property rights that is artificially erected around a creative work will disappear. The consequence, thus, is that the work – regardless of whether it involves a (new) creation or a performance – will have to be marketed from the moment of its announcement onwards. We will nuance this position further on in the chapter when we discuss the second option. What is essential is that the entrepreneurial patron, artist, or producer obtains a competitive advantage by creating or performing a work (Picciotto 2002: 225). This renders additional protection unnecessary.

What we have now is a first-mover advantage. The first person to bring a work to market can use the advantage to reap revenues. The entrepreneur thus has 'lead-time'. What we propose is not completely new. In 1934 Plant stated 'that copyright encourages moral hazard in publishers (firms in the creative industries) without sufficiently rewarding authors (creators) who supply the creative input. He believed that publishers should rely on the temporary monopoly of lead time to establish new products in the market.' (in Towse 2003: 19) This time gives the first mover a lead over possible competitors, the opportunity to skim the market for the new cultural product, ask a good price for it, and thus earn a return on investment. After all, it will take several months before, say, the same play or music piece will see its opening night elsewhere or the same chair is eligible for production in another location. It should be understood that the work falls immediately in the public domain; thus can be used by others as well, and everybody is free to adapt this work creatively. The competitive advantage that most artists possess in one form or other is put at the very core of our new system. If such advantages are allowed and able to do their work, ancillary forms of protection, like copyright, will be unnecessary.

The counter argument, however, might be that, with an eye on digitization, reality is that lead-time is only a couple of minutes or perhaps hours (Towse 2003: 19)! Does this mean that there are almost no works that can benefit from a competitive advantage? We do not believe so. Apart from the first-mover advantage, many artists are able to add value or create advantages in other ways. In order to understand this, we should keep in mind that cultural production and distribution will reshuffle considerably after the abolition of copyright. For instance, in the field of music concerts and performances will become much more important, also as a source of income for the artists. Live, direct contact with an audience generates inimitable value. Performing qualities are even now, in the present era, of decisive importance for long and lasting careers of musicians. This is what gives them a good reputation. Reputation creates value. Reputation has a signalling effect. It indicates guaranteed quality. Customers are more loyal and are willing to pay higher prices for cultural products from artists with a good reputation and it makes them aficionados (Fombrun 1996). In the part of this chapter where we test our proposals in the different fields of the arts – see below – we will come back to how cultural production and distribution will change in a world without copyright. But let us at this point stress that service qualities of artistic works will become much more important than the individual product.

From what we have stated before about the philosophically doubtful concept of the originality of the author, it is clear that we claim that any artistic creation or performance belongs to the public domain. It is derived from the commons, based on the works of predecessors and contemporaries, and therefore, from its moment of conception onwards it takes its place in the public domain. We use the concepts public domain and commons without distinction. However, we know that in legal traditions there may be differences between the two concepts. We define the public domain or the commons as the space in any society that *belongs* to all of us and can be *used* by all of us. It is a misunderstanding to think that the commons, or the public domain, is an unregulated space. Of course not: always in history and in all societies those common spaces have been regulated one way or another, for example on the conditions of their usage. In our alternative we return to the commons what has always belonged to it – no more and no less. We give back to all of us what has been privatised in the fields of creativity and knowledge in the Western world over the last centuries (Hemmungs Wirtén 2004: 133,4).

5. A NEW CULTURAL MARKET AND A LEVEL PLAYING FIELD

With our new system a new cultural market will emerge. The first observation is that with the abolition of copyright cultural conglomerates will lose their grip on the agglomeration of cultural products, with which they determine the outlook of our cultural lives to an ever-increasing extent. Because what will they lose? They have to give up control over huge chunks of the cultural markets. They lose the monopolistic exclusivity over broad cultural areas because everyone is allowed to exploit artistic materials that are not protected by temporary usufruct and absolutely no limitations are put on creatively adapting works of art. With these new conditions, the rationale is then lost for cultural conglomerates to make substantial investments in blockbusters, bestsellers, and stars. After all, by making creative adaptation respectable again and by undoing the present system of copyright, the economic incentives to produce at the present scale will diminish. However, it will not be forbidden for a cultural entrepreneur to invest millions of dollars or euros in, for instance, a film, game, CD or DVD. Of course not, but the investment will no longer be made under an endless wall of protection.

There will once again be room to manoeuvre in cultural markets for a variety of entrepreneurs, who are then no longer pushed out of the public's attention by blockbusters, bestsellers, and stars. Those plentiful artists are more likely to find audiences for their creations and performances in a normal market that is not dominated by a few large players. There is not a single reason to believe that there would be no demand for such an enormous variety of artistic expressions. In a normalized market, with equal opportunities for everyone, this demand can be fulfilled. This increases the possibility that a varied flock of artists would be capable of extracting a decent living from their endeavours.

A second observation is about cultural adaptation and how the market should be regulated with respect to fraud and plagiarism. We stress the fact that we do not like theft. We of course do not propose that X can attach his or her name to Y's book or film, suggesting to be the author of that work. That is plain misrepresentation or fraud. If that is found out, and that is bound to happen sooner or later, then the lazy fraudster will receive his or her fair penalty in the court of public opinion; we do not need a copyright system to accomplish that. It is up to all of us not to be afraid to publicly accuse artists of misrepresentation or fraud. This will only happen if we are culturally alert, and we have to be if we want to do without judgments of the courts, which have made us culturally lazy in the past! We should critically discuss what we consider culturally inappropriate use.

What we have suggested thus far is that it is quite feasible to have a flourishing cultural domain without the existence of a copyright system, while at the same time many artists in the Western and non-Western countries alike can make a reasonable income from their labours. However, it is evident that the completely new approach as we propose it does not immediately eradicate all conceivable problems. With this we come to our third observation. If cultural enterprises can no longer control the market with copyright in hand, they must resort to a second protective mechanism, which they will then attempt to apply with even greater force than is presently the case. That is the far-reaching control over distribution and promotion of cultural expression they possess and wield.

This too must be limited with metes and bounds, as has been analysed already before. After all, from a democratic perspective it is impermissible that a limited number of cultural giants is able to determine the contents of artistic and cultural communications, using traditional as well as new media. Democracy is not the privilege of a few cultural conglomerates. It is a necessity to use ownership and content regulations to organize the cultural market in such a way that cultural diversity gets the best possible chance. First of all, there should not be dominant modes of distribution. It cannot be the case that a single owner dominates, controls, or concerts the market for music, films, or books. Vertical integration and other forms of cross ownership must be condemned.

Content regulations may take the form of diversity prescriptions. That is to say: diversity in terms of genre, musicians' backgrounds, and geographical diversity, and the latter representing diversity from the home country, neighbouring countries, and many other parts of the world. Of course there will be outlets specializing in a certain genre that want to be known for it. These too will be subject to diversity prescription, albeit within that genre (Smiers 2004). This type of regulation does not take anything away from a free market economy. To the contrary, these rules, while in need of further elaboration, serve to create a free market, or differently put, to 'normalize' the market and to bring about a level playing field. No one should be able to dominate the cultural market or to have such a strong position that cultural diversity will be suppressed, pushed aside, or taken away from the public attention.

This demands some regulations: on the one hand the elimination of the control mechanism 'copyright' and on the other hand the instalment of some regulations concerning ownership and content that protect and promote the flourishing of artistic diversity.

BIBLIOGRAPHY

Barthes, Roland (1968), *La mort de l'auteur*, Manteia, no. 5, 4e trimestre 1968. Also published in: Roland Barthes, *Oeuvres complètes*, Tome II, 1966–73, Paris 1994 (Editions du Seuil): 491–5.

Bettig, Ronald V. (1996), *Copyrighting Culture. The Political Economy of Intellectual Property* (Boulder: Westview Press).
Bollier, David (2003), *Silent Theft. The Private Plunder of Our Common Wealth* (New York and London: Routledge).
Boyle, James (1996), *Shamans, Software, and Spleens. Law and the Construction of the Information Society* (Cambridge, MA and London: Harvard University Press).
Coombe, Rosemary J. (1998), *The Cultural Life of Intellectual Properties. Authorship, Appropriation, and the Law* (Durham and London: Duke University Press).
Correa, Carlos M. (2000), *Intellectual Property Rights, the WTO and Developing Countries. The TRIPS Agreement and Policy Options* (London/Penang: Zed Books/Third World Network).
Drahos, Peter (2002), with John Braithwaite, *Information Feudalism. Who Owns the Knowledge Economy?* (London: Earthscan).
Drahos, Peter, and Ruth Mayne (2002a), *Global Intellectual Property Rights. Knowledge, Access and Development* (Basingstoke (Hampshire) and New York: Palgrave Macmillan and Oxfam).
Fombrun, C.J. (1996), *Corporate Reputation: How Companies Realise Value from the Corporate Brand* (Boston MA: Harvard Business School Press).
Frith, Simon (ed.) (1993), *Music and Copyright* (Edinburgh: Edinburgh U.P.).
Frith, Simon, and Lee Marshal (eds) (2004), *Music and Copyright. Second Edition* (Edinburgh: Edinburgh U.P.).
Grosheide, Willem, and Jan Brinkhof (ed.) (2002), *Articles on the Legal Protection of Cultural Expressions and Indigenous Knowledge (*Antwerp: Intersentia).
Hauser (1972), *Sozialgeschichte der Kunst und Literatur* (München: C.H. Beck).
Hemmungs Wirtén, Eva (2004), *No Trespassing. Authorship, Intellectual Property Rights, and the Boundaries of Globalization* (Toronto: University of Toronto Press).
Kretschmer, Martin (1999), 'Intellectual Property in Music: A Historical Analysis of Rethoric and Institutional Practices', special issue Cultural Industry (ed. P. Jeffcutt), *Studies in Cultures, Organizations and Societies*, 6: 197–223.
Kretschmer, Martin and Friedemann Kawohl, (2004), 'The History and Philosophy of Copyright', in Frith and Marschall (2004): 21–53.
Lessig, Lawrence (2002), *The Future of Ideas. The fate of the commons in a connected world* (New York: Vintage Books).
Lessig, Lawrence (2004), *Free Culture. How Big Media Uses Technology and the Law to Lock Down Culture and Control Creativity* (New York: The Penguin Press).
Lewinski, Silke von (2002), *Indigenous Heritage and Intellectual Property. Genetic Resources, Traditional Knowledge and Folklore* (The Hague: Kluwer Law International).
Litman, Jessica (2001), *Digital Copyright*, (Amherst, New York: Prometeus Books).
McChesney, Robert W. (1999), *Rich Media, Poor Democracy. Communication Politics in Dubious Times* (Urbana and Chicago: University of Illinois Press).
Mitsui, Tôru (1993), 'Copyright and Music in Japan. A Forced Grafting and its Consequences', in Frith 1993: 125–45.
Motavalli, John (2002), *Bamboozled at the Revolution. How Big Media Lost Billions in the Battle for the Internet* (New York: Viking).
Perelman, Michael (2002), *Steal this Idea. Intellectual Property Rights and the Corporate Confiscation of Creativity* (New York: Palgrave).
Picciotto, Sol (2002), 'Defending the Public Interest in TRIPS and the WTO', in Drahos 2002a: 224–43.
Rifkin, Jeremy (2000), *The Age of Access. The New Culture of Hypercapitalism, Where All of Life is a Paid-for Experience* (New York: Jeremy P. Tarcher/Putnam).

Schiller, Dan (2000), *Digital Capitalism. Networking the Global Market System* (Cambridge (MA)/London: The MIT Press).
Shiva, Vandana (1997), *Biopiracy. The Plunder of Nature and Knowledge* (Boston MA: South End Press).
Shiva, Vandana (2001), *Protect or Plunder? Understanding Intellectual Property Rights* (London: Zed Books).
Shulman, Seth (1999), *Owning the Future* (New York: Houghton Mifflin Company).
Smiers, Joost (2001), 'La propriété intellectuelle, c'est le vol! Pladoyer pour l'abolition des droits d'auteur', in *Le Monde Diplomatique*, septembre 2001.
Smiers, Joost (2003), *Arts Under Pressure. Promoting Cultural Diversity in the Age of Globalisation* (London: Zed Books).
Smiers, Joost (2004), *Artistic Expression in a Corporate World. Do We Need Monopolistic Control?* (Utrecht: Utrecht School of the Arts).
Towse, Ruth (2003), 'Copyright and Cultural Policy for the Creative Industries', in Grandstrand 2002: 1–10.
Vaidhyanathan, Siva (2003), *Copyrights and Copywrongs. The Rise of Intellectual Property and How It Threatens Creativity* (New York and London: New York University Press).

7. Intellectual property rights, human rights and the right to health

Duncan Matthews*

1. INTRODUCTION

> *The allocation of rights over intellectual property has significant economic, social and cultural consequences that can affect the enjoyment of human rights.*[1]

In many respects, this statement by the United Nations Committee on Economic, Social and Cultural Rights in 2001 encapsulates the tensions between intellectual property rights, human rights and the right to health that will be examined in this chapter. These tensions are driven by the manner in which creative works, cultural heritage, and scientific knowledge are turned into property which, subsequently, has significant human rights implications,[2] particularly the right to health. Accordingly, this chapter undertakes an analysis of the tensions between intellectual property rights, human rights and the right to health.

To achieve this, the chapter is divided into four parts. The first part of the chapter engages with the debate on whether intellectual property rights are

---

* Reader in Intellectual Property Law, Centre for Commercial Law Studies, Queen Mary, University of London, 67–69 Lincoln's Inn Fields, London WC2A 3JB. Email: d.n.matthews@qmul.ac.uk. The author would like to thank Tina Loverdou of Davenport Lyons Solicitors and Viviana Munoz-Tellez of South Centre for invaluable insights and advice. Any errors or omissions remain the responsibility of the author.

1 Statement by the Committee on Economic and Cultural Rights, *Substantive Issues Arising in the Implementation of the International Covenant on Economic, Social and Cultural Rights. Follow-up to the day of general discussion on article 15.1(c), Monday 26 November 2001, Human Rights and Intellectual Property*. United Nations Committee on Economic, Social and Cultural Rights, E/C.12/2001/15, 14 December 2001, para 1.

2 For a lengthy discussion on this point see *Implementation of the International Covenant on Economic, Social and Cultural Rights*. Discussion paper submitted by Dr Audrey R. Chapman, American Association for the Advancement of Science (AAAS), Washington, USA, to the United Nations Committee on Economic, Social and Cultural Rights, E/C.12/2000/12, 3 October 2000.

human rights. It will reappraise, in particular, Article 27 of the Universal Declaration of Human Rights, Article 15(1) the International Covenant on Economic, Social and Cultural Rights, and the report of the High Commissioner on Human Rights on the impact of the Agreement on Trade-Related Aspects of Intellectual Property Rights (TRIPS). The second part of the chapter then examines the tensions between intellectual property rights and the right to health, specifically in relation to whether a rights-based approach to health can be used as a mechanism to facilitate access to medicines. To do this, the second part of the chapter re-examines Article 25 of the Universal Declaration of Human Rights and Article 12 of the International Covenant on Economic, Social and Cultural Rights. The third part of the chapter then discusses the implications of the right to health for intellectual property rights with reference to the experiences of using a human rights-based discourse to assert the right to health in the context of pharmaceutical product patents, compulsory licences and access to medicines, particularly anti-retroviral drugs for people living with HIV/AIDS in two developing countries: Brazil and South Africa. In the light of this analysis of rights-based discourse and implications of the right to health for access to medicines, the fourth part of the chapter then concludes by drawing attention to the World Health Organisation's Resolution on Public Health, Innovation and Essential Health Research and Intellectual Property Rights of 27 May 2006, which reasserted the significance of intellectual property rights as human rights at a time when concerns about access to medicines reached a new level of prominence. In doing so, the chapter concludes that the WHO Resolution has brought back to the fore tensions between intellectual property rights, human rights and the right to health that are likely to persist for the foreseeable future.

2. INTELLECTUAL PROPERTY RIGHTS AND HUMAN RIGHTS

At the heart of the debate on intellectual property rights and human rights lies a distinction between individual rights and community rights. Three possible interpretations are available: the first is that intellectual property rights have no human rights dimension and are purely legal rights; the second is that intellectual property rights are human rights, with the emphasis on property rights and individual concerns; the third interpretation is that some aspects of intellectual property rights have potentially adverse implications for human rights.[3]

[3] See also 3D: Trade-Human Rights-Equitable Economy (2005) *Background Note: Intellectual Property, Human Rights and the Drafting of the General Comment on Article 15(1)(c) ICESCR*, Geneva: 3D.

The first interpretation, namely that intellectual property rights have no human rights dimension and are purely legal rights appears incorrect given that, with regard to copyright at least, the little-known solemn declaration by the States members of the Assembly of the Berne Union for the Protection of Literary and Artistic Works that, in 1986, asserted clearly and unambiguously that 'copyright is based on human rights and justice and that authors, as creators of beauty, entertainment and learning, deserve that their rights in their creations be recognized and effectively protected both in their country and in all other countries of the world'.[4]

With regard to the second interpretation, namely that intellectual property is essentially the same as property in tangible assets and must therefore be secured by the same legal guarantees, Tom Giovanetti and Merrill Matthews assert that the protection of intellectual property rights has long been recognised as a basic human right and those concerned about human rights made a conscious and concerted effort to ensure that intellectual property rights were protected.[5] In support of this claim, they draw on the Constitution of the United States[6] and the American Declaration on the Rights and Duties of Man.[7] This is the rationale for arguing that provisions made by international human rights documents with regard to property cover intellectual property, with the latter elevated to the status of 'fundamental rights'.

Foremost amongst the international human rights documents that are often claimed to regard property as covering intellectual property are the Universal Declaration of Human Rights and the United Nations International Covenant on Economic, Social and Cultural Rights.

The Universal Declaration of Human Rights,[8] in Article 17(1), recognises that '[e]veryone has the right to own property alone as well as in association with others' and, in Article 17(2), that '[no] one shall be arbitrarily deprived of his property'. The Universal Declaration of Human Rights then goes on, in

[4] 'Solemn Declaration' by the Assembly of the Berne Union of 9 September 1986.

[5] Giovanetti, T. and M. Matthews (2005) *Intellectual Property Rights and Human Rights* (Lewisville, Texas: Institute for Policy Innovation).

[6] 'To promote the progress of science and useful arts, by securing for limited times to authors and inventors the exclusive rights to their respective writings and discoveries.' US Constitution Article 1, Section 8, Clause 8.

[7] 'He likewise has the right to the protection of his moral and material interests as regards his inventions or any literary, scientific or artistic works of which he is the author.' American Declaration of the Rights and Duties of Man, Article 13.

[8] Universal Declaration of Human Rights *Adopted and proclaimed by General Assembly Resolution 217 A (III) of 10 December 1948*, G.A. Res217A (III) 3 U.N. GAOR (Resolutions, part 1) at 71, U.N. Doc. A/810 (1948). Available at: http://www.un.org/Overview/rights.html (visited on 4 April 2007).

Article 27, to state that: '(1) Everyone has the right to freely participate in the cultural life of the community, to enjoy the arts and to share in scientific advancement and its benefits. (2) Everyone has the right to the protection of the moral and material interests resulting from any scientific, literary or artistic production of which he is the author.'

Article 15(1) of the United Nations International Covenant on Economic, Social and Cultural Rights (ICESCR), 1966,[9] contains similar provisions to the Universal Declaration of Human Rights: 'The States Parties to the present Covenant recognise the right of everyone: (a) to take part in cultural life; (b) to enjoy the benefits of scientific progress and its applications; (c) to benefit from the protection of the moral and material interests resulting from any scientific, literary or artistic production of which he or she is the author.'

For Audrey Chapman, author of a discussion paper entitled 'Implementation of the International Covenant on Economic, Social and Cultural Rights' that was presented to the United Nations Committee on Economic, Social and Cultural Rights in 2000, intellectual property rights should be viewed as human rights because the three provisions of Article 15(1) ICESCR were viewed by drafters as intrinsically interrelated to one another; the rights of authors and creators are not just good in themselves but were understood as essential preconditions for cultural freedom and participation and scientific progress.[10] However, Chapman goes on to point out that, conversely, human rights considerations impose conditions on the manner in which authors' rights are protected in intellectual property regimes. For Chapman, to be consistent with the provisions of Article 15, intellectual property law must assure that intellection property protections complement, fully respect, and promote other components of Article 15, so that the rights of authors and creators facilitate rather than constrain cultural participation on the one side and scientific progress and access on the other. The language of the Covenant underscores the importance of the obligation to respect the moral and material interests of the author, artist, inventor and creator but, in contrast with the individualism of intellectual property law, Chapman argues that a human rights approach also recognises that an author, artist, or creator can be a group or a community as well as an individual.

Chapman also points out that intellectual property rights have an intrinsic value as an expression of human dignity and creativity and that, put another way, artistic and scientific works are not first and foremost economic commodities whose value is determined by their utility and economic price

---

9 International Covenant on Economic, Social and Cultural Rights, adopted 16 December 1966, 993 U.N.T.S. 3 (entered into force 3 January 1976), G.A. Res. 2200 (XXI), 21 U.N. GAOR Supp. (No. 16) at 49, U.N. Doc.A/6316 (1966).

10 Chapman, above n. 2 at para 23.

tag.[11] A human rights approach takes what is often an implicit balance between the rights of inventors and creators and the interests of the wider society within intellectual property paradigms and makes it far more explicit and exacting – for Chapman, from a human rights perspective, the rights of the creator are not absolute but conditional on contributing to the common good and welfare of society.[12] Chapman concludes that, because a human rights approach also establishes a different and often more exacting standard for evaluating the appropriateness of granting intellectual property protection, in order for intellectual property to fulfil the conditions necessary to be recognised as a universal human right, intellectual property regimes and the manner they are implemented first and foremost must be consistent with the realisation of the other human rights, particularly those enumerated in the Covenant.[13]

This leads us to the third interpretation of intellectual property rights and human rights, namely that some aspects of intellectual property rights have potentially adverse implications for human rights. The report of the High Commissioner on Human Rights on the impact of the Agreement on Trade-Related Aspects of Intellectual Property Rights on human rights of 27 June 2001, acknowledged that Article 15 ICESCR identifies a need to balance the protection of both public and private interests.[14] On the one hand, Article 15 recognises the right of everyone to take part in cultural life and to enjoy the benefits of scientific progress and its applications. On the other hand, the same article recognises the right of everyone to benefit from the protection of the moral and material interests resulting from any scientific, literary or artistic production of which he or she is the author. Taking these two aspects of Article 15 together, the ICESCR could be said to bind States to design intellectual property systems that strike a balance between promoting general public interests in accessing new knowledge as easily as possible and in protecting the interests of authors and inventors in such knowledge. Of course, as the report of the High Commissioner on Human Rights points out, the balance between public and private interests found under Article 15 ICESCR (and under Article 27 of the Universal Declaration) is one familiar in intellectual property law. For the report of the High Commissioner on Human Rights, there is consequently a degree of compatibility between Article 15 and traditional intellectual property systems, but the question is essentially where to strike the right balance,

---

11 Chapman, above n. 2 at para 26.

12 Chapman, above n. 2 at para 27.

13 Chapman, above n. 2 at para 28.

14 United Nations Commission on Human Rights (2001) *Economic, Social and Cultural Rights: The Impact of the Agreement on Trade-Related Aspects of Intellectual Property Rights on Human Rights. Report of the High Commissioner*, 27 June 2001, E/CN.4/Sub.2/2001/13, page 5.

namely whether greater emphasis should be given to protecting interests of inventors and authors or to promoting public access to new knowledge.[15]

The Charter of Fundamental Rights of the European Union also states, in Article 17, that: '(1) Everyone has the right to own, use, dispose of and bequeath his or her lawfully acquired possessions. No one may be deprived of his or her possessions, except in the public interest and in the cases and under the conditions provided for by law, subject to fair compensation being paid in good time for their loss. The use of property may be regulated by law in so far as is necessary for the general interest.' Article 17 goes on to state explicitly that: '(2) Intellectual property shall be protected'.

The drafting committee responsible for the Charter commented on sub-paragraph (2) as follows: 'Protection of intellectual property, one aspect of the right of property, is mentioned explicitly in paragraph 2 because of its growing importance and Community secondary legislation. Intellectual property covers not only literary and artistic property but also patent and trademark rights and associated rights. The guarantees laid down in paragraph 1 shall apply *as appropriate* to intellectual property' (emphasis added). What, then, would be the *appropriate* application of property rights under the EU Charter in the context of intellectual property rights? The answer to this question would appear to be of crucial importance to determining the appropriate balance between public and private interests that the High Commissioner on Human Rights on the impact of the Agreement on Trade-Related Aspects of Intellectual Property Rights on human rights of 27 June 2001 had highlighted.

It will be recalled that Article 15(1)(c) of the Covenant sets out the right of everyone to benefit from the protection of the moral and material interests resulting from any scientific, literary or artistic production of which he is the author. On 21 November 2005, the UNHCR Committee on Economic, Social and Cultural Rights adopted General Comment 17 on the right of everyone to benefit from the protection of the moral and material interests resulting from any scientific, literary or artistic production of which he is the author (Article 15, paragraph 1(c) of the Covenant).[16] General Comment 17 noted that the

---

15 Ibid, page 5.

16 General Comment No. 17 on the right of everyone to benefit from the protection of the moral and material interests resulting from any scientific, literary or artistic production of which he is the author (Article 15(1)(c) of the Covenant), adopted by the UNHCR Committee on Economic, Social and Cultural Rights on 21 November 2005 (E/C.12/2005/GC/17). The earlier title of the draft document was General Comment No. 18. This draft document, for which Eibe Riedel (CESCR member, Germany) was Rapporteur, was ultimately adopted by the Committee on Economic, Social and Cultural Rights on 21 November 2005 and re-numbered as General Comment No. 17 (confusingly, a separate General Comment No. 18 now relates to the right to work (Article 6 of the Covenant).

right of everyone to benefit from the protection of the moral and material interests resulting from any scientific, literary or artistic production of which he or she is the author is a human right, which derives from the inherent dignity and worth of all persons. General Comment 17 notes that this fact distinguishes Article 15, paragraph 1(c) and other human rights from most legal entitlements recognisable in intellectual property systems. It stated that human rights are fundamental, inalienable and universal entitlements belonging to individuals and, under certain circumstances, groups of individuals and communities. General Comment 17 also noted that human rights are fundamental as they are inherent in the human person as such, whereas intellectual property rights are first and foremost means by which States seek to provide incentives for inventiveness and creativity, encourage the dissemination of creative and innovative productions, as well as the development of cultural identities, and preserve the integrity of scientific, literary and artistic productions for the benefit of society as a whole.[17]

General Comment 17 goes on to suggest that, in contrast with human rights, intellectual property rights are generally of a temporary nature, and can be revoked, licensed or assigned to someone else. While under most intellectual property systems, intellectual property rights, with the exception of moral rights, may be allocated, limited in time and scope, traded, amended and even forfeited, human rights are timeless expressions of fundamental entitlements of the human person. Whereas the human right to benefit from the protection of the moral and material interests resulting from one's scientific, literary and artistic productions safeguards the personal link between authors and their creations, and between peoples, communities, or other groups and their collective cultural heritage, as well as their basic material interests which are necessary to enable authors to enjoy an adequate standard of living, intellectual property regimes primarily protect business and corporate interests and investments. Moreover, the General Comment stated that the scope of protection of the moral and material interests of the author provided for by Article 15(1)(c) does not necessarily coincide with what is referred to as intellectual property rights under national legislation or international agreements.[18]

3. INTELLECTUAL PROPERTY RIGHTS AND THE RIGHT TO HEALTH

With regard to the relationship between intellectual property rights and the

---

17 Ibid, para 1. See also n. 1, above, at para 6.
18 Above, n. 16, para 2. See also above, n. 1 at para 6.

right to health, on the one hand, under Article 27(1) of the TRIPS Agreement, patents must be available for all fields of technology. This scope of coverage includes the availability of patents for pharmaceutical products. However, when considering the availability of patents for pharmaceutical products, one must also take into account the right to health. Article 25 of the Universal Declaration of Human Rights, 1948, states explicitly that '(1) Everyone has the right to a standard of living adequate for the health and well-being of himself and his family, including food, clothing, housing and *medical care* . . .' (emphasis added). This principle of the right to health is underpinned by Article 12 of the United Nations International Covenant on Economic, Social and Cultural Rights, 1966, which states that '(1) The States Parties to the present Covenant recognize the right of everyone to the enjoyment of the highest attainable standard of physical and mental health'.

UN Committee on Economic, Social and Cultural Rights has also elaborated, in General Comment 14, adopted on 11 May 2000,[19] on the concept of the highest attainable standard of health, as set out in Article 12 of the Covenant. General Comment 14 sets out the content of the right, obligations on States to respect, and fulfil the right, the elements of international cooperation relevant to implement the right, as well as acts constituting violations of the right. In particular, General Comment 14 states that health is a fundamental human right indispensable for the exercise of other human rights.[20] General Comment 14 also makes clear that the reference to Article 12(1) of the Covenant to 'the highest attainable standard of physical and mental health' is not confined to the right to health care and that, on the contrary, the wording of Article 12.1 acknowledges that the right to health embraces a wide range of socio-economic factors that promote conditions in which people can lead a healthy life and extends to the underlying determinants of health, such as food and nutrition, housing, access to safe and potable water and adequate sanitation, safe and healthy working conditions, and a healthy environment.[21] In this regard, General Comment 14 makes specific reference to the promotion of research, access to affordable treatments, in particular essential drugs; HIV/AIDS; national measures for the promotion of the right to health; clarification of international obligations; and acts that constitute violations of the right to health. Furthermore, General Comment 14 notes that, while the notion of 'the highest attainable standard of health' in Article 12(1) of the Covenant must be understood as taking into account both the individual's biological and socio-economic preconditions and a State's available resources, the right to health must be understood as a right to the enjoyment of a variety of facilities,

---

19 General Comment No. 14 E/C.12/2000/4.

20 Ibid, para 1.

21 Above, n. 19, para 4.

goods, services and conditions necessary for the realisation of the highest attainable standard of health.[22]

According to the report of the High Commissioner on the impact of TRIPS on human rights,[23] States are bound to promote the right to health through the ensuring of access to affordable treatments. The right to health contains certain essential elements to be applied by States according to the prevailing national conditions. These elements include ensuring the availability, accessibility, and quality of health facilities, goods and services. States are also bound to ensure the availability, accessibility acceptability and quality of health facilities, goods and services. The report of the High Commissioner goes on to state that accessibility also includes the notion of affordability, namely that health facilities, goods and services must be affordable to all, whether privately or publicly owned.

General Comment 14 also examines the specific steps that States should undertake in fulfilment of their obligations, particularly in the context of Article 12(2)(c) ICESCR, which indicates that States parties to the Covenant must undertake steps necessary for 'the prevention, treatment and control of epidemic, endemic, occupational and other diseases'. The control of diseases refers to States' individual and joint efforts to make available relevant technologies and the promotion of strategies of infectious disease control.[24]

Furthermore, the right to health includes a right to facilities, goods and services, under Article 12(2)(d). This obliges States to provide equal and timely access to basic preventive, curative and rehabilitative health services and appropriate treatment of prevalent diseases, injuries and disabilities, preferably at the community level. The right to facilities, goods and services also includes the provision of essential drugs.[25]

The right to health obliges States to take into account HIV/AIDS in respecting, protecting and fulfilling the right to health. General Comment 14 notes that formerly unknown diseases, such as HIV/AIDS and others, as well as the rapid growth of the world population have created new obstacles to the realisation of the right to health which need to be taken into account when interpreting Article 12.[26]

General Comment 14 goes on to set out some of the national measures that States must take to implement the right. It notes that, as with other rights, States are obliged to respect, protect and fulfil the right to health. It states that '(t)he obligation to respect requires States to refrain from interfering directly

---

22 Above, n. 19, para 9.
23 E/CN.4/Sub.2/2001/13.
24 Above, n. 19, para 16.
25 Above, n. 19, para 17.
26 Above, n. 19, para 10.

or indirectly with the enjoyment of the right to health. The obligation to *protect* requires States to take measures that prevent third parties from interfering with Article 12 guarantees. Finally the obligation to *fulfil* requires States to adopt appropriate legislative, administrative, budgetary, judicial, promotional and other measures towards the full realisation of the right to health'.[27]

General Comment 14 sets out international obligations under the right to health. Specifically, States parties should recognise the essential role of international cooperation and comply with their commitment to take joint and separate action to achieve the full realisation of the right to health, taking into account the gross inequality in the health status of people, particularly between developed and developing countries.[28] States parties should ensure that the right to health is given due attention in international agreements and States parties should take steps to ensure that these instruments do not adversely impact upon the right to health.[29] Similarly, States parties have an obligation to ensure that their actions as members of international organisations take due account of the right to health.[30] General Comment 14 recognises that while States are ultimately responsible for compliance with the Covenant, all members of society, including the private business sector, have responsibilities regarding the realisation of the right to health.[31] States parties to the Covenant also have international obligations to 'provide essential drugs, as from time to time defined under the WHO Action Programme on Essential Drugs' and to 'take measures to prevent, treat and control epidemic and endemic diseases'.[32] Further, international organisations, including WHO and WTO, should cooperate effectively with States to build on their respective expertise in relation to the right to health.[33]

Finally, General Comment 14 notes certain acts that constitute violations of the right to health. Violations of the right to health can be the result of the actions of States, or the actions of other entities insufficiently regulated by the State.[34] Violations of the obligation to protect the right to health include the failure to regulate individuals, groups or corporations so as to prevent them from violating the right to health of others.[35] Violations of the obligation to fulfil the right to health include, amongst others, the failure to adopt or implement a national health policy designed to ensure the right to health of all;

27 Above, n. 19, para 36.
28 Above, n. 19, para 38.
29 Above, n. 19, para 39.
30 Above, n. 19, para 39.
31 Above, n. 19, para 42.
32 Above, n. 19, paras 43 and 44.
33 Above, n. 19, para 64.
34 Above, n. 19, para 64.
35 Above, n. 19, para 51.

insufficient expenditure which results in non-enjoyment of the right; and the failure to take measures to reduce the inequitable distribution of health facilities, goods and services.[36]

Furthermore, the United Nations Sub-Commission on the Promotion of Human Rights affirmed, in Resolution 2000/7,[37] that the right to protection of the moral and material interests resulting from any scientific, literary or artistic production of which one is the author is, in accordance with Article 27(2) of the Universal Declaration of Human Rights and Article 15 of the Covenant (ICESCR) a human right, subject to limitations in the public interest.[38]

The United Nations Sub-Commission on the Promotion of Human Rights also declared, in Resolution 2000/7, that 'since the implementation of the TRIPS Agreement does not adequately reflect the fundamental nature and indivisibility of all human rights, including the right of everyone to enjoy the benefits of scientific progress and its applications, the right to health, the right to food and the right to self-determination, there are apparent conflicts between the intellectual property rights regime embodied in the TRIPS Agreement, on the one hand, and international human rights law, on the other'.[39]

The United Nations Sub-Commission on the Promotion of Human Rights, in Resolution 2000/7, also encouraged the Committee on Economic Social and Cultural Rights (CESCR) to 'clarify the relationship between intellectual property rights and human rights, including through the drafting of a general comment on this subject';[40] and recommended to the World Intellectual Property Organisation, the World Health Organisation, the United Nations Development Programme and other relevant United Nations agencies that they continue and deepen their analysis of the impacts of the TRIPS Agreement, including a consideration of its human rights implications.[41]

In addition, the United Nations Sub-Commission on the Promotion of Human Rights, in Resolution 2000/7, commended the Conference of Parties to the Convention on Biodiversity for its decision to assess the relationship between biodiversity concerns and intellectual property rights in general, and between the Convention on Biodiversity and TRIPS, in particular, and urged it also to consider human rights principles and instruments in undertaking this

36 Above, n. 14, para 39.

37 United Nations High Commission for Human Rights Sub-Commission on Human Rights Resolution 2000/7: Intellectual property rights and human rights.

38 Above, n. 37, para 1.

39 Above, n. 37, para 2.

40 Above, n. 37, para 11.

41 Above, n. 37, para 12.

assessment.[42] It also encouraged the relevant civil society organisations to promote with their respective governments the need for economic policy processes fully to integrate and respect existing human rights obligations, and to continue to monitor and publicise the effects of economic policies that fail to take such obligations into account.[43]

The starting point for a consideration of the operational aspects of intellectual property systems with regard to access to drugs is that access to essential drugs is a human right. While the protection and enforcement of intellectual property rights can provide a more secure environment for the transfer of technology to developing countries, it can also provide a basis for charging higher prices for drugs and for technology transfer which can restrict access to the poor.[44]

In this respect, although Cornides asserts that intellectual property rights only interact with human rights where the question involves making available the most recent results of medical research to a greater public, or the funding of new research,[45] in fact intellectual property rights are an issue for human rights and access to medicines precisely because the UNHCR has made them so.

This can be seen clearly in the Statement of the UN Committee on Economic, Social and Cultural Rights (CESCR), 2001, which addressed explicitly this link between human rights and the right to health. The Statement presents a substantial argument that is worthy of particular note here since, I think, it addresses the central issues of this chapter:

> 5. Human rights derive from the inherent dignity and worth of all persons, with the human person as the central subject and primary beneficiary of human rights. The moral and legal guarantees of fundamental freedoms, protections and entitlements both derive from and support people's self-respect and dignity . . . To be consistent with obligations in respect of international human rights, intellectual property regimes must promote and protect all human rights, including the full range of rights guaranteed in the Covenant.
> 6. The fact that the human person is the central subject and primary beneficiary of human rights distinguishes human rights, including the right of authors to the moral and material interests in their works, from legal rights recognized in intellectual property systems . . . Human rights are fundamental, inalienable and universal entitlements belonging to individuals, and in some situations groups of individuals and communities . . . Human rights are fundamental as they derive from the human person as such, whereas intellectual property rights derived from intellectual property

---

42 Above, n. 37, para 13.

43 Resolution 2000/7, para 14.

44 Above, n. 14, para 42.

45 Cornides, J. (2004), 'Human Rights and Intellectual Property: Conflict or Consensus', *Journal of Intellectual Property*, 7(2): 135 at 162.

> systems are instrumental, in that they are a means by which States seek to provide incentives for inventiveness and creativity from which society benefits . . . In contrast with human rights, intellectual property rights are generally of a temporary nature and can be revoked, licensed or assigned to someone else. While intellectual property rights may be allocated, limited in time and scope, traded, amended and even forfeited, human rights are timeless expressions of fundamental entitlements of the human person . . .
>
> Whereas human rights are dedicated to assuring satisfactory standards of human welfare and well-being, intellectual property regimes, although they traditionally provide protection for individual authors and creators, are increasingly focused on protecting business and corporate interests and investments . . . Moreover, the scope of protection and the moral and material interests of the author provided under article 15 of the Covenant does not necessarily coincide with what is termed intellectual property rights under national legislation or international agreements . . .
>
> 8. A human rights-based approach focuses particularly on the needs of the most disadvantaged and marginalized individuals and communities. Because a human right is a universal entitlement, its implementation is evaluated particularly by the degree to which it benefits those who hitherto have been the most disadvantaged and marginalized and brings them up to the mainstream level of protection . . . Thus, in adopting intellectual property regimes, States and other actors must give particular attention at the national and international levels to the adequate protection of human rights of disadvantaged and marginalized individuals and groups, such as indigenous peoples.

So, did the CESCR Statement resolve once and for all the tensions between human rights and intellectual property rights? Well, it certainly set out a manifesto for those who seek to promote the balance between the rights of the disadvantaged and marginalised in society on the one hand and the rights of intellectual property owners on the other, over intellectual property rights.

4. INTELLECTUAL PROPERTY RIGHTS AND THE RIGHT TO HEALTH: THE BRAZILIAN AND SOUTH AFRICAN EXPERIENCES

In the light of the foregoing debate it is instructive to note that, at the nation state level, there are indeed particular tensions underpinning the debate on intellectual property rights and human rights. I shall explain the practical manifestations of these tensions by using examples from human rights-based discourse and the access to medicines campaign of non-governmental organisations (NGOs) in two developing countries: Brazil and South Africa.

As acknowledged in the Report of the High Commissioner on the impact of the TRIPS Agreement,[46] the tensions between provisions on the fundamental

---

[46] Above, n. 14, para 55.

right to health and the view that intellectual property rights are human rights can be seen clearly in the Brazilian context, with Article 196 of the Brazilian Constitution, 1988, stating that 'Health is a right of all and a duty of the State and shall be guaranteed by means of social and economic policies aimed at reducing the risk of illness and other hazards and at the universal and equal access to actions and services for its promotion, protection and recovery'.

As the Brazilian experience demonstrates, the debate on whether to override the patent rights of pharmaceutical companies by the use of compulsory licences has been inextricably linked to the right to health as enshrined in Article 196 of the Brazilian Constitution.

Throughout the late 1980s and 1990s, Article 196 of the Brazilian Constitution was used by groups representing people living with HIV/AIDS in Brazil as justification for advocating the right to free anti-retroviral drugs produced by the State, if necessary produced using compulsory licences which limit the rights of the patentee in relation to particular pharmaceutical products. The linkage between the right to health as a human right underpinned arguments in favour of providing free anti-retroviral drugs when, in 1990, the Federal Government began free delivery of AZT, one of the first anti-retroviral drugs, to the citizens of Brazil. Initially, the Brazilian Federal Government purchased anti-retroviral drugs from the multinational proprietary pharmaceutical companies that had undertaken research and development work and had subsequently been granted patents on these drugs. However, given the high costs associated with the Brazil purchasing large consignments of these patented drugs at the market price, in 1993 the Federal Government instead began to purchase anti-retroviral drugs manufactured by Brazilian pharmaceutical companies which produced cheaper, but equally effective, generic versions of the patented medicines. In the pre-TRIPS era, this was permissible under international law because Brazil was not required to grant patents to all areas of technology, such as pharmaceuticals.

However, in 1996, a year after the TRIPS Agreement had come into force, Brazilian Industrial Property Law 9279/96 was introduced to provide for the protection of pharmaceutical products by patent law. In so doing, Brazil, as a WTO member with developing country status, came forward early to offer patent protection for pharmaceutical products since it was only required to do so, under the transitional arrangements of the TRIPS Agreement, on 1 January 2000. Nevertheless, attempts are apparent within Law 9279/96 to achieve a balance between the patent rights accorded to pharmaceutical products and the right to health, in particular the provision of anti-retroviral drugs to people living with HIV/AIDS in Brazil.

Brazilian Law 9279/96 allows a government authority to issue a compulsory licence where a patent holder exercises patent rights in an abusive manner, or by means of an abuse of economic power proven by an administrative or court decision. There are certain other instances where compulsory licences may be issued, including under Article 71, in cases of national emergency or public interest (Intellectual Property Law (1996) Brazil, No. 9279/96, Article 71 of which states: 'In cases of national emergency or public interest, declared in an act of the Federal Authorities, insofar as the patentee or his licensee does not meet such demand, a temporary non-exclusive compulsory license for the exploitation of the patent may be granted, without prejudice to the rights of the respective patentee.') The terms 'national emergency' and 'public interest' are defined in the Presidential Decree on Compulsory Licensing (1999) (Presidential Decree on Compulsory Licensing (1999) Brazil, No. 3201, Article 2): '(a) national emergency is understood to be a condition of impending danger to the public, even if existing only in a part of the national territory'. Further, '(t)here are considered to be within the public interest those facts, among others, related to the public health, nutrition, protection of the environment, as well as those of primordial importance to the technological or social and economic development of this country'.

As a further safeguard designed to address the right to health in Brazil, 1996 also saw the introduction of Federal Law 9313/96 to guarantee federal responsibility in providing ARV treatment to all Brazilian citizens. Yet Law 9313/96 had the effect of putting Brazil back in the position it had been prior to 1993 when it had begun to purchase generic versions of anti-retroviral drugs from Brazilian pharmaceutical manufacturers at prices far lower than the market price of patented drugs available from multinational pharmaceutical companies. As a result, in 1999 Presidential Decree 3201 was issued which defines situations of national and public interest in which compulsory licences can be issued for product patents, thus increasing significantly the likelihood that lower cost generic versions of anti-retroviral drugs subject to product patents could still be produced by Brazilian pharmaceutical companies in specified circumstances.

However, in 2001 the United States initiated a complaint to the WTO Dispute Settlement Body against Brazil in relation to Decree 3201 on grounds that this measure was not TRIPS compliant because it envisaged failure to work the patent locally through manufacture as sufficient grounds for the issuance of a compulsory licence to a pharmaceutical manufacturer in Brazil. Law 9279/96, the United States argued, was contrary to the provisions of Article 27.1 TRIPS, which requires patents to be available within the territories of WTO members without discrimination as to their place of manufacture.

In response to the US complaint in 2001, NGOs such as Grupo de Incentivo a VIDA (GIV) and the Council of the Brazilian Interdisciplinary AIDS Association (ABIA) representing people living with HIV/AIDS articulated their opposition to the United States complaint by using the language of human rights and the right to health, as enshrined in Article 196 of the Brazilian Constitution, when they demonstrated outside US Consulates in Brazil – initially in Sao Paulo and then elsewhere in the country – claiming that the complaint by the United States to the WTO had the potential to infringe their human rights. The United States and Brazil subsequently notified the WTO Dispute Settlement Body that a mutual agreed understanding had been reached to settle the dispute but, in effect, the US had stepped back from further confrontation on this issue, subject to a bilateral understanding to the effect that, should Brazil seek to issue a compulsory licence on grounds of failure to work the patent locally, it would consult the United States before doing so.[47]

The continued existence of the safeguard provisions on compulsory licences in Brazil was considered by the Report of the UN High Commissioner on the impact of the TRIPS Agreement as being helpful in improving the implementation of the Brazilian HIV treatment programme.[48] While no compulsory licence was issued under Brazilian Law 9279/96 until 2007, the provisions were nevertheless useful in negotiating lower prices with the owners of patents on pharmaceutical products. The Report of the High Commissioner concluding that: 'On the facts that have been provided by the Government of Brazil, it is possible to say that the Brazilian case demonstrates how the provisions of the TRIPS Agreement can be implemented in ways that respect, protect and fulfil the right to health. Through careful legislative implementation of TRIPS provisions . . . the Brazilian IP law supports the implementation of national health policy aimed at providing essential drugs to those who need them.'[49]

In South Africa, HIV/AIDS activists allied to the Treatment Action Campaign (TAC) have similarly framed their struggle for anti-retroviral treatment in terms of the human rights of people living with HIV/AIDS. TAC insists that access to life-saving combination anti-retroviral treatment for all HIV positive people is a human right.[50] TAC's formation in 1988 was based on a distinctly post-apartheid period when human rights issues were particularly to the fore. Accordingly, TAC's successes in advocating wider access to anti-retroviral drugs has utilised the human rights discourse to good effect,

---

47 Raghavan, Chakravarthi (2001), 'US to withdraw TRIPS dispute against Brazil, South–North Development Monitor' (SUNS). Available at: http://www.twnside.org.sg/title/withdraw.htm (visited on 1 August 2007).

48 Report of the High Commissioner (2001) above n. 14 above at para 56.

49 Report of High Commissioner (2001) above n. 14 above at para 58.

50 Mbali, M. (2005), *The Treatment Action Campaign and the History of Rights-Based, Patient-Driven HIV/AIDS Activism in South Africa*, Research Report No. 29, University of Kwazulu-Natal Centre for Civil Society, page 2. Available at: http://www.ukzn.ac.za/ccs/files/RReport_29.pdf (visited on 30 July 2007).

using the language of socio-economic rights and human rights enshrined in the South African constitution, which include the right to life set out in Article 11 of the constitution and the right of everyone to have access to health care services set out in Article 26 of the constitution.[51] In this respect, TAC shares historical continuities with the late 1980s and early 1990s anti-apartheid gay rights activism, particularly the emphasis on human rights-based discourse. However, this use of human rights-based discourse is based on the presumption that such rights are absolute, true and universal rather than contested, constructed and given different meanings and contexts.[52] This, however, is by no means clear-cut.

Boulle and Avafia identify the two main roles of TAC as being, first, a campaign for treatment, prevention of new infections and transforming the public health care system to provide a higher quality and a more comprehensive level of health care; and, secondly, to make a contribution to developing a culture of human rights and democracy in South Africa.[53] For Boulle and Avafia, how the two main roles relate to one another is at the heart of the debate on whether TAC is focused on issue-based campaigning or whether it is a broad-based human rights movement. A human rights focus allows for a holistic approach and sustainable long term solution for people living with AIDS, given that treatment is but one of several required conditions for people living with AIDS to live healthy lives. A human rights approach is also considered to widen the opportunities with partnerships. On the other hand, a human rights approach dilutes the clarity and power of the message, requires a more politicised support base and limits the quality and depth of the commentary and interventions, as the scope is so wide that it is not possible to be an expert in every area. An access to treatment focus would allow TAC to undertake a single issue campaign that enables more targeted campaigns and delivery and enables the organisation to develop a real base of expertise in the area and become experts in the advocated field, and prevents the organisation from being stretched too thinly, which in turn facilitates the achievement of results. On the negative side, a single issue campaign does not allow a holistic approach to addressing HIV/AIDS, which cannot be separated from other

---

[51] Constitution of the Republic of South Africa, 1996. Available at: http://www.constitutionalcourt.org.za/site/theconstitution/english.pdf (visited 30 July 2007).

[52] Mbali, above n. 50 at 3.

[53] Boulle, J. and T. Avafia (2005), *Treatment Action Campaign (TAC) Evaluation*, internal TAC report, page 23. Available at: http://www.tac.org.za/Documents/FinalTACEvaluation-AfaviaAndBoulle-20050701.pdf (visited 11 July 2007).

complex socio-economic issues impacting on the lives of poor people, especially those who are HIV-positive.[54]

Similarly, in the international context, human rights have been central in discourses to debates on the link between the TRIPS Agreement and access to medicines. In January 1999, for instance, senior staff of Médecins Sans Frontières (MSF) wrote, in the Journal of the American Medical Association, that '[t]he lack of access to essential drugs or vaccines because of economic reasons raises new human rights issues in a world that remains divided among wealthy countries, developing countries, and the rest of the world'.[55]

In the subsequent WTO negotiations on access to medicines, commencing with the Doha Declaration on the TRIPS Agreement and Public Health of 14 November 2001, through to the 30 August 2003 Decision on Implementing Paragraph 6 of the Doha Declaration and resulting in the agreement on 6 December 2005 to amend the TRIPS Agreement, the process of seeking to facilitate access through the compulsory licensing provisions of the TRIPS Agreement was very much underpinned by the human rights-based, right to health discourse.

Academic commentators have also acknowledged the significance of the human rights-based discourse. For Lang, the UN work programme on human rights and intellectual property described in this chapter can itself be understood in part as a response to civil society pressure.[56] Lang stresses that the important place of civil society in the trade and human rights debate can be seen in a number of different developments: the diffusion of human rights language into the work of NGOs primarily interested in trade matters; the trend among human rights NGOs to develop new expertise in, and pursue activities related to, international economic questions.

As Lang explains, if human rights norms and values are to be a source of substantive guidance for trade policy makers, it is necessary for human rights norms to undergo a degree of elaboration if they are to provide meaningful guidance to trade policy makers.[57] For Lang, re-framing the analysis in terms of the right to health *does* perform a number of potentially important functions, although human rights norms are not providing substantial policy guid-

---

54 Boulle and Avafia, above n. 53 at 24.

55 Pécoul, B., P. Chirac, P. Trouiller, J. Pinel (1999) 'Access to Essential Drugs in Poor Countries – A Lost Battle?' *Journal of American Medicine Association*, 281(4).

56 Lang, A. (2007) 'The Role of the Human Rights Movement in Trade Policy-Making: Human Rights as a Trigger for Social Learning', *New Zealand Journal of Public and International Law*, 5: 147–72.

57 See, for example, Abbott, F. (2005), 'The "Rule of Reason" and the Right to Health: Integrating Human Rights and Competition Principles in the Context of TRIPS' in T. Cottier, E. Bűrgi and J. Pauwelyn (eds) *Human Rights and International Trade*, 279 at 294.

ance and are not a source of new policy ideas, and do not provide a means of choosing between competing ideas.

To the extent that the human rights movement can mobilise actors and interest groups presently marginalised in trade debates, and provide effective tools to augment their political influence, it follows that the human rights movement may be able to achieve real change. Although it is difficult to measure the precise impact, there is at least some indication already of such an important part in the negotiations leading to the 30 August 2003 WTO Decision. Human rights institutions and actors added weight to the campaign for the modification of TRIPS commitments by lending additional legitimacy, new constituencies and (to a certain extent) further resources to those groups pressuring for change.

The deployment of human rights language also helped to frame the debate as a *moral* issue, and through the mobilisation of moral outrage, thereby helped to generate a widespread sense that the TRIPS Agreement in its current form could not be justified. While Lang makes it clear that he does not think 'human rights' themselves necessarily provide a vision of the most appropriate ends towards which the trade regime ought to be striving, he suggests that human rights actors have nevertheless been instrumental in generating a renewed critical debate about the social purposes of the international trading system and, although he acknowledges that no-one would suggest that the human rights movement is solely responsible for shifts which are already observable, in his view human rights have contributed to this process by providing resources and institutional space for the production and dissemination of this knowledge, and a ready-made audience for it.

When human rights actors produce their numerous commentaries on the 'human rights impact' of the trading system, Lang's observation is that one of the most important functions they are performing is facilitating the production of social knowledge: generating shared narratives; synthesising some kind of consensus about how certain aspects of the trading system operate; the selecting, reframing and imparting new meaning to information produced by various kinds of trade policy experts.

5. THE WORLD HEALTH ASSEMBLY RESOLUTION ON PUBLIC HEALTH, INNOVATION AND ESSENTIAL HEALTH RESEARCH AND INTELLECTUAL PROPERTY RIGHTS

So how is this human rights-discourse in relation to intellectual property rights and the right to health likely to develop in the future? One indication of the shape of the debate to come can be found in the World Health Assembly

Resolution on Public Health, Innovation and Essential Health Research and Intellectual Property Rights of 27 May 2006. In this Resolution, the World Health Assembly appears to have reignited the debate on the relationship between human rights and the right to health, asserting the significance of intellectual property rights as human rights by 'Stressing that the Universal Declaration of Human Rights provides that "everyone has the right freely to participate in the cultural life of the community, to enjoy the arts and to share in scientific advancement and its benefits" and that "everyone has the right to the protection of the moral and material interests resulting from any scientific, literary or artistic production of which he is the author".'

In many respects, therefore, the debate appears to have run full circle. Tensions remain between, on the one hand, the interpretation of intellectual property as a human right in terms of property and ownership and, on the other hand, the right to health as a human right, with all this implies for intellectual property rights and access to medicines.

How intellectual property rights, human rights and the right to health are interpreted in developing countries where problems of access to medicines is most acute will largely depend on the capacity of those developing countries' governments to utilise the language of human rights to their best advantage. In this respect, as the General Comment 14 on the right to health confirmed, it is particularly incumbent on all those in a position to assist, to provide 'international assistance and cooperation, especially economic and technical' in order to enable developing countries to fulfil their core obligations under the Convention.[58] 'Accordingly, it is incumbent upon developed States and other actors in a position to assist, to develop international intellectual property regimes that enable developing States to fulfil at least their core obligations to individuals and groups within their jurisdictions.'[59]

BIBLIOGRAPHY

3D: Trade-Human Rights-Equitable Economy (2005) *Background Note: Intellectual Property, Human Rights and the Drafting of the General Comment on Article 15(1)(c) ICESCR*, Geneva: 3D.

Abbott, F. (2005), 'The "Rule of Reason" and the Right to Health: Integrating Human Rights and Competition Principles in the Context of TRIPS' in T. Cottier, E. Bűrgi and J. Pauwelyn (eds), *Human Rights and International Trade*, 279.

Assembly of the Berne Union (1986) 'Solemn Declaration' of 9 September 1986.

Boulle, J. and T. Avafia (2005), *Treatment Action Campaign (TAC) Evaluation*, internal TAC report.

58 Above, n. 19, para 45.

59 Above, n. 1, para 13.

Chapman, A.R. (2000), American Association for the Advancement of Science (AAAS), Washington, USA, to the United Nations Committee on Economic, Social and Cultural Rights, E/C.12/2000/12, 3 October 2000.

Cohen, J.C. and K.M. Lybecker (2005), 'AIDS Policy and Pharmaceutical Patents: Brazil's Strategy to Safeguard Public Health', *World Economy*, 28(2): 211–30.

Cornides, J. (2004), 'Human Rights and Intellectual Property: Conflict or Consensus', *Journal of Intellectual Property*, 7(2): 135.

Giovanetti, T. and M. Matthews (2005), 'Intellectual Property Rights and Human Rights' (Lewisville, Texas: Institute for Policy Innovation).

Lang, A. (2007), 'The Role of the Human Rights Movement in Trade Policy-Making: Human Rights as a Trigger for Social Learning', *New Zealand Journal of Public and International Law*, 5: 147–72.

Mbali, M. (2005) 'The Treatment Action Campaign and the History of Rights-Based, Patient-Driven HIV/AIDS Activism in South Africa', Research Report No. 29, University of Kwazulu-Natal Centre for Civil Society.

Pécoul, B., P. Chirac, P. Trouiller and J. Pinel (1999), 'Access to Essential Drugs in Poor Countries – A Lost Battle?', *Journal of American Medicine Association*, 281(4).

Raghavan, C. (2001), *US to Withdraw TRIPS Dispute Against Brazil, South–North Development Monitor* (SUNS).

United Nations (1948) Universal Declaration of Human Rights *Adopted and proclaimed by General Assembly Resolution 217 A (III) of 10 December 1948*, G.A. Res217A (III) 3 U.N. GAOR (Resolutions, part 1) at 71, U.N. doc. A/810.

United Nations (1966) International Covenant on Economic, Social and Cultural Rights, adopted 16 December 1966, 993 U.N.T.S. 3, G.A. Res. 2200 (XXI), 21 U.N. GAOR Supp. (No. 16) at 49, U.N. Doc. A/6316.

United Nations Economic and Social Committee (2000) General Comment No. 14 on the right to the highest attainable standard of health (Article 12 of the International Covenant on Economic, Social and Cultural Rights). Committee on Economic, Social and Cultural Rights, Twenty-second session, Geneva, 25 April–12 May 2000, E/C.12/2000/4.

United Nations High Commission for Human Rights Sub-Commission on Human Rights (2000) Resolution 2000/7: Intellectual property rights and human rights.

United Nations Committee on Economic and Cultural Rights (2001) Substantive Issues Arising in the Implementation of the International Covenant on Economic, Social and Cultural Rights. Follow-up to the day of general discussion on article 15.1(c), Monday 26 November 2001, Human Rights and Intellectual Property. United Nations Committee on Economic, Social and Cultural Rights, 14 December 2001, E/C.12/2001/15.

United Nations Commission on Human Rights (2001) Economic, Social and Cultural Rights: The Impact of the Agreement on Trade-Related Aspects of Intellectual Property Rights on Human Rights. Report of the High Commissioner, 27 June 2001, E/CN.4/Sub.2/2001/13.

United Nations Commission on Human Rights Committee on Economic, Social and Cultural Rights (2005) General Comment No. 17 on the right of everyone to benefit from the protection of the moral and material interests resulting from any scientific, literary or artistic production of which he is the author (article 15(1)(c) of the Covenant), 21 November 2005, E/C.12/2005/GC/17.

World Health Assembly (2006) *Public Health, Innovation, Essential Health Research and Intellectual Property Rights: towards a global strategy and plan of action*, Fifty-Ninth World Health Assembly, WHA59.24, 27 May 2006.

World Health Assembly (2008) *Global Strategy and Plan of Action on Public Health, Innovation and Intellectual Property*, Sixty-First World Health Assembly, WHA61.21, 24 May 2008.

8. On patents and human rights

Jan Brinkhof*

1. INTRODUCTION

Duncan Matthews' clear and balanced contribution on 'Intellectual Property Rights, Human Rights and the Right to Health' has inspired me to make a few observations. I will limit myself to patent law and human rights law. There are two reasons warranting such a restricted reply. First, it may not be helpful to talk about Intellectual Property Rights (IPRs) in general terms as this might give rise to the impression that they are more or less homogenous rights, and that would be a misunderstanding of IP law. That is to say, considerable differences exist between the rights protected in IP law, the aims pursued by the law, the ways in which rights are gained or granted, and the extent to which and the length of time during which the economic freedoms of third parties are restricted. To make matters more complex still, the various types of IP rights also differ in their relationships with the various categories of human rights.[1] Given this diversity, tarring IP rights with the same brush carries with it the risk of arriving at incorrect comments and policy prescriptions. A second reason to restrict the scope of my reply is that I have a better understanding of patent law than the other IP rights – and I hasten to add, I am not a specialist in human rights.

* Jan Brinkhof is Professor of Patent Law at the Centre for Intellectual Property Law (CIER), Molengraaff Institute for Private Law, Utrecht University and attorney at law with Brinkhof, Amsterdam.

[1] Take, for example, copyright and trademark law. Traditionally, continental copyright law was closely linked to the person of the author. Apart from the rather recent expansion of the copyright domain to works which show hardly any traces of the personality of the maker, continental copyright law protects the personal expression of a person. The inalienable moral rights mentioned in Article 6bis of the Berne Convention fit within this approach. Clearly, the human rights aspects of trademark law are less obvious since this is a branch of IP law concerned not so much with the intellectual achievements of individuals, but rather with the regulation of competition through the prevention of confusion arising between participants in a market.

2. MY EXPERIENCE WITH THIS SUBJECT IS LIMITED

When I was a judge, I only once considered an issue which, with the benefit of hindsight, related to the subject of this contribution. The dispute concerned the infringement of a patent that had been granted to a balloon catheter used in clearing partially occluded arteries. The patentee had petitioned the Dutch court to grant an injunction stopping the defendant from infringing the patent. Of course, the defendant invited the court not to grant this request. The defendant claimed that the patent was not being infringed. The defendant also added that if the court would find against him on the issue of patent infringement, then the court was invited not to grant the injunction on the ground of the likely effect on patients. To support this buttress of the defence, the defendant relied on witness statements made by various medical specialists. The specialists described their good experiences with the defendant's allegedly infringing catheter, and noted that there was no equivalent catheter on the market. Even though they had worked with the plaintiff's patented catheter, they were of the opinion that it was not as good as the catheter produced by the defendant. The specialists took the view, therefore, that patients would be disadvantaged if, by virtue of the injunction, the defendant's catheter could no longer be used in treatment.

Although I held that the defendants had indeed infringed the patent, I refused to grant the injunction. I was of the opinion that to grant the injunction would jeopardise the interests of patients. I was also of the view that those interests should be given greater weight than the rights granted to the patent holder. I felt that it would be more appropriate for the claimant to be granted relief in the form of damages rather than by way of an injunction. My decision relied on Article 168 of Book 6 of the Dutch Civil Code, which allows a judge to refuse an injunction where the acts giving rise to an injunction are viewed as tolerable because of some interest which is fundamental to society ['*zwaarwegend maatschappelijk belang*'].[2] Thus, even though the claimant would in effect lose its right to an injunction, it would not be deprived of its right to damages. I note that a number of years later, and in a separate case, the Dutch Supreme Court[3] went on to rule that the rights of third parties, such as patients, should not be protected by permitting a patent infringement to continue.

---

[2] Article 6:168 Netherlands Civil Code: 'The judge may reject an action to obtain an order prohibiting unlawful conduct on the ground that such conduct should be tolerated for reasons of important societal interests. The victim retains his right to reparation of damage (. . .).' (Haanappel, P.P.C. and Ejan Mackaay (1990), *New Netherlands Civil Code, Patrimonial Law* (Deventer/Boston: Kluwer Law International).)

[3] *Boehringer v Kirin Amgen*, judgment of the Dutch Supreme Court [*Hoge Raad*] 21 April 1995, NJ 1996, 462. See also the critical annotation by D.W.F. Verkade.

Two recent events, however, spurred me to reflect further on the interface between patent law and human rights law. Both arose in the context of being an academic. The first was the defence of a doctorate at which the researcher, Arie Rijlaarsdam, claimed that the wording of the Dutch Patents Act infringed an instrument of human rights law, namely the International Covenant on Economic, Social and Cultural Rights. The allegedly infringing provision of the Dutch Patents Act was Article 12(3), which states:

> Where the invention has been made by a person carrying out research in the service of a university, college or research institute, the university, college or research institute shall be entitled to the patent.

According to Rijlaarsdam, Article 15(1)(c) of the International Covenant grants a researcher 'economic and cultural rights' and that this entails that 'a researcher working for a university is entitled to patents on his inventions and that it is up to him to decide whether and when he publishes his inventions'. This view leads to the inexorable exhortation that a Dutch judge should not be legally bound by the wording of Article 12(3) of the Dutch Patents Act.[4]

The second fillip to thinking about an apparent relationship between patent law and human rights was a paper by Audrey Chapman. Chapman's paper was entitled 'Approaching Intellectual Property as a Human Right: obligations related to Article 15(1)(c)'.[5] Paragraph 18 of the text stated:

> The drafters of the UDHR[6] and ICESCR[7] decided to recognize the intellectual property claims of authors, creators, and inventors as a human right.

The purpose of this chapter, therefore, is to examine critically this growing body of literature and to show that it is mistaken. It does this by searching for the rationale behind patent legislation. It then considers the historical context to, the wording of, and the rationale behind the international instruments recognising fundamental human rights. Since these texts only make very isolated and specific references to intellectual property law, and make no reference at all to inventors and patents, this chapter reveals that the standpoint adopted by these authors cannot be backed up by the law. It concludes,

---

4 Rijlaarsdam, A. (2005), *Octrooi en dienstbetrekking (Patents and Employment)* (Delft: VSSD), p. 168.

5 Discussion paper for the Twenty-fourth session of the United Nations Economic and Social Council, Committee on Economic, Social and Cultural Rights (13 November–1 December 2000).

6 Universal Declaration of Human Rights (10 December 1948).

7 International Covenant on Economic, Social and Cultural Rights (3 January 1976).

therefore, by making a number of general observations on the utility of any debate on patent law and the protection of human rights.

3. THE RATIONALE BEHIND PATENT LEGISLATION

The first known patent legislation is that of the 1474 Act in Venice. Although the rule is extremely short, it contains pretty much every element found in modern patent acts. The statute contains the following consideration:

> We have amongst us men of great genius, apt to invent and discover ingenious devices . . . now if provision were made for the works and devices discovered by such persons, so that others who may see them could not build them and take the inventor's honour away, more men would then apply their genius, would discover, and would build devices of great utility and benefit to our commonwealth.[8]

From this it is clear what the Venetian legislature had in mind: the legislature foresaw that it was in the interest of the Venetian Republic that ingenious people should come to Venice and develop their creativity there – this would serve the general interest.

This desire to serve the general interest is also the rationale underpinning the English legislation of the 1624 Statute of Monopolies:

> VI. Provided also and be it declared and enacted that any declaration before mentioned shall not extend to any letters of patent and grants of privilege for the term of fourteen years or under, hereafter to be made, of the sole working or making of any manner of new manufactures within this realm, to the true and first inventor and inventors of such manufactures which others at the time of making such letters patent and grants shall not use, so also they be not contrary to the law or mischievous to the state, by raising prices of commodities at home, or hurt of trade, or generally inconvenient.[9]

From this fragment, it is clear that the recognition of monopolies must be justified and that it may also not bring any harm in terms of trade, or to society more generally.

That patent law is also a means to serve the general interest is also apparent from the wording of Section 8 of the Constitution of the United States of America (1787):

---

[8] Citation from Mandich (1948), 'Venetian Patents (1450–1550)', 30 *JPOS* 166, at pp. 176–7.

[9] See *Terrell on the Law of Patents*, 16th edn (2006), I-11, and P. Kurz (2000), *Weltgeschichte des Erfindungsschutzes* (Köln: Carl Heymanns Verlag), p. 168.

> Section 8
> The Congress shall have Power
> (. . .)
> To promote the Progress of Science and useful Arts, by securing for limited Times to Authors and Inventors the exclusive Right to their respective Writings and Discoveries;

The words of George Washington spoken to Congress in 1790 provide further illustration as to the rationale behind the American law:

> Nor am I less persuaded that there is nothing which can better deserve your patronage than the promotion of science and literature. Knowledge is in every country the surest basis of public happiness.

These three pieces of legislation give the distinct impression that the aim of patent legislation is to encourage and develop the general interest and the means by which this is achieved is through the granting of exclusive rights to inventors. From the wording of the Venetian Statute, it is also apparent that they had realised that it was the granting of exclusive rights that would be so attractive to inventors.

Patents had been granted in the Netherlands from the end of the sixteenth century. However, these were not granted by legislation. Governments granted a patent at the request of inventors – providing that it served the general interest.[10]

In post-Revolution France, the situation appeared at first blush to be different. That is to say, the Preamble to the French Patent Act (1790/1791) stated:

> that every novel idea whose realisation or development can become useful to society belongs primarily to him who conceived it, and there would be a violation of the rights of man in their very essence if an industrial invention were not regarded as the property of its creator.[11]

From these words, it might be inferred that the claim of the inventor to protect the invention was indeed described as a human right. However, a little relativity might not appear out of place. That is to say, it should be remembered that privileges were contrary to the conceptual ideals of the Revolution. In light of this, how would it be possible to get the Assemblée Nationale to

---

[10] See for instance the patent granted to Henrick de Keyser in 1596, quoted in: in Drucker, W.H. (1924), *Handboek voor de studie van het Nederlandsche Octrooirecht* [Textbook for the study of Dutch Patent Law] (The Hague: Nijhoff), p. 66.

[11] Machlup and Penrose (1950), 'The Patent Controversy in the Nineteenth Century', 10 *Journal of Economic History*, 1, at 11; French text in: Foyer, J. and M. Vivant (1991), *Le droit des brevets*, (Paris: Presses Universitaires de France), 12.

vote for a patent law that granted inventors a temporary monopoly even if this would be desirable from an economic point of view? After all, the granting of a monopoly looks very much like a privilege, and thus a legal intervention doomed to fail. In the political climate of the day, therefore, the argument that a patent concerned a '*droit de l'homme*' therefore had at least the power of persuasion and conviction.[12] However, it is submitted that Boufflers, the initiator of the French Patents Act, was not so much preoccupied by the need to recognise it as a human right but was rather guided by the desire to revive the health of French industry for, at this time, France had begun to lag behind Great Britain. Indeed, it can be said that the economic powerhouses of Britain and the United States and their patent laws were of exemplary importance to Boufflers, and the resulting architecture of the French Patent Act of 1790/1791.

The inextricable link between patent law and the health of a nation's economy was not merely the product of eighteenth century thought. The nineteenth century witnessed the rise and spread of the Anti-Patent Movement. In the middle of the nineteenth century, there were economists who took the view that patents formed a barrier to free trade and as such were harmful to economic progress. Partly influenced by these economists, in 1869 the Dutch decided no longer to grant patents. Economic theory was only part of the story, however. What was also important for the Dutch was the fact that, at the time, the perceived need to preserve free trade was greater than the protection to patents (the Dutch industrial revolution not having achieved very much at this point). The Dutch industrial revolution only got going towards the end of the nineteenth century. Dutch industry then was unencumbered by patent law and became a copier's paradise – much to the chagrin of its industrial neighbours. It is perhaps not without a tinge of irony, therefore, that one of the earliest contracting states to sign the Paris Convention in 1883 was the Netherlands – a country then viewed as a nation of pirates ('un peuple de brigands'). It was only when the Dutch economy expected to gain a greater advantage from protecting its industrial patents at the expense of preserving free trade that it was decided to introduce modern patent legislation. This took the form of the Dutch Patents Act 1910.

Curiously, the golden years of the nineteenth century 'patent-free' period coincide with those in which many of today's European multinationals were created. In the Netherlands, it was Philips, and the Dutch part of today's Unilever, Jurgens and Van Den Bergh.[13] In Switzerland, another patent-free country, it was the time in which the Swiss chemical companies of Geigy,

---

[12] Compare R. Kraßer (2004), *Patentrecht*, 5th edn (Münich: CH Beck Verlag), p. 36. See also P. Kurz, op. cit. at p. 239.

[13] Kurz, op. cit. pp. 388–93.

Sandoz, and Hoffmann-La Roche experienced considerable commercial growth, partly at the expense of the German chemical industry, whose inventions could not be protected under Swiss law.

On the basis of these historical facts, the interim conclusion must be that patent law has been viewed primarily as an instrument of economic policy. The aim of patent legislation was to encourage technological innovation. This was considered as serving the general interest. The means to achieve this end was the grant of temporary, exclusive rights to inventors. In the parlance of economists: monopolies. If this goal was not going to be attained, or if as in the nineteenth century when the Netherlands took the view that it was better off without patents, then legislatures abolished their patent systems. This, too, was done with a view to serving the general interest.

Against this historical backdrop, the fact that Chapman views IP law as a human right and not as an instrument of economic policy is rather surprising. Equally striking is that Rijlaarsdam takes the view that the Dutch Patents Act, as a matter of human rights law, must not presume to entitle universities to any inventions arising from the labour relationships it has with its researchers.[14] Perhaps I must readjust my opinions in light of the wording of the international legal instruments?

4. INSTRUMENTS OF HUMAN RIGHTS LAW

Proponents of the idea that the claim to a patent is a human right rely on the Universal Declaration of Human Rights (UDHR) and the International Covenant on Economic, Social and Cultural Rights (ICESCR). In order to avoid any misunderstanding I wish to emphasise that what I am going to deal with here is the entitlement to a patent, and that this has nothing to do with the scope of protection offered by a granted patent. The protection offered by a granted patent can be described in terms of human rights, but this goes to the heart of a different human right, namely, the right to own property. It is an essential difference perhaps made clear by way of an example. That is to say, do I, as a Dutchman, have a human right to a bicycle, or do I have an entitlement in human rights law to the protection of my property in the bicycle that I own? It is useful to be clear about the wording of the international legal texts.

In 1945, the Charter of the United Nations was signed. Phrases inserted into the Preamble include:

---

[14] One issue he fails to address is whether the scope of this provision goes too far in failing to make any distinction between the invention and the nature of the research actually conducted under the auspices of the university.

> to save succeeding generations from the scourge of war, which twice in our lifetime has brought untold sorrow to mankind . . . to reaffirm faith in fundamental human rights, in the dignity and worth of the human person, in the equal rights of men and women and of nations large and small.

It should be noted that human rights per se were not elaborated in this Charter.

In 1948, the General Assembly of the United Nations proclaimed the Universal Declaration of Human Rights (UDHR). Voted in by 48 states, with no state voting against the Declaration, and only eight states abstaining (the countries of the Soviet Bloc, Saudi Arabia, and South Africa[15]), the proclamation concerned:

> a common standard of achievement for all peoples and all nations, to the end that every individual and every organ of society, keeping this Declaration constantly in mind, shall strive by teaching and education to promote respect for these rights and freedoms and by progressive measures, national and international, to secure their universal and effective recognition and observance, both among the peoples of Member States themselves and among the peoples of territories under their jurisdiction.[16]

The point to note is that this is not a convention that was signed by the states parties and whereby the signing results in their becoming legally bound.

The UDHR contains one express provision governing property. Article 17 states:

> (1) Everyone has the right to own property alone as well as in association with others.
> (2) No one shall be arbitrarily deprived of his property.

One further provision relevant to the present discussion is Article 27, which states:

> (1) Everyone has the right freely to participate in the cultural life of the community, to enjoy the arts and to share in scientific advancement and its benefits.
> (2) Everyone has the right to the protection of the moral and material interests resulting from any scientific, literary or artistic production of which he is the author.

Reading the wording of these provisions, it becomes apparent that Article 27(2) makes no reference to either the word 'patents' or 'inventions'. Article 27(2) specifically covers 'scientific production' but this cannot be understood

---

15 Bien étonnés de se trouver ensemble.

16 For completeness, I note that the Islamic countries produced their own declaration on human rights: Cairo Declaration on Human Rights in Islam.

as being a synonym for an 'invention'. These precise points aside, it should be noted that the overall tenor of the human rights provisions is one of extreme vagueness as to what might be understood to form part of the content of 'the right to protection'.

In 1976, the ICESCR was ratified. The relevant recitals in the Preamble read as follows:

> The States Parties to the present Covenant,
> Considering that, in accordance with the principles proclaimed in the Charter of the United Nations, recognition of the inherent dignity and of the equal and inalienable rights of all members of the human family is the foundation of freedom, justice and peace in the world,
> Recognizing that these rights derive from the inherent dignity of the human person,
> Recognizing that, in accordance with the Universal Declaration of Human Rights, the ideal of free human beings enjoying freedom from fear and want can only be achieved if conditions are created whereby everyone may enjoy his economic, social and cultural rights, as well as his civil and political rights.

From this wording it can be seen that this is a covenant which is binding upon those states parties which had signed up to it. In this convention, the rights mentioned in the Charter are elaborated. The rights elaborated are described as inalienable rights deriving from the inherent dignity of the human person.

The language used here is figurative. Rights are formulated by people. In a certain sense, the very notion that an individual can claim that his/her inalienable rights must be respected by states is itself the product of human invention. Naturally, it is an invention to be cherished. Nevertheless, the wording remains the product of human invention, in much the same way as the infringement of human rights is also the activity of humans, for which humans alone are responsible. According to this vision, human rights are ascribed a very special status. In the lexical hierarchy of legal sources, human rights cannot be equated with those rules which structure the economic ordering of the production process.

Whereas the ICESCR is a binding obligation between the states parties to the convention, it also imposes specific positive obligations. Article 2(1) states:

> Each State Party to the present Covenant undertakes to take steps, individually and through international assistance and co-operation, especially economic and technical, to the maximum of its available resources, with a view to achieving progressively the full realization of the rights recognized in the present Covenant by all appropriate means, including particularly the adoption of legislative measures.

A better idea about the true nature of Article 2(1) can be gained by reference to General Comment 3, indent 8, which states:

> (. . .) the Committee reaffirms that the rights recognized in the Covenant are susceptible of realization within the context of a wide variety of economic and political systems, provided only that the interdependence and indivisibility of the two sets of human rights, as affirmed inter alia in the preamble to the Covenant, is recognized and reflected in the system in question.[17]

Article 15 is also relevant, and is expressly relied upon by Chapman:

> 1. The States Parties to the present Covenant recognize the right of everyone:
>   (a) To take part in cultural life;
>   (b) To enjoy the benefits of scientific progress and its applications;
>   (c) To benefit from the protection of the moral and material interests resulting from any scientific, literary or artistic production of which he is the author.[18]
>
> 2. The steps to be taken by the States Parties to the present Covenant to achieve the full realization of this right shall include those necessary for the conservation, the development and the diffusion of science and culture.
> 3. The States Parties to the present Covenant undertake to respect the freedom indispensable for scientific research and creative activity.
> 4. The States Parties to the present Covenant recognize the benefits to be derived from the encouragement and development of international contacts and co-operation in the scientific and cultural fields.

Reading the wording of Article 15 carefully, it can be seen that there is hardly a difference with that used in Article 27(2) UDHR. Thus, the same points can be made. Aritcle 15(1)(c) mentions neither patents nor inventions. Scientific production is not synonymous with patents. And the provision is extremely vague as to the intended end-result.[19]

In light of the above I am of the opinion that neither the UDHR nor the ICESR provides sufficient legal basis for the view that the entitlement to a patent ought to belong to human rights. The standpoint that a national piece of legislation cannot deem inventions flowing from a university researcher as

---

17 ICESCR General comment 3 (General Comments), The nature of States parties' obligations (Art. 2, para.1): 14/12/90, contained in document E/1991/23.

18 Indent number 5 of the same General Comment says the following about Article 15(3) ICESCR, '. . . there are a number of other provisions in the International Covenant on Economic, Social and Cultural Rights, including articles 3, 7(a)(i), 8, 10(3), 13(2)(a), (3) and (4) and 15(3) which would seem to be capable of immediate application by judicial and other organs in many national legal systems.' The point to note is that this does not mention Article 15(1).

19 In the former Soviet Union, inventors were rewarded not with the grant of an exclusive right but rather with a provision of a certificate. This author has not been able to find any evidence that the Soviet Union introduced a reservation to Article 15 so it seems likely that providing the inventor with a certificate was considered sufficient for the purposes of this international legal provision.

belonging to the university is one which therefore seems incorrect. It is almost inconceivable that the General Assembly of the United Nations would have described an entitlement to a patent as an inalienable right at a time when it was driven by the desire to prevent a repeat of the unimaginable horror of two world wars. Indeed, it might even be wondered whether the recognition of such an inalienable right would have contributed one iota to the realisation of the goals of the UDHR. There is simply not a sign of this anywhere. This situation is no different when considering the context to the ICESCR.

I can find no explanation for the apparently self-evident way in which Chapman reads Articles 27(2) and 15(1)(c) ICESCR as meaning that every inventor is entitled to patent protection especially given the stark reality that neither provision mentions the words patent or invention. Chapman, however, is not the only academic to subscribe to this point of view. In the Netherlands, Rijlaarsdam has uttered the same sentiment, as has Birgit Kramer in Germany.[20]

Approaching sacred legal texts in this way reminds me of what happened when one episode in the Bible was incorrectly translated into Latin.[21] That is to say, whereas Moses descended Mount Sinai with the Ten Commandments in hand, and 'the skin on his face shone', the translator mistranslated radiating (light), to mean 'grew horns'. As a result, when the legendary Michelangelo came to sculpt the giant statue of Moses, two intriguing horns were incorporated and protrude from Moses' head.[22]

In Duncan Matthews' chapter, there is extensive citation of the Statement made by the Committee on Economic Social and Cultural Rights, which I do not propose to reproduce here.[23] That said, there is to my mind one statement

---

[20] Kramer, Birgit (2007), *Patentschutz und Zugang zu Medikamenten*, (Köln: Carl Heymanns Verlag) who at page 85 writes:

> *Nach Art. 15 Abs. 1. lit. c CESCR erkennen die Staaten ein Recht des Autors oder Erfinders an, den Nutzen aus dem Schutz der moralischen und materiellen Interessen, die aus wissenschaftlichen, literarischen und künstlerischen Produkten stammen, zu ziehen. Die Mitgliedstaaten müssen also den Schutz von Immaterialgüterrechten gewährleisten.* ['According to Article 15(1)(c) ICESCR, the states recognise the right of authors or inventors to use the moral and material interests which derive from scientific, literary and artistic products. The contracting states must therefore guarantee the protection of intellectual property rights'.]

[21] Exodus 34:29.

[22] The impressive statue is to be seen in the Church of Saint Peter in Chains in Rome (San Pietro in Vincoli).

[23] Committee on Economic, Social and Cultural Rights, 14 December 2001, E/C.12/2001/15, Agenda item 3, Twenty-seventh session.

which explains why patent law cannot be seen as a human right. The following excerpt is from number 6:

> Human rights are fundamental as they derive from the human person as such, whereas intellectual property rights derived from intellectual property systems are instrumental, in that they are a means by which States seek to provide incentives for inventiveness and creativity from which society benefits. In contrast with human rights, intellectual property rights are generally of a temporary nature, and can be revoked, licensed or assigned to someone else.[24]

The point I wish to emphasise is the reference to the fact that intellectual property rights are instrumental.

In 1950, the Convention for the Protection of Human Rights and Fundamental Freedoms, also known as the European Convention on Human Rights (ECHR), was adopted under the auspices of the Council of Europe. The ECHR does not contain a single provision on intellectual property. The First Protocol only recognises a provision protecting property. The provision makes no reference to intellectual property. On this point, the European Court of Human Rights in Strasbourg has held:

> 6. The Court observes at the outset that intellectual property as such incontestably enjoys the protection of Article 1 of Protocol No. 1. That was the view taken by the European Commission of Human Rights with regard to patents in (. . .) *Smith Kline*[25] decision. However, with regard to an application for a patent that had been rejected by the competent national authority, the Commission expressed the following opinion in the case of *British-American Tobacco Company Ltd*:
>
> > . . . the applicant company did not succeed in obtaining an effective protection for their invention by means of a patent. Consequently, the company were denied a protected intellectual property right but were not deprived of their existing property' (*British-American Tobacco Company Ltd v The Netherlands*, Series A no. 331, judgment of 20 November 1995, opinion of the Commission, p. 37, §§ 71–72).

---

[24] Reference is made to the Report of the High Commissioner on the impact of the Agreement on Trade-Related Aspects of Intellectual Property Rights on Human Rights, E/CN.4/Sub.2/2001/13, 27 June 2001, paragraph 14 which contains the following passage: '. . . it is important to note the differing characteristics of intellectual property rights (IPRs) – copyright, patents, trademarks and so on – on the one hand, and human rights such as cultural rights on the other. Intellectual property rights are granted by the State according to well-defined criteria and so are more akin to a privilege. Those criteria are defined by national legislation. IPRs can be licensed or assigned to someone else, they can be revoked, and they eventually expire. Similarly, IPRs can be – and often are – held by corporations. Human rights, on the other hand, are inalienable and universal. They are not granted by the State, they are recognized.'

[25] 4 October 1990. Decisions & Reports 66, 1990.

> 15. The Court thus considers that, while it is clear that a trade mark constitutes a 'possession' within the meaning of Article 1 of Protocol No. 1, this is only so after final registration of the mark, in accordance with the rules in force in the State concerned.

In this way, the Court in *Anheuser-Busch Inc v Portugal* allowed a registered trademark to be considered to be property within the meaning of the First Protocol.

The latest addition to the legal texts recognising fundamental rights within the legal order of the European Union is the Charter of Fundamental Rights in Europe (2000).[26] This Charter says precious little about intellectual property:

> Article 17
> Right to property
> 1. Everyone has the right to own, use, dispose of and bequeath his or her lawfully acquired possessions. No one may be deprived of his or her possessions, except in the public interest and in the cases and under the conditions provided for by law, subject to fair compensation being paid in good time for their loss. The use of property may be regulated by law in so far as is necessary for the general interest.
> 2. Intellectual property shall be protected.

The protection of intellectual property forms a part of the provision dedicated to the right to property. In this provision, there is no reference to inventors being entitled to patents, nor is there any indication that patents are to be considered as human rights. In this respect, the EU Charter does not differ from the ECHR.

Given that these instruments of fundamental human rights law derive directly or indirectly from Article 27 UDHR, it should be noted that the European Patent Office's Enlarged Board of Appeal has commented on Article 27 only once. The comment arose in the context of a dispute involving priority rights:

> 7.2 . . . It takes the view, however, that this [Article 27 UDHR] provides a guarantee that States should provide their citizens with patent and copyright laws to protect their interests and endorses the opinion of the Legal Board of Appeal that the obligation to recognise priority rights laid down in the TRIPs Agreement cannot be considered to impinge on the fundamental rights of the persons involved (point 5.2 of the reasons for the referring decision).[27]

In view of the legal analysis outlined above, I suspect that the Enlarged Board of Appeal in believing that States are required to have a patent act on their statute books, may have read too much into the wording of Article 27 UDHR.

---

26 OJ [2000] C 364/01.
27 Case G2/02 (26 April 2004), Official Journal EPO [2004], 483.

5. CONCLUSION

From the brief analysis of the history of patent law, it can be seen that patent legislation was introduced in order to encourage technological innovation and to reinforce the health of a nation's economy. Patent law can be considered as an instrument of economic policy. It is not an aim in itself but only a means to an end. The end is to serve the general interest. The general interest, and how it has been defined, has altered the duration of a patent which is always finite, and has often involved the State reserving to itself various rights.

Today's patent acts do not differ in essence from the patent acts of the past. Perhaps the difference is only the extent to which the 'higher' interests are drafted more explicitly, and in greater detail. In this respect, it is helpful to consider the rules and exceptions surrounding what is understood to be patentable material, or the conditions by which a compulsory licence may be granted in the general interest.

The analysis of the instruments of human rights law has revealed that it is indefensible in law to claim that an entitlement to patent protection is a human right. Those who defend such a proposition are reading things into the text which are simply not there. They ignore the fact that the words inventors and patents are not even mentioned in the very provisions they rely on. The fact that the provisions make no reference to inventors and patents is explicable by the fact that patent rights miss the very characteristics by which human rights are recognised, namely, they are not inalienable, nor are they universal. Indeed, it is not even likely that in 1948 the General Assembly of the United Nations would have even considered patent rights as really necessary and thereby ascribe them the status of human rights in accordance with the goals of the UDHR – the human suffering occasioned by two world wars cannot be linked to a paucity of patent law.

Patents which have been granted, of course, qualify as property and therefore enjoy the protection of fundamental human rights.

I am of the opinion that patent rights miss the status of being human rights. Is this a situation to be bemoaned? I do not think so. Indeed, it would appear to me to be good for both patent law and human rights law. Patent law is subordinate to human rights. In the event of a collision between the two areas of the law, patent law must give way. Describing patents as human rights only leads to an unnecessary complication. We cannot make any progress by pursuing this line of thought. Indeed, I consider it of great importance that human rights remain restricted really to the universal rights which are closely linked to human dignity, for to do otherwise only imperils the status of, and respect for, human rights in our societies. Irrespective of the economic importance of patent law in industrialised countries, it can in no way be said to touch human dignity.

Indeed, it might even be said that whereas we can live without patent rights, we cannot live without human rights.[28]

BIBLIOGRAPHY

Brinkhof, Jan (2004), 'Wish List in the Area of Patent Law', 35 *IIC* 416.
Drucker, W.H. (1924), *Handboek voor de studie van het Nederlandsche Octrooirecht* [Textbook for the study of Dutch Patent Law] (The Hague: Nijhoff), p. 66.
Foyer, J. and M. Vivant (1991), *Le droit des brevets* (Paris: Presses Universitaires de France), p. 12.
Haanappel, P.P.C. and Ejan Mackaay (1990), *New Netherlands Civil Code, Patrimonial Law* (Deventer/Boston: Kluwer Law International).
Kramer, Birgit (2007), *Patentschutz und Zugang zu Medikamenten* (Köln: Carl Heymanns Verlag), p. 85.
Kurz, P. (2000), *Weltgeschichte des Erfindungsschutzes* (Köln: Carl Heymanns Verlag), p. 168.
Kraßer, R. (2004), *Patentrecht*, 5th edn (Münich: CH Beck Verlag), p. 36.
Machlup and Penrose (1950), 'The Patent Controversy in the Nineteenth Century', 10 *Journal of Economic History*, 1, at 11.
Mandich (1948), 'Venetian Patents (1450–1550)', 30 *JPOS* 166, at pp. 176–7.
Rijlaarsdam, A. (2005), *Octrooi en dienstbetrekking (Patents and Employment)* (Delft: VSSD), p. 168.

---

[28] Brinkhof, Jan (2004), 'Wish List in the Area of Patent Law', 35 *IIC* 416.

9. Current patent laws cannot claim the backing of human rights

Wendy J. Gordon[1]

1. INTRODUCTION

Many of the world's countries (one exception being the United States) has undertaken a commitment at the level of human rights to protect the interests of persons who author 'scientific . . . production[s]'.[2] This commit-

[1] This article is © 2010 by Wendy J. Gordon. Wendy Gordon is the Philip S. Beck Professor of Law at Boston University School of Law in the US. Very significant help toward this article was contributed by Keren Ben Shahar, BU LLM 2007.

The initial draft of this chapter, then titled 'Patent and Human Rights: The Case of the Second to Invent', was prepared for the conference on The Human Rights Paradox in Intellectual Property Law organized by the Centre for Intellectual Property Law (CIER) at Utrecht University. Professor Gordon presented a revised draft at 'Tackling Global Health Issues Through Law & Policy', the Annual Symposium of *The American Journal of Law and Medicine* (Boston University, 2 February 2008.) She appreciates the feedback of the participants at both conferences.

She also thanks Giuseppina D'Agostino, Brook Baker, Willem Grosheide, Mike Meurer, Kevin Outterson, Giovanni Ramello, Rob Sloane and David Sugarman for their helpful comments, and Naomi Baumol and Sarah Kaskel for their excellent research assistance. For general discussion, she thanks Geertrui Van Overwalle, Christopher Ricks, and Bruce Sunstein.

[2] Such a right is recognized in a number of international and regional human rights instruments. The most prominent document is the International Covenant on Economic, Social and Cultural Rights which recognizes in Article 15.1(c) the right of everyone 'to benefit from the protection of the moral and material interests resulting from any scientific, literary, or artistic production of which he is the author'. International Covenant on Economic, Social and Cultural Rights, Art. 15.1(c), 16 December 1996, 993 U.N.T.S 3 [hereinafter ICESCR], available at http://www2.ohchr.org/english/law/pdf/cescr.pdf.

The United States signed but did not ratify the ICESCR. See http://treaties.un.org/Pages/ViewDetails.aspx?src=TREATY&mtdsg_no=IV-3&chapter=4&lang=en#bottom. Nearly identical language to that of the ICESCR is included in its declaratory predecessor, The Universal Declaration of Human Rights. See Universal Declaration of Human Rights, G.A. Res. 217A, art. 27(2), U.N. GAOR, 3d Sess., 1st

ment[3] is embodied in the International Covenant on Economic, Social and Cultural Rights (ICESCR), which recognizes in Article 15.1(c) the rights of everyone 'to benefit from the protection of the moral and material interests resulting from any scientific, literary or artistic production of which he is the author.'[4]

This chapter aims to clarify the relationship between the 'interests of authors', protected in Article 15.1(c) of the ICESCR, and national patent legislation. Specifically, it intends to dispel the notion that current patent laws are the manifestation of the human right commitment to authors under the ICESCR.

The claim that patent rights are human rights – the claim whose error[5] this article seeks to reveal – has the potential for being used as a weapon to expand

---

plen. mtg., U.N. Doc A/810 (10 December 1948) [hereinafter UDHR]. (On the issue of whether the UDHR has attained the status of customary law, see, for example, Yu, Peter K. (2007), 'Reconceptualizing Intellectual Property Interests in a Human Right Framework', 40 *U.C. Davis L. Rev.* 1039 at 1060–1). Similarly, the human right of authors is recognized in Article 13.2 of The American Declaration of the Rights and Duties of Man of 1948, available at http://www1.umn.edu/humanrts/oasinstr/zoas2dec.htm; Article 14.1(c) of the Additional Protocol to the American Convention on Human Rights in the Area of Economic, Social and Cultural Rights.

3 The ICESCR is generally recognized as one of the building blocks of what is referred to as 'the international bill of rights', along with the UDHR and the International Covenant on Civil and Political Rights [ICCPR]. Strossen, Nadine (1992–93), 'United States Ratification of the International Bill of Rights: A Fitting Celebration of the Bicentennial of the U.S. Bill of Rights', 24 *U. Tol. L. Rev.* 203, 203. The ICESCR is probably more controversial than the other two components. The United States has ratified the ICCPR (although with strong limitations, see Strossen at id.*)*, and has signed and not ratified the ICESCR. See http://treaties.un.org/Pages/ViewDetails.aspx?src=TREATY&mtdsg_no=IV-3&chapter=4&lang=en#bottom.

4 Article 15.1 of the ICESCR, *supra* note 2, provides:

1. The States Parties to the present Covenant recognize the right of everyone:
   (a) To take part in cultural life;
   (b) To enjoy the benefits of scientific progress and its applications;
   (c) To benefit from the protection of the moral and material interests resulting from any scientific, literary or artistic production of which he is the author.

5 That patent laws have significant differences from human rights under Article 15 can be seen, for example, in *The Impact of the Agreement on Trade-Related Aspects of Intellectual Property Rights on Human Rights*, E/CN.4/Sub.2/2001/13, 27 June 2001 – available at http://www.unhchr.ch/Huridocda/Huridoca.nsf/Symbol/E.CN.4.Sub.2.2001.13.En?Opendocument. The *Impact* document sees distinct differences between enacted intellectual-property law ('more akin to a privilege'; can be 'licensed or assigned', id. at paragraph 14) and human rights ('inalienable', id.).

patent rights[6] against the desires of impoverished peoples to manufacture or distribute inexpensive versions of patented drugs. When those peoples claim that their human right to health[7] and to share in scientific progress[8] mandates allowing them cheap access to patented medications,[9] supporters of strong patent rights sometimes point to an imagined countervailing human right to patents. Thus, one pair of commentators went so far as to state that 'expropriation of others' [intellectual] property . . . is, ironically, one of the most "anti-human rights" actions governments could take'.[10]

This chapter contends that a fundamental disconnect exists between ICESCR Article 15.1(c) and current national laws on patent. I join Rochelle Dreyfuss in her contention that a human rights approach has little expression in national patent legal systems.[11] This chapter illustrates the extent to which

---

6 See, for example, Helfer, Lawrence (2007), 'Toward A Human Rights Framework For Intellectual Property', 40 *U.C. Davis L. Rev*. 971, 1015 (discussing the possibility of the ICESCR being used to expand intellectual-property rights).

7 UDHR, *supra* note 2, at Art. 25(1). ('Everyone has the right to a standard of living adequate for the health and well-being of himself and of his family, including food, clothing, housing and medical care and necessary social services, and the right to security in the event of unemployment, sickness, disability, widowhood, old age or other lack of livelihood in circumstances beyond his control.'); ICESCR, *supra* note 2, at Art. 12.1. ('The States Parties to the present Covenant recognize the right of everyone to the enjoyment of the highest attainable standard of physical and mental health'.)

8 ICESCR, *supra* note 2, at Art. 15.1(b).

9 Supporters of strong access rights include Balasubramaniam, Kumariah (2002), 'Access to Medicines: Patents, Pieces and Public Policy – Consumer Perspectives', in Drahos, Peter and Ruth Mayne (eds), *Global Intellectual Property Rights: Knowledge Access and Development* 90, and Outterson, Kevin (2005), 'Pharmaceutical Arbitrage: Balancing Access And Innovation in International Prescription Drug Markets', 5 *Yale J Health Pol Law & Ethics* 193. For a general discussion see 'Patent Versus Patients – five Years After the Doha Declaration', Oxfam Briefing Paper 95 (November 2006) available at http://www.maketradefair.com/en/assets/english/doha5_101106.pdf; Mayne, Ruth (2002), 'The Global NGO Campaign on Patents and Access to Medicines: an Oxfam Perspective', in Drahos and Mayne (2002), *supra*, at 244; Chapman, Audrey R. (2001), 'Approaching intellectual property as a human right: obligations related to Article 15(1)(c)', 35(3) *Copyright Bull*. 4, 26 available at http://unesdoc.unesco.org/images/0012/001255/125505e.pdf.

10 Giovanetti, Tom and Merrill Matthews (2005), 'Intellectual Property Rights and Human Rights', 34 *IPI Ideas*, September 2005, available at http://www.ipi.org/ipi/IPIPublications.nsf/PublicationLookupFullText/FF5BC1CE33A784E2862570880053B054, quoted in Yu, *supra* note 2, at 1085 and n. 176.

11 Dreyfuss, Rochelle C., 'Patents and Human Rights: Where is the Paradox?', Chapter 4 of this volume. I agree with Dreyfuss' central point: that the human rights vision of ICESCR is not the basis on which 'the world's patent rights are structured. Instead, the perspective is purely utilitarian'. Id. at 80. This point is made clear in General Comment 17, Article 1: 'Human rights are fundamental as they are inherent to the human person as such, whereas intellectual property rights are first and foremost

the two paradigms are foreign to each other by examining a fundamental element of Article 15 – the nature of authorship. The chapter concludes that current laws' allocation of patent ownership bears an insufficient relationship to any plausible human right conception of who should count as a scientific author.

Commentators have argued that current patent and copyright laws award authors and inventors protections *in excess* of what the human rights obligation seems to require.[12] For example, I have argued that the natural rights theory of John Locke does not justify copyright's current reach.[13] In addition, of course, many commentators point to the provisions in the ICESCR that give the public rights to health[14] and to participate in culture and benefit from science,[15] and to the free speech rights in the International Covenant on Civil and Political Rights,[16] to demonstrate that any claim by an author or inventor

---

means by which States seek to provide incentives for inventiveness and creativity . . . for the benefit of society as a whole.' U.N. Econ. & Soc. Council [ECOSOC], Comm. on Econ., Soc. & Cultural Rights, General Comment No. 17: 'The Right of Everyone to Benefit from the Protection of the Moral and Material Interests Resulting from any Scientific, Literary or Artistic Production of Which He Is the Author (Article 15, Paragraph (1)(c) of the Covenant)', U.N. Doc. E/C.12/GC/2005/5 (21 November 2005) [hereinafter General Comment No. 17], available at http://www.unhchr.ch/tbs/doc.nsf/898586b1dc7b4043c1256a450044f331/03902145edbbe797c125711500584ea8/$FILE/G0640060.pdf.

At one point, Dreyfuss's excellent paper for some reason (perhaps rhetorical) treats the notion of an author's human rights claim as if it might embody entitlement to 'all' benefits. Id. at 80. This is a bit of a straw man. For example, even a stalwart defender of property rights like philosopher Robert Nozick saw a natural-right justification for cutting off patent duration. Nozick, Robert (1974), *Anarchy, State and Utopia* (New York: Basic Books) at 178–82.

12 See, for example, Yu, *supra* note 2 at 1077: '[S]ome attributes of intellectual property rights are protected in international or regional human rights instruments, while other attributes do not have any human rights basis at all.'

13 Gordon, Wendy J. (1993), 'A Property Right in Self-expression: Equality and Individualism in the Natural Law of Intellectual Property', 102 *Yale L.J.* 1533. See also, Shiffrin, Seana (2004), 'Lockean Arguments for Private Intellectual Property', in Stephen R. Munzer (ed), *New Essays in the Legal and Political Theory of Property* 138, 142 (while authors might deserve a right to reward, under a Lockean approach they would not deserve a full property right.)

14 ICESCR, *supra* note 2, at art. 12.1.

15 General Comment 17, *supra* note 11, paragraph 6 states that Article 15 of the ICESCR enumerates in paragraph 1, 'three rights covering different aspects of cultural participation', including authorial right, the right of the public to 'take part in cultural life', and the right of the public 'to enjoy the benefits of scientific progress and its applications'. See ICESCR, *supra* note 2, at Art. 15.1(a), 15.1(b).

16 ICCPR, Art. 19.2, 16 December 1966, 999 U.N.T.S. 171 ('Everyone shall have the right to freedom of expression; this right shall include freedom to seek, receive and impart information and ideas of all kinds, regardless of frontiers, either orally, in writing or in print, in the form of art, or through any other media of his choice').

to a 'human right' benefit from her work must be *limited* by the countervailing human rights of the public.[17] Along a similar line, as mentioned above, I have argued that the Lockean natural-rights approach mandates a strong right of access in the public as against the holders of copyrights and patents.[18] But the point of the instant chapter is somewhat different from any of these contentions: here I argue that current patent laws are actually in discord with the most plausible notion of a scientist's human rights. The chapter thus takes fundamental issue with those commentators who cite the human rights of authors as support for strong patent protection.

This chapter seeks to highlight how erroneous such claims are; patent owners should not rely on the ICESCR human rights commitment to bolster their position. While many reasons might disqualify current patent laws from the backing of the ICESCR,[19] this chapter highlights one: that current laws grant patents to people who are not 'authors' whom the human rights regime is designed to protect.

2. THE IMPORTANCE OF IDENTIFYING THE AUTHOR TO THE HUMAN RIGHTS SCHEME

The ICESCR in Article 15.1(c) speaks of the rights of 'authors'. The significance of correctly identifying the 'author' is evident in the language adopted by the Committee on Economic, Social and Cultural Rights (hereinafter the 'Committee'), which is the United Nations body responsible for monitoring

---

17 See, for example, Hestermeyer, Holger (2007), *Human Rights and the WTO: The Case of Patents and Access to Medicines* (Oxford: Oxford University Press) at 152–3 and *passim*; Yu (2007), *supra* note 2, at 1124; Drassinower, Abraham, 'Labour and Intersubjectivity: Notes on the Natural Law of Copyright', on page 4, available at http://papers.ssrn.com/sol3/papers.cfm?abstract_id=275470.

18 Gordon, *A Property Right in Self-expression*, *supra* note 13, at 1561–2. Some of the Lockean concern for public access could be accommodated if copyright law imposed liability only in the presence of certain types of 'intent'. However, copyright law does not do so as a general matter. Copyright civil liability is strict. See Gordon, Wendy (2008), 'Moral Philosophy, Information, Technology, and Copyright: The Grokster Case', in Weckert and van den Hoven (eds), *Moral Philosophy and Information Technology* 270, 295 (Cambridge: Cambridge University Press).

19 For additional arguments suggesting that Article 15 does not enshrine patent law, see Hestermeyer, *supra* note 17, at 152–8; also see id. at 30 (which includes an argument similar to the point about 'authorship' made herein). For one list of proposed human-rights requirements against which a patent law might be measured, see Chapman, Audrey R. (2002), 'Core Obligations Related to ICESCR Article 15(1)(c)', in Audrey Chapman and Sage Russell (eds), *Core Obligations: Building a Framework for Economic, Social and Cultural Rights*, 305.

the implementation of the ICESCR by Member States. In its General Comment number 17, a document designed to give substantive meaning to the Covenant's provision recognizing the rights of authors, the Committee explained that 'only the "author", namely the creator . . . can be the beneficiary of the protection of Article 15, paragraph 1 (c)'.[20]

It would therefore seem that for a patent system to even aspire to ICESCR backing,[21] it would have to properly identify and give patents to those 'creators' whom the ICESCR subprovision is designed to protect. Yet this chapter will show that the various patent legal systems are in discord over this primary point among themselves, and take approaches inconsistent with how a 'creator' might be identified under a plausible human rights inquiry. The result is that whatever human rights claims might or might not be maintainable for scientists in some abstract realm, in the real world ICESCR Article 15.1(c) cannot appropriately be used to support strong patent enforcement.

3. SEARCHING FOR A PLAUSIBLE HUMAN-RIGHTS CONCEPTION OF AUTHORSHIP

Who, then, is the author protected under Article 15? The ICESCR uses the term 'author' to indicate a 'creator'[22] of 'scientific, literary or artistic productions'.[23] The focus on the individual creator or groups of creators is dictated by the nature of human rights as derived from 'the inherent dignity and worth of all persons'[24] and specifically the nature of the 'rights of authors' as designed to 'safeguard[] the personal link between authors and their creations'.[25] Therefore a regime that does not give rights to 'creators' could not satisfy the subprovision's mandate.

---

20 General Comment 17, *supra* note 11, at paragraph 7.

21 Even were patent laws to resolve the identification of authors satisfactorily, it is of course far from clear that strong patent laws would deserve ICESCR recognition as against public claims to health. To offer a brief reminder: Subprovision 15.1(b) 'recognize[s] the right of everyone . . . (b) to enjoy the benefits of scientific progress and its applications.' ICESCR, *supra* note 2, at Art. 15.1. As explained in one drafting history of the provision, '15 (1) (c) does not seem to have been written as an intentional limit on the rights of all [the public] to benefit.' Green, Maria, Int'l Anti-Poverty L. Ctr., Drafting History of the Article 15(1)(c) of the International Covenant, Paragraph 46, U.N. Doc. E/C.12/2000/15 (9 October 2000), available at http://www.unhchr.ch/tbs/doc.nsf/0/872a8f7775c9823cc1256999005c3088/$FILE/G0044899.pdf.

22 The Comment uses the term 'creator'. General Comment 17, *supra* note 11.

23 General Comment 17, *supra* note 11, paragraph 7.

24 General Comment 17, *supra* note 11, paragraph 1.

25 General Comment 17, *supra* note 11, paragraph 2. Note, however, that the role of the 'personal link' in patent can be questioned. The General Comment makes a

The term 'creator' is of course ambiguous. One ambiguity results from creators' need to draw on what came before. It is important to remember that human creators are not divinely capable of creating 'out of nothing'.[26] 'Creation' and 'making' are recognized as often resulting from acts of addition to the common heritage or remixing common-heritage elements. But still a host of issues remain.[27]

Many nations distinguish between 'authors' and 'inventors'. An 'authorial' effort is usually thought to be one that is original, in the sense that some aspect (the aspect in which authorship is claimed) is not copied from predecessors. Under this view, anticipation does not erode authorship. As a United States Court of Appeals wrote, 'If by some magic a man who had never known it were to compose anew Keats's Ode on a Grecian Urn, he would be an "author"'.[28] In examining who 'deserves' rewards such as property rights, philosopher Lawrence Becker has persuasively suggested that this approach to authorship is the ethically correct view: that priority in time is irrelevant to desert.[29]

---

distinction between the 'moral' interests of creators (such as rights of attribution) and their 'material' interests (such as a right to remuneration). Patent law is linked more closely to the material than the dignitary, and 'personality' may be correspondingly less important, according to the authors of the Comment. They state, 'Unlike other human rights, the material interests of authors are not directly linked to the personality of the creator, but contribute to the enjoyment of the right to an adequate standard of living'. Id. at paragraph 15.

The implications of this are unclear. Nevertheless, to the extent that a right to material remuneration makes sense as a human right, it would have to be linked to actual authors rather than to persons who are not authors. For example, Peter Yu argues that a focus on the rights of the individual creator has the potential to 'encourage the development of an author-centered regime', rather than the current 'publisher centered' copyright regime. Yu, *supra* note 2, at 1131.

[26] See, for example, Litman, Jessica (1990), 'The Public Domain', 39 *Emory L.J.* 965, 1008 (arguing that while romantic ideas of authorship imagine that artists create 'out of nothing', in fact everything is created from utilizing an existing heritage); also see Zemer, Lior (2007), *The Idea of Authorship in Copyright* (London: Ashgate) (focusing on the public's contribution to authorship).

[27] See, for example, the important review of issues canvassed in Becker, Lawrence C. (1993), 'Deserving to Own Intellectual Property', 68 *Chi.-Kent L. Rev.* 609.

[28] *Sheldon v Metro-Goldwyn Pictures Corporation*, 81 F.2d 49, 54 (2nd Cir. 1936) (citing *Bleistein v Donaldson Lithographing Co.*, 188 U.S. 239, 249 (1903)). In the US, copyright is said to inhere in all authors, including authors who by coincidence create something identical to a pre-existing work of which they had no knowledge. However, since even 'subconscious copying' can give rise to liability and preclude ownership, the independent second author may face difficulties of proof, particularly if the prior work was publicly disseminated. See, for example, *Three Boys Music Corp. v Michael Bolton*, 212 F.3d 477 (9th Cir. 2000).

[29] '[T]emporal primacy alone seems a red herring.' Becker, *supra* note 27, at

Becker sets out a set of tentative but attractive desert-based arguments that suggest that an award of property rights should not depend on whether creators' subjectively-original productions happen to duplicate an existing work from which they did not copy.[30]

By contrast, the notion of 'invention' seems to imply something new and significantly different from what has come before. Under this approach, a creator counts as an inventor only if he or she is the *first* person to make or create something. Subjective originality would be an insufficient basis on which to claim rights.

The ICESCR speaks not of 'inventors' but of scientific 'authors'.[31] This may imply that a scientific author is anyone who independently makes or creates, in Becker's sense that even if her act of creation was later in time than someone else's, she is an 'author' if she did not copy the element she claims as the invention from the predecessor.[32] This interpretation would give rights under the ICESCR to a host of authors, including independent inventors who were second in time. But some commentators would probably disregard the

618. Becker does, however, suggest that 'the antiquity of a thing' can sometimes 'revise [] our estimate of its singularity'. Id.

30 Becker, *supra* note 27, at 622–3 (principle of non-preclusion: 'Surely it would be odd to accept a desert basis for one person that precluded other equally deserving people from getting a similar reward.') , 626–8. 'Honoring the non-preclusion principle would introduce significant changes into intellectual property law. For example, far from being excluded from rewards for their work, authors who can show their intellectual independence from patented products would be entitled to share the property rights in them.' Id. at 629.

31 At least one of the documents that preceded the ICESCR does speak of 'invention', however. Article 13 of the American Declaration on the Rights and Duties of Man, Organization of American States, 2 May 1948, OEA/Ser. L./V./II.23, doc. 21 rev. 6 (1948), provides as follows:

> Article XIII. Every person has the right to take part in the cultural life of the community, to enjoy the arts, and to participate in the benefits that result from intellectual progress, especially scientific discoveries.
>
> He likewise has the right to the protection of his moral and material interests as regards his inventions or any literary, scientific or artistic works of which he is the author.

The passage of the Declaration may have played some role in the adoption of Article 27(2) of the UDHR, see Yu, *supra* note 2, at 1053–8, which Article in turn affected the language of the ICESCR.

32 A corollary of the second approach would be a rule that freed inventors from liability so long as their inventions did not result from copying. Two quite different but thoughtful philosophers have argued that a proper conception of rights would not impose liability on someone who independently invents. See Becker, *supra* note 27, at 628–9; Nozick, *supra* note 11, at 182.

linguistic and desert issues, and substitute for 'author' the notion of 'inventor'. If adopted, this interpretation would give rights under the ICESCR only to those persons who were first to invent.

So current law has two primary conceptions of who counts as a creator: subjective originality versus being objectively 'first'. As this essay will show, patent legal systems do not consistently follow *either* conception.

Given the centrality of the 'creator' to a human rights notion of a scientific authors' rights, the current legal systems' lack of consistency about *who* counts as a creator should be a shocking divergence from human rights. But if the divergence does not shock, that is because virtually everyone recognizes at some level what was pointed out by the Committee's General Comment 17: that the foundations for existing legal regimes like copyright and patent differ strongly from the foundations of an authorial right under the ICESCR, and that 'it is important not to equate' current intellectual-property rights to authors' human rights under subprovision 15(1)(c).[33] (In fact, the most accessible drafting history of Article 15 suggests that the subprovision's primary goal was not to secure authors a right to payment from persons benefiting from creative work, but rather to secure authors and scientists from governmental repression.[34])

[33] See General Comment 17, *supra* note 11, especially paragraph 2. As noted above, General Comment 17 distinguishes between on the one hand, 'human rights' that are 'fundamental, inalienable and universal', and, on the other hand 'intellectual property rights' which 'seek to provide incentives' and serve other purposes for the 'benefit of society as a whole'. As Rochelle Dreyfuss cogently argues in Chapter 4 of this volume, the history and structure of patent law makes it a poor fit for human rights. Also see, for example, Hestermeyer, *supra* note 18, at 153–8.

[34] Article 15(1)(c) may not even have been adopted with a focus on issues of copyright and patent. For those legal regimes, the primary conflict is among nongovernmental claimants, but 'the subtext to the entire discussion [of 15(a)(c)] was the issue of *government* control over science and art, and scientists and artists'. Green, *supra* note 21, paragraph 42 (emphasis added). Green writes:

> The provision on authors' rights, judging from the exchanges between the USSR, Czechoslovakia, and Uruguay, became associated with protection for authors' freedom from state intervention. Any substantive issues to be worked out on the relation between the 'benefits' clause and the 'authors' clause never had a real chance for discussion. The final vote was straight down cold war faultlines, with the opposed roster holding Romania, Ukrainian Soviet Socialist Republic, USSR, Albania, Bulgaria, Byelorussian Soviet Socialist Republic, Czechoslovakia, Hungary, and Iraq . . . .

Green, *supra* note, paragraph 43. Also see the discussion in Yu, *supra* note 2, at 1067–70.

By focusing on the *specific* issue of *who* is entitled to rights, it will become clear that current patent laws cannot claim to be implementing the ICESCR provision that seeks to secure the 'material interests' of scientific authors.

4. DO PATENTS GO TO THE FIRST TO INVENT?

The vast majority of countries, the United States being probably the only exception, subscribe to the first to file system.[35] Under a first to file system, the patent is given to the first person to file a patent application, regardless of whether the filer was the first to conceive of the invention. Such a rule is motivated by the desire to enable the public to capture the benefit of prompt disclosure of new scientific findings and by bureaucratic considerations such as ease of administration. When nations make 'first to file' the test for inventorship it is possible that many persons who are the first to conceive of an invention, or even the first to reduce it to practice, will be denied patents.

The United States does not adopt the 'first to file' approach. Instead, it grants patent rights according to a 'first to invent' rule.[36] Does the US approach satisfy the ICESCR concern with linking the 'material interests' flowing from an invention to its true 'author'? On the surface, the 'first to invent' rule has the promise of being consistent with at least one plausible notion of authorship, namely, 'being first' to conceive or make something, and seems fairer to individual scientists than a 'first to file' rule.

When one takes a closer look, however, the United States system also fails to seek a true 'author'. For example, is the true 'author' the first to *conceive* an invention? Under US law, the first to conceive of a new invention may forfeit his rights if he is less than diligent in reducing his invention to practice.[37] Is the true 'author' the one who first reduces the invention to practice? Under US law, even if a person is first to both conceive a new invention *and* reduce it to practice, she may also forfeit her rights to another, if she 'with-

---

[35] Lemley, Mark A. and Colleen V. Chien (2003), 'Are the U.S. Patent Priority Rules Really Necessary?', 54 *Hastings L.J.* 1299, 1303.

[36] 35 USC § sec 102 (2006). Although it can be debated the extent to which the two systems result in different ownership awards, Lemley and Chien find 'that the first person to file is usually, but by no means always, also the first to invent. In over 40% of the cases, the first to invent is the last to file.' Lemley and Chien *supra* note 35, at 1300. Although even in the US first filers often win priority contests, Lemley and Chien conclude that 'the U.S. first to invent system has a significant effect on outcomes.' Id. at 1333.

[37] 35 USC § sec 102(g); see Mueller, Janice (2006), *An Introduction to Patent Law* (New York: Aspen Publishers)) at 162–3.

holds h[er] invention from the public'.[38] The reasoning seems to be that as the public will not benefit from a concealed invention, the law is justified in stripping the first inventor of her right in favor of a subsequent inventor who disclosed his invention to the public. But both are inventors.

Public disclosure leads to a third area in which US law grants patents in ways that diverge from notions of 'authorship': a person who authors an invention, but who practices it publicly, or discloses it in a publication, after a year cannot claim patent protection in it.[39] This may make sense from a utilitarian perspective,[40] but the result is that an 'author' lacks rights.

A striking example of an authorial inventor not receiving a patent can be found in the decision of the PTO Board of Interference in the case of *Lassman v Brossi*.[41] The Board held that when two inventors file a patent application on the same day, and it is impossible to establish priority based on the date of conception, neither of the inventors gets a patent. Such result does not seem to comport with a principle of authors' rights.

In addition, of course, both the 'first to file' and 'first to invent' systems often deny patent rights to independent inventors, even though, as Becker argues, even second inventors can be authorial creators in a very real and strong sense.[42] That is the topic of the next section.

---

38 *Mason v Hepburn*, 13 App.D.C. 86, 96 (D.C. Cir. 1898) (quoting with approval from a prior case). Such is the result today under 35 USC §102. That section reads in part: 'a person shall be entitled to a patent unless . . . before such person's invention thereof, the invention was made in this country by another inventor who had not abandoned, suppressed or concealed it' §102(g)(2).

39 35 U.S.C. § 102(b).

40 I should take note here of a possible counter-argument. One might distinguish between two kinds of authorial inventors: those who do not apply for a patent because they expect to garner sufficient revenue and control without a patent (for example, by using trade secret law), and those who do not apply for a patent for other reasons, such as ignorance about legal requirements. It could be argued that the 'human rights' concerns of the first group are met even without the assistance of patent law, and therefore that this group's failure to qualify for patent protection does not create a divergence between human rights law and the current legal pattern. I take no position on such an argument.

But as for members of the second group, especially those whom a patentee may deprive of any ability to benefit from their invention, divergence between most human rights notions and patent practice seems clear.

41 *Lassman v Brossi*, 159 U.S.P.Q. 182, 185–6 (BD. Pat. INT'F. 1967).

42 See Becker, *supra* note 27, at 618 (arguing that notions of deservingness imply that a predecessor invention should not preclude a second but independent inventor from having title).

5. DO PATENTS GO TO ALL INDEPENDENT AUTHORS?

What of the second possible meaning for 'author', namely, independent creation? This essay has suggested that an author under a plausible and attractive human rights conception might be anyone who has added or remixed some elements *independently,* in ways he did not copy from others, even if he happens to duplicate a previous invention.

No patent system that I know of grants patents to second inventors simply because they invented independently. The US patent system, for example, employs a 'winner takes all' approach. While a first to file system seems to yield results that are arbitrary from a human-rights perspective, it might be argued that 'the U.S. first to invent system is not particularly "fairer" than a first to file alternative, since [in any kind of winner-takes-all system,] regardless of who wins, the loser is an independent inventor who will likely have made substantial investment in developing its invention before learning of another party's priority'.[43]

Not only does only one inventor get a patent; the other independent inventor often gets sued. In the United States, there is no general 'independent inventor' defense. Admittedly, many other nations provide prior independent inventors some limited defenses, and even the United States has adopted a limited form of such a defense for one class of patents.[44] But that still does not give equal treatment to all independently authorial inventors.

The rejection of 'independent creation' as a sufficient basis for patent ownership may make sense in utilitarian or economic terms. Inventions are often made by many researchers near-simultaneously.[45] If all the independent researchers each received a patent, or even if independent inventors merely received a defense, the various independent inventors would compete with

---

43 Lemley and Chien, *supra* note 35 at 1326 (discussing a possible implication of the closeness of reported invention dates in their data).

44 The harshness of patent races is moderated in European countries. They typically recognize some prior users' rights, granting those who independently develop an invention 'a limited right to continue using it even after another party's patent issues'. Lemley and Chien, *supra* note 35, at 1326. In the US, if two persons independently invent, and one person obtains a patent, the other is an infringer. The only exception is a narrow category of business-method patents. 35 U.S.C. § 273(b)(3) (2000).

45 Lemley, Mark (2007), 'Should Patent Infringement Require Proof of Copying?', 105 *Mich. L. Rev*. 1525, 1528; Merges, Robert P. and Richard R. Nelson (1990), 'On the Complex Economics of Patent Scope', 90 *Colum. L. Rev* 839, 884. The *locus classicus* of this observation is Merton, Robert K. (1973), *The Sociology of Science* (Chicago: University of Chicago Press), especially at 365.

each other and drive down the price of the invention or its products to a level that might provide insufficient incentive for new research to take place.[46] Therefore, a 'winner take all race' may be necessary for providing researchers sufficient incentives to create what the public needs. But this is a utilitarian or economic concern, and as General Comment 17 recognizes, that is quite a separate matter from what the ICESCR 15.1(c) seeks to protect.[47] In sum: a 'winner takes all' approach may be necessary for incentives, but it is inconsistent with rewarding all authors.

The conclusion seems clear. On either plausible conception of creator – being the 'first' to make or create, or being an 'independent' creator or maker – current patent laws do not fit.[48]

6. ASSIGNEES AND CORPORATIONS AS OWNERS

In addition to the issues of first to file versus first to invent, and independent authorship versus initial inventorship, there is the issue of whether a corporation or assignee can claim the protection of human rights. It is likely that most patent rights are held by corporations, who may hold them by assignment from the actual, human creators.[49] Patent laws in the US require that the actual creator be granted patent rights, which she in turn may assign to her employer. The very fact that a right holder is merely an assignee, ipso facto prevents him from seeking human rights protection to its interests. At least that is so in the eyes of the Committee, which states that human rights are by nature 'inalienable';[50] if inalienable, they cannot be held by an assignee.

Perhaps based on the asserted inalienable nature of human rights, or perhaps for other reasons,[51] General Comment 17 interprets the ICESCR to

---

[46] Samson Vermont has challenged this traditional economic argument, suggesting that giving a defense to second inventors might be compatible with incentive goals. Vermont, Samson (2006), 'Independent Invention as a Defense to Patent Infringement', 105 *Mich. L. Rev.* 475; compare Lemley (2007), *supra* note 45, at 1525.

[47] In emphasizing the nonutilitarian basis of the human rights document, I do not contend that the ICESCR is blind to the way the even private IP rights can assist the public.

[48] Nor does current copyright law fit, for quite different reasons. See, for example, Gordon, *A Property Right in Self-Expression*, *supra* note 13.

[49] There are conceptions of natural right that would allow one to delegate physical 'creation' and still claim 'authorship', as in the Lockean reference to the 'turfs my servant has cut'. John Locke (1690), *Two Treatises of Government*, 307 (Laslett, Peter (ed.) (1967), Cambridge University Press). I do not enter that particular bramble.

[50] General Comment 17, *supra* note 11, paragraph 1.

[51] One cannot be sure how far the Committee would extend the inalienability notion. For example, the Committee expressed the view that human rights should be

exclude legal entities such as corporations.[52] Corporations' rights under positive existing law are of 'different nature [and] are not protected at the level of human rights'.[53] Yet, as mentioned, it appears that the majority of patents are held by corporations. This is further evidence that current patent holders have little valid claim to the backing of the ICESCR. The Committee even cites the fact that 'intellectual property regimes primarily protect business and corporate interests and investments'[54] as part of the reason for the Committee's conclusion that it is 'important not to equate intellectual property rights with the human right recognized in article 15'.[55]

7. CONCLUSION

In the dispute over the enforcement of pharmaceutical patents, the ICESCR at first appears Janus-headed. On the one hand, it provides for 'the right of everyone' '[t]o enjoy the benefits of scientific progress and its applications'.[56] On the other hand, it provides for 'the right of everyone' '[t]o benefit from the protection of the moral and material interests resulting from any scientific, literary or artistic production of which he is the author'.[57]

Tension may arise between those provisions, or between those provisions and other human rights, like the right to health, within ICESCR and otherwise. But the actual patent laws of actual nations do not rise to a level that would require resolving any such tension. The nations of the world recognize as patent holders people who would not be entitled to human rights as authorial inventors; and the nations of the world refuse to recognize as patent holders people who would indeed be authorial inventors. The 'first to file' systems may be the most obvious offenders against a search for authors, but any

---

extended to allow communities and other groups to benefit from 'their collective cultural heritage'. General Comment 17, *supra* note 11, at paragraph 2; also see paragraph 9 ('knowledge, innovations, and practices of indigenous and local communities'). Presumably, under this interpretation, a community could have rights in creations originating before any of the inhabitants were born. This suggests a kind of alienability, or transfer among individuals, albeit one not mediated by a market.

52 Contrast this with the European Convention on Human Rights, which at protocol 1, Article I (the right to property), provides that 'Every natural *or legal* person is entitled to the peaceful enjoyment of his possessions.' (Emphasis added).

53 General Comment 17, *supra* note 11, paragraph 7.

54 General Comment 17, *supra* note 11, at paragraph 2.

55 General Comment 17, *supra* note 12, paragraph 3 ('It is therefore important . . .') See also Hestermeyer, *supra* note 17, at 153–8.

56 ICESCR, *supra* note 2, at Art. 15.1.(b).

57 ICESCR, *supra* note 2, at Art. 15.1.(c).

system is suspect that denies patents to independent inventors. Given the crucial importance of 'authorship' to the ICESCR subprovision that grants 'material' rights to scientists, and given the relative *un*importance of 'authorship' to national patent laws, it makes little sense for patent holders to claim a presumptive gloss of 'human rights' for their claims.

BIBLIOGRAPHY

Additional Protocol to the American Convention on Human Rights in the Area of Economic, Social and Cultural Rights, Article 14.1(c).

American Declaration of the Rights and Duties of Man of 1948, Article 13.2. Available at http://www1.umn.edu/humanrts/oasinstr/zoas2dec.htm.

Anheuser Busch v Portugal [GC], no. 73049/01, § 63, 11 January 2007.

Article 13 of the American Declaration on the Rights and Duties of Man, Organization of American States, Article 13, 2 May 1948, OEA/Ser. L./V./II.23, doc. 21 rev. 6 (1948).

Balasubramaniam, Kumariah (2002), 'Access to Medicines: Patents, Pieces and Public Policy – Consumer Perspectives', in Peter Drahos and Ruth Mayne (eds) *Global Intellectual Property Rights: Knowledge Access and Development* (Basingstoke: Palgrave Macmillan).

Becker, Lawrence C. (1993), 'Deserving to Own Intellectual Property', 68 *Chi.-Kent L. Rev.* 609.

Bleistein v Donaldson Lithographing Co., 188 U.S. 239, 249 (1903).

Chapman, Audrey R. (2001), 'Approaching intellectual property as a human right: obligations related to Article 15(1)(c)', 35(3) *Copyright Bull.* 4, 26. Available at http://unesdoc.unesco.org/images/0012/001255/125505e.pdf.

Chapman, Audrey R. (2002), 'Core Obligations Related to ICESCR Article 15(1)(c)', in Audrey Chapman and Sage Russell (eds) *Core Obligations: Building a Framework for Economic, Social and Cultural Rights* (Antwerp: Intersentia), p. 305.

Drassinower, Abraham, 'Labour and Intersubjectivity: Notes on the Natural Law of Copyright', on page 4. Available at http://papers.ssrn.com/sol3/papers.cfm?abstract_id=275470.

Dreyfuss, Rochelle C., 'Patents and Human Rights: Where is the Paradox?', Chapter 4 of this volume.

European Convention on Human Rights, Protocol 1, Article I.

Giovanetti, Tom and Merrill Matthews (2005), 'Intellectual Property Rights and Human Rights', 34 *IPI Ideas*, September 2005. Available at http://www.ipi.org/ipi/IPIPublications.nsf/PublicationLookupFullText/FF5BC1CE33A784E2862570880053B054.

Gordon, Wendy (2008), 'Moral Philosophy, Information, Technology, and Copyright: The Grokster Case', in Weckert and van den Hoven (eds), *Moral Philosophy and Information Technology* (Cambridge: Cambridge University Press).

Gordon, Wendy J. (1993), 'A Property Right in Self-expression: Equality and Individualism in the Natural Law of Intellectual Property', 102 *Yale L.J.* 1533.

Green, Maria (2000), Int'l Anti-Poverty L. Ctr., Drafting History of the Article 15(1)(c) of the International Covenant, Paragraph 46, U.N. Doc. E/C.12/2000/15

(9 October 2000). Available at http://www.unhchr.ch/tbs/doc.nsf/0/872a8f7775c9823cc1256999005c3088/$FILE/G0044899.pdf.

Helfer, Lawrence (2007), 'Toward A Human Rights Framework For Intellectual Property', 40 *U.C. Davis L. Rev*. 971, 1015.

Hestermeyer, Holger (2007), *Human Rights and the WTO: The Case of Patents and Access to Medicines* (Oxford: Oxford University Press).

'The Impact of the Agreement on Trade-Related Aspects of Intellectual Property Rights on Human Rights', E/CN.4/Sub.2/2001/13, 27 June 2001.

International Covenant on Economic, Social and Cultural Rights, 16 December 1966, available at http://www2.ohchr.org/english/law/pdf/cescr.pdf.

Lassman v Brossi, 159 U.S.P.Q. 182, 185–6 (BD. Pat. INT'F. 1967).

Lemley, Mark (2007), 'Should Patent Infringement Require Proof of Copying?' 105 *Mich. L. Rev*. 1525.

Lemley, Mark A. and Colleen V. Chien (2003), 'Are the U.S. Patent Priority Rules Really Necessary?' 54 *Hastings L.J.* 1299.

Litman, Jessica (1990), 'The Public Domain' 39 *Emory Law L.J.* 965, 966.

Locke, John (1690), *Two Treatises of Government* 307 (Peter Laslett (ed) (1967), (Cambridge: Cambridge University. Press), p. 307.

Mason v Hepburn, 13 App.D.C. 86,96 (D.C. Cir. 1898).

Mayne, Ruth (2002), 'The Global NGO Campaign on Patents and Access to Medicines: an Oxfam Perspective', in Peter Drahos and Ruth Mayne (eds) *Global Intellectual Property Rights: Knowledge Access and Development* (Basingstoke: Palgrave Macmillan).

Merges Robert P. and Richard R. Nelson (1990), 'On the Complex Economics of Patent Scope', 90 *Colum. L. Rev* 839.

Merton, Robert K. (1973), *The Sociology of Science* (Chicago: University of Chicago Press).

Mueller, Janice (2006), *An Introduction to Patent Law* (New York: Aspen Publishers).

Nozick, Robert (1974), *Anarchy, State, and Utopia* (New York: Basic Books), p. 182.

Outterson, Kevin (2005), 'Pharmaceutical Arbitrage: Balancing Access And Innovation In International Prescription Drug Markets', 5 *Yale J Health L Pol Law & Ethics* 193.

'Patent Versus Patients – Five Years After the Doha Declaration', Oxfam Briefing Paper 95 (November 2006). Available at http://www.maketradefair.com/en/assets/english/doha5_101106.pdf.

Shiffrin, Seana (2004), 'Lockean Arguments for Private Intellectual Property', in Stephen R. Munzer (ed), *New Essays in the Legal and Political Theory of Property* (Cambridge: Cambridge University Press).

Strossen, Nadine (1992–93), 'United States Ratification of the International Bill of Rights: A Fitting Celebration of the Bicentennial of the U.S. Bill of Rights', 24 *U. Tol. L. Rev*. 203.

U.N. Econ. & Soc. Council [ECOSOC], Comm. on Econ., Soc & Cultural Rights, General Comment No. 17: 'The Right of Everyone to Benefit from the Protection of the Moral and Material Interests Resulting from Any Scientific, Literary or Artistic Production of Which He Is the Author' (Article 15, Paragraph 1(c) of the Covenant)', U.N. Doc. E/C.12/GC/17 (12 January 2006), available at http://www.unhchr.ch/tbs/doc.nsf/898586b1dc7b4043c1256a450044f331/03902145 edbbe797c125711500584ea8/$FILE/G0640060.pdf.

Universal Declaration of Human Rights, G.A. Res. 217A, art. 27(2), U.N. GAOR, 3d Sess., 1st plen. mtg., U.N. Doc A/810 (10 December 1948).

Vermont, Samson (2006), 'Independent Invention As A Defense To Patent Infringement', 105 *Mich. L. Rev.* 475.
Yu, Peter K. (2007), 'Reconceptualizing Intellectual Property Interests in a Human Right Framework', 40 *U.C. Davis L. Rev.* 1039.
Zemer, Lior (2007), *The Idea of Authorship in Copyright* (Aldershot: Ashgate).

PART III

Human rights as restrictions to intellectual property rights

10. Introduction

Lucky Belder*

The third part of this book on the nexus between intellectual property rights and human rights regards the effects of human rights provisions as restricting the scope and the exercise of intellectual property rights.

The process of globalisation and liberalisation of trade is of great importance in the fight against poverty and the improvement of access to food and medicines. The development and the production of these essentials is increasingly controlled by economic interests that are protected by intellectual property rights. At the same time, the development of new technology, new media and uses of these media has resulted in a fast forwarding of adaptation of legislation to secure interests by intellectual property right holders. The access to these media and the information communicated by these media is the cause of an increasing digital divide, in which economic interests decide the access to and the content of the new media economy. A third aspect is the complex relationship between (representatives of) indigenous communities as holders of traditional cultural expressions and traditional knowledge, and the agricultural, pharmaceutical and creative industries that are in search of new sources of information. The question today is how to reconcile these interests in international legislation and regulate recognition and remuneration for these original communities.[1]

All of these developments have made it necessary to rethink the scope of intellectual property rights and the balance between private and public interests.

The codification of both intellectual property rights and human rights finds its justification in arguments based on a utilist perspective as well as a rights based perspective. The rights based perspective has a focus on the codification of the protection of the inherent dignity of every person and his personal

* Lucky Belder is Associate-Professor of Intellectual Property Law at the Centre for Intellectual Property Law (CIER), Molengraaff Institute for Private Law, Utrecht University.

1 See on the status of work on the protection of traditional cultural expressions done by the WIPO Intergovernmental Committee on Intellectual Property and Genetic Resources, Traditional Knowledge and Folklore WIPO/GRTKF/IC/12/4(a),(b),(c), Issued 6 December 2007.

sphere, and the protection of his personality rights. This perspective is reflected in the concept of just reward for all efforts made in the creation of artistic and scientific works and the knowledge, skills and funds that contribute to new inventions and investments.

The utilist perspective, on the other hand, emphasises the effects of the codification and allocation of rights. In a human rights discourse the focus is on the promotion of welfare for all and the contribution to a democratic society, whereas intellectual property rights are considered as economic tools that may serve as an incentive to further create, invent or invest, and thereby contribute to the public interest.

In intellectual property rights these values have been internalised, as the legislation recognises limitations and exceptions to the allocation and exercise of intellectual property rights. From the start in the nineteenth century codification of intellectual property rights in international law, a distinction is made between the rights pertaining to the fruits of creativity in the Berne Convention and the results of industry in the Paris Convention. These Conventions provide the core content of obligations in the TRIPS Agreement, regulating the Trade-Related Aspects of Intellectual Property Rights.[2]

The Berne Convention reserves protection for creative works from the moment they have come into existence, but leaves the ideas on which they are based freely available. This protection is only allocated for a restricted period of time, and provides for exceptions and limitations in national legislation to permit certain uses of protected works which have already been lawfully made available to the public without permission of the right holder. Also, the moral rights of the author are given protection, although it remains the prerogative of the national state to choose to grant this protection (Article 6bis).

The Paris Convention concerns the protection of industrial rights, and provides intellectual property rights to patents, utility models, industrial designs, trademarks, service marks, trade names, indications of source or appellations of origin, as well as the obligation for the countries of the Union to secure effective protection against unfair competition and dishonest trade practices (Article 1; Article 10bis). After a procedure of filing and registration, the duration of protection of intellectual property rights and therefore the

---

[2] The TRIPS Agreement 1994 refers in Article 1.3 to the nature and scope of the obligations, that the Members of the WTO shall accord the treatment provided for in the 1886 Berne Convention for the Protection of Literary and Artistic Works, last revision 1971; the 1883 Paris Convention for the Protection of Industrial Property, last revision Stockholm 1967; as also the International Convention for the Protection of Performers, Producers of Phonograms and Broadcasting Organisations, the Rome Convention of 1961 and the Treaty on Intellectual Property in Respect of Integrated Circuits signed in Washington in 1989.

exclusivity of the exploitation of the commercial exploitation of the objects of these rights is limited. In recognition of his personal contribution, the inventor has the right to be mentioned as such in the patent (Article 4ter). Importantly, the Paris Convention allows for compulsory licenses for patents to prevent the abuse of exercise of patent rights (Article 5.A.2). Also, a country may deny the registration of a trademark or have it invalidated when it can be considered to be contrary to morality or public order (Article 6 quinquis B.3).

Human rights are instrumental in providing external limitations to the exercise of intellectual property rights. International law on human rights as codified in the UN Universal Declaration on Human Rights[3] stakes out a protected sphere, in which fundamental rights and freedoms are not to be violated. Further enshrined in the International Covenant on Civil and Political Rights (ICCPR) and the International Covenant of Social, Economic and Cultural Rights (ICSECR),[4] human rights contain the obligation of national states to respect, protect and fulfil the right to participation in cultural life, to benefit from scientific progress and to benefit from the moral and material interests in a work of which he is the author (UDHR Article 27; ICCPR Article 27; ICESCR Article 15). Many understand this to be a right to the protection of intellectual property, although there is debate on whether this human right to the protection of intellectual property is identical to today's intellectual property right as protected under the TRIPS regime.[5] While the focus of human rights is on the protection of individual rights, the 2007 UN Declaration on the Rights of Indigenous Peoples proclaims that indigenous peoples have the right, as individuals as well as a collective, to the full enjoyment of human rights in international human rights law (Article 1).[6]

Contributing to the realisation of these human rights and relevant to the exercise and enforcement of intellectual property rights are instruments like the Convention on Biological diversity,[7] the ILO Convention No. 169 concerning Indigenous and Tribal Peoples in Independent Countries[8] and in normative instruments by other UN specialised agencies like UNESCO in the Convention on the Protection of Intangible Heritage of 2003[9] and the

---

3 United Nations Declaration on Human Rights 1948.

4 Both Conventions were adopted in 1966, and entered into force 1976.

5 See also the contribution by Brinkhof, J. 'On Patents and Human Rights' (Chapter 9 of this volume).

6 UN Doc. A /61/ L.67. The Declaration was adopted by the UN General Assembly in September 2007.

7 The Convention on Biological Diversity was adopted in 1992, entered into force 1993.

8 The International Labour Organisation adopted this Convention in 1989, entered into force 1991.

9 Adopted in 2003, entered into force 2006.

Convention on the Protection and Promotion of the Diversity of Cultural Expressions of 2005.[10]

In the first of the following three chapters, Charlotte Waelde and Abby Brown report a recent expert's discussion on a fictitious copyright case, in which the University, as copyright holder, refuses publication of a study on historical facts, and thereby acts against the wishes of the author to publish his text and the public interest in the access to this new information. In search of the outcome that would best serve the public interest, Waelde and Brown first discuss the potential of the internal limitations to the exercise of the copyright of the University. Next, the external limitations by the exercise of freedom of expression, and also the balance with the right to the protection of the property rights, are evaluated. Emphasis is given to the potential role of auxiliary instruments of competition law and contract law, and their influence on the exercise of intellectual property rights.

The next chapter by Geertrui Van Overwalle concentrates on patent law as a tool to foster both private and public interests, by stimulating economic expansion and technological progress. The paper postulates a normative claim in patent law, as it seeks to make a reassessment of the notion of public interest. This deconstruction leads to 'a mosaic encompassing ordre public, morality, public security, protection of the consumer, health safety, protection of public health, and the protection of the lives of persons, animals and plants'.

Van Overwalle sees human rights reflected in public interest considerations on human dignity and the right to food that are limiting the existence of patent rights. At the same time human rights are reflected in the right to informed consent and the right to protection and remuneration to holders of traditional knowledge that burden the existence of human rights. As for the exercise of patent rights, the right of access to public health, to education and research, and to information call for a full account of human rights considerations.

The following chapter by Charles McManis also emphasises the common moral foundation of intellectual property rights and human rights. His paper presents an emerging human right of individual holders of traditional knowledge and/or genetic resources to give consent and receive equitable remuneration for the use of such knowledge and resources by others as well as a proposal on how this right could be accommodated in existing legal regimes. This analysis leads to the conclusion that the existing intellectual property regimes should be adapted and the TRIPS Agreement should be modified to include the requirement of a disclosure of origin and evidence of prior informed consent to use information that is obtained from holders of traditional knowledge and/or genetic resources.

---

10 Adopted in 2005, entered into force 2007.

In these chapters we may detect three main ideas. The first is that we should realise that shared values of human dignity and legal certainty are underpinning both human rights and intellectual property rights. The second is the importance of human rights provisions in their role as a limitation to the exercise of intellectual property rights. And third is that intellectual property rights should adapt to the steady development of an increasing body of international public law that enables both individuals and communities to protect their interests against appropriation and misuse of knowledge and information triggered by economic interests of intellectual property rights holders.

Copyright law and patent law: to its enforcement – differing views

11. A practical analysis of the human rights paradox in intellectual property law: Russian Roulette[1]

Charlotte Waelde* and Abbe E.L. Brown**

1. INTRODUCTION[2]

Exploration of the relationship between intellectual property ('IP') and human rights which were at least once strange bedfellows[3] has been steadily increasing in both academic and activist fields. The CIER Utrecht event 'The Human Rights Paradox in Intellectual Property Law' is a welcome contribution to this debate. However, to the same extent that the relationship between IP and human rights is relevant to addressing legal and practical problems, so is consideration of the interaction of these fields with still others, most notably competition and contract law.

The purpose of this chapter is to:

- describe a research project at the AHRC (Arts and Humanities Research Council) Research Centre for Studies in Intellectual Property and Technology Law at the University of Edinburgh ('the Centre') examining

[1] This chapter is based on a paper delivered at the conference 'The Human Rights Paradox in Intellectual Property' held at the University of Utrecht, the Netherlands, 3 and 4 July 2006. The authors are grateful to all organisers and participants.

* Professor, School of Law, University of Edinburgh and Co-Director AHRC Research Centre for Studies in Intellectual Property and Technology Law.

** Lecturer, School of Law, University of Edinburgh and Associate, AHRC Research Centre for Studies in Intellectual Property and Technology Law.

[2] As is apparent from the body of the text, this chapter draws heavily from the meetings of the Intellectual Property, Competition and Human Rights Network of the Centre. The authors are most grateful to all participants and members for their significant and valuable contributions and involvement. Errors in this chapter are, of course, the responsibility of the authors.

[3] Helfer, Laurence R. (2003), 'Human Rights and Intellectual Property: Conflict or Coexistence?' *Minnesota Journal of Law, Science & Technology*, Vol. 5, p. 47.

the interfaces between Intellectual Property, Competition and Human Rights ('the Project');
- report on an expert meeting of network members of the Project that took place in Edinburgh on 23–24 March 2006;
- consider the extent to which human rights law might be used to achieve agreed outcomes in relation to a specific set of facts in which copyright law plays a prominent role; and
- analyse the extent to which competition law, or other doctrines, might be used to further achieve the desired goals together with, or instead of, human rights.

The Centre was funded by the AHRC in 2002 to build upon and expand work underway in the domains of IP, information technology and medical law as they touch upon technology in its widest sense. One of the anchor projects of the first phase of the Centre's work[4] was Intellectual Property, Cultural Heritage and the Public Domain, of which the Project forms part. The aims of the Project are as follows:

> . . . to investigate and develop the increasing international debate as to the role played by intellectual property rights, and whether the power now exercised by right owners is inconsistent with encouragement of innovation and diffusion and furthering of knowledge. Key aspects of the work are considering the impact of intellectual property rights in jurisdictions in the developed world and considering the negotiation and history of the TRIPS agreement, potential opportunities for application of TRIPS and the reaction of the developed world to this, and the impact of this for the developing world and international trade.
>
> The project also reviews the role played to date by competition law, in particular the use of compulsory licences and misuse of market power legislation in fettering the power of right owners; the extent to which such use of such principles is consistent with the fundamentals tenets of competition law; and other means for potential use of competition principles in this field, both nationally and through international bodies.
>
> In addition, the project is reviewing the relevance of normative human rights instruments in this field, and the extent to which a legal regime could be created where relevant human rights, particularly the right to property, the right to life and freedom of expression can be further used to create appropriate limits on the impact of intellectual property rights.
>
> The final aspect of the project is to consider the extent to which there is the need and potential for cohesion between the above principles, and for a new international regime to be created which allows appropriate incentives to create, innovate and develop, while also encouraging wider development and international trade.

---

[4] We are delighted that the AHRC Centre has been awarded second phase funding for five years from April 2007. Key project themes will be Openness and Secrecy; Regulation and Trust.

The Project proceeded apace.[5] In 2004 a meeting took place, to which experts from the fields of IP, human rights and competition were invited, to examine and analyse overlaps and interfaces between the three domains – both in theory and in relation to a set of practical scenarios. The stimulating dialogue resulted in publication of an edited note of the meeting,[6] and a set of papers published in SCRIPT-ed (the Centre's on-line journal) in December 2005.[7]

Network members agreed that the discussion was well worth continuing. A second, closed, expert meeting took place in Edinburgh in March 2006. This had the specific remit of discussing a set of fictional case studies with a view to exploring the possibility of bringing together thinking within the three domains, to reach mutually acceptable solutions to scenarios raising a variety of issues. This meeting was again agreed to be highly successful, with the case studies enabling complex, novel and evolving issues to be considered from new and challenging perspectives. A lightly edited note of these discussions and the text of the case studies are available on the project blog, where the work is the subject of wider comment and debate.[8]

The following discussion sets out and analyses just one of the case studies explored at the meeting.[9] The facts bring to the fore the interfaces between copyright, human rights and also competition in the publishing and education fields – consistent with the communication and culture themes of the CIER Utrecht conference. The chapter concludes with an assessment of the future impact of the relationship between copyright and human rights and the place for further work.

2. THE CASE STUDY

2.1 The Facts: Russian Roulette

- An academic in Russia writes, in both Russian and in English, an alternative narrative on the assassination of the last Tsar and his family ('the work'). The work suggests that not only did many of the family escape,

---

5 See also the project webpage: http://www.law.ed.ac.uk/ahrb/research/view.asp?ref=3 and the Project blog 'ipedinburgh' http://ipedinburgh.blogspot.com/.

6 http://www.law.ed.ac.uk/ahrb/publications/online/ipcomphrnote.doc.

7 http://www.law.ed.ac.uk/ahrb/script-ed/issue2-4.asp.

8 http://ipedinburgh.blogspot.com/ – post of 25 September 2006.

9 Minor stylistic amendments have been made to the text of the case study; the name of the offending fictional website has also been changed to 'freeducation.edu.uk' from 'freeducation.edu'. It must be reiterated that the case study is entirely fictitious and no comment is made in respect of any institution, company or individual apparently identified.

as has been suggested, but that they reached agreement with the Bolsheviks and continued, from a safe house in Vladivostock, to exert influence over Russia until the late 1920s.

- Although a substantial piece of political history, the work attracts much international media attention; this, more than the work itself, provokes the ire of the Russian government.
- Undeterred, the academic puts the work on the internet – from which it is promptly removed by the Russian government. All hard copies of the work are also seized. The academic manages to send a further copy to colleagues at Oxford University, and it is published on their website. In return, Oxford University demands assignment of copyright.
- The work is extremely popular amongst students and becomes a standard text. Russia complains to the UK government.
- The UK civil servant contacted isn't quite sure what can be done but calls the master of his old college and asks them to take down the work. This is done.
- In outrage, students contact the author who sends them further copies which they put on 'freeinformation.edu.uk'. The University threatens an action for copyright infringement.

2.2 The Format

At the Edinburgh 2006 meeting, participants were split into three groups to consider the case studies from one of an IP, competition or human rights perspective; then groups considered collectively how the problem might be solved: first seeking to identify what the public interest(s) dictate(s) should be the outcome of the problem, and then assessing whether a combination of IP, competition and human rights law could deliver that outcome. Discussions throughout the meeting covered the legal and political position in jurisdictions from developed and developing regions. However, given the facts in this case study, the focus here was on an adversarial scenario, pursued using the law and jurisdictions of the UK and Europe.

Given the importance of the work, the network members agreed that it should be published online in return for some form of payment There was, however, less consensus as to whom the payment should be made to – whether the University as (apparent) copyright owner,[10] or to the author. This chapter will now review and develop a number of the means identified at the expert meeting for achieving these goals.

---

10 See contractual arguments below.

Strategy 1 Attack the Contract

Introduction

The author could challenge his assignment of copyright to the University. If this could be set aside on the basis of being voidable, the copyright would return to the author. The author could then agree to the work being published online under licence. Alternatively, it could be argued that the assignment was unenforceable. If this was so, and the author simply published the work, the University would be unable to rely on the assignment to found a copyright infringement action. Both of these approaches could be pursued proactively by seeking a declaration of unenforceability or applying for the contract to be set aside; or the enforceability of the contract could be raised as part of a defence to copyright infringement.

Setting aside contracts, on whatever basis, is a challenge. In England, however, there have been a number of cases, mostly in the music recording industry, in which assignments and licences between artists and the recording industry have been attacked. Grounds have included common law doctrines of restraint of trade, public policy and undue influence. Although the facts provided here do not narrate the terms of the assignment as between the author and the University, the following arguments might prove useful.

Restraint of trade

Schroeder Music Publishing v Macaulay[11] concerned a standard form agreement in which the artist assigned the copyright in his works to a publisher for five years (and, if the royalties exceeded £5000, for a further five year period); there was no requirement for the publisher to exploit the works. The House of Lords declared that this agreement was unenforceable as it was in restraint of trade: it was unreasonable for the artist's work to be 'sterilised' over the period, without any possibility of the artist recovering the copyright if there was no exploitation.[12]

If the Russian Roulette contract exhibits a similar one sided nature (as it may well do given that the University seems to be able to refuse permanently to publish the work) then it may be found to be in restraint of trade and unenforceable. However, this doctrine might be viewed as exceptional. In another case the appeal to restraint of trade was not successful. Panayiotou (aka George Michael) claimed that his contract with Sony Music Entertainment[13] was unenforceable on grounds of restraint of trade. The parties had a complex

---

[11] [1974] 1 WLR 1308 [1974] 3 All ER 616. See also *Elton John v James* (1983) [1991] FSR 397.

[12] Ibid at 1315.

[13] *Panayiotou and Others v Sony Music Entertainment* [1994] EMLR 229.

history, and there had been a number of changes to their contractual relationship. With both freedom of trade and freedom of contract in the public interest, the High Court refused on public policy grounds to find the agreement unenforceable, given the relationship between the parties, their respective bargaining power and the provisions of the agreement. Russian Roulette would seem closer to the first authority.

Undue influence

On the facts here, it appears that the Russian author may have been in a particularly vulnerable position, desperate to secure publication of his work. It could be argued that there had been abuse of relationship, or unconscionable conduct, rendering the contract voidable. This would resonate with the situation in *O'Sullivan and Another v Management Agency*[14] where an artist entered into various contracts with a management agency and publishing company, without receiving independent advice. The Court of Appeal held that in such circumstances, the onus was on those asserting validity to show that the agreements had been entered into with full information as to the nature of the transaction. If this could not be done (as in *O'Sullivan*) the contracts would be voidable.[15]

Here, it could be argued that 'full information' means it is for the University to show that the Russian author was aware that the work might be withdrawn from circulation with no prospect of being made available again. Admittedly this may be a difficult task, particularly given the background facts.

Public policy

Remaining with public policy, it is notable that this has been a recurrent theme in decisions of the UK courts in controversial and borderline IP cases.[16] The

---

14 [1985] QB 428 (*O'Sullivan*).

15 In *O'Sullivan* restituto in integrum was not possible. Nonetheless the Court was able to do what was just to set aside the agreements.

16 The next section is based on a paper given by Abbe Brown at the Bileta conference, Belfast, 2005: 'Guarding the guards: the practical impact of human rights on protection of innovation and creativity', available at http://www.bileta.ac.uk/Document%20Library/1/Guarding%20the%20Guards%20-%20the%20Practical%20Impact%20of%20Human%20Rights%20on%20Protection%20of%20Innovation%20And%20Creativity.pdf (last accessed 29 August 2007) ('Brown Guards'). See also Brown, A.E.L. 'Power, responsibility and norms: could and should human rights be used as a curb on intellectual property rights', www.law.ed.ac.uk/AHRB/publications/online/ipandhumanrights.doc (last accessed 29 August 2007), at 25; and MacQueen, H.L. (1995) (2nd ed) *Copyright, Competition and Industrial Design* Hume Papers on Public Policy: Vol. 3 No. 2, Edinburgh University Press, Edinburgh, 64.

seminal case was the decision of the House of Lords in *British Leyland Motor Corporation v Armstrong Patents Company Limited ('British Leyland')*[17] regarding whether spare parts for a car could be obtained from sources other than the original manufacturer. With some judicial innovation, the court developed the principle of an implied right to repair and also the concept of non derogation from grant.[18] In *Canon Kabushiki Kaisha v Green Cartridge Company (Hong Kong) Limited ('Canon')*,[19] however, faced with an attempt to apply the doctrine to printer cartridges, the Privy Council held that there was no legal basis for these concepts. It considered that the *British Leyland* decision should be seen as one of 'public policy', with limited effect outside its own facts;[20] and that it was 'constitutionally questionable'[21] for a court to declare public policy and use this as a basis to override express legislation. This move to place parameters around the potentially far reaching implications of reliance on public policy was reiterated in *Mars UK Ltd v Teknowledge Ltd* ('*Mars*').[22] Here the court held that the right to repair exception had not been retained by new relevant legislation;[23] Parliament had not chosen to deal with the alleged exception, and in these new circumstances, there was no basis for the court to support its continued existence.[24] The court then went to on state that if the concept did, in fact, exist, then it was to be interpreted in line with (somewhat ironically) public policy grounds; it should be applied only when 'the court [was] reasonably certain that no-right thinking member of society would quarrel with the result'.[25]

These cases suggest that there is a place (albeit a very limited one) for public policy approaches in legislation and common law based arguments in the IP field. In Russian Roulette, it could be argued that it would be contrary to public policy to enforce the assignment where the University declined to publish the work or to give consent to others to do so.

The impact of the UK Human Rights Act 1998 ('HRA')

These common law doctrines (created and developed without specific reference

---

[17] [1986] RPC 279.

[18] The case concerned the interface between industrial designs and copyright before the Copyright Designs and Patents Act 1988 ('CDPA'). See *British Leyland* at 361, 374, 376.

[19] [1997] FSR 817.

[20] With the facts in the printer case not warranting its application.

[21] See *Canon* at 824.

[22] [2000] ECDR 99.

[23] Section 171(3) CDPA – considered in detail below.

[24] See *Mars* at 105–7.

[25] Ibid, 108. See also Llewellyn, G. (1999), 'Does Copyright Law Recognise a Right to Repair', *European Intellectual Property Review* 21(11), 596–9.

to human rights law) provide the first opportunity in this chapter to explore the impact of the HRA in court actions in the UK jurisdictions.

Human rights per se are not new to these jurisdictions. For many years there were principles of rather vague, but fundamental, common law rights, which could be overridden by express legislative wording. Since 1953, the UK has been a signatory to the European Convention on Human Rights (ECHR). However, the UK did not incorporate the ECHR into UK law and as such the ECHR could not be relied upon directly in the courts of the UK. Reference could be made to the ECHR (and all other unincorporated treaties) when interpreting ambiguous legislation or applying common law principles; and when considering the ECHR, English courts saw it as dynamic and evolving, reflecting society.[26] In all such cases, it was assumed that the UK Parliament had not intended to legislate inconsistently with its international obligations, although this could be overridden by clear legislative wording.[27]

Despite much rhetoric,[28] the HRA still did not wholly incorporate the ECHR[29] into the laws of the UK. However, s. 3 HRA imposes interpretative obligations on courts for legislation to be read and given effect in a way compatible with Convention rights,[30] so far as it is possible to do so;[31] and

---

[26] *Tyrer v UK* (A/26) (1979–80) 2 EHRR 1, para 31.

[27] For an overview of these matters, see Clayton, R. and H. Tomlinson (2000), *The Law of Human Rights* (Oxford: Oxford University Press) ('Clayton/Tomlinson'), at 25–31, 36–8, 72–4, 75 (commenting on *Garland v British Rail* [1983] 2 AC 751) 89, 99–102, and Jayawickrama, N. (2002) *The Judicial Application of Human Rights Law. National, Regional and International Jurisprudence* (Cambridge: Cambridge University Press) ('Jayawickrama'), 61, 84–5, 96–7, 99–102, 109–10. See also *Malone v Metropolitan Police Commissioner (no. 2)* [1979] Ch 344.

[28] For example, UK White Paper 'Bringing Rights Home', see http://www.archive.official-documents.co.uk/document/hoffice/rights/intro.htm (last accessed 29 August 2007).

[29] For background overview see Jayawickrama, 109–111. For early analysis see Hooper. A. (1998), 'The impact of the Human Rights Act on judicial decision-making' E.H.R.L.R. 6, 676–86 and Lord Cooke of Thorndon (1999), 'The British embracement of human rights' E.H.R.L.R. 3, 243–60.

[30] Most, but not all, of the ECHR rights. See s. 1(1) and Sch. 1 HRA, listing Articles 2–12 and 14, Articles 1–3 of the First Protocol and Articles 1 and 2 of the Sixth Protocol, all as read with Articles 14–16.

[31] Section 3 HRA: (1) So far as it is possible to do so, primary legislation and subordinate legislation must be read and given effect in a way which is compatible with the Convention rights. (2) This section (a) applies to primary legislation and subordinate legislation whenever enacted; (b) does not affect the validity, continuing operation or enforcement of any incompatible primary legislation; and (c) does not affect the validity, continuing operation or enforcement of any incompatible subordinate legislation if (disregarding any possibility of revocation) primary legislation prevents removal of the incompatibility.

s. 6 HRA makes it unlawful for courts as public authorities to act in a way incompatible with Convention rights when, essentially, an alternative course exists.[32] The s. 6 HRA obligation would also cover common law based arguments. Further, the obligations conferred on courts by s. 6 HRA, together with an open and increasingly unquestioning approach from the courts to consideration of human rights,[33] has meant that fears, at least of some, that the HRA could not impact upon disputes between private parties have proved unfounded.[34]

The HRA also provides that courts must also take into account decisions of the European Court of Human Rights (ECtHR) in interpreting Convention rights.[35] This could also result in greater effect being given to decisions of other human rights bodies and of courts in other jurisdictions, often consulted by the ECtHR.[36] UK courts are not, however, obliged to follow these decisions. Commentators have argued that since the HRA, courts are more open to human rights approaches and authorities from elsewhere, and as such greater

---

[32] Section 6 HRA: (1) It is unlawful for a public authority to act in a way which is incompatible with a Convention right. (2) Subsection (1) does not apply to an act if (a) as the result of one or more provisions of primary legislation, the authority could not have acted differently; or (b) in the case of one or more provisions of, or made under, primary legislation which cannot be read or given effect in a way which is compatible with the Convention rights, the authority was acting so as to give effect to or enforce those provisions. (3) In this section 'public authority' includes (a) a court or tribunal, and (b) any person certain of whose functions are functions of a public nature, but does not include either House of Parliament or a person exercising functions in connection with proceedings in Parliament. (4) In subsection (3) 'Parliament' does not include the House of Lords in its judicial capacity. (5) In relation to a particular act, a person is not a public authority by virtue only of subsection (3)(b) if the nature of the act is private. (6) 'An act' includes a failure to act but does not include a failure to (a) introduce in, or lay before, Parliament a proposal for legislation; or (b) make any primary legislation or remedial order.

[33] See, for example, *Ashdown v Telegraph Group Ltd* [2001] EWCA Civ 1142 [2002] Ch 149 ('*Ashdown*'), *Campbell v Mirror Group Newspapers Ltd* [2004] UKHL 22 [2004] 2 AC 457 ('*Campbell*') *HRH Prince of Wales v Associated Newspapers Ltd* [2006] EWCA Civ 1776 [2007] 3 WLR 222.

[34] See, for example, Phillipson, G. (1999), 'The Human Rights Act, "horizontal effect" and the common law: a bang or a whimper?' *M.L.R.* 62(6), 824–49 and Mead, D. (2003), 'Swallowing the camel, straining at the gnat: the implications of *Mendoza v Ghaidan*', *E.H.R.L.R.* 5, 501–14.

[35] Section 2(1) HRA: a court or tribunal determining a question which has arisen in connection with a Convention right must take into account any (a) judgment, decision, declaration or advisory opinion of the European Court of Human Rights.

[36] Examples of ECtHR references to comparative systems at http://www.echr.coe.int/ECHR/EN/Header/Case-Law/Case-law+information/Selective+comparative+law+case+list/ (last accessed 29 August 2007).

regard will be had to these sources.[37] But these sources are already being consulted, albeit with caution,[38] and it may be that this practice will continue.

With Russian Roulette, it would seem that s. 6 HRA does provide a basis for human rights arguments to be explored in respect of the contract. It is unlikely, however, that they would make a significant contribution: essential concepts in restraint of trade and undue influence are public policy, public interest and unconscionable conduct. These suggest that the question of fairness, broadly speaking, lies at the heart of the doctrines, in creating those limited circumstances in which it would be appropriate for courts to interfere with contractual certainty. Although resonant of human rights theory, such general concepts are not in fact listed in the Convention rights.

There is also no Convention right to work and its benefits, which may have been relevant to the restraint of trade argument. The right to work is included in the European Social Charter ('ESC'),[39] which the UK has signed but not incorporated. The right to work could therefore form part of an argument based on using unincorporated treaties to inform and interpret common law.[40] Freedom of expression, and the corollary of access to information, are, however, Convention rights.[41] It could be argued that the right of the author to

---

[37] Note that there is no need for an ambiguity before human rights can enter this arena. This has led to much debate and concern that the HRA could enable and require courts to engage in what could be seen as judicial activism, subverting the will of Parliament in respect of legislation and introduce new approaches to authority and analysis (see, for example, Gearty, C. (2004), *Principles of Human Rights Adjudication* (Oxford: Oxford University Press) ('Gearty') at 22–3, 42–8, 179–180 and 196; Lord Irvine of Lairg (1999), 'Activism and restraint: human rights and the interpretative process', *E.H.R.L.R.* 4, 350–72, Gearty, C. (2002), 'Reconciling Parliamentary democracy and human rights', *L.Q.R.* 118(Apr), 248–69, Phillipson, G. (2003) '(Mis)-reading section 3 of the Human Rights Act', *L.Q.R.* 119(Apr), 183–8, Gearty, C. (2003), 'Revisiting section 3(1) of the Human Rights Act', *L.Q.R.* 119(Oct), 551–3 and Debeljak , J. (2003), 'The Human Rights Act 1998 (UK): The Preservation of Parliamentary Supremacy in the Context of Rights Protection', 9 *Australian Journal for Human Rights* 183–235.

[38] Clayton/Tomlinson 7–8, 12 (see in particular use made of sources in *R v D.P.P. ex p Kebilene* [1999] 3 WLR 972 and *Reynolds v Times Newspaper*s [2001] 2 AC 127). Note also *Murray v Express Newspapers Plc* [2007] EWHC 1908 (Ch) in the field of privacy, holding that a decision of the House of Lords must be followed, notwithstanding a potentially inconsistent decision of the ECtHR.

[39] http://www.coe.int/T/E/Human_Rights/Esc/ (last accessed 29 August 2007). See Article 1.

[40] See above, p. 190.

[41] Article 10 ECHR: (1) Everyone has the right to freedom of expression. This right shall include freedom to hold opinions and to receive and impart information and ideas without interference by public authority and regardless of frontiers. This article shall not prevent States from requiring the licensing of broadcasting, television or

express himself, and the right of others, particularly students, to access the work, should inform public policy. However, the limits on Article 10 ECHR include restrictions as prescribed by law as necessary in a democratic society for the protection of the rights of others. These would include contract. The additional force of the human rights aspect of the argument must therefore be questionable.

As noted above, it has been argued that increased human rights litigation since the HRA has sensitised the courts to broader, less restricted approaches to legislation and common law based on human rights.[42] However, once the HRA/ECHR door has been opened in the IP field, it may prove difficult to close. It should be borne in mind that not all human rights arguments would favour publication and the attack of the contract. Article 1 Protocol 1 ECHR provides a right to the enjoyment of possessions, albeit subject to greater limitations than the other ECHR rights.[43] In *Anheuser-Busch, Inc. v Portugal*[44] the ECtHR confirmed that industrial property rights are 'possessions' within Article 1 Protocol 1. Further, the ECtHR has considered cases involving human rights of companies.[45] Human rights arguments could likely be advanced, therefore, by the University to protect their own rights to property as copyright owners. On the facts here, the argument is unlikely to be determinative in favour of the University; yet it does confirm that the HRA will not be a straightforward panacea.

Further support for arguments in respect of unenforceability and voidability could be based on the human rights of the Russian author. Article 15(1)(c) International Covenant on Economic Social and Cultural Rights ('ICESCR') 1966 to which the UK is a party, recognises the right of the author to benefit from the moral and material interests resulting from their work.[46] Similar

---

cinema enterprises. (2) The exercise of these freedoms, since it carries with it duties and responsibilities, may be subject to such formalities, conditions, restrictions or penalties as are prescribed by law and are necessary in a democratic society, in the interests of national security, territorial integrity or public safety, for the prevention of disorder or crime, for the protection of health or morals, for the protection of the reputation or the rights of others, for preventing the disclosure of information received in confidence, or for maintaining the authority and impartiality of the judiciary.

42 See Gearty, 81–3, 179–85, 197–202.

43 Every natural or legal person is entitled to the peaceful enjoyment of his possessions. No one shall be deprived of his possessions except in the public interest and subject to the conditions provided for by law and by the general principles of international law. See consideration in *Sporrong and Lonnroth v Sweden* (1982) 5 EHRR 35.

44 [2007] ETMR 24.

45 For example in the field of commercial expression *Markt Intern Verlag GmbH v Germany* (A/164) (1990) 12 EHRR 161.

46 The relevant text of Article 15 ICESCR provides '(1) The States Parties to the present Covenant recognize the right of everyone: (c) To benefit from the protection of

rights[47] were included in the 1948 Universal Declaration of Human Rights.[48] The University's preventing the work from being published could mean that the Russian author cannot benefit from the moral interests resulting from the work in terms of prestige and reputation. The court could have regard to this on the basis of an obligation under an unincorporated treaty to which the UK is a signatory,[49] in particular one to which the ECtHR has had regard in interpreting the ECHR.[50]

Summary

There may be room to challenge the assignment on the basis of restraint of trade and/or undue influence.[51] It does not appear that the University entered into any further licences or assignments in respect of the copyright; therefore, no questions of third party rights arise.[52]

---

the moral and material interests resulting from any scientific, literary or artistic production of which he is the author'.

[47] Article 27(2) Universal Declaration on Human Rights ('UDHR') 'Everyone has the right to the protection of the moral and material interests resulting from any scientific, literary or artistic production of which he is the author'.

[48] These provisions have been the cornerstone of the growing debate on IP as a human right. This argument is controversial, and has been challenged firstly for diluting the proper status to be accorded to human rights, and secondly for potentially providing a response for IP owners to human rights based arguments for those challenging IP and its exercise. See Chapman, A.R. (2001), 'Approaching intellectual property as a human right: obligations related to Article 15(1)(c)', *Copyright Bulletin*, vol. XXXV, No. 3, July–September 2001, UNESCO Publishing, http://unesdoc.unesco.org/images/0012/001255/125505e.pdf (last accessed 29 August 2007); Drahos, P. (1999), 'Intellectual property and human rights', *I.P.Q.* 3, 349–71; and Ricketson, S. (2002), 'Intellectual Property and Human Rights', 187–213 in S. Bottomley and D. Kinley (eds) (2002), '*Commercial Law and Human Rights*' (Hampshire, England and Virginia, USA: Ashgate Publishing, Dartmouth Publishing Company). See also consideration by Abbe Brown in Brown, A.E.L. (2005), 'Socially responsible intellectual property: a solution?', 2:4 *SCRIPT-ed* 485 @: http://www.law.ed.ac.uk/ahrc/script-ed/vol2-4/csr.asp ('Brown Responsible') and (2006) 'Human rights: in the real world', *Journal of Intellectual Property Law & Practice* Vol. 1, Issue 9, 603–13 ('Brown').

[49] See above, p. 190 and see also *Experience Hendrix LLC v Purple Haze Records Ltd* 2007 WL 1484095, paras 6–9, 27–33, 34–6, 60–2.

[50] It has also been argued (see Nwauche, E.S. (2005), 'Human Rights – Relevant Considerations in respect of IP and Competition Law', 2:4 *SCRIPT-ed* 467 @: http://www.law.ed.ac.uk/ahrc/script-ed/vol2-4/enyinna.asp) that, in the context of claims based on constitutional rights in South Africa, international human rights should properly form part of the public policy considerations weighed by courts when considering the validity of a contract.

[51] Note that the doctrines of restraint of trade and undue influence may be subject to acquiescence *Zang Tumb Tuum Records Ltd v Johnson* [1993] EMLR 61, but given the time frame here this would not seem relevant.

[52] See for example the discussion in *O'Sullivan* above.

If the contract is unenforceable on the basis of restraint of trade (possibly, although unlikely, augmented by human rights arguments), the University would be unable to rely on the assignment to object to publication by the author, the students, or anyone else. If the assignment is instead found to be voidable on the basis of undue influence, then the copyright will revert to the author. As noted above, this is only of practical value if the Russian author would then grant the students a licence to publish. The author may not, of course, choose to do so – particularly if he has now been the subject of domestic political pressure.

Accordingly, contractual arguments cannot be relied upon to deliver the solution. Even if they could, is it sensible for the author to take the initiative, and incur the risk, in raising court proceedings? It may be more sensible for students to publish the work again, and try to raise the issues considered as defences.[53] But in any event, this analysis suggests that a comparatively simple and effective solution to the problem might exist – and be a solution which does not depend on IP or, directly, on human rights.

Strategy 2 Publish and . . .?

Introduction

If the aim is for the work to be published, perhaps this should simply be done, irrespective of possible clashes with copyright: but by whom? The facts suggest that the 'students' publish the work on 'freeinformation.edu.uk'. However, the Russian author appears to be alive and in contact with the students. Would it be preferable, if he wishes to do so, for the Russian author himself to place the work on the website?

If the author publishes and is sued for copyright infringement, he could again consider advancing human rights arguments based on 'authorship', drawing to some extent from the ICESCR. However, as the HRA does not enable the arguments to be pursued in a vacuum,[54] a context is needed: an exception or defence to copyright infringement, pursuant to which Convention rights (in particular Article 10 ECHR), and thus the ICESCR rights, may be considered. Possibilities are the Copyright Designs and Patents Act 1988

---

[53] If human rights arguments were considered to have force, either the author or the students as affected victims would also be entitled to complain about this conduct in a separate action (s. 7(1)(b) HRA and Article 34 ECHR); see also s. 8 HRA re possible remedies if there is a finding of unlawful conduct in that separate action. It has been considered unlikely that this potential for victims to complain will lead to development of a new set of case law outside established causes of action: see Gearty at 80–1, 161–4 and 178–9.

[54] Although see above at p. 190 regarding residual possibilities based on common law and unincorporated treaties.

(CDPA) 'internal' fair dealing provisions which provide a defence to an action of infringement in certain circumstances[55] and/or the CDPA 'external' public interest provision.[56]

But in any event, the impact will be limited. There is an argument that copyright can satisfy the rights conferred by Article 15(1)(c) ICESCR: copyright confers on the author the right to control reproduction of the work and to recover royalties from this. Accordingly, the fact that the Russian author here chose (subject to the arguments above) to assign that copyright and is now unhappy with the outcome might not be attractive to the court.

Further, if the author publishes work on the internet from Russia, then the author would not be carrying out a potentially infringing act in the UK.[57] Although this may remove the Russian author from the threat of a UK court action, this does not in itself achieve the desired outcome of the work being published: if the work is downloaded in the UK there still may be infringing acts there by students; and this could lead directly or indirectly to orders for the material to be removed from the website by the operators of freeducation.edu.uk, likely based in the UK or their (again, likely UK based) service providers.[58]

Accordingly, if the work is published notwithstanding the assignment and the position of the University, arguments based on the CDPA and freedom of

---

[55] For the purposes of this discussion the provisions relating to reporting current events and criticism and review are relevant. The text is as follows: CDPA s. 30 (1): Fair dealing with a work for the purpose of criticism or review, of that or another work or of a performance of a work, does not infringe any copyright in the work provided that it is accompanied by a sufficient acknowledgement and provided that the work has been made available to the public. (1A) For the purposes of subsection (1) a work has been made available to the public if it has been made available by any means, including (a) the issue of copies to the public; (b) making the work available by means of an electronic retrieval system; (c) the rental or lending of copies of the work to the public; (d) the performance, exhibition, playing or showing of the work in public; (e) the communication to the public of the work, but in determining generally for the purposes of that subsection whether a work has been made available to the public no account shall be taken of any unauthorised act. (2) Fair dealing with a work (other than a photograph) for the purpose of reporting current events does not infringe any copyright in the work provided that (subject to subsection (3)) it is accompanied by a sufficient acknowledgement. (3) No acknowledgement is required in connection with the reporting of current events by means of a sound recording, film or broadcast where this would be impossible for reasons of practicality or otherwise.

[56] Section 171(3) CDPA.

[57] Section 16 CDPA.

[58] Electronic Commerce (EC Directive) Regulations 2002 (SI 2002/2013) reg. 19. See Edwards, L. (2005), 'Articles 12–15 ECD: ISP Liability. The Problem of Intermediary Service Provider Liability' in Edwards, L. (ed), *The New Legal Framework for E-Commerce in Europe* Ch. 4, pp. 93–136.

expression/information could be advanced by either the author or the students. Additional human rights author based arguments might also be available if the author publishes such that he would be open to a UK action. However, it is unlikely that these will have significant impact on the outcome. The next section will explore the available legal arguments in the context of Russian Roulette, the CDPA and all relevant human rights.

Legal analysis

The linkages between copyright, human rights, publication and litigation between private parties have been considered in the English cases of *Ashdown v Telegraph Ltd ('Ashdown')*[59] and *HRH Prince of Wales v Associated Newspapers Ltd ('HRH')*.[60]

Ashdown kept diaries while leader of a political party. In preparation for their publication, he showed documents, protected by copyright, to publishing houses. Substantial extracts from one particular document were subsequently published in the Telegraph newspaper in November 1999. Ashdown successfully sought an injunction. Considering the matter, the Court of Appeal made a number of key observations on the intersection between freedom of expression and copyright. In the light of the HRA, the fair dealing provision of the CDPA should be applied so as to reflect the (limited) right to freedom of expression in Article 10 ECHR. Concerning the 'external' provision relating to the public interest[61] the Court of Appeal noted that:

> . . . the circumstances in which public interest may override copyright are not capable of precise categorisation or definition. Now that the HRA is in force, there is the clearest public interest in giving effect to the right of freedom of expression in those rare cases where this right trumps the rights conferred by the 1998 Act. In such circumstances, we consider that s171(3) permits the defence of public interest to be raised.

The Court of Appeal considered the law of copyright already reflected freedom of expression, in that protection is limited to the expression of a work and not the ideas embodied within it.[62] However, in 'rare cases' in which the public interest in giving effect to the right of freedom of information should prevail over rights conferred by the CDPA (including its more specific exceptions), the

---

59 See above, p. 191. While the facts arose prior to the coming into force of the HRA, the court nonetheless tackled the intersection between two.

60 High Court [2006] EWHC 522 ('*HRH High Court*'); Court of Appeal [2006] EWCA Civ 1776 [2007] 3 WLR 222 ('*HRH Court of Appeal*').

61 CDPA s. 171(3): Nothing in this Part affects any rule of law preventing or restricting the enforcement of copyright, on grounds of public interest or otherwise.

62 *Ashdown* para 39.

court must apply the CDPA in a manner that accommodates freedom of expression[63] – but again only so far as it is able.[64] A need for reproduction of the precise text of a document, as in *Ashdown*, would be such a rare case; and the public interest preserved by s. 171(3) CDPA could provide a vehicle to enable the CDPA to accommodate and deliver free expression.

Without this vehicle, however, there would be no basis for this to occur, irrespective of other considerations.[65] The s. 171(3) CDPA 'vehicle' could in fact be termed a gateway: the public interest provision[66] expressly preserving any existing possibilities is, through the HRA, turned into a means for delivering priority to human rights, with the public interest provision itself remaining unchanged for application to new scenarios.

However, in a rare case, how is free expression to be delivered once the vehicle has been identified? The Court of Appeal in *Ashdown* considered that free expression could be accommodated by refusing an injunction, rather than there being a finding of non infringement.[67] This would enable rights of the copyright owner to be acknowledged by an award of damages as '[f]reedom of expression should not normally carry with it the right to make free use of another's work'.[68] Damages would not be awarded, however, if they could have a 'chilling effect' on free speech.[69] Here, however, this concern is irrelevant, given the level of interest in the work – and thus the potential for some funds to be raised – and the view that some payment should indeed be made.

The creative approach to remedies in *Ashdown* is a significant shift in judicial thinking since the HRA. Freedom of expression will not necessarily prevail over the interests of the copyright owner – but the focus is now to accord appropriate weight to freedom of expression, and how to deliver and

---

63 Ibid, para 45.

64 This point later being made clearly in *Levi Strauss & Co. v Tesco Stores Ltd* [2003] RPC 18, para 44. See also Brown.

65 For further analysis of *Ashdown* see Johnson, P. (2005), 'The public interest: is it still a defence to copyright infringement?' *Ent. L. R.* 16(1), 1–6; Griffiths, J. (2002), 'Copyright law after Ashdown – time to deal fairly with the public', *I.P.Q.* 3, 240–64; Birnhack, M.D. (2003), 'Acknowledging the conflict between copyright and freedom of expression under the Human Rights Act', *Ent. L.R.* 14(2), 24–34; and also Brown.

66 For detailed analysis and history see Sims, A. (2006), 'The public interest defence in copyright law: myth or reality?' *E.I.P.R.* 28(6), 335–43 ('Sims').

67 *Ashdown* para 27 et seq (court considering, however, that this need to consider such factors did not produce a significant change in approach) and para 59. See s. 12 HRA regarding grant of injunctions when freedom of expression issues are raised, and *Cream Holdings Ltd v Banerjee* [2004] UKHL 44, [2005] 1 AC 253 and *Miss World Ltd v Channel 4 Television Corp.* 2007 WL 1292609.

68 *Ashdown* paras 46, 67–97; Regarding the public interest 'defence' in respect of damages and injunctions, see again Sims.

69 *Ashdown* paras 67–9.

accommodate it as necessary. The otherwise fundamental fact in copyright litigation – whether there is infringement – is no longer accorded pre-eminence.

The English courts' growing openness to dealing with direct confrontation between copyright and freedom of expression is seen in *HRH Prince of Wales v Telegraph (HRH High Court and Court of Appeal).*[70] Prince Charles, as heir to the throne, attends many official engagements and recorded his thoughts about these events in private journals. These journals were then photocopied and made available to a limited audience specified by Prince Charles with the originals remaining under lock and key. The *Mail on Sunday* (a national newspaper) printed extracts from these photocopies; Prince Charles raised actions for breach of confidence and copyright infringement in the High Court. An application was then made for summary judgment. Part of the claim considered breach of confidence (or privacy/misuse of personal information),[71] pursuant to Article 8 ECHR. There was also a claim in copyright, bringing freedom of expression claims in direct conflict with the copyright in the journals.

The High Court found that the journal was indeed protected by copyright, that this was owned by the Prince of Wales[72] and that there was the necessary reproduction for copyright infringement.[73] Attempted reliance on the exclusion from infringement of reporting of current events[74] was unsuccessful, as the events were not considered current[75] or the taking fair in the circumstances;[76] and arguments based on fair dealing for criticism and review were also unsuccessful as the journal had not been made available lawfully to the public – a prerequisite for the exclusion from infringement under the CDPA.[77] This was upheld in the Court of Appeal.

There was also detailed argument on the impact of human rights jurisprudence to the operation of reporting of current events provision on these facts; however, applying *Ashdown*, the court considered that the facts and conduct here were not such that the public interest in expression and information should prevail over the interests of the copyright owner. On the same basis, the court dismissed the public interest defence, considering it could add nothing to the analysis.[78]

---

[70] See references above at pp. 197 and 198.

[71] See *HRH High Court* paras 49, 88–137; *Campbell.*

[72] After an argument about the finer points of Crown copyright *HRH High Court* paras 151–4.

[73] Ibid, paras 161–2.

[74] See also *HRH Court of Appeal* considered below at p. 204.

[75] *HRH High Court*, para 168.

[76] Ibid, paras 169–74.

[77] Ibid, para 176 – otherwise the court indicated this defence might have been successful. See also the discussion below on *HRH* in the Court of Appeal.

[78] Section 171(3) CDPA. *HRH High Court* paras 179–80.

The newspaper also challenged any reliance on copyright, based on an argument by the academic commentator Barendt:[79] '[t]he use of copyright to protect personal privacy can be regarded as an abuse of the former right . . . It is surely wrong to allow a copyright action to succeed, when it acts as a surrogate for a privacy claim which would, rightly or wrongly, almost certainly fail.' The court dismissed this argument, seeing copyright as a property right, subject to relevant exceptions including any residual public interest defences; the copyright owner did not need to justify its assertion.[80]

There is an indication in *HRH*, however, that freedom of expression arguments, when raised in juxtaposition with claims to copyright, may have some broader force. Most of the time in the High Court was taken up with the Hong Kong journal – and this was the only issue under appeal in the Court of Appeal. However, the Prince was not only concerned with this journal. He also wanted seven other journals returned to him, to enable, inter alia, prevention of publication of further extracts. The fate of these other journals were the subject of only skeleton arguments in the High Court case, but Counsel for the Prince argued that as the journals were protected by copyright, it was entirely standard to ask for their return, and to expect the journals to be returned, on that basis. Counsel for the *Mail on Sunday* pointed out that in no case had a court required the return of a work on the basis that it was protected by copyright where it was possible that there was information contained in that work which was in the public interest,[81] and that the *Mail on Sunday* should retain the journals until a decision on publication had been taken. The court held that it would not order return of the journals until it knew what was in them, and

---

[79] Barendt, E. (1987) *Freedom of Speech* (2nd edn Oxford: Clarendon Press), p. 262.

[80] *HRH High Court* para 183. The matter was not fully argued in the Court of Appeal. Counsel for the Prince argued that as he (the Prince) had no intention of publishing the journal, so no commercial interest was at stake. The only point of raising the CDPA was to protect privacy. He should not be able to rely on copyright to protect privacy. 'If he was not in a position to complain of publication by the assertion of his Article 8 rights, because these gave way before the Article 10 rights of the Newspaper and the public, it could not be right that he should be able to rely upon his copyright in order to protect his privacy' (para 83). The Court of Appeal thought these arguments interesting and novel, but did not feel it necessary to consider them further because the Prince had a valid claim based on his Article 8 rights and breach of confidence (para 84). The reference, however, to the arguments being 'interesting' and 'novel' suggests that the Court, given the right circumstances, may be prepared to consider the merits. See analysis of decision in the AHRC Centre's blog 'ipedinburgh' 20 March 2006: http://ipedinburgh.blogspot.com/2006_03_01_ipedinburgh_archive.html.

[81] *HRH High Court*, para 191. The term 'public interest' was used there in the more general sense, without reference to s. 171(3) CDPA.

whether freedom of expression might support disclosure in one of the *Ashdown* rare cases. There was insufficient time to explore this at the hearing;[82] the matter was not further dealt with in the Court of Appeal.

Had the High Court preferred the copyright claim over freedom of expression, notably given that the journals were unpublished, then there should have been no hesitation in ordering the return of the journals to the Prince. The 'external' human right argument to freedom of expression, using the s. 171(3) CDPA provision as a vehicle for its existence, thus potentially has force in relation to unpublished works. The key factor will be the public interest in access to the content or indeed particular words, balanced against the interests of the copyright owner. The latter will not automatically prevail.

Freedom of expression: basic principles

What is in fact meant by 'freedom of expression'? Are all forms of expression or speech to be accorded the same protection when balanced against the more proprietorial aspects of copyright? Russian Roulette involves speech of a different nature from that considered in *HRH* and *Ashdown*. There is some consensus between courts that political speech should be accorded the most weight when considering claims of freedom of expression, with intellectual, educational and artistic, and then commercial, speech following thereon.[83]

Commentators have argued that greater weight should also be given to freedom of expression claims where there is no substitute for a work:[84] in particular for those works that make a unique contribution to public understanding and debate. The example is given of atrocities committed by US personnel during the Vietnam War.[85] Such reproduction would, on this argument, be limited to photographs of the events in question. Support for this approach can also be drawn from United States decisions enabling publication in the general interest in cases involving extreme factual scenarios, such as images of President Kennedy's assassination.[86] Other commentators have taken this further, arguing that there are certain works that have a particular association

---

82 *HRH High Court*, paras 147, 192.

83 *Campbell*, paras 19, 148. See also *Markt Intern Verlag GmbH v Germany* (1989) 12 EHRR 161; *Casado Coca v Spain* (1994) 18 EHRR 1.

84 See broader analysis of this field by Netanel, N.W. (2005),'Copyright and "Market Power" in the Marketplace of Ideas' in F. Leveque and H. Shelanski (eds), *Antitrust, Patents and Copyright. EU and US Perspectives* (Cheltenham, UK and Northampton, MA, USA: Edward Elgar Publishing) 149 et seq.

85 Nimmer on *Copyright* (2003), (US: Matthew Bender & Company), para 1197.

86 See *Time Inc. v Geis* 293 F. Supp 130 and *Rosemount Enterprise v Random House* 366 F.2d. 303 (2nd Cir 1966), considered in Brown Guards, 7.

or carry a special meaning for which it would be impossible 'to find an adequate alternative vehicle'.[87]

The concept of such special cases where freedom of expression should be accorded greater weight is resonant of the *Ashdown* rare cases. It also introduces into copyright analysis principles familiar to competition law – substitutability and the availability of an alternative source of supply. Competition questions per se, and their interaction with copyright and human rights, are considered further below. However, their presence here is an insight into, and confirmation of, the fact that essential principles of competition, copyright and human rights are closely linked, and that a holistic approach to combining the three fields merits consideration.

Application to facts

While the text in Russian Roulette might be considered political speech, on the facts it is claims for educational use that highlight the tensions between control and freedom; claims which are not, according to the proposal referred to above, as weighty as freedom of expression in respect of political discourse.

This approach suggests it is unlikely that these facts would produce a rare case of a conflict between copyright and freedom of expression, where freedom of expression should prevail. However, this would be inconsistent with the work in question being unique, innovative and much in demand, which suggests that there is no alternative means of sharing information which can make a valuable contribution to public understanding and debate. Further, given the passage of time, there are few survivors of the Russian Revolution, and records might have been destroyed. An alternative is therefore unlikely to be developed.

This approach to the question, combined with the education and limited political speech arguments available, might suggest that there was indeed a conflict between copyright and free expression, such that the *Ashdown* approach to remedies could be pursued. Accordingly, adding competition based arguments and perspectives to human rights and IP might increase the prospect of achieving the desired outcome.[88]

A more straightforward approach – just re-write it . . .

Does the whole of the text need to be published to provide access to the underlying ideas? Might this not be a work that could be as well expressed in a different form (such as the Russian author penning a new edition which he

---

[87] Spence, M. (1988), 'Intellectual Property and the Problem of Parody', 114 *LQR* 594, 611.

[88] Note that this is quite distinct from using competition law, which is considered below at pp. 205 et seq.

might then publish) rather than infringing the rights of the copyright owner? The difficulty for the author, of course, is that the dividing line between ideas and expression is hard to fathom.[89] In any 'second edition' it is likely, or inevitable, that the same author would express the same ideas, views and research in similar language in a similar structure.[90] It might be possible to rewrite the alternative narrative using different words; the question then is whether the underlying theme of the narrative is so strong that it would dwarf the language chosen. If this is so, however, it would render the idea/expression dichotomy worthless in respect of ground breaking works.

The trusted internal controls?

Could the whole of this work in fact have been published under copyright law, either looking to fair dealing defences or the public interest defence referred to above (without need for the additional arguments afforded by the HRA?).

This could not be done under current UK copyright law as interpreted by the English courts. Both the fair dealing and public interest defences considered above refer only to *parts* of a work protected by copyright, albeit that those parts are substantial in copyright terms such that the reproduction could otherwise infringe. *Ashdown* and *HRH* considered this argument as, in common with other similar cases where a fair dealing or public interest defence has succeeded,[91] only part, and not the whole, of the work had been copied and re-used. Although it has been suggested that in order to use parts of a work for fair dealing the whole of the work might be copied,[92] that differs markedly from arguing that the whole of the work may be published relying on fair dealing and/or the public interest defence.

But if it is challenging to argue that the whole of the text should be reproduced, what then about using substantial parts for the purpose of criticism and review, part of the fair dealing internal parameter? Through reliance on the fair dealing provision, it could be that at least large parts of the text would become known to the interested readership (albeit filtered through the words and reflecting the views of a third party critic and reviewer).

---

89 For detailed analysis and references, see Waelde, C. (2006), 'Copyright, Corporate Power and Human Rights: Reality and Rhetoric', in F. Macmillan (ed), *New Directions in Copyright Law*, vol. 2 (Cheltenham, UK and Northampton, MA, USA: Edward Elgar Publishing), 291–310.

90 On the difficulty in determining the dividing line between ideas and expression for artistic works see *Designers' Guild Ltd v Russell Williams (Textiles) Ltd* [2000] 1 WLR 2416; and for literary works, *Baigent & Anor v The Random House Group Ltd* [2007] EWCA Civ 247.

91 For example, *Pro Sieben Media v Carlton Television* [1999] EMLR 109.

92 Ibid at p. 127.

CDPA s 30(1) has been mentioned above. It provides that fair dealing for the purposes of criticism and review applies 'provided that the work has been made available to the public' (no account being taken of any unauthorised act). The requirement of publication stems from the Infosoc Directive.[93] However, previous case law shows that the UK fair dealing provision did not even then operate to the same extent where a claim had been made in relation to an unpublished work. Some courts considered that the defence would not apply at all: '[it] would be manifestly unfair that an unpublished work should, without the consent of the author, be the subject of public criticism, review or newspaper summary'[94] – a view that has changed over the years: 'an unpublished work is not automatically excluded from the defence of fair dealing, it is yet a much more substantial breach of copyright than publication of a published work.'[95]

But has the work in Russian Roulette been published? Certainly, it would seem that it had been, on the internet and in hard copy form, when the Russian author owned the copyright. It has become popular amongst students and in the wider community – this very popularity giving rise to Russian disquiet. Difficulties would arise, however, if that popularity had in fact only arisen as a result of the unauthorised publication of the work by the students. As mentioned above, in *HRH*, the criticism and review defence failed because the journals had not been made available with consent to the public – merely to a select few recipients.[96]

When *HRH* was heard in the Court of Appeal[97] that court spent most time on the breach of confidence claim. In relation to the claim for copyright infringement and in an attempt to get around the argument that the work had not been lawfully made available to the public, counsel for Associated Newspapers argued that the work should have been regarded as first published under CDPA s. 30(2), which provides that the publication of a substantial part of a work for the purpose of reporting current events does not infringe copyright so long as the dealing is fair.[98] The claimed defence to fair dealing for the purposes of criticism and review would then be in relation to the work that had been published within the parameters of reporting current events. The appeal court seemed unimpressed by this saying that for the argument to work there would have to be two publications; the first falling under s. 30(2) and the

---

93 Directive 2001/29/EC of the European Parliament and of the Council of 22 May 2001 on the harmonisation of certain aspects of copyright and related rights in the information society.

94 *British Oxygen Co. Ltd v Liquid Air Ltd* [1925] Ch D 383 at 393.

95 *Beloff v Pressdam Ltd* [1973] 1 All ER 241 at 263.

96 See footnote 77.

97 *HRH Court of Appeal*. See consideration above, p. 199.

98 See above at footnote 55 for the wording of this subsection.

second under s. 30(1) criticising and reviewing the content of the first publication. As the publication fell outwith the parameters of publication of current events, and because there had only been one publication, the defence failed.[99]

A right of distribution by the author

The WIPO Copyright Treaty (WCT), Article 6 (right of distribution) states that 'authors of literary and artistic works shall enjoy the exclusive right of authorising the making available to the public of the original and copies of their works through sale or other transfer of ownership'.

This seems remarkably close to a positive right of 'making available' conferred, by the WCT, on the author of a work. This would be similar to the moral right of divulgation which exists in some civil law countries, although not the UK.[100] Read literally, it might enable our Russian author to compel the making available of his work, resonant of some aspects of the international human rights argument considered above, and apparently irrespective of the copyright position. However, hurdles arise. This provision has not been incorporated in the CDPA, which simply provides that the communication to the public of a work is an act restricted by copyright[101] which 'includes the making available to the public of the work'.[102] As noted above, although it is assumed that the UK Parliament did not intend to legislate contrary to its obligations under international treaty, this is merely an interpretative tool; and here, there is no scope for interpreting communication to the public as an act restricted by copyright as conferring rights on an author who is not the copyright owner. Further, this argument would doubtless be met with a right to enjoyment of property argument based, as considered above, on the copyright.

. . . Call for the Competition Cavalry?

Introduction

If copyright law and human rights cannot necessarily enable the courts to decide that the publication in Russian Roulette should not be met with an injunction, is there a further role for competition law and principles?

In this context, references to competition law are to the UK Competition Act 1998 ('CA') and Article 82 EC Treaty ('Article 82'),[103] as distinct from

---

99 *HRH Court of Appeal* para 82.

100 For example, French Law No. 57-298 of 11 March 1957 Article 19, 'droit de divulgation'.

101 CDPA s. 20(1).

102 CDPA s. 20(2)(b).

103 The facts not suggesting an agreement which would raise Article 81 EC Treaty issues.

the common law doctrine of restraint of trade considered above. Section 18 CA and Article 82 both prohibit the abuse of a dominant position: which one is applicable depends on whether the conduct will have an impact on trade between EC member states (interpreted broadly),[104] or within the UK.[105] Both can be applied directly by national courts,[106] and legislation provides that so far as possible both must be approached in the same way and applied together.[107] However, which provision is initially to be used does have some (possibly formal) relevance.

Both ss. 3 and 6 HRA apply in respect of courts interpreting and making decisions in respect of s. 18 CA. But as s. 3 HRA applies just to UK legislation, only s. 6 HRA is relevant when the English courts are applying Article 82.[108] However, when applying Article 82 the English courts must act as Community courts[109] and should have regard to the EC doctrine of fundamental rights. The ECJ has looked to these in interpreting EC Treaty provisions,[110] and in identifying the rights, has been willing to look more broadly than the ECHR, including to human rights traditions of member states (now acknowledged in the Treaty on European Union)[111] and other human rights treaties.[112] Accordingly, regard to EC fundamental rights imposes an equiva-

---

[104] Article 82 EC Treaty; see Commission Guidelines on the effect on trade concept contained in Articles 81 and 82 of the Treaty [2004] O.J. C101/81, *Societe Technique Miniere v Maschinenbau Ulm* [1966] ECR 235.

[105] Section 18(1) CA.

[106] Article 82 having direct effect in the courts of the UK and as such may be invoked before them – see *BRT v Sabam* [1974] ECR 51; *Van Gend en Loos* [1963] ECR 1.

[107] Section 60(1) and (2) CA; Council Regulation (EC) No. 1/2003 of 16 December 2002 on the implementation of the rules on competition laid down in Articles 81 and 82 of the Treaty OJ L 1, 4.1.2003, pp. 1–25 ('Regulation 1/2003') Article 3(1).

[108] Section 3 HRA applying only to interpretation of legislation which, as defined, does not include articles of the EC Treaty.

[109] *CILFIT Srl v Ministero della Sanita* (283/81) [1982] ECR 3415 [1983] 1 CMLR 472 – and as part of this consider whether it is appropriate to make a reference to the ECJ.

[110] See *Internationale HandelsgesellschaftGmbH v Einfuhr- und Vorratsstelle fur Getreide und Futtermittel* 1970 ECR 1125; *Hauer v Land Rheinland-Pflaz* [1979] ECR 3727; *Society for the Protection of the Unborn Child Ireland v Grogan* [1991] ECR I-4685; *Wachauf v Germany* (C5/88) [1989] ECR 2609; see also Clayton/Tomlinson 32–4, 81 et seq.

[111] Treaty on European Union (consolidated text) Official Journal C 321E of 29 December 2006, Article 6(2); see also Brown. See application in *Roquette Freres SA v Directeur General de la Concurrence* [2002] ECR I-9011, para 25.

[112] See *Eugen Schmidberger Internationale Transporte Planzuge v Austria* (C112/00) [2003] ECR I-5659 considered in Facenna, G. (2004), 'Eugen Schmidberger

lent obligation on national courts in respect of Article 82 as s. 3 HRA does in respect of s. 18 CA. Notwithstanding ongoing uncertainty as to the precise scope of fundamental rights, it is likely that these will encompass both expression/information and property, subject to exceptions. These exceptions (at least on the basis of the ECHR) will encompass other measures necessary in a democratic society – which could include Article 82 goals.

More significantly, however, if Article 82 is used, it is, as is well established, supreme over inconsistent national law such as the CDPA.[113] If the CA applies, there would merely be a potential conflict between pieces of national legislation, and a balancing act required. The requirement from the legal perspective that the provisions are to be approached in the same way, and from a practical perspective are argued together and in the alternative without distinction,[114] means that this may have little substantive effect. However, it is still proper to establish here which competition provision is applicable.

On the present facts, a text on such an important event for Europe is likely to be of interest throughout the member states, and persons might be willing to pay for and publish the work.[115] Although the facts do not deal with this specifically, it can be assumed that all rights to produce the work, including to translate[116] and publish it, and the copyright in respect of all countries, were assigned to the University. Any abuse of a dominant position by the University which restricts dealings with the work will therefore have an impact on trade between member states. Accordingly, Article 82 should apply.

The role of the cavalry

A steadily growing body of English case law over the years has now firmly established the possibility of what had been termed a Euro-defence (on the basis of Article 82) in IP enforcement actions.[117] That said, the consideration

---

International Transporte Planzuge Austria: Freedom of Expression and Assembly vs Free Movement of Goods' *E.H.R.L.R.* 1, 73–80.

113 *Costa v ENEL* [1964] ECR 1141; *R v Secretary of State for Transport ex p Factortame (No. 2)* [1991] 1 AC 603, at 659. See also Ward, T. and K. Smith (eds) (2005), *Competition Litigation in the UK* (London: Thomson/Sweet & Maxwell) ('Ward/Smith'), 383–4.

114 Article 3(1) Regulation 1/2003 and s. 60(1) CA – see footnote 107. For an example, see *Intel Corp v Via Technologies Inc.* 2003 FSR 33 ('*Intel v Via*'), H4.

115 Although again 'effect on trade' is broadly interpreted, and includes potential effect. See Ward/Smith 380 and *Miller v Commission* [1978] ECR 131.

116 Regarding translation in respect of developing countries, consider the Appendix to the Berne Convention. This is not, however, directly raised by the facts in question here.

117 There has also been a growth in s. 18 CA actions – see attempts in *Hewlett-Packard v Expansys* 2005 WL 1748806 (see H7 and paras 16–18); *BHB Enterprises v Victor Chandler* 2005 WL 1248417; *PIK Facilities Ltd v Watson's Ayr Park Ltd* 2005

of IP and competition together has not been uncontroversial. A useful example is the view of Slaughton LJ in *Chiron v Murex*, who considered that as the goal was to bring the abuse to an end, the appropriate remedy is not to refuse relief to the IP owner as this was disproportionate and would create uncertainty regarding future enforcement. He considered that the appropriate remedy should be in the competition arena – parallel and separate.[118] Indeed, Euro-defences have at least to an extent become established because of a reluctance on the part of the courts to exclude their possibility in what is, as will be seen below, an ever evolving area of Community law.[119]

The initial challenge for those advancing such defences is to identify, and plead with sufficient detail, a relevant abuse.[120] A purely formulaic approach will not suffice; there must be a nexus between the alleged abuse (by the IP owner), and the alleged infringing act (of the defendant). The courts have been clear that one act of abuse of a dominant position in respect of an IP right should not turn the IP owner into an 'outlaw', permanently unable to enforce that IP right against anyone at all.[121]

In most cases heard by the courts there has been no such nexus (for example, unrelated excessive pricing could not act as a counter to a passing off action)[122] or at least none which was properly pleaded.[123] On the facts here, however, this should not pose a problem: the alleged infringing act would be publication of the work on the freeducation.edu.uk website; the alleged abuse of a dominant position would be refusal by the University, as copyright owner, to permit the work to be published on this website.

Market definition

Even if the most common hurdle of pleading could be overcome here, more

SLT 1041; and *P&S Amusement Ltd v Valley House Leisure Ltd* 2006 WL 1783201. If these arguments were made, the possibility of a reference to the ECJ on their interpretation would likely remain – *Oscar Bronner GMbH & Co. KG v Mediaprint* [1998] ECR 1-7791 [1999] 4 CMLR 112, and Ward/Smith, 397.

118 *Chiron Corporation v Murex Diagnostics (No. 2)* [1994] FSR 187 ('*Chiron*'), see headnote para 2 and pp. 199–200.

119 For example, *Chiron*; *Intel v Via* [2003] FSR 33, paras 29, 39, 48–9, and 95; *Sportswear v Ghattaura* [2006] ETMR 66 ('*Sportswear*') para 71.

120 The IP aspects of an action, validity and infringement, should be considered before competition matters, given that these assume that the IP right is valid and infringed; *Ingman*, paras 7 and 13 and *Intel v Via* para 95.

121 *ICI v Berk* [1981] FSR 1, at 6. See also *Pitney Bowes Inc. v Francotyp – Postalia GmbH* [1991] FSR 72, submission at 77.

122 *ICI v Berk* [1981] FSR 1.

123 *Lansing Bagnall v Buccaneer* [1984] FSR 241 and also *Chiron* at 195 pleadings in respect of the impact of alleged abuse (no access to potentially life saving kit) was said to be mere speculation.

fundamental difficulties remain. A Euro-Defence requires firstly, a dominant position; and secondly, an abuse of that dominant position. The presence of a dominant position will be assessed by reference to the relevant market.

Market definition is vital: if a market is narrowly defined, there will be fewer market players, and one will more readily be dominant, than if the market is more widely defined – consider a market for jeans as opposed to a market for clothing. Here, is the market for books about history? Books about communism? Jurisprudence of the ECJ and the EC Commission, and, building on this, guidance from the EC Commission[124] have established market definition criteria. The essential principles are substitutability of supply, substitutability of demand, geographical factors.

Given the facts here, with publication online, the possibility of translations and the suggested global interest in the book, it seems likely that competition in respect of the work would operate in similar fashion throughout the world, and that the market would be global. If it was considered, however, that the demand and attempts to meet it may differ between the UK and France, or the UK and Russia, then the geographical aspect of the market would be so restricted.

In terms of supply side substitutability, the key questions are how easy it would be to source, research or publish an alternative to this work, given, as noted, that the original protagonists are dead and it is difficult to obtain records. Could publishers or writers of Russian history, or Russian literature, supply alternative texts? If so, these actual and potential texts would be included in the market. Regarding substitutability of demand, relevant questions are how easily others, say researchers, students and readers of the French Revolution, or the fall of Communism, could turn their attention to the Russian Revolution, or indeed whether students of the Russian revolution would be satisfied with existing more conventional accounts of the period. If it were established that they may do so easily, then the market might be one of works on European revolutionary politics, or indeed the Russian revolution, which may contain many publishers, writers, copyright owners and readers.

On the facts here, however, it is at least arguable that the market, properly defined, is the narrow 'alternative narratives of Russian history in the 1920s'. Substitutes are unlikely on both the supply and demand side, given the lack of

---

[124] See Commission Notice on the definition of the relevant market for the purposes of Community competition law [1997] O.J. C372/03; see also UK Office of Fair Trading *Market Definition* OFT 403. For an example of the Commission perspective on market analysis in the IP context, see Fagerlund, N. and S.B. Rasmussen (2005), 'Astra Zeneca: the first abuse case in the pharmaceutical sector' Commission Competition Policy Newsletter Autumn 2005, http://ec.europa.eu/comm/competition/publications/cpn/cpn2005_3.pdf (last accessed 4 September 2007), Section 4.

records and witnesses and the controversial and individual nature of the work. If the market is to be so defined, and no other candidates for market presence exist (likely so, given the popularity of the book and the extreme government reaction), the book is the only product in the market: and the copyright owner is the only person able to permit and control publication of the text. The market properly defined, therefore, could be the market for publication of the work; and the University, as copyright owner, would be dominant in that market as its only member.[125]

Is there abuse?

Being dominant is not in itself a breach of Article 82. The question is whether there has been an abuse of this dominant position. The ECJ has defined abuse as behaviour which weakens competition in the market and hinders its maintenance and growth.[126] Importantly here, however, it has been established that it can be abuse to unjustifiably refuse to supply goods, or to provide access to what could be termed an essential facility; and in exceptional circumstances to refuse to license copyright. Could the refusal to license in respect of Russian Roulette, which has led to the alleged infringement and the action, be an abuse on this basis?

Relevant EC cases are *Commercial Solvents Corp. v Commission*,[127] *Volvo AB v Erik Veng (UK) Ltd*,[128] *RTE and ITP v EC Commission* ('*Magill*'),[129] *Oscar Bronner GMbH & Co. KG v Mediaprint*,[130] *IMS Health GmbH & Co. OHG v NDC Health GmbH & Co. KG*[131] and *Microsoft*.[132] A variety of approaches – not always consistent – have been developed in these cases by the Commission, the CFI, Advocates General and the ECJ, and the following

---

125 In more 'contested' situations, the question of dominance is whether an undertaking has a position of economic strength to enable them to hinder the maintenance of effective competition in the relevant market by allowing it to behave to an appreciable extent independently of competitors, customers and consumers: see *Michelin v Commission* [1983] ECR 3461, *OFT Guidelines Assessment of Market Power* OFT 415.

126 *Hoffman-La Roche & Co. AG v Commission*, 1979 E.C.R. 461, para 91.

127 [1974] ECR 223 ('*Commercial Solvents*').

128 [1988] ECR 6211, [1989] 4 CMLR 122 ('*Volvo*').

129 *RTE and ITP v EC Commission* [1995] ECR I-743, [1995] 4 CMLR 718.

130 [1998] ECR 1-7791, [1999] 4 CMLR 112 ('*Oscar Bronner*').

131 *IMS Health GmbH & Co. OHG v NDC Health GmbH & Co. KG (Case C-418/01)* [2004] ECR I-5039 ('IMS').

132 Case COMP/C-3/37, available via http://ec.europa.eu/comm/competition/antitrust/cases/decisions/37792/en.pdf (last accessed 3 September 2007) ('*Microsoft*') and also the decision of the CFI in respect of an application to annul the decision, *Microsoft Corp. v Commission of the European Communities* (T-201/04) [2007] 5 CMLR 11 ('CFI Microsoft').

principles can be distilled. It is not abuse to own an IP right,[133] nor is it abuse to refuse to license it, unless there are exceptional circumstances.[134]

These circumstances will include (possibly cumulatively, and possibly exclusively):[135] a refusal to supply[136] a product protected by an IP right, which is indispensable (in the sense that there is no economically viable substitute for use by a competitor the same size as the dominant undertaking) rather than inconvenient for them[137] to use in the development of a new product or technical development,[138] for which there is unmet consumer demand;[139] which supply would enable this access seeker[140] (or possibly anyone)[141] to compete with the IP owner in a second downstream market, such that the refusal would reserve that second market to the IP owner (or possibly lead to a risk of elimination of viable competition there);[142] and where there is no objective justification for the refusal.[143]

The requirement for a new product or even technical development is difficult for Russian Roulette, given the desire to publish an existing work, rather than develop a new one. The requirement has attracted much criticism, for having greater regard for the interests of competitors, rather than providing increased consumer access to existing important products, such as the work.[144]

---

133 Nor does 'mere ownership' in itself made one dominant – see *Magill*, para 46.

134 See *Volvo*, paras 7–9 and *Magill*, para 50.

135 See Korah, V. (2005), 'The Interface Between Intellectual Property Rights and Competition in Developed Countries', 2:4 *SCRIPT-ed* 429 @: http://www.law.ed.ac.uk/ahrc/script-ed/vol2-4/korah.asp ('Korah'), section 3.2.2.

136 First addressed in *Commercial Solvents*, in the context of refusal to supply an existing customer paras 3 and 25.

137 *Oscar Bronner*, paras 41–5; *IMS* para 28, 37. See comprehensive overview provided by the Advocate General in *Oscar Bronner* [1998] ECR I-7791 AGO paras 33–53 in respect of this and the so-called essential facilities doctrine. For further on this see 'Proceedings and reports of the Competition and Intellectual Property Law and Policy in the Knowledge-Based Economy – Joint Hearings of the Federal Trade Commission and Department of Justice' http://www.ftc.gov/opp/intellect/ and 'Antitrust Enforcement and Intellectual Property Rights: Promoting Innovation and Competition: A Report Issued By the U.S. Department of Justice and the Federal Trade Commission' (April 2007) http://www.ftc.gov/opa/2007/04/ipreport.shtm (both last accessed 30 August 2007) and also Hovenkamp, H., M.D. Janis and M.A. Lemley (2006), 'Unilateral Refusals to License', *J.C.L. & E.* 2(1), 1–42.

138 *Magill*, para 54; *IMS*, para 49; *CFI Microsoft*, para 647.

139 *Magill*, para 54; *IMS*, para 49.

140 *Commercial Solvents*, paras 3 and 25; *Oscar Bronner* paras 41 and 47.

141 *Magill*, paras 55–6; *IMS* para 37.

142 *CFI Microsoft*, paras 421 and 620.

143 *Magill*, para 55; *Oscar Bronner*, para 41; *IMS*, para 37.

144 See Stothers, C. (2004), 'IMS Health and its implications for Compulsory Licensing in Europe', *E.I.P.R.* 26(10), 467–72, at 470–1; Derclaye, E. (2004), 'The

Here, however, it could be argued that as the work is not at present on the market, publication would indeed enable a new product to be made available. Alternatively, commentary could be added to the work, or translations made, to develop a new product.

Yet a further problem for Russian Roulette would be that demand for the work would exist on the same market as that on which it was previously published. However, the finding in *IMS* that an upstream market could be hypothetical[145] might support the argument that there is a hypothetical market for a license, with the real market being for publication of the work itself (which could not occur without the licence).

It is also unclear what might be 'objective justification' for a refusal to license. Safety and financial solvency considerations have been mentioned, as well as encouraging of research and development and protection of trade secrets.[146] Bare reliance on an IP right as a reward for investment in innovation was found in Microsoft to be insufficient justification.[147] However, despite human rights arguments having been raised in *IMS*, the human rights aspect of the IP owner's rights (based on ECHR Article 1 Protocol 1 arguments) has been not considered in this line of cases.[148]

On the facts here, it could be argued that the lack of objective justification could be established by a failure to publish, in response to political pressure, a work which the University had previously been willing to publish; in circum-

---

IMS Health Decision and the Reconciliation of Copyright and Competition Law', *E.L. Rev.* 29(5), 687–97, at 691, 692, 695–6; Ong, B. (2005), 'Building Brick Barricades and Other Barriers to Entry: Abusing a Dominant Position by Refusing to License Intellectual Property Rights', *E.C.L.R.* 26(4), 215–24, at 220–4; Korah sections 3.2.2 and 4; and McCann, D. (2006), 'European Union: competition law – abuse of dominant position', *I.C.C.L.R.* 17(4), N27–31.

145 *IMS*, paras 42–4.

146 The Advocate General in *Synetairismos Farmakopoion Aitolias & Akarnanias (SYFAIT) v Glaxosmithkline Plc* (C53/03) [2005] ECR I-4609, para 71 rejected the Commission's argument that a narrow approach should be adopted to objective justification; and see Korah section 4.2.

147 Regarding the complex questions of IP and innovation in this context, see, for example, *Microsoft*, para 709, Advocate General *Oscar Bronner*, para 64 and *CFI Microsoft*, paras 267–89, 666–703. See also Ridyard, D. (2004), 'Compulsory access under EC competition law – a new doctrine of "convenient facilities" and the case for price regulation', *E.C.L.R.* 25(11), 669–73 ('Ridyard') at 670–1; Vezzoso, S. (2006), 'The incentives balance test in the EU Microsoft case: a pro-innovation "economics-based" approach?' *E.C.L.R.* 27(7), 382–90; Eagles, I. and L. Longdin (2008), 'Microsoft's refusal to disclose software interoperability information and the Court of First Instance', *E.I.P.R.* 30(5), 205–8 and Ghidini, G. (2006) *Intellectual Property and Competition Law: The Innovation Nexus* (Cheltenham, UK and Northampton, MA, USA: Edward Elgar Publishing).

148 See details in IMS Advocate General *IMS v NDC* [2004] ECR I-5039 ('*IMS AGO*'), para 37, p. 1559.

stances where the work has been identified as rare and important; and without which competition would be reduced in respect of the work.

Further, the decision of the Commission in *Microsoft* seems to herald a return for the Commission[149] to a more flexible approach to 'exceptional circumstances' than the rigid criteria seen in *Magill* and *IMS*. The Commission stressed the need for special circumstances for a refusal to license to be abusive; but also stated that all such circumstances would form part of the assessment.[150] The CFI's decision in *Microsoft* took a different approach, rather focusing on whether the existing Magill and IMS tests were met,[151] and, as noted, likely expanded them in the process. As a result, however, it could still be argued that a more flexible approach is correct; and that, after regard to all the circumstances, refusal to permit publication could be abuse of a dominant position by the copyright owner.

Students: Eurodefence

An alternative Euro-Defence, however, could be that the action itself (rather than the underlying refusal to license) was an abuse of a dominant position.

ITT Promedia v Commission ('*Promedia*')[152] concerned the defendant in an ongoing court action complaining to the Commission that the raising of the court action was abuse of a dominant position. The Commission declined to investigate. The CFI confirmed the Commission's approach[153] that it could be abuse of a dominant position to raise proceedings. This would, however, only be so if (a) the proceedings could not reasonably be considered an attempt to assert the rights of the dominant undertaking, the proceedings being objectively manifestly unfounded and serving to harass the opposing party; and (b) the proceedings were conceived in the framework of a plan whose goal was to eliminate competition.[154]

---

149 See also proposals under discussion in the ongoing Article 82 Review, full details of this at http://ec.europa.eu/comm/competition/antitrust/art82/index.html including the Staff Discussion Paper and EGAP report, and the comments of the Max Planck Institute for Intellectual Property, Competition and Tax Law http://ec.europa.eu/comm/competition/antitrust/art82/047.pdf (last accessed 30 August 2007).

150 *Microsoft*, pp. 146–7.

151 *CFI Microsoft*, paras 103–6, 108–10, 118–53, 207–66, 337–422, 560–703. For discussion, see Howarth, D. and K. McMahon (2008), 'Windows has performed an illegal operation: the Court of First Instance's judgment in Microsoft v Commission', *E.C.L.R.* 29(2), 117–34.

152 [1998] ECR II-2937.

153 *Promedia*, paras 57–8. The CFI set out the criteria applied by the Commission but was not invited by the parties to comment on their correctness – just their application in this case.

154 *Promedia*, paras summary 1, 30, 56, 73.

Even if this were so, however, there should only be a finding of abuse in, once again, exceptional circumstances.[155] Harassment and lack of foundation and unmeritorious litigation in themselves would not suffice: there must also be an impact on competition.[156] Further, these criteria must be interpreted and applied restrictively in a manner which does not frustrate general access to the courts.[157] The CFI considered that the ability to assert rights in courts is a fundamental principle in the constitutional traditions of member states, and also recognised by Articles 6 and 13 ECHR.

Promedia could be used to create a direct response to an IP infringement action.[158] It was pleaded in *Intel v Via* that the raising of the action was abuse of a dominant position. No substantive decision was made on the point, although more generally the Court of Appeal was reluctant to restrict the circumstances in which there could be abuse.[159] In contrast, in *SanDisk Corp. v Koninklijke Philips Electronics NV* ('*Sandisk*')[160] in 2007 the English High Court considered alleged abuse in respect of preliminary procedural steps taken in Germany, Italy and the Netherlands prior to any action having been raised. The court declined jurisdiction;[161] however, it suggested obiter that the more specific *Promedia* test should be applied in such a situation.[162]

In Russian Roulette, it would seem manifestly unreasonable for the University to be able to prevent publication of such an important work, with its implications for human rights to information. The action would also be harassing the author, by likely causing distress by preventing publication of his work, in circumstances when the University had previously published it.

---

155 Ibid, paras summary 1, 60.

156 Ibid, paras summary 6, 56 (per Commission), 140. This is resonant of the application of the US *Noerr-Pennington* doctrine to litigation. This shield from antitrust action conferred on government actions, including litigation, does not apply to sham litigation. See 'Federal Trade Commission Staff Report: Enforcement Perspectives on the Noerr-Pennington Doctrine', http://www.ftc.gov/reports/P013518enfperspectNoerr-Penningtondoctrine.pdf (last accessed 30 August 2007).

157 *Promedia*, paras summary 1, 61.

158 See Preece, S. (1999), 'ITT Promedia v EC Commission: Establishing an Abuse of Predatory Litigation' *E.C.L.R.* 20(2), 118–122.

159 *Intel v Via*, H4, H5 and paras 48–9 when the Court of Appeal refused to limit the circumstances when there might be a breach of Article 82 to those considered in *Magill* and *IMS;* similar pleadings were also included in *HM Stationery Office v Automobile Association Ltd* [2001] ECC 34 ('*HMSO*') paras 9 and 12, although these did not survive attack. Note also *Microsoft Corp. v Ling* [2006] EWHC 1619, 2006 WL 1887046 para 21, where alleged abuse in respect of licensing practices must be established, and cannot be presumed.

160 [2007] FSR 22.

161 *Promedia* H15, 17, 18, paras 20, 22–5, 30 and 34.

162 Ibid. H27, paras 43–6.

The facts suggest a political, rather than objective reason for refusing publication and raising the action.

However, the action would here still very much be an attempt to assert copyright, which could reasonably be considered to be owned by the University. Further, although there would be an impact on competition, the objective of the action is to prevent publication of the work per se: the impact on competition is a corollary, albeit an inevitable one, given the prevention of emergence of a market for work. It is unlikely, therefore, notwithstanding the impact of the action on rights to information and expression, that the *Promedia* criteria would be satisfied here, particularly given the human rights of the IP owner to enjoyment of property and concerns regarding access to courts.

A final point in respect of all types of Euro-Defences is their impact: are they indeed to be defences, or rather relevant to relief and appropriate outcome, similar to the approach adopted in *Ashdown*.[163] The case law to date, as considered above, has focused on whether the pleading of the defence can survive a preliminary attack. No decision has yet had to be made as to outcome;[164] and the variety of indications of approach so far (which range from the conduct being invalid,[165] an injunction being inappropriate,[166] no relief should be awarded,[167] and elision of questions of defence and relief[168]) suggests that courts may not find it easy to do so.

Further, it should be borne in mind that the aim of the parties is to obtain and avoid relief.[169] The basis need not necessarily be made clear, albeit that

163 This approach can also be compared to the proposed 'pliability' approach explored in United States literature – see Bell, A. and G. Parchomovsky (2002), 'Pliability Rules' October, 101 *Mich. L. Rev.* 1. At a more practical level, an award of damages would follow established procedures in infringement actions; it would also be similar to the compulsory licences and negotiations requirements imposed by the Commission in *Magill*, *IMS* and *Microsoft*, see pp. 210–13 and 224–5.

164 *Sportswear* para 67, referring to Laddie J in *Glaxo v Dowelhurst* [2000] FSR 371 considering whether an Article 81 claim could be defence as well as a counterclaim and noting problems in identifying the appropriate relief; also *Sportswear* at first instance, 2006 FSR 11, para 24 (competition arguments could be relevant to relief granted) and para 25 (noting it was unclear whether the defendants' arguments distinguished between a defence and a refusal as a matter of discretion to grant injunctive relief).

165 *Parke, Davis* [1968] CMLR 47.

166 *British Leyland v T.I. Silencers* [1981] FSR 213, 217.

167 *Chiron*, see headnote para 2 and pp. 199–200.

168 *Intel v Via* para 80 – if there is conduct contrary to Article 82 then such illegality might constitute a defence to any liability for infringement or any remedies.

169 See, for example, Thorley, S. et al (2000) (15th rev. edn), *Terrell on the Law of Patents* (London: Sweet & Maxwell) precedents for IP pleadings (there, patents) at p. 573; see details of pleadings in *Intel v Via*, extracts set out at paras 15 and 21 and *HMSO* summary at paras 9, 12.

the pleadings will have set out legal positions in respect of infringement and non-infringement. The legal complexity and judicial equivocation on the issue suggests that if this question does not need to be addressed by the courts, it will not be.

More broadly, *Promedia* introduces questions of what may be reasonable action on the basis of an IP right. This is resonant of the misuse of IP doctrine developed in the US,[170] which is quite distinct from antitrust/competition.[171] The circumstances in which there has been misuse tend to be the inverse of those which have survived the direct Euro-Defence nexus test, involving wider anti-competitive conduct such as requiring products to be bought together, or requiring entering into anti-competitive agreements. In such cases, courts have 'with[held] their aid where the plaintiff is using the right asserted contrary to the public interest',[172] restricting the circumstances in which IP might be enforced in the light of equity and the public interest.[173] This more fluid, internal approach has been raised by some commentators[174] as an alternative to the introduction of competition into IP actions.[175] However, the analysis above in respect of the *British Leyland* public policy line of cases, and indeed *Ashdown*, suggests that here, even this approach would also not make a significant difference.

---

170 See comprehensive analysis in Cotter, T.F. (2006),'The Procompetitive Interest in Intellectual Property Law' (27 January) Berkeley Center for Law and Technology *Law and Technology Scholarship (Selected by the Berkeley Center for Law & Technology)*. Paper 15. http://repositories.cdlib.org/cgi/viewcontent.cgi?article=1016&context=bclt (last accessed 30 August 2007) ('Cotter').

171 See Cotter, esp. pp. 17–21.

172 *Morton Salt Co. v G.S. Suppiger Co.* 312 U.S. 488 (1942) – patented products licensed on condition used in conjunction with non patented items; held patent unenforceable when defendant not a party to that licence, see quote at p. 492; also *Lasercomb v Reynolds* 911 F.2d 970 (4th Cir 1990) ('*Lasercomb*') where court developed the misuse of copyright defence, when the copyright owner had a standard licence agreement which the court considered objectionable in respect of its impact on others' abilities to develop ideas – see paras 6, 10–22.

173 See *Lasercomb* para 7 – action would be barred from succeeding if misuse defence was made out.

174 Ong, B. (2004), 'Anti Competitive Refusals to Grant Copyright Licences: Reflections on the IMS Saga' *E.I.P.R.* 26(11), 505–14 at 508–11.

175 The more direct converse of misuse of IP can be found in the doctrine of abuse of rights, where particular malicious or antisocial exercise of a right can give rise to liability, as opposed to a defence or relief from remedy – see Reid, R. (2004), 'The Doctrine of Abuse of Rights: Perspective from a Mixed Jurisdiction', vol. 8.3 *Electronic Journal of Comparative Law*, (October 2004), <http://www.ejcl.org/83/art83-2.html> (last accessed 3 September 2007). Again this involves a different assessment of the impact of the exercise of IP and is outside the scope of this chapter.

A further role for human rights?

Coming full circle, human rights could contribute to delivering the desired outcome using a competition route. Section 6 HRA and EC fundamental rights could enable regard to be had to human rights consequences in considering how to approach decision making in respect of Article 82.

A first possibility could be to influence market definition, for example by favouring a narrow approach to market definition if there was a reasonable (albeit not otherwise compelling) argument for this based on economic and factual evidence.

Human rights could also support a more purposive approach to Article 82. This would mean greater focus being placed on preventing objectionable conduct, rather than market definition and dominance, enabling these potential preliminary obstacles to a finding of abuse to be overcome. Indeed, the ability to engage in such objectionable conduct could be indicative of a dominant position.

An example is the Australian case of *ACCC v Boral Besser Masonry*[176] ('*Boral*'). This case involved an allegation of misuse of market power in what was known as predatory pricing. The relevant legislation[177] prohibited a corporation with a substantial degree of market power taking advantage of that power for a prohibited purpose. There was possible evidence of the necessary purpose, but the first instance judge found no substantial degree of market power, so other questions did not arise.[178] The Full Federal Court[179] considered that the ability to engage in problematic conduct for that purpose was evidence of market power.[180] This approach was strongly criticised, however, by the majority of the High Court[181] as inconsistent with established authority.[182] A dissenting High Court judge also adopted a more fluid purposive construction, considering that the provision should be viewed and applied as a whole, rather than step by step.[183] This approach does have some academic support.[184]

---

176 [2003] HCA 5.

177 Section 46 Trade Practices Act 1974 (Cth).

178 *Boral*, para 86.

179 First appeal court.

180 *Boral*, paras 108–11, 113–7, 182–3, 185–7.

181 The final appeal court.

182 *Boral*, paras 120–21, 132, 133–41, 143, 169–70, 172, 179–81, 184, 245–54, 320.

183 *Boral*, paras 382, 389.

184 See consideration and references at Ward/Smith, 442 footnote 34. See analysis in McMahon, K. (2006), 'Competition Law, Adjudication and the High Court' 30 (3) *Melbourne University Law Review* pp. 782–836.

However this approach, even if attractive to a court, is difficult to apply to IP cases. The objectionable conduct would be reliance on the IP right to refuse to license or raise an action. But this is consistent with owning an IP right; and it is well established as considered above that owning an IP right should not in itself lead to a dominant position – and that exercising it will only be abusive in exceptional circumstances.

A purposive and human rights based approach may be more attractive in courts preferring the more flexible approach of the ECJ in *Volvo* and the Commission in *Microsoft*, rather than the often confused rigidity of *Magill*, *IMS* and *Promedia*. However, the weight of authority remains against this.

These suggestions assume that human rights arguments would support the students. But arguments based on rights to information and expression must take into account exceptions to these rights, and also the human right to property of the IP owner. Accordingly, this human rights perspective may only have a marginal contribution to a new approach. This may still be enough, however, to support a narrow market definition, or suggest a more fluid approach, similar to *Volvo* and more consistent with regard for rights to expression and information.

Summary

If the work is published and a copyright infringement action awaited, it is possible that the action would be unsuccessful. Arguments exist on the basis of the internal and external balance in copyright, fuelled by freedom of expression in the light of the HRA, and also by competition law arguments, possibly also assisted by human rights arguments. The competition arguments would have a greater prospect of success, although they are dependent upon market definition; and in any event their prospects could be rated no more highly than reasonable, given *IMS*, *Magill* and *Promedia*. If these arguments were successful they would likely mean there was no infringement, although it might be possible to build on an *Ashdown* analogy to deliver both publication and payment.

Strategy 3 The Proactive Human Rights Approach

Introduction

If the above approaches are unsuccessful, the students may still be outraged that they are unable to access what they see as a valuable educational text. Once all national remedies have been exhausted,[185] a student could make a

[185] Article 35 ECHR. See also Protocol 11 to the ECHR.

complaint to the ECtHR[186] that the UK was, given the decisions of its national courts, in breach of its obligations to 'secure to everyone within [its] jurisdiction' the ECHR rights.[187]

The students might hope that the human rights starting point of the ECtHR, (seeking to assess whether there has been a failure to secure these human rights) rather than the copyright or indeed contractual starting point of the English court might produce an additional shift in the balance in their favour. But this would be a time consuming[188] and expensive process, notwithstanding ongoing efforts by the ECtHR to improve its processes generally.[189]

Arguments

The key issue for the ECtHR would be the extent to which the English court's finding in respect of copyright or contract came properly within the exceptions to the Article 10 ECHR rights to information and expression, particularly bearing in mind the limited human rights to enjoyment of property of the copyright owner.

The ECtHR has been said to take a more fluid approach to previous interpretations of Convention provisions than the courts of the UK, and to seek to deliver what it sees as an appropriate outcome, given the human rights interests involved and the social and moral values of society at the time.[190] However, in Russian Roulette a careful balancing would have been carried out at national level, between copyright and human rights from the internal and external perspective, and also between contract and other matters including human rights. It is unlikely, therefore, that the ECtHR would consider that there was a breach of obligation on the part of the UK.

---

186 Article 34 ECHR. For initial guidance on procedures, see http://www.echr.coe.int/ECHR/EN/Header/Applicants/Information+for+applicants/Frequently+asked+questions/ (last accessed 29 August 2007).

187 Article 1 ECHR.

188 For example, *Bosphorus v Ireland* (2006) 42 EHRR 1 ('*Bosphorus*') was completed eight years after the relevant events.

189 See Lord Woolf et al (December 2005) 'Review of the Working Methods of the European Court of Human Rights' http://www.echr.coe.int/Eng/Press/2005/Dec/LORDWOOLFSREVIEWONWORKINGMETHODS.pdf (last accessed 30 August 2007); 'Interim Report of the Group of Wise Persons to the Committee of Ministers' CM (2006) 88 10 May 2006, https://wcd.coe.int/ViewDoc.jsp?id=998185&BackColorInternet=9999CC&BackColorIntranet=FFBB55&BackColorLogged=FFAC75 (last accessed 30 August 2007); and the Opinion of the Court on the Wise Persons Report as adopted 2 April 2007 http://www.echr.coe.int/NR/rdonlyres/26457EAB-2840-4D71-9ED7-85F0F8AE0026/0/OpinionoftheCourtontheWisePersonsReport.pdf (last accessed 30 August 2007).

190 Gearty at 179 and 197–202; see also Clayton/Tomlinson, 1535.

Further, if, contrary to the suggested analyses above, the Euro-Defence did succeed, the copyright owner could itself complain about the impact upon its enjoyment of rights to property in copyright. This would then be analogous to the situation considered by the ECtHR in *Bosphorus*:[191] can the UK be found to be in breach of its ECHR obligations because of decisions made in the light of mandatory obligations under other international instruments?

Given the EC fundamental rights doctrine considered above, the ECtHR has held there to be a rebuttable presumption that a state did not depart from its obligations under the ECHR in complying with its obligations under the EC Treaty.[192] Once again, the complex interrelationship of the interests envisaged in Russian Roulette and the detailed balancing act which will have been carried out at national level suggest that it is unlikely that the ECtHR would consider the presumption rebutted here.

Margin of appreciation

Even if this were not so, however, the ECtHR's view of the appropriate balance between copyright, contact, competition and each human right in each case is not the end of the matter. One of the essential principles of ECtHR jurisprudence is the margin of appreciation.[193] The ECtHR is reluctant to intervene in a state's internal affairs by declaring a state to have breached its ECHR obligations in questions which essentially involve consideration of national policy.

The striking of the balances involved in Russian Roulette may come within this category. The ECtHR will only overcome this reluctance if it considers that the conduct of the UK through the decision of the English courts in this case was not proportionate and legitimate.[194] This may return the debate to the initial balancing act: there are at least alleged benefits of copyright and, as would have been seen at the national stage, the balances are finely struck.

Remedies

If, notwithstanding the above assessments, the students were to be successful in Strasbourg, what would be achieved? The ECHR provides a right to an

---

[191] See footnote 188.

[192] See *Bosphorus* H17, pp. 148–56 and 159–60; Parga, A.H. (2006), 'Bosphorus v Ireland and the Protection of Fundamental Rights in Europe', *E.L.Rev*. 31(2), 251–9, esp. at 254–5, and Banner, C. and A. Thomson (2005), 'Human Rights Review of State Acts Performed in Compliance with EC law – Bosphorus Airways v Ireland', *E.H.R.L.R*. 6, 649–59 esp. at 654–6.

[193] See *Handyside v UK* (1979–80) 1 EHRR 737 – also a freedom of expression case.

[194] See further analysis in Clayton/Tomlinson at 273–86; and Gearty, 122–9.

effective remedy.[195] The question returns to UK law – can this allow full reparation? It would already have been established that UK law, as applied by the English courts in Russian Roulette, would not permit publication. Further, the remedy must be available from a body 'sufficiently independent' of that which has been judged to have breached ECHR rights: an order from a differently constituted English court may not be acceptable.[196]

In such circumstances, the ECtHR may 'afford just satisfaction to the injured party'.[197] On the facts here, 'just satisfaction' would appear to require an order that the work is published, possibly with some payment being made. This would be unusual, with ECtHR reparation tending to focus on financial compensation,[198] and being reluctant to quash decisions of national courts[199] or require new legislation.[200] However, there are indications that this could be achieved. Key principles would include the facts and urgency of the matter, the need for the remedy (with payment in itself not being adequate), and enforceability and practicality.[201] One set of cases concerns restitution of property where there had been extreme violation of an ECHR right, and reparation was not possible;[202] and another line of cases involves repeated and systemic violation of an ECHR right, without appropriate remedial action being taken by the state in question.[203]

It could be argued that the approach of the English court in Russian Roulette is indicative of a systemic imbalance between copyright and freedom of expression and information, and that the legislation could be ordered by the ECtHR to be revisited. However, the existence of international obligations

---

195 Clayton/Tomlinson 1471–6; Article 13 ECHR (not a Convention right) and *K v Camden & Islington Health Authority* [2002] QB 198 (CA).

196 Clayton/Tomlinson 1471–6, and see *Silver v UK* (1983) 5 EHRR 347, para 116.

197 Article 41 ECHR; see also Clayton/Tomlinson at 1544.

198 See Clayton/Tomlinson at 1422–8, 1554; see importantly Leach, P. (2005), 'Beyond the Bug River. A New Dawn for Redress Before the European Court of Human Rights', *E.H.R.L.R.* 2, 148–64 ('Leach') – overview of traditional approach at 148–50 – for example, *Lyons v UK* App No. 15227103 decision 8 July 2003.

199 See, for example, Clayton/Tomlinson at 1554 – reference made to *Brozieck v Italy* (1989) 12 EHRR 371.

200 See eg *Lundvall v Sweden* App No. 38629/97 decision 12 November 2002.

201 See Leach, 163 and references.

202 See Leach, 151–4 and references; also *Papamhalopoulos v Greece* (1990) 21 EHRR 439 and *Brumarescu v Romania* (2001) EHRR 35.

203 See Leach, 159–61 and references; see Committee of Ministers Recommendation to Member States on Improvement of Domestic Remedies Rec (2004) 6, https://wcd.coe.int/ViewDoc.jsp?id=743317&BackColorInternet=9999CC&BackColorIntranet=FFBB55&BackColorLogged=FFAC75 (last accessed 30 August 2007). No such review has been carried out in respect of copyright.

under TRIPS[204] mandating legislation of at least similar nature to the CDPA, and careful analysis of national courts rather than any flagrant disregard for human rights, would support a less interventionist approach. This might lead instead to the quashing of the specific decision and an order for publication on specific terms.

Once an order is made, the UK has undertaken to comply with it – thus concerns in respect of the impact on national sovereignty, particularly regarding legislation, do not apply.[205] Compliance will be supervised by the Committee of Ministers, and the UK would need to report to it.[206]

Summary

Complaints could be to the ECtHR made by the party which is unsuccessful in the national courts. If the complaint is made by the students, it might be possible for the ECtHR to reach a decision which favours the free expression/information argument rather than the property/copyright arguments. The prospects of this are, however, slim. Likewise, if the Euro-Defence succeeded, it is unlikely that the ECtHR would consider the presumption to be rebutted such that this decision was in breach of ECHR obligations. If the ECtHR found a court decision to result in a breach of rights under the ECHR, there is also only a slim likelihood of an order being made that the work is published, with or without payment.

Strategy 4 The Positive Competition Approach

Introduction

The analysis of strategies 1–3 suggests that human rights and copyright in themselves, and when combined with competition law and argument in the adversarial context, cannot be relied upon to deliver publication, at all or with a payment. As an alternative to publishing and then waiting to be sued, the students could choose to take a proactive approach based on competition law. As was the case with Strasbourg, it would be interesting to note whether the starting point of competition law, rather than copyright law, could have any impact on the end result.

The first option is through regulatory avenues. The students could notify competition regulators and hope that they investigate and impose a remedy which is acceptable to the students. The basis for complaint would be that the

[204] Articles 9–14 http://www.wto.org/english/docs_e/legal_e/27-trips.pdf.

[205] Article 46(1) ECHR.

[206] See also Clayton/Tomlinson, 1566; and for regular updates see http://www.coe.int/T/E/Human_rights/execution/ (last accessed 30 August 2007).

refusal to permit publication through licence or mere tolerance of proactive publication, or the raising of any court proceedings, was abuse of a dominant position.

One advantage is that the regulatory approach would proceed at no cost to the complainant.[207] If a regulator chose to pursue the complaint, however, it is unlikely that any decision would be reached quickly – and, unlike the case in court proceedings, the parties could not decide to resolve the matter amongst themselves. As an example, the EC Microsoft investigation began in 1999, there was a Commission decision in 2004, and the decision of the CFI was published in September 2007.[208]

Procedure

Complaints could be made to the EC Commission, or the UK Office of Fair Trading ('OFT') requesting that they pursue the matter. The analysis above of the relationship between Article 82 and Section 18 suggests that either basis could be adopted here, with Article 82 more likely applicable.

The present system for allocation of business between national regulators (such as the OFT) and the EC Commission proceeds on the basis of subsidiarity. Most matters should be pursued at national level although the Commission can investigate even if there is an ongoing national investigation (a network of interagency collaboration has been established),[209] if it considers this would be in the Community interest.[210] The likely EC wide interest in the work and the controversial nature of its subject matter suggest that this would be a case where the EC Commission would consider it appropriate to proceed. From the EC perspective, *Magill*, *IMS* and *Microsoft* suggest that the Commission may be interested given the legal subject matter. However, the nature of the work (relatively obscure literature as opposed to software and TV listings) may make it a matter of lower priority. No similar cases have yet been pursued by the OFT, although it is beginning to take an interest in other IP matters.[211]

---

207 See similar points made in Sackville, R (Justice) (2005), 'Monopoly versus freedom of ideas: The expansion of intellectual property', 16 *AIPJ* 65 at 74–5.

208 See press overview in http://news.zdnet.co.uk/itmanagement/0,1000000308,39287406,00.htm (last accessed 30 August 2007). The CFI decision is expected on 17 September 2007, and inter alia p. 210.

209 See Council Regulation 1/2003 articles 11, 13; see also Ward/Smith, 321 et seq and http://www.oft.gov.uk/oft_at_work/partnership_working/international/ (last accessed 30 August 2007).

210 There is no clear guidance as to when the Commission should act – Ward/Smith, 331.

211 See acceptance by OFT of undertaking to license IP in respect of cheese making equipment in lieu of referring a merger to the Competition Commission http://www.oft.gov.uk/news/press/2006/118-06 (last accessed 29 August 2007).

If a regulator does investigate, once there is a decision, appeals would be possible. In the UK, this would be to the Competition Appeals Tribunal ('CAT') in the first instance[212] and then to the courts, starting with the High Court;[213] and in the EC initially to the Court of First Instance by way of judicial review and then to the ECJ.[214]

The regulator may choose, however, not to pursue the matter. Developments in the UK supermarket sector confirm that the students could challenge such a decision of the OFT before the CAT, which could ultimately lead to an investigation.[215] A similar decision of the Commission could be challenged and annulled.[216] However, this would clearly involve cost, time and other resources without immediate substantive results, although it may put pressure on the University to take a new approach.

Possible outcome

If a regulator did find there to be an abuse of a dominant position, they could impose financial and also more positive behavioural and structural remedies.[217] These could include publication, requiring the abusive conduct to be brought to an end. The key question is whether the remedies are proportionate and necessary, which would likely to satisfied here if there was reasonable royalty.[218] But calculating a reasonable royalty can be problematic, as can establishing other terms of the licence. Requiring this has been criticised as an unsuitable intervention of courts and regulators into commercial relations, appropriate only in cases of chronic market breakdown.[219]

In Russian Roulette, however, there has arguably been market breakdown, with the market being unable to deliver the work to satisfy consumers.[220]

---

212 Section 43(3)(i) CA; Ward/Smith 89 et seq.

213 Section 49 CA (as amended); Ward/Smith 157 et seq.

214 Article 230 EC Treaty; see also Ward/Smith 354 et seq.

215 OFT announced an investigation in May 2006. For full overview of developments and links to sources see http://www.breakingthearmlock.com/index.php?option=com_content&task=view&id=11&Itemid=15 (last accessed 30 August 2007).

216 *Micro Leader v EC Commission* [2000] ECDR 217.

217 For full overview and references from the UK perspective, see http://www.oft.gov.uk/advice_and_resources/resource_base/legal/competition-act-1998/consequences (last accessed 30 August 2007). From the EC perspective, see analysis of *Microsoft* in Ridyard, and also footnote 219.

218 Sections 33(1), (3) and section 34 CA (if order not complied with an application can be made to court); Council Regulation 1/2003 Article 7.

219 Ridyard at 671–2.

220 See again Ridyard at 671–3; and see Geradin, D. (2004), 'Limiting the Scope of Article 82 EC: what can the EU learn from the U.S. Supreme Court's Judgment in Trinko in the Wake of Microsoft, IMS and Deutsche Telekom', *CML Rev* 41: 1519–53, at 1543–53 – more detailed guidance should be provided.

Further, the Commission has moved to imposing, with increasing specificity, requirements for parties to negotiate to reach agreement for reasonable and non-discriminatory terms for a licence or supply of information, with the dominant party not to extract strategic value and leverage in its licensing fee from its dominant position in the market of supply;[221] for proposals to be submitted to the Commission;[222] and also, sensibly, for independent experts to become involved, reporting to the Commission.[223] This possibility of a licence is more consistent with the agreed objectives in respect of Russian Roulette than a complete Euro-Defence.

Following any finding of abuse, an application for damages could also be made at national level to the CAT or the High Court.[224] There is a question as to who could properly be established to have suffered damage as a result of an abuse.[225] It is likely here that the original students who had been seeking access could raise a claim; but this would in itself not address the objective of publication.

Human rights implications

As with the Euro-Defence, there is place for a more central role for human rights in regulatory action.

The OFT is a public authority within s. 6 HRA. Accordingly, in assessing whether there is a breach of Article 82 (or s. 18 CA), it is obliged, so far as possible, to have regard to Convention rights. The points made above in respect of courts, therefore, also apply here. The Commission is an institution of the EC and the EC fundamental rights considered above therefore underpin its conduct in assessing abuse.[226] Accordingly, whichever regulatory approach

221 See *Microsoft* pp. 298–301, and also pp. 275–81 and 289–91 re remedies and monitoring.

222 Council Regulation 17/62, para 3(1) being the basis for this order – see Commission Decision 89/205/EEC of 21 December 1988 O.J. 1989 L78/43, [1989] 4 CMLR 757, paras 26 et seq.

223 *NDC Health v IMS Health* Case COMP D3/38.044 (OJ 2002) L 59, p. 18. Available via http://ec.europa.eu/comm/competition/antitrust/cases/decisions/38044/en.pdf#search=%22NDC%20Health%20v%20IMS%20Health%20Case%20COMP%20D3%2F38.044%20Decision%203%20July%202001%22 (last accessed 30 August 2007) para 215.

224 On the basis of breach of statutory duty ss. 47A, 58A CA.

225 *Masterfoods Ltd. (t/a Mars Ireland) v HB Ice Cream Ltd.* [2000] ECR I-11369. See also *Garden Cottage Foods v Milk Marketing Board* [1984] AC 130 and *Crehan v Courage* [2001] ECR I-6297, and Ward/Smith, 260 et seq. The future of damages action is the subject of an ongoing consultation, which touches on some of the issues raised here: see http://ec.europa.eu/comm/competition/antitrust/others/actions_for_ damages/index_en.html (last accessed 30 August 2007).

226 See Articles 5 and 6(2) Treaty on European Union. For consideration of the possi-

were chosen, and bearing in mind the requirements that the two provisions be interpreted consistently, there would be some comfort that regard should once again be had by the regulator to human rights even when considering competition matters. As has been seen, however, this might not have a substantial impact.

Court avenue

Alternatively, the students or even the author could choose to retain control, to bear cost and risk, and to raise a competition action in the English court. The claim would, again, be for an abuse of a dominant position in Article 82 (and s. 18 CA) based on the objections by the University to publication or indeed proposed publication. There have been a growing number of direct competition actions; and although there has not yet been one involving IP per se, *Attheraces Ltd v British Horseracing Board* involved abuse of a dominant position in respect of the pricing of data.[227]

The principles considered above in respect of Euro-Defences and ss. 3 and 6 HRA would be applied by the English court in considering the competition questions. In competition actions, as in the later Euro-Defence cases considered above, the English courts have declined to take a limited view of the circumstances in which there might be abuse. In *Attheraces*, the court thought it to be irrelevant that the access seeker was not a competitor;[228] and it confirmed that the greater the power, and the closer the incumbent was to monopoly status, the greater the responsibility imposed on the dominant undertaking.[229] The court also indicated that a welfare view of economics (rather than one more focused on efficiency and the property rights in question) might be relevant in assessing whether there was an objective justification for refusal to allow access to (here) the work,[230] although the Court of Appeal in the same case took a different approach.[231]

---

ble future direct relevance in this regard of the EU Charter, see MacCormick, N. (2005), 'Human Rights and Competition Law: Possible Impact of the Proposed EU Constitution', 2:4 *SCRIPT-ed* 444 @: http://www.law.ed.ac.uk/ahrb/script-ed/vol2-4/maccormick.asp; MacQueen, H.L. (2005), 'Towards Utopia or Irreconcilable Tensions? Thoughts on Intellectual Property, Human Rights and Competition Law', 2:4 *SCRIPT-ed* 466 @: http://www.law. ed.ac.uk/ahrb/script-ed/vol2-4/hlm.asp; and Brown, A. and C. Waelde (2005), 'Intellectual Property, Competition and Human Rights: the past, the present and the future', 2:4 *SCRIPT-ed* 422 @: http://www.law.ed.ac.uk/ahrb/script-ed/vol2-4/utopia.asp.

227 [2005] WLR 3590086 ('*Attheraces*').

228 Ibid, H12-3, paras 30–2.

229 Ibid, H33, paras 240–54, 256–8.

230 Ibid, paras 182, 185, 188–9, 199.

231 *Attheraces Ltd v British Horseracing Board Ltd* [2007] EWCA Civ 38 [2007] UKCLR 309 [2007] ECC 7, which took a different approach to assessment of fair price and did not consider welfare.

In a competition action, in addition to damages[232] an injunction could be sought to bring the anticompetitive conduct to an end.[233] Here, this would mean the grant of a licence or the cessation of objections to publication by another, with the latter negative order more attractive to the court.[234] To secure payment, however, the court would need to pursue an approach similar to that in *Ashdown*, building on s. 6 HRA, and find that there should be publication and payment.

Summary

A proactive competition approach might succeed, either through a regulatory remedy, or an order for publication for payment in a private action. However, this slim increase in prospects of success is unlikely to outweigh the risk entailed in raising court proceedings. The regulatory route might prove more fruitful – although it is perhaps unlikely that Russian Roulette would be accorded regulatory priority, and matters might therefore move slowly.

Strategy 5 The 'Alternative' Approach

The above analyses have explored several legal options. A more fundamental course, however, is to pursue a different route entirely. Students and author could liaise with a respected and established 'free speech' NGO, for example the Open Society Institute,[235] and encourage them to approach the media and demand publication. Freed from the constraints of enforceability and relevance in national or ECtHR case law and procedure, reference could be made to all the freedom of expression and information related human rights referred to above.

This approach,[236] which has had success in other fields, such as Brent

---

232 See, for example, *Wireless Group Plc v Radio Joint Audience Research Ltd* 2004 WL 3111423 (action unsuccessful).

233 Successful attempts at the interim stage in competition actions have concerned the posting of job advertisements on a site when those same advertisements were also posted on a competitor's site (*Network Multimedia v Jobserve* 2001 WL 1479864) and restrictions on the design of tennis clothing (*Adidas-Salmon v Draper* 2006 WL 1546637). See also *Getmapping v Ordnance Survey* 2002 WL 820137.

234 Section 12 HRA is again relevant, however, as the grant of the injunction would affect the exercise of freedom of expression.

235 http://www.soros.org/initiatives/issues/education (last accessed 30 August 2007).

236 Exploration of which has developed into a field of its own, even overview of which is outside the scope of this chapter – see, for example, Wild, L. (2006), 'Strengthening Global Civil Society', http://www.globalpolicy.org/ngos/intro/general/2006/04strengthening. pdf (last accessed 30 August 2007); Florini, A.M. (ed.) (2000) *The Third Force: The Rise of Transnational Civil Society*, Japan Center for International Exchange, Tokyo, Japan; and McBarnet, D. (2007), 'Corporate Social

Spar,[237] Nestle/milk substitutes[238] and Nike/labour conditions,[239] might be effective here. Although the University in this hypothetical scenario would have different publicity concerns from the companies concerned in those cases, it may be concerned at suggestions that it is acting contrary to the interests of free speech and academic freedom.[240]

Reference could also be made to the UN Business Norms.[241] Although the Norms are aimed primarily at multinational corporations, they could be interpreted as extending to universities, as 'other business enterprises'.[242] To the extent that these Norms do have impact and can be enforced, therefore, it could be argued that the University has some international human rights obligations.

These approaches, strongly based in human rights values and rhetoric, but outside the direct legal process, might be most effective. It is, however, more difficult to manage. If the work is to be published, it is likely to be demanded to be made available for no charge, and to all. This might not appeal to students or the author. One should consider, before opening Pandora's Box, if one will be happy with what might result.

Responsibility beyond law, through law, for law' chapter 1, pp. 9–56 in D. McBarnet et al (eds) (2007) *The New Corporate Accountability Corporate Social Responsibility and the Law* (Cambridge: Cambridge University Press).

237 Lubbers, E. (1998) 'The Brent Spar Syndrome' http://www.medialounge.net/lounge/workspace/nettime/DOCS/zkp5/pdf/local.pdf (last accessed 30 August 2007).

238 For example, Multinational Monitor July/August 2002 interview with J. Richter vol. 23 Nos 7 & 8 'Corporate Codes of Conduct Regulation, Self-Regulation and the Lessons from the Baby Food Case' http://multinationalmonitor.org/mm2002/02july-aug/july-aug02interviewrichter.html (last accessed 30 August 2007); http://www.babymilkaction.org/pages/boycott.html (last accessed 30 August 2007).

239 See, for example, http://www.ethicalcorp.com/content.asp?ContentID=5181 (last accessed 30 August 2007).

240 Witness, for example, criticism for Google for being seen to accede to what was seen as Chinese censorship – for example, http://www.rsf.org/article.php3?id_article=16262 (last accessed 30 August 2007).

241 See http://www1.umn.edu/humanrts/links/commentary-Aug2003.html and http://www.business-humanrights.org/Gettingstarted/UnitedNationsNorms (both last accessed 29 August 2007). For details and commentary, see Kinley, D. and R. Chambers (2006), 'The UN human rights norms for corporations: the private implications of public international law', *HRL Rev.* 6(3), 447–97 and Kinley, D. et al (2007), '"The Norms are dead! Long live the Norms!" The politics behind the UN Human Rights Norms for corporations', chapter 15, 459–75, in D. McBarnet et al (eds) *The New Corporate Accountability Corporate Social Responsibility and the Law* (Cambridge: Cambridge University Press); see also Brown Responsible.

242 UN Business Norms, A 1.

3. CONCLUSION

It may be possible to achieve publication of the work: the contractual route may be successful and the author amenable to grant of a licence, proactive competition approaches might lead to a licence, the ECtHR might be unusually creative and require not only publication but some form of payment as 'just reparation', or an *Ashdown* type 'damages only' finding might be made.

A regulatory competition approach, building on *IMS*, *Microsoft* and *Magill* and incorporating human rights arguments would seem to be the most sensible means of achieving the outcome sought. It is also possible that publication could be brought about through a complete defence to infringement or a finding of abuse of a dominant position and an injunction requiring cessation of objections. This would mean that the work would be published to all for no fee – an outcome inconsistent with the public interest goals identified at the outset.

From the perspective of the AHRC Centre Project, this analysis confirms the substantial interface between IP, competition and human rights, at theoretical, legislative and practical levels. At least within the legislative and instrumental context, none of the rights conferred or interests protected by these fields are absolute. They contain exceptions, must be balanced, and depending on the fora and starting point, some may appear likely to be accorded greater weight than others.

A recurrent theme in the analysis from each perspective, however, was the right to freedom of expression and information. Human rights are, or should be, centre stage in IP and competition analysis, at least in the UK and the EC. This does not mean that outcomes consistent with human rights to expression and information will invariably be delivered, at least within the adversarial judicial context. A more fundamental revision of the relationship between the fields and accordance of practical supremacy to human rights would require further development in international human rights policy making, treaty and legislation. The battle for this goes on. In the meantime, the human rights contest within IP goes on – against the backdrop of competition law and policy.

BIBLIOGRAPHY

Books

Anderman, S.D. (ed) (2007) *The Interface between Intellectual Property Rights and Competition Policy* (Cambridge, UK: Cambridge University Press).

Bottomley, S. and D. Kinley, (eds) (2002) *Commercial Law and Human Rights* (Virginia, USA: Dartmouth Publishing Company and Aldershot, UK: Ashgate Publishing).

Clayton, R. and H. Tomlinson (2000) *The Law of Human Rights* (Oxford, UK: Oxford University Press).
Gearty, C. (2004) *Principles of Human Rights Adjudication* (Oxford, UK: Oxford University Press).
Ghidini, G. (2006) *Intellectual Property and Competition Law: The Innovation Nexus* (Cheltenham, UK and Northampton, MA, USA: Edward Elgar Publishing).
Govaere, I. (1996) *The Use and Abuse of Intellectual Property Rights in E.C. Law* (London, UK: Sweet & Maxwell).
Jayawickrama, N. (2002) *The Judicial Application of Human Rights Law. National, Regional and International Jurisprudence* (Cambridge, UK: Cambridge University Press).
Kallay, D. (2004) *The Law and Economics of Antitrust and Intellectual Property* (Cheltenham, UK and Northampton, MA, USA: Edward Elgar Publishing).
McBarnet, D. et al (eds) (2007) *The New Corporate Accountability Corporate Social Responsibility and the Law* (Cambridge, UK: Cambridge University Press).
MacQueen, H.L. (1995) (2nd edn) *Copyright, Competition and Industrial Design* (Edinburgh, UK: Hume Papers on Public Policy: Vol. 3 No. 2, Edinburgh University Press).
Nimmer on *Copyright* (2003) (USA: Matthew Bender & Company).
Ward, T. and K. Smith (eds) (2005) *Competition Litigation in the UK* (London, UK: Thomson/Sweet & Maxwell).

Articles

Banner, C. and A. Thomson (2005), 'Human Rights Review of State Acts Performed in Compliance with EC law – Bosphorus Airways v Ireland', *E.H.R.L.R.* 6, 649–659.
Bell, A. and G. Parchomovsky (2002), 'Pliability Rules', October, 101 *Mich. L. Rev.* 1.
Birnhack, M.D. (2003), 'Acknowledging the conflict between copyright and freedom of expression under the Human Rights Act', *Ent. L.R.* 14(2), 24–34.
Brown, A.E.L. (2005), 'Socially responsible intellectual property: a solution?', 2:4 *SCRIPT-ed* 485, available at: http://www.law.ed.ac.uk/ahrc/script-ed/vol2-4/csr.asp.
Brown, A.E.L. (2006), 'Human rights: in the real world', *Journal of Intellectual Property Law & Practice* Vol. 1, Issue 9, 603–613.
Brown, A. and C. Waelde (2005), 'Intellectual property, competition and human rights: the past, the present and the future', 2:4 *SCRIPT-ed* 422, available at: http://www.law.ed.ac.uk/ahrb/script-ed/vol2-4/utopia.asp.
Chapman, A.R. (2001), 'Approaching intellectual property as a human right: obligations related to Article 15(1)(c)', *Copyright Bulletin*, vol. XXXV No. 3, July–September 2001 UNESCO Publishing.
Lord Cooke of Thorndon (1999), 'The British embracement of human rights', *E.H.R.L.R.* 3, 243–260.
Cotter, T.F. (2006), 'The procompetitive interest in intellectual property law', (27 January) Berkeley Center for Law and Technology *Law and Technology Scholarship (Selected by the Berkeley Center for Law & Technology)*. Paper 15, http://repositories.cdlib.org/cgi/viewcontent.cgi?article=1016&context=bclt.
Debeljak, J. (2003), 'The Human Rights Act 1998 (UK): The preservation of Parliamentary supremacy in the context of rights protection', 9 *Australian Journal for Human Rights* 183–235.

Derclaye, E. (2004), 'The IMS Health Decision and the Reconciliation of Copyright and Competition Law', *E.L. Rev.* 29(5), 687–697.

Drahos, P. (1999), 'Intellectual property and human rights', *I.P.Q.* 3, 349–371.

Eagles, I. and L. Longdin (2008), 'Microsoft's refusal to disclose software interoperability information and the Court of First Instance', *E.I.P.R.* 30(5), 205–208.

Facenna, G. (2004), 'Eugen Schmidberger International Transporte Planzuge Austria: freedom of expression and assembly vs free movement of goods', *E.H.R.L.R.* 1, 73–80.

Gearty, C. (2002), 'Reconciling Parliamentary democracy and human rights', *L.Q.R.* 118(Apr), 248–269.

Gearty, C. (2003), 'Revisiting section 3(1) of the Human Rights Act', *L.Q.R.* 119(Oct), 551–553.

Geradin, D. (2004), 'Limiting the Scope of Article 82 EC: what can the EU learn from the U.S. Supreme Court's Judgment in Trinko in the Wake of Microsoft, IMS and Deutsche Telekom', *CML Rev* 41, 1519–1553.

Helfer, Laurence R. (2003), 'Human Rights and Intellectual Property: Conflict or Coexistence?', *Minnesota Journal of Law, Science & Technology*, Vol. 5, p. 47.

Hooper. A. (1998), 'The impact of the Human Rights Act on judicial decision-making', *E.H.R.L.R.* 6, 676–686.

Hovenkamp, H., M.D. Janis and M.A. Lemley (2006), 'Unilateral refusals to license', *J.C.L. & E.* 2(1), 1–42.

Howarth, D. and K. McMahon (2008), 'Windows has performed an illegal operation: the Court of First Instance's judgment in *Microsoft v Commission*', *E.C.L.R.* 29(2), 117–134.

Lord Irvine of Lairg (1999), 'Activism and restraint: human rights and the interpretative process', *E.H.R.L.R.* 4, 350–372.

Johnson, P. (2005), 'The public interest: is it still a defence to copyright infringement?', *Ent. L.R.* 16(1), 1–6.

Korah, V. (2005), 'The interface between intellectual property rights and competition in developed countries', 2:4 *SCRIPT-ed* 429, available at: http://www.law.ed.ac.uk/ahrc/script-ed/vol2-4/korah.asp.

Leach, P. (2005), 'Beyond the bug river. A new dawn for redress before the European Court of Human Rights', *E.H.R.L.R.* 2, 148–164.

MacCormick, N.M. (2005), 'Human rights and competition law: possible impact of the proposed EU Constitution', 2:4 *SCRIPT-ed* 444, available at: http://www.law.ed.ac.uk/ahrb/script-ed/vol2-4/maccormick.asp.

MacQueen, H.L. (2005) 'Towards utopia or irreconcilable tensions? Thoughts on intellectual property, human rights and competition law', 2:4 *SCRIPT-ed* 466, available at: http://www.law.ed.ac.uk/ahrb/script-ed/vol2-4/hlm.asp.

McCann, D. (2006), 'European Union: competition law – abuse of dominant position', *I.C.C.L.R.* 17(4), N27–31.

McMahon, K. (2006), 'Competition law, adjudication and the High Court', 30(3) *Melbourne University Law Review*, 782–836.

Mead, D. (2003), 'Swallowing the camel, straining at the gnat: the implications of *Mendoza v Ghaidan*', *E.H.R.L.R.* 5, 501–514.

Nwauche, E.S. (2005), 'Human Rights – Relevant considerations in respect of IP and competition law', 2:4 *SCRIPT-ed* 467, available at: http://www.law.ed.ac.uk/ahrc/script-ed/vol2-4/enyinna.asp.

Ong, B. (2004), 'Anti competitive refusals to grant copyright licences: reflections on the IMS saga', *E.I.P.R.* 26(11), 505–514.

Ong, B. (2005), 'Building brick barricades and other barriers to entry: abusing a dominant position by refusing to license intellectual property rights', *E.C.L.R.* 26(4), 215–224.

Parga, A.H. (2006), 'Bosphorus v Ireland and the protection of fundamental rights in Europe', *E.L.Rev.* 31(2), 251–259.

Phillipson, G. (1999), 'The Human Rights Act, "horizontal effect" and the common law: a bang or a whimper?', *M.L.R.* 62(6), 824–849.

Phillipson, G. (2003), '(Mis)-reading section 3 of the Human Rights Act', *L.Q.R.* 119(Apr), 183–188.

Preece, S. (1999), 'ITT Promedia v EC Commission: Establishing an Abuse of Predatory Litigation', *E.C.L.R.* 20(2), 188–122.

Ridyard, D. (2004), 'Compulsory access under EC competition law – a new doctrine of "convenient facilities" and the case for price regulation', *E.C.L.R.* 25(11), 669–673.

Sackville, R. (Justice) (2005), 'Monopoly versus freedom of ideas: The expansion of intellectual property', 16 *AIPJ* 65 at 74–5.

Sims, A. (2006), 'The public interest defence in copyright law: myth or reality?', *E.I.P.R.* 28(6), 335–343.

Spence, M. (1988), 'Intellectual property and the problem of parody', 114 *LQR* 594.

Stothers, C. (2004), 'IMS Health and its implications for compulsory licensing in Europe', *E.I.P.R.* 26(10), 467–472.

Vezzoso, S. (2006), 'The incentives balance test in the EU Microsoft case: a pro-innovation "economics-based" approach?', *E.C.L.R.* 27(7), 382–390.

Chapters in Books

Netanel, N.W. (2005), 'Copyright and "Market Power" in the Marketplace of Ideas', in F. Leveque and H. Shelanski (eds), *Antitrust, Patents and Copyright. EU and US Perspectives* (Cheltenham, UK and Northampton, MA, USA: Edward Elgar Publishing).

Waelde, C. (2006), 'Copyright, Corporate Power and Human rights: Reality and Rhetoric', in F. Macmillan (ed), *New Directions in Copyright Law*, vol. 2 (Cheltenham, UK and Northampton, MA, USA: Edward Elgar Publishing).

Legislation

Council Regulation (EC) No. 1/2003 of 16 December 2002 on the implementation of the rules on competition laid down in Articles 81 and 82 of the Treaty OJ L 1, 4.1.2003.

Sections 16, 21, 30, 171(3) Copyright Designs and Patents Act 1988 (UK).

Sections 18 and 60 Competition Act 1998 (UK).

Sections 2, 3, 6, 12 Human Rights Act 1998 (UK).

Treaties

Article 82 EC Treaty.

Article 10 and Protocol 1 Article 1 European Convention on Human Rights 1951.

Article 15 International Covenant on Economic Social and Cultural Rights 1966.

Article 27(2) Universal Declaration of Human Rights 1948.

Agreement on Trade-Related Aspects of Intellectual Property Rights (TRIPS) Annex 1C to the WTO Agreement.
Norms on the Responsibilities of Transnational Corporations and Other Business Enterprises with Regard to Human Rights (and Commentary) http://www1.umn.edu/humanrts/links/commentary-Aug2003.html.
Treaty on European Union (consolidated text) Official Journal C 321E of 29 December 2006.

Guidelines

Commission Notice on the definition of the relevant market for the purposes of Community competition law [1997] O.J. C372/03.
Commission Guidelines on the effect on trade concept contained in Articles 81 and 82 of the Treaty [2004] O.J. C101/81.
UK Office of Fair Trading *Market Definition* OFT 403.
UK Office of Fair Trading *Assessment of Market Power* OFT 415.

Cases – England

Adidas-Salmon v Draper 2006 WL 1546637.
Ashdown v Telegraph Ltd [2002] Ch 149.
Attheraces Ltd v British Horseracing Board [2005] WL 3590086.
Attheraces Ltd v British Horseracing Board Ltd [2007] EWCA Civ 38, [2007] UKCLR 309, [2007] ECC 7.
British Leyland Motor Corporation v Armstrong Patents Company Limited [1986] RPC 279.
British Leyland v T.I. Silencers [1981 FSR 213, 217.
Campbell v Mirror Group Newspapers Ltd [2004] 2 AC 457.
Canon Kabushiki Kaisha v Green Cartridge Company (Hong Kong) Limited [1997] FSR 817.
Chiron Corporation v Murex Diagnostics (No. 2) [1994] FSR 187.
Getmapping v Ordnance Survey 2002 WL 820137.
Glaxo v Dowelhurst [2000] FSR 371.
HRH Prince of Wales v Associated Newspapers Ltd [2006] EWHC 522 and [2006] EWCA Civ 1776, [2007] 3 WLR 222.
Hewlett-Packard v Expansys 2005 WL 1748806.
HM Stationery Office v Automobile Association Ltd [2001] ECC 34.
ICI v Berk [1981] FSR 1.
Intel Corp. v Via Technologies Inc [2003] FSR 33.
Mars UK Ltd v Teknowledge Ltd [2000] ECDR 99.
Microsoft Corp. v Ling [2006] EWHC 1619, 2006 WL 1887046.
Murray v Express Newspapers Plc [2007] EWHC 1908 (Ch).
Network Multimedia v Jobserve 2001 WL 1479864.
Panayiotou and Others v Sony Music Entertainment [1994] EMLR 229.
R v Secretary of State for Transport ex p Factortame (No. 2) [1991] 1 AC 603.
SanDisk Corp v Koninklijke Philips Electronics NV [2007] FSR 22.
Schroeder Music Publishing v Macaulay[1974] 1 WLR 1308, [1974] 3 All ER 616.
Sportswear v Ghattaura [2006] ETMR 66.
Wireless Group Plc v Radio Joint Audience Research Ltd 2004 WL 3111423.

Cases – EC

BRT v Sabam [1974] ECR 51.
CILFIT Srl v Ministero della Sanita (283/81) [1982] ECR 3415 [1983] 1 CMLR 472.
Commercial Solvents Corp. v EC Commission [1974] ECR 223.
Commission of the European Communities v Microsoft Case COMP/C-3/37 available via http://ec.europa.eu/comm/competition/antitrust/cases/decisions/37792/en.pdf.
Costa v ENEL [1964] ECR 1141.
Crehan v Courage [2001] ECR I-6297.
Eugen Schmidberger Internationale Transporte Planzuge v Austria (C112/00) [2003] ECR I-5659.
F Hoffmann La Roche & Co. AG v Commission of the European Communities [1979] ECR 461.
Garden Cottage Foods v Milk Marketing Board [1984] AC 130.
IMS Health GmbH & Co. OHG v NDC Health GmbH & Co. KG [2004] ECR I-5039.
Internationale HandelsgesellschaftGmbH v Einfuhr- und Vorratsstelle fur Getreide und Futtermittel 1970 ECR 1125.
ITT Promedia v EC Commission [1998] ECR II-2937.
Michelin v Commission [1983] ECR 3461.
Micro Leader v EC Commission [2000] ECDR 217.
Microsoft Corp. v Commission of the European Communities (T-201/04) [2007] 5 CMLR 11.
Oscar Bronner GMbH & Co. KG v Mediaprint [1998] ECR 1-7791, [1999] 4 CMLR 112.
Parke Davis & Co. v Probel (24/67) [1968] CMLR 47.
Roquette Freres SA v Directeur General de la Concurrence [2002] ECR I-9011.
RTE and ITP v EC Commission [1995] ECR I-743.
Society for the Protection of the Unborn Child Ireland v Grogan [1991] ECR I-4685.
Synetairismos Farmakopoion Aitolias & Akarnanias (SYFAIT) v Glaxosmithkline Plc (C53/03) [2005] ECR I-4609.
Van Gend en Loos [1963] ECR 1.
Volvo AB v Erik Veng (UK) Ltd [1988] ECR 6211.

Cases – ECtHR

Bosphorus v Ireland (2006) 42 EHRR 1.
Casado Coca v Spain (1994) 18 EHRR 1.
Handyside v UK (1979–80) 1 EHRR 737.
Markt Intern Verlag GmbH v Germany (A/164) (1990) 12 EHRR 161.
Sporrong and Lonnroth v Sweden (1982) 5 EHRR 35.

Cases – US

Lasercomb v Reynolds 911 F.2d 970 (4th Cir 1990).
Morton Salt Co. v G.S. Suppiger Co. 312 U.S. 488 (1942).
Rosemount Enterprise v Random House 366 F.2d. 303 (2nd Cir 1966).
Time Inc. v Geis 293 F. Supp 130.

Cases – Australia

ACCC v Boral Besser Masonry [2003] HCA 5.

Enquiries and Reports

'EC Commission review of Article 82 and Exclusionary Abuses', full details at http://ec.europa.eu/comm/competition/antitrust/art82/index.html.

'Committee of Ministers Recommendation to Member States on Improvement of Domestic Remedies' Rec(2004)6 https://wcd.coe.int/ViewDoc.jsp?id=743317&BackColorInternet=9999CC&BackColorIntranet=FFBB55&BackColorLogged=FFAC75.

'Federal Trade Commission Staff Report: Enforcement Perspectives on the Noerr-Pennington Doctrine' http://www.ftc.gov/reports/P013518enfperspectNoerr-Penningtondoctrine.pdf.

'Proceedings and reports of the Competition and Intellectual Property Law and Policy in the Knowledge-Based Economy – Joint Hearings of the Federal Trade Commission and Department of Justice' http://www.ftc.gov/opp/intellect/.

'Antitrust Enforcement and Intellectual Property Rights: Promoting Innovation and Competition: A Report Issued By the U.S. Department of Justice and the Federal Trade Commission' (April 2007) http://www.ftc.gov/opa/2007/04/ipreport.shtm.

12. Human rights' limitations in patent law

Geertrui Van Overwalle*

INTRODUCTION

The relationship between human rights and intellectual property (IP) rights has been undertheorized for a long period. IP rights have remained a 'normative backwater' in the burgeoning post-World War II human rights movement.[1] Only over the last decade, human rights discourse has gained wider attention and commentators have started to explore the relationship between IP and human rights in more detail.[2] Two major approaches can be witnessed. A first school of thought takes the view that human rights and IP are in fundamental *conflict*. Strong IP protection is undermining, and therefore incompatible with, a broad spectrum of human rights obligations, especially in the area of economic, social and cultural rights. This approach can be witnessed in Resolution 2000/7, which stipulates that 'Actual or potential conflicts exist between the implementation of the TRIPs Agreement[3] and the realization of

* Professor of Intellectual Property Law at the University of Leuven, the University of Brussels and the University of Liège (Belgium); and professor of Patent Law and New Technologies at the University of Tilburg (The Netherlands). The present research was supported by the the Vancraesbeeck Fund. Special thanks go to Paul Lemmens for his valuable comments on an earlier draft of this chapter.

[1] Helfer, L.R. (2006), 'Toward a Human Rights Framework for Intellectual Property', Vanderbilt University Law School Public Law and Legal Theory. Working Paper 06-03 (available at http://ssrn.com/abstract=891303, last visited June 2009).

[2] Cf. Helfer, L.R. (2003), 'Human Rights and Intellectual Property: Conflict or Coexistence?' *Minnesota Intellectual Property Review*, Fall 2003 (available at http://law.vanderbilt.edu/faculty/pubs/helfer-humanrights.pdf?abstract_id=459120, last visited June 2009).

[3] The multilateral trade negotiations in the GATT Uruguay Round, which were concluded in 1993 and resulted in the formation of the WTO, encompassed for the first time discussions on aspects of intellectual property rights. The result of those negotiations was embodied in the Agreement on Trade-Related Aspects of Intellectual Property Rights (TRIPS Agreement), contained in an Annex to the WTO Agreement

economic, social and cultural rights'.[4] Resolving this conflict lies in the recognition of the primacy of human rights law over IP law and in viewing IP as instruments designed to fulfil human rights objectives.[5] A second way of thinking claims that human rights and IP are essentially compatible and can *coexist*. Indeed, human rights and IP focus on the same fundamental question and share the same goal. Both human rights and IP rights aim at enhancing welfare and the benefit for society.[6] Both legal regimes equally try to define the appropriate scope of private rights, while safeguarding public interest. A clear exponent of this attitude is reflected in the International Covenant on Economic, Social and Cultural Rights (ICESCR).[7]

The present chapter aims at exploring the delicate relationship between the human rights pantheon and the patent framework in more depth. The normative perspective underlying the present chapter is that human rights can coexist with IP rights. Human rights are valuable and necessary complements of patent rights. Human rights serve as a counter balance of patent rights when centering too one-sidedly on trade, access to markets and economic calculus. For patent law to be widely accepted and generally recognized as a tool fostering both private and public interest, it is vital that current patent law regimes are inextricably linked with human rights discourse, and that human rights assist in defining the utter limits of patent rights. Patent law should be moulded as a human rights compliant legal framework to promote innovation. The normative claim put forward in the present chapter is based on a reassessment of the notion of public interest in patent law and an analysis of human rights treaties. Human rights can be factored into patent law, through the gateway of public interest. A post-modern interpretation of public interest will

(see http://www.wto.org/english/tratop_e/trips_e/t_agm0_e.htm, last visited June 2009). Membership in the WTO implies adherence to the TRIPS Agreement.

4 United Nations, Sub-Commission on the Promotion and Protection of Human Rights, Resolution 2000/7, 'Intellectual property rights and human rights', 17 August 2000 (available at http://www.unhchr.ch/Huridocda/Huridoca.nsf/0/c462b62cf8a07b13c12569700046704e?Opendocument, last visited June 2009).

5 This is the view taken by Drahos, P. (1999), 'The Universality of Intellectual Property Rights: Origins and Development', Intellectual Property and Human Rights, Conference organised by the WIPO in collaboration with the Office of the UN High Commissioner for Human Rights to commemorate the 50th Anniversary of the Universal Declaration of Human Rights, Geneva, 9 November 1998. The paper presented at the WIPO Conference was later published under the title 'Intellectual Property Rights and Human Rights' in *I.P.Q.*, 349–371.

6 This is the view taken by Geiger, C. (2006), 'Constitutionalising Intellectual Property Law? The Influence of Fundamental Rights on Intellectual Property in the European Union', 37 *IIC*, 371–500.

7 International Covenant on Economic, Social and Cultural Rights, adopted by the General Assembly, resolution 2200A (XXI) of 16 December 1966, and entered into force on 3 January 1976.

prove to offer a more than skeletal basis for taking into account human rights in patent law, and to have prompted new human rights standards in the patent law system.

The present chapter focuses on human rights and human values, and draws attention to civil, political, economic and social, as well as cultural, rights. Human rights and values which are considered here as particularly relevant are human dignity, the right to food, the right to informed consent, the right to protection, the right of access to public health, the right to education and research, and the right of access to information. These human rights and values fulfil different functions in a patent law context. Some rights and values, such as human dignity and the right to food, act as a basis to limit the coming into *existence* of patent rights in certain fields (Section 2). Other rights, such as the right to informed consent and the right of protection as translated in an origin requirement, act as a means to implement *procedural* guarantees in the patent application procedure (Section 3). Yet other human rights, such as the right of access to public health and the right to education and research serve as limitations with regard to the *exercise* of patent rights (Section 4). Although the right of access to information fits into this last category at first sight, it has a somewhat ambiguous position in the human rights and patent rights debate. Before embarking on a further analysis, some clarification regarding the concepts and terminology used is offered (Section 1).

1. CONCEPTS AND CLASSIFICATIONS

1.1. Human Rights

The classification of human rights appears to be rather complex. Some scholars make a distinction between ordinary rights and fundamental human rights, the latter being of such importance that 'no legislative organ may lawfully take these rights away from citizens'.[8] The qualification of rights as fundamental human rights mainly depends on the stage of development of a society. Other scholars claim that human rights can be broken up in three generations: civil and political rights (first generation), economic, social and cultural rights (second generation) and solidarity rights (third generation) encompassing the right to development, the right to peace, the right to environment and the right to humanitarian assistance.[9] Yet, other authors categorize human rights

---

[8] Schermers, H.G., 'The international protection of the right of property', in F. Matscher and H. Petzold (eds) (1988), *Protecting Human Rights: the European Dimension* (Köln: Carl Heymanns), 1988, 565–580.

[9] Vasak, K. (1984), 'Pour une troisième génération des droits de l'homme', in

according to the type or level of obligations they impose on states, and observe the obligations to respect, protect and fulfil. The obligation to respect requires that States refrain from interfering directly or indirectly with the enjoyment of the right. The obligation to protect requires States to take measures that prevent third parties from interfering with the rights. The obligation to fulfil requires States to adopt appropriate legislative, administrative, budgetary and other appropriate measures towards the full realization of the right.[10] Likewise, some thoughtful observers distinguish between human rights and human values. In their view, concepts such as dignity are underlying values, but not rights as such. They serve as guidelines for interpreting the rights.[11] The present chapter will review a set of rights and values which serve human interest. In doing so, the chapter will not only identify pertinent civil rights and values, but also focus on social and economic rights. Assessing the implications of social and economic rights in patent law will prove to be of particular importance in the field of health and food.

The identification and recognition of (new) human rights in international law seems rather delicate as well. The human rights regime is expanding. As a result of the expansion of human rights, many more interests become the subject matter of rights claims. New rights claim to be recognized as human rights. For a long time it was unclear to what extent new rights fit into the conceptual framework and deserve the status of human rights.[12] Quality

---

C. Swinarski (ed), *Studies and Essays on International Humanitarian Law and Red Cross Principles in Honour of Jean Pictet* (The Hague: Martinus Nijhoff), 1984, 837–845; Vasak, K. (1990), 'Les différentes catégories des droits de l'homme', in A. Lapeyre, F. de Tinguy and K. Vasak (eds) *Les dimensions universelles des droits de l'homme* (Brussels: Bruylant), vol. I, 297–316.

[10] HRC, General comment on obligations of States – cf. Eide, A. (1989), 'The human right to adequate food and freedom from hunger', FAO (available at http://www.fao.org/docrep/w9990e/w9990e03.htm, last visited June 2009); Eide, Asbjorn (1989), 'The Right to Adequate Food as a Human Right', Study Series No. 1. (Geneva and New York: United Nations Center for Human Rights); Eide, A. (1996), 'Human Rights Requirements to Social and Economic Development', *Food Policy*, 23–39; Eide, A., W. B. Eide, S. Goonatilake, S. Gussow and J. Omawale (eds) (1984), *Food as a Human Right* (Tokyo: United Nations University); Eide, A., A. Oshaung and W.B. Eide (1991), 'Food Security and the Right to Food in International Law and Development', *Transnational Law and Contemporary Problems*, 1(2), 416–467.

[11] Cf. Fierens, J. (2002), 'La dignité humaine comme concept juridique', J.T., 577–582; Hermeren, G., 'European Values, Ethics and Law. Present Policies and Future Challenges', in *Jahrbuch für Wissenschaft und Ethik*, (5), 8–9 and footnote 10 in particular: 'A distinction is sometimes made between values and human rights. . . . I would be inclined to think that we have agreed on certain human rights and codified them in international documents, because these human rights promote or protect certain important values'.

[12] The discussion is especially strong with regard to the third generation of

control on the origination of such rights was suggested.[13] As yet, this debate has greatly faded away and little willingness is left to recognize new rights as human rights. The present chapter will review a series of widely recognized human rights, such as the right to food, the right to informed consent, the right of access to public health, the right to education and research, and the right of access to information, as well as generally accepted values, such as human dignity.

The foundational, international document, which shaped or 'constitutionalized' the human rights regime is the Universal Declaration of Human Rights of 1948 (UDHR).[14] However, the UDHR is just a declaration, lacking enforceability. The rights of the UDHR were further developed and given greater specificity in the ICESCR, as well as enforceability in those states which ratified the Covenant. The present chapter will scrutinize both the UDHR and the ICESCR, as well as some other, highly relevant, international and European conventions and treaties.

1.2 Patent Law

Patent law was once introduced to create incentives to develop new goods and services and to disclose underlying technologies, by granting the patentee a temporary monopoly on the patented invention in return for the disclosure of the description of the invention. In doing so, patent law aimed at serving both private and public interest. The *private* interest of the inventor is guaranteed through the grant of a limited monopoly right as a reward for creativity and inventiveness, including necessary investments in research and development efforts.[15] The *public* interest is served through the dissemination of the technical information related to the patent and the development of accessible goods and services. Although the debate on the legitimation of IP and patent systems has a long and turbulent history, the present consequentialist, utilitarian justification, focusing on both the incentive to invent/innovate and the incentive to disclose argument,[16] is probably most accepted to date.

---

collective rights. For more, see Crawford, J. (ed) (1988), *The Rights of Peoples* (Oxford: Clarendon Press).

13 Alston, P. (1984), 'Conjuring up New Human Rights: a Proposal for Quality Control', AJIL, 607.

14 On 10 December 1948 the General Assembly of the United Nations adopted and proclaimed the Universal Declaration of Human Rights.

15 Gervais, D. (2003), *The TRIPs Agreement. Drafting History and Analysis* (London: Sweet & Maxwell), p. 81, point 2.10.

16 For more on this theory, as well as the other justifications theories, see Sterckx, S. (2005), 'The Ethics of Patenting – Uneasy Justifications', in P. Drahos (ed), *Death of Patents* (Oxon: Lawtext Publishing), 175–211.

Human rights contribute to the basic concepts of patent law in a twofold way. First and foremost, human rights feed into the *private* interest component of patent law. It can be argued that Article 27 (2) UDHR and Article 15(1)(c) ICESCR act as a *foundation* for claiming that patent rights are human rights. Article 27 (2) stipulates that 'Everyone has the right to the protection of the moral and material interests resulting from any scientific, literary or artistic production of which he is the author', and Article 15(1)(c) ICESCR equally says that signatory states recognize the right of everyone 'To benefit from the protection of the moral and material interests resulting from any scientific, literary or artistic production of which he is the author'. In the same vein, the Grand Chamber of the European Court of Human Rights (ECHR) recently confirmed that Article 1 of Protocol No. 1, guaranteeing the right to the protection of property, equally applies to intellectual property as such (*Anheuser-Busch Inc. v Portugal*).[17] [18] This line of reasoning will not be further developed here,[19] only to the extent that the right to protection for biodiversity and traditional knowledge holders, complicates the coming into existence of the right to protection of patent holders (see Section 3.2).

Additionally, human rights add to the *public* interest component of patent law. In that regard, the present chapter will analyse how human rights discourse can contribute in establishing a post-modern approach to the public interest component in patent law, and how certain human rights can act as *limits* to patent rights.

1.3 Public Interest

Traditionally, the public interest component of patent law has been given a rather economic interpretation. Patent law was a tool for promoting – both private and – public interest, public interest being understood in terms of

---

[17] ECHR, Grand Chamber, 11 January 2007, *Anheuser-Busch Inc. v Portugal* (Application no. 73049/01) (see http://cmiskp.echr.coe.int/tkp197/view.asp?item=2&portal=hbkm&action=html&highlight=ANHEUSER-BUSCH%20%7C%20PORTUGAL&sessionid=11307840&skin=hudoc-en, last visited 14 February 2007).

[18] In doing so, the Grand Chamber reinforced the case law of the European Commission of Human Rights (ECHR) in *Smith Kline and French Laboratories Ltd v The Netherlands*, from 4 October 1990 (Application no. 12633/87): 'The Commission notes that under Dutch law the holder of a patent is referred to as the proprietor of a patent and that patents are deemed, subject to the provisions of the Patent Act, to be personal property which is transferable and assignable. The Commission finds that a patent accordingly falls within the scope of the term "possessions" in Article 1 of Protocol No. 1' (see http://cmiskp.echr.coe.int, last visited June 2009).

[19] The first question, whether patent rights can be qualified – yes or no – as human rights, is the topic of the contributions from Jan Brinkhof (Chapter 8) and Martin Adelman (Chapter 14) in this book.

economic expansion and technological progress. Witness, for example, the intervention of Charles Rogier, the then Minister of Internal Affairs who submitted the first proposal for a patent act to the Belgian Parliament in 1854:[20] *'Il y a, messieurs, dans ce projet de loi deux grands intérêts à protéger: c'est d'abord l'intérêt des inventeurs qui ont droit à jouir du produit de leur invention; en second lieu l'intérêt du travail national, qui se confond avec l'intérêt de la société'*.[21] This economic interpretation prevailed for quite some time in legal doctrine as well.[22]

A mainly economic approach seems to be unfit to date. There is a clear need for a wider, contemporary interpretation of the public interest component in patent law. One approach to update the public interest concept, is to consult theological, philosophical, politicological or economic writings. However, this literature often deploys a *holistic* perspective, with a high level of abstraction and rather unwieldy notions.[23] An alternative approach to contemporize the public interest component, is to 'desacralize' this concept and to anatomize it in its various *concrete* emanations in a series of legislation. An analysis of the public interest concept in legal discourse, more in particular in civil law, judicial law, administrative law, medical law, economic law and competition law, both at the national and the European level,[24] clearly demonstrates that the public interest is a mosaic encompassing *ordre public*, morality, public security, protection of the consumer, health safety, protection of public health and

---

[20] Belgian Patent Act [Wet op de uitvindingsoctrooien], 24 May 1854, Official Gazette [Belgisch Staatsblad], 25 May 1854.

[21] Parliamentary Proceedings [Handelingen], 1853–54, 8 December 1853, 181.

[22] See for Belgium: Gotzen, F. (1989), 'Industriële eigendomsrechten', in R. Dillemans and Van Gerven, W. (eds), *Beginselen van Belgisch Privaatrecht, XIII, Handels- en economisch recht, Deel I, Ondernemingsrecht*, volume A (Brussels: Story), (287), 309; Remouchamps, L. (1969), 'Octrooien', in *Algemene Praktische Rechtsverzameling*, (Brussels: Larcier), 55. See for Germany: Benkard, G. (1993), 'Patentgesetz', in *Beck'sches Kurz Kommentare*, 4 (München: Beck), 46–47; Bernhardt, W. and R. Krasser (1986), *Lehrbuch des Patentrechts* (München: Beck), 24–25. See for the Netherlands: Brinkhof, J. (2000), 'Clinical trials. De situatie in Nederland', in G. Van Overwalle (ed.), *Octrooirecht en geneesmiddelen* (Brussel: Bruylant), (93), 95; Schutjens, M.-H. D.B. (1993), *Octrooirecht en geneesmiddelen. Een rechtsvergelijkende studie naar de juridische aspecten van medisch-farmaceutische uitvindingen in het octrooirecht* (Apeldoorn: Maklu), 1.

[23] See Van Overwalle, G. (2000), 'Klinische proeven en volksgezondheid. Naar een herijking van het algemeen belang in het octrooirecht', *Tijdschrift voor Privaatrecht (TPR)*, 899–968. Also see Van Overwalle, G. (2008a), 'L'intérêt général, le domaine public, les commons et le droit des brevets d'invention', in *L'intérêt général et l'accès à l'information en propriété intellectuelle* (Brussel: Bruylant) 149–175.

[24] Such a survey has previously been undertaken by the author in Van Overwalle, references previous footnote.

protection of the lives of persons, animals and plants. The list of human rights coming to the fore here might be expanded to other human rights. Re-interpreting the notion of public interest can be realized through a further elaboration of human rights discourse in patent law through the gateway of public interest. The human rights pantheon offers a welcome supplement to the current public interest concept in patent law, and adds notions such as human dignity, personal integrity, food security, informed consent, access to health care and access to information. Human rights offer concepts essential to a contemporary interpretation of the public interest component in patent law. Patent law serves the public interest if it does not focus too one-sidedly on market access, economic welfare and technological progress, but equally pays attention to social welfare.

The aforementioned human rights are all articulated in the UDHR and/or the ICESCR. This catalogue of human rights restricts and limits patent law on a double level. First of all, human rights limit the coming into being, the *existence* of patent rights (see Section 2). Second, human rights limit the *exercise* of patent rights (see Section 4). Furthermore, human rights add additional procedural requirements in patent law (see Section 3).

2. HUMAN RIGHTS LIMITING THE EXISTENCE OF PATENT RIGHTS

2.1 Human Dignity

Human dignity appears as a pivotal concept in the *preamble* of a variety of international and European conventions. The UDHR already underlined in 1948 that 'recognition of the inherent dignity and of the equal and inalienable rights of all members of the human family is the foundation of freedom, justice and peace in the world'. Although the notion of human dignity has no literal equivalent in the European Convention for the Protection of Human Rights and Fundamental Freedoms of 1950 (ECHR), the notion is well established in case law.[25] The notion is implemented expressis verbis in the Charter of

---

[25] See, for example, ECHR, 22 November 1995, *S.W. v U.K.*, Publ. Cont., Series A, vol. 335-B, § 44, where the Court underlined that 'the abandonment of the unacceptable idea of a husband being immune against prosecution for rape of his wife was in conformity not only with a civilised concept of marriage but also, and above all, with the fundamental objectives of the Convention, the very essence of which is respect for human dignity and human freedom'. Also see ECHR, 22 November 1995, C.R. v U.K., Publ.. Cont., Series A, vol. 335-C, § 42ff.

Fundamental Rights of the European Union (European Charter)[26] which recalls that 'the Union is founded on the indivisible, universal values of human dignity, freedom, equality and solidarity and that it is based on the principles of democracy and the rule of law'. The concept of human dignity equally appears in a context of research on and use of the human body and the human genome, more in particular in the Convention for the Protection of Human Rights and Dignity of the Human Being with regard to the Application of Biology and Medicine[27] (Oviedo Convention) which announces that 'Convinced of the need to respect the human being both as an individual and as a member of the human species and recognising the importance of ensuring the dignity of the human being', and which warns that 'the misuse of biology and medicine may lead to acts endangering human dignity' (Preamble Oviedo Convention).

Human dignity is explicitly taken up as a *full provision* in a limited series of international and European conventions as well. In a general sense, the European Charter stipulates in its first article that 'Human dignity is inviolable. It must be respected and protected'. In order to protect human dignity in a context of increasing research on the human body, some international instruments also came about. More in particular, the Universal Declaration on the Human Genome and Human Rights,[28] underlines that 'The human genome underlies the fundamental unity of all members of the human family, as well as the recognition of their inherent dignity and diversity. In a symbolic sense, it is the heritage of humanity' (Article 1). The Oviedo Convention equally stipulates in its first article that signatory states 'shall protect the dignity and identity of all human beings and guarantee everyone, without discrimination, respect for their integrity and other rights and fundamental freedoms with regard to the application of biology and medicine'.

As becomes clear from the foregoing, the concept of the inherent dignity of the human person is well established, both in international and European law. The connection between human dignity and patent law, however, is quite recent. That should not come as a surprise, as developments in human genet-

---

[26] Charter of Fundamental Rights of the European Union, (2000/C 364/01), Official Journal of the European Communities C, 364/1, 18 December 2000.

[27] Convention for the Protection of Human Rights and Dignity of the Human Being with regard to the Application of Biology and Medicine – Convention on Human Rights and Biomedicine, Oviedo, 4 April 1997.

[28] The Universal Declaration on the Human Genome and Human Rights was adopted unanimously and by acclamation at UNESCO's 29th General Conference on 11 November 1997. The following year, the United Nations General Assembly endorsed the Declaration (the text is available at http://portal.unesco.org/shs/en/ev.php-URL_ID=1881&URL_DO=DO_TOPIC&URL_SECTION=201.html, last visited June 2009).

ics and subsequent debates on patentability have mainly emerged over the last two decades. In response to these developments and debates, the scope of subject matter in patent law has expanded significantly and the twentieth century has exponentially seen new subject matter added to patent law. Especially in the field of natural and biological sciences, patent law has adapted itself to the new reality of genetics by extending protection to biological material. At present, patent protection is available for micro-organisms, plants, animals and elements isolated from the human body, including genes. Patent offices as a matter of routine grant patents related hitherto and the patenting of genetic engineering products has often been presented as a natural and logical application of the basic principles of patentability, simply extended to biotechnology.

Predicated by the centrality of protecting and nurturing human dignity, a human rights approach has irrefutably led to some significant limitations and restrictions to the expansionary tendency in patent law. The subject matter of patent law has been limited when human dignity is at stake, and a proposed invention is denied patent protection if it is inconsistent with the inherent dignity of the human person. This reflex of human dignity in patent law appeared for the first time in the European Community in the *proposal* for an EU Biotechnology Directive in 1988.[29] The proposal stated that 'processes for modifying the genetic identity of the human body for a non-therapeutic purpose which is contrary to the dignity of man' are unpatentable (for example, implicit reference to cloning and chimera-production). The article was implemented to preserve human genetic integrity, and more in particular, in an attempt to exclude the patenting of processes eliminating flaws or enhancing human potential (eugenics) making use of patented gene sequences. The notion was also implemented in the *final* EU Biotechnology Directive of 1998,[30] yet only as a recital. Recital 16 stipulates that 'patent law must be applied so as to respect the fundamental principles safeguarding the dignity and integrity of the person' and that 'it is important to assert the principle that the human body, at any stage in its formation or development, cannot be patented'. In turn, recital 38 echoes the first proposal and underlines that 'processes, the use of which offend against human dignity, such as processes to produce chimeras from germ cells or totipotent cells of humans and animals, are obviously also

[29] Proposal for a Council Directive on the legal protection of biotechnological inventions, October 1988, Official Journal EC C, 13 January 1989, 10/3. The proposal was eventually rejected by the European Parliament on 1 March 1995 (see Official Journal EC C, 20 March 1995, 68/26).

[30] Directive 98/44/EC of 6 July 1998 of the European Parliament and of the Council on the legal protection of biotechnological inventions, Official Journal EC L 213/13 of 30/07/1998 13 (available at http://europa.eu.int, last visited June 2009).

excluded from patentability'. It may seem strange that the first-ever reference to the principle of respect for human dignity was made in a Directive on patents. It can be seen as an indication of the concern aroused by certain developments in the fields of human genetics and medicine.

The link between human dignity and patent law, was also explored in depth by the European Group on Ethics in Science and New Technologies (EGE), and its predecessor the Group of Advisers to the European Commission on the Ethical Implications of Biotechnology (GAEIB).[31] The task of the Group is to examine ethical questions arising from science and new technologies and on this basis to issue Opinions to the European Commission in connection with the preparation and implementation of Community legislation or policies. Examining the various opinions of the GAEIB/EGE clearly demonstrates that this advisory body supports the integration of a human rights approach in patent law, especially in the context of human genetics. Reference is explicitly made to the respect for human rights and fundamental freedoms,[32] the respect for 'fundamental rights of the human person'[33] and the respect for human dignity.[34] In its very first Opinion of 1993, the GAEIB admitted that in pursuit of its economic and social objectives, it is essential for the Community to harmonize patent law relating to biotechnology. The GAEIB underlined that the need to protect human dignity does not contravene patenting, and that there are no ethical objections to the patenting of biotechnological inventions per se.[35] In its second opinion, the GAEIB brings to mind Article 6 of the Treaty on the European Union, underlining that (1) the Union is founded on the principles of liberty, democracy, respect for human rights and fundamental freedoms, and the rule of law, principles which are common to the Member States, and that (2) the Union shall respect fundamental rights, as guaranteed by the ECHR and as they result from the constitutional traditions common to the

---

[31] The EGE is a neutral, independent, pluralist and multidisciplinary body, composed of experts appointed by the Commission for their expertise and personal qualities, representing a broad range of professional competences in different disciplines such as, biology and genetics, medicine, pharmacology, agricultural sciences, ICT, law, ethics, philosophy, and theology. Further information at http://ec.europa.eu/european_group_ethics/index_en.htm (last visited June 2009).

[32] GAEIB, Opinion. no. 8, referring to Article F2 of the Treaty of the European Union.

[33] GAEIB, Opinion no. 8, para. 1.6.

[34] GAEIB, Opinion no. 3, para. 2.2.3; GAEIB, Opinion no. 8, para. 2.1; EGE, Opinion no 16, referring to Article 1 of the European Charter.

[35] GAEIB, Opinion no. 3, 30 September 1993, Ethical questions arising from the Commission Proposal for a Council Directive on Legal Protection for Biotechnological Inventions (also available at http://ec.europa.eu/european_group_ethics/index_en.htm, last visited June 2009).

Member States, as general principles of Community law.[36] [37] The GAEIB equally underlines that the EU Biotechnology Directive aims to actualize and adapt patent law to the specific case of biotechnological inventions which, when they are based on elements of human origin, involve the issue of fundamental rights of the human person. More in particular, the GAEIB takes the view that whatever is the nature of the biotechnological invention involving elements of human origin, the Directive must give sufficient guarantee so that refusal to grant a patent on an invention in so far as it infringes the rights of the person and the respect of human dignity should be legally founded.[38] The affirmation of the citizen's rights in the European Union implies that the economic advantages derived from biotechnological developments should in no way affect the respect for ethical requirements.[39]

The relationship between human dignity and patent law, and the extent to which the respect for human dignity can limit patent law, was also subject of debate in the Committee on Economic Social and Cultural Rights of the United Nations, which monitors the ICESCR. The implementation of the ICESCR was hampered by unclarities about definition and scope of rights.[40] In an attempt to interpret some concepts and the scope of the ICESCR, especially Article 15 which is highly relevant in the context of the present paper, the UN Committee recently issued a General Comment no. 17.[41] The Committee confirms that States should prevent the use of scientific and technical progress for purposes contrary to human rights and dignity, including the rights to life, health and privacy, for example by excluding inventions from patentability whenever their commercialization would jeopardize the full realisation of these rights.[42]

---

36 GAEIB, Opinion no. 8, 25 September 1996, Ethical aspects of patenting inventions involving elements of human origin.

37 Article 6 (formerly Article F2) of the Treaty on European Union, Official Journal of the European Communities C , 325/11, 24 December 2002 (available at http://europa.eu.int/eur-lex/lex/en/treaties/index.htm, last visited June 2009).

38 GAEIB, Opinion no. 8, 25 September 1996, Ethical aspects of patenting inventions involving elements of human origin, para. 2.1.

39 GAEIB, Opinion no. 8, 25 September 1996, Ethical aspects of patenting inventions involving elements of human origin, para. 2.7.

40 See Alston, P. (1987), 'Out of the Abyss: the Challenges Confronting the New U.N. Committee on Economic, Social and Cultural Rights', *Human Rights Quarterly*, 332–384; Chapman, A.R. (1996), 'A "Violations Approach" for Monitoring the International Covenant on Economic, Social and Cultural Rights', *Human Rights Quarterly*, 23–66.

41 General Comment on Article 15(1)(c) of the Covenant (General Comment no. 17), Committee on Economic Social and Cultural Rights, Geneva, 7–25 November 2005, para. 32 [E/C.12/GC/17 12 January 2006] (see www.unhchr.ch, last visited June 2009).

42 General Comment no. 17, 2005, para. 35 (see footnote 41).

Legal scholars have confirmed that including the criterion of human dignity in a patent discourse does not overstep the appropriate role of a (liberal) state. Some claim that even if the main purpose of the patent system is to promote technological advances, 'there is no reason why it cannot recognize limitations based upon the need to respect legitimate moral constraints . . . Neither institutional considerations, nor considerations of political policy prohibit the protection of human dignity by the patent office'.[43] With regard to gene patenting, it is reiterated that it is legitimate to limit patent rights in human genes in order to preserve human dignity. Gene patenting does not generally run counter to human dignity, apart from two cases: both patents encompassing an entire set of genes, and patents on genetic modifications should be rejected because of human dignity considerations.

2.2 Right to Food

A human right which is highly relevant these days as well, is the right to food, which is proclaimed in the ICESCR. Indeed, the right to the protection of the moral and material interests resulting from any scientific, literary or artistic production of which one is the author, is subject to limitations and must be balanced with other rights recognized in the ICESCR, more in particular with the right of everyone to an adequate standard of living for himself and his family, including adequate food, clothing and housing, and to the continuous improvement of living conditions (Article 11(1) ICESCR). In view of 'the right of everyone to be free from hunger', the states shall take the measures which are needed 'to improve methods of production, conservation and distribution of food by making full use of technical and scientific knowledge' (Article 11(2) ICESCR). Likewise, states should ensure that their protection regimes constitute no impediment to their ability to comply with their core obligations in relation to the rights of food, health, and education.[44] Ultimately IP is a social product and has a social function.[45]

Discussing the right to food in a patent context is not new by a long way. In some countries it was a matter of debate in the nineteenth century whether inventions related to nutrition could be barred from patent protection, for reasons of hindering food supply. Fierce debates took place in legal doctrine

---

[43] Brody, B.A. (1999), 'Protecting Human Dignity and the Patenting of Human Genes', in *Perspectives on Gene Patenting: Science, Religion, Industry, and Law in Dialogue* (Washington: AAAS).

[44] General Comment no. 17, 2005, para. 35 (see footnote 41).

[45] Ibid.

and parliament in the Netherlands,[46] Belgium,[47] Germany[48] and in the US.[49] Echoing these concerns, the first German Patent Act of 1877 explicitly excluded food products from patentability.[50] However, most food exemptions in patent law were repealed afterwards.[51]

The debate on the right to food was recently re-opened, at the event of the development of genetically modified crops. Suggestions were raised to support the right to food by limiting patent protection for (genetically modified) plants and plant seeds, or by preventing unreasonably high costs for access to plant seeds or other means of food production. It is abundantly evident that such an approach could be based at present on Article 27(3)(b) *first* sentence of the TRIPS Agreement, which stipulates that Members may exclude from patentability plants and animals other than micro-organisms, and essentially biological processes for the production of plants or animals other than non-biological and microbiological processes. Various countries have indeed used the flexibility of this provision to limit what constitutes patentable subject matter and have excluded plants and animals from patent protection, adopted a restrictive definition of micro-organisms, or even prohibited the patenting of genetic material.[52] A typical example are the Andean Pact

---

[46] Van Leeuwen, J.C. (1951), 'Tussenkomst op het Symposium betreffende gebieden waarover de bescherming door octrooien zich behoort uit te strekken', *BIE*, (106), 107.

[47] The controversy found its origin in a passage from the report from the Parliamentary Commission, which said that products, such as chocolate, macaroni, gingerbread, and so on should not be patentable as they were in fact nutrition. See Van Overwalle, G. (1996), *Octrooieerbaarheid van plantenbiotechnologische uitvindingen. Een rechtsvergelijkend onderzoek naar een rechtvaardiging van een uitbreiding van het octrooirecht tot planten. – Patentability of Plant Biotechnological Inventions. A Comparative Study towards a Justification of Extending Patent Law to Plants (Substantive Summary)* (Brussels: Bruylant), p. 739; Van Overwalle, G. (1997), *The Legal Protection of Biotechnological Inventions in Europe and in the United States. Current Framework and Future Developments* (Leuven: Universitaire Pers), p. 78.

[48] Marx, W. (1952), 'Zur Patentierung von Pflanzenzüchtungen', *GRUR*, (456), 458.

[49] Lesser, W. (1987), 'International Patent Agreements for Protecting Biotechnology Products and Processes Worldwide', *Agribusiness*, vol. 3, (351), 363.

[50] In the same train of thought, the US Plant Variety Protection Act (PVPA) explicitly excluded six crops, viz. ocra, celery, tomatoes, peppers, carrots and cucumbers from its field of application, the so-called crop exemption. See Van Overwalle, G. (1999), 'Patent Protection for Plants: a Comparison of American and European Approaches', 39 *IDEA-Journal of Law and Technology* (US), 143–194.

[51] See Van Overwalle, references in footnote 47.

[52] Cf. *Integrating Intellectual Property Rights and Development Policy*, Report from the Commission on Intellectual Property Rights established by the Secretary of State for International Development of the British Government in May 2001, London,

Countries, that stipulate that 'the entirety or part of living beings as encountered in nature, natural biological processes, biological material existing in nature or which may be isolated, including the genome or germplasm of any natural living being'[53] shall not be considered inventions. The same is true of Brazil and Argentina.[54] However, the optional nature of the *first* sentence of Article 27(3)(b) of the TRIPS Agreement has equally led to a different approach with regard to the patent protection of plants and animals. Some countries, amongst which are all EU Member States, find patents on biological resources useful and do not opt for the implementation of the exclusionary TRIPS provision in their patent law. They have established patent protection for biological material, plants and animals mirroring the EU Biotechnology Directive. Under such a regime, patent protection is available for subcellular fragments (such as gene sequences, vectors, plasmids and so on), microorganisms, plant cells, animal cells, plants *per se*, plant seeds *per se* and animals *per se*. The underlying argument for admitting patent claims on food was put forward in a decision of the European Patent Office (EPO), long before. The EPO ruled that, given that the nutritive value of genetically modified plants exceeds that of conventionally obtained plants, and the fact that those plants may give rise to a better management of food shortage in the world, exploitation of such genetically modified plants cannot consequently be considered immoral or against public order.[55,56]

Besides Article 27 of the TRIPs Agreement, Article 8 of the TRIPs Agreement might also serve as a welcome basis to restrict the patentability of food. Article 8(1) clearly stipulates that Members may, in formulating or

---

September 2002, p. 114 (available at http://.iprcommission.org/graphic/documents/final_report.htm, last visited June 2009).

[53] Article 15(b) of the Subregional Integration Agreement of the Andean Community (Cartagena Agreement), Decision 486 – Common Provisions On Industrial Property (14 September 2000), see http://www.wipo.int/clea/docs_new/en/ac/ac005en.html (last visited June 2009).

[54] For more, see Van Overwalle, G. (2008b), 'Biotechnology and Patents: Global Standards, European Approaches and National Accents', in Daniel Wüger (ed), *Genetic Engineering: Challenges Posed by a New Technology to the World Trading System* (Cambridge: Cambridge University Press), pp. 77–108.

[55] Opposition Division, 31 March 1992, concerning European patent application bearing publication number 122.791, Lubrizol (Plant Gene Expression).

[56] Opposition Division, 15 December 1992, concerning European patent application bearing publication number 242.236, IIC, 1993, 618; Technical Board of Appeal, 21 February 1995 (T 356/93) (Appeal on the decision of the Opposition Division, 15 December 1992), Plant Genetic Systems case. For more, see Van Overwalle, references in footnote 47; Van Overwalle, G. (1993), 'Protecting Innovations in Plant Biotechnology: Patents or Plant Breeders' Rights?', Mededelingen van de Faculteit Landbouwwetenschappen Universiteit Gent (Proceedings of the Sixth Forum for Applied Biotechnology, Brugge), vol. 57, 1521–1536.

amending their laws and regulations, adopt measures necessary to protect public health and nutrition, and to promote the public interest in sectors of vital importance to their socio-economic and technological development, provided that such measures are consistent with the provisions of the Agreement. Over the last years, this provision has been widely used to discuss public health issues in patent law and prevent potentially obstructive effects of patents.[57] It might be equally important to bring this provision into action to secure the right to food.

3. HUMAN RIGHTS BURDENING THE EXISTENCE OF PATENT RIGHTS

Another approach which can be observed in factoring human rights in a patent law context is the addition of extra conditions for the grant of patents.

3.1 Right to Informed Consent

The right to informed consent is equally present in the current human rights landscape. Opinions differ, however, on how the right to informed consent should be qualified. One school of thought claims that the right of informed consent is an accessory right of another – fundamental – human right, more in particular the prohibition of torture and inhuman or degrading treatment or punishment. This – major – right is guaranteed in the UDHR, which proclaims that 'No one shall be subjected to torture or to cruel, inhuman or degrading treatment or punishment' (Article 5 UDHR). This right is also articulated in the Convention for the Protection of Human Rights and Fundamental Freedoms, as amended by Protocol No. 11, Rome, 4 November 1950, which states that 'No one shall be subjected to torture or to inhuman or degrading treatment or punishment' (Article 3). The right is equally articulated in the European Charter stating that 'No one shall be subjected to torture or to inhuman or degrading treatment or punishment' (Article 4). Other human rights scholars take the view that the right of informed consent is an accessory right of the right for respect of physical integrity, which is proclaimed in the European Charter: '1. Everyone has the right to respect for his or her physical and mental integrity 2. In the fields of medicine and biology, the following must be respected in particular, the free and informed consent of the person concerned, according to the procedures laid down by law, the prohibition of eugenic practices, in particular those aiming at the selection of persons, the

[57] For more, see Van Overwalle, reference in footnote 54.

prohibition on making the human body and its parts as such a source of financial gain, and, the prohibition of the reproductive cloning of human beings' (Article 3). Yet another school of thought claims that the right to informed consent is an accessory right of the right 'to respect for his or her private and family life, home and communications' (Article 7 European Charter), the latter right implying respect for physical integrity and personal autonomy.[58]

Not awaiting the outcome of academic debates on the exact legal basis of the right of informed consent, this right has been given an autonomous basis in the context of human health and genetics in Article 5 of the Oviedo Convention, which stipulates that 'An intervention in the health field may only be carried out after the person concerned has given free and informed consent to it. This person shall beforehand be given appropriate information as to the purpose and nature of the intervention as well as on its consequences and risks. The person concerned may freely withdraw consent at any time'. Furthermore, the Convention stipulates that 'When in the course of an intervention any part of a human body is removed, it may be stored and used for a purpose other than that for which it was removed, only if this is done in conformity with appropriate information and consent procedures' (Article 22). As was equally demonstrated in US case law, more in particular in the trendsetting *Moore* case, sources of human biological materials have a right to informed consent on the further use of their bodily material.[59] Also on an international level consensus is growing that sources of tissue should consent to the secondary use of their tissue.[60]

The link between the right to informed consent and patent law is quite recent. The debate emerged at the advent of modern medicine, as new medical developments have increased the use of human tissue, especially for research purposes and subsequent innovations. Various patent legislators tried to give something to hold on to people, who in the framework of a diagnosis or treatment, give body material, which material is subsequently being used for scientific research and forms the basis of a new drug or therapy, for which patent protection is requested and granted. In this aim, recital 26 of the EU Biotechnology Directive stipulates that 'if an invention is based on biological material of human origin or if it uses such material, where a patent application is filed, the person from whose body the material is taken must have had an opportunity of expressing free and informed consent thereto, in accordance

---

58 Cf. Trouet, C. (2003), *Van lichaam naar lichaamsmateriaal. Recht en het nader gebruik van cellen en weefsels* (Intersentia), p. 503.

59 *John Moore v The Regents of the University of California*, Supreme Court of California, decided 9 July 1990, 793, P2d, 479.

60 See Trouet, C. (2003), 'Informed consent for the research use of human biological materials', *Med Law.* 22(3), 411–419.

with national law'. Recital 26 attempts to embed the general principle of free and informed consent of the donor of body material as proclaimed in Article 22 of the Oviedo Convention, in the context of biotech-patenting.[61]

Discussions emerged on the binding nature of recital 26 on national authorities in EU Member States.[62] In the past, the EGE[63] has already explicitly expressed the view that the ethical principle of informed and free consent of the person from whom retrievals are performed, must be respected. The EGE has underlined that this principle includes that the information of this person is complete and specific, in particular on the potential patent application on the invention which could be made from the use of this element. An invention based on the use of elements of human origin, having been retrieved without respecting the principle of consent will not fulfil the ethical requirements.[64] In addition, the Council of Europe has issued an Additional Protocol relating to the informed consent-requirement in the framework of use of human tissue outside the traditional physician–patient relationship (so called 'further use'), for example, in the framework of scientific research.[65] Free and informed consent is also required in those circumstances[66] on the basis of the right to

---

61 Article 22 (Disposal of a Removed Part of the Human Body): 'When in the course of an intervention any part of a human body is removed, it may be stored and used for a purpose other than that for which it was removed, only if this is done in conformity with appropriate information and consent procedures.'

62 See Van Overwalle, G. (2005a), 'Legal and Ethical Aspects of Bio-Patenting: Critical Analysis of the EU Biotechnology Directive', in Drahos, P. (ed.), *Death of Patents* (Oxon: Lawtext Publishing), 212–227.

63 On the EGE, see footnote 31.

64 European Group on Ethics in Science and New Technologies (EGE), Opinion no. 8, 'Ethical aspects of patenting inventions involving elements of human origin', 25/09/1996.

65 Council of Europe, Additional Protocol to the Convention on Human Rights and Biomedicine Concerning Biomedical Research, Strasbourg, 25 January 2005, European Treaties Series, no. 195 (see http://conventions.coe.int/Treaty/en/Treaties/html/195.htm, last visited June 2009). Also see Council of Europe, Steering Committee on Bioethics, Explanatory Report to the Additional Protocol to the Convention on Human Rights and Biomedecine Concerning Biomedical Research, Strasbourg, 25 January 2005 (see http://www.coe.int/ViewDoc.jsp?id=747439&Site=COE, last visited June 2009). Similarly, Council of Europe, Recommendation Rec(2006)4 of the Committee of Ministers to member states on research on biological materials of human origin, 15 March 2006 (available at https://wcd.coe.int/ViewDoc.jsp?id=747439&Site=COE, last visited June 2009).

66 See Article 14(1) of the Protocol: 'No research on a person may be carried out, without the informed, free, express, specific and documented consent of the person'; see Article 10(2) of Recommendation 2006(4): 'Information and consent or authorisation to obtain such materials should be as specific as possible with regard to any foreseen research uses and the choices available in that respect'.

dignity and integrity.[67] Informed consent is also required for any foreseen potential further uses, including commercial uses, of the research results, data or biological materials.[68] By extension, one can argue that the informed consent is also required for patenting, which falls under commercialisation. Although this Protocol has not yet entered into force,[69] the Protocol holds great attraction to apply the free and informed consent in a patent context.

Besides the right of informed consent in the field of health and genetics, a right of informed consent is also articulated in the context of use of genetic resources from plant and animal origin, and related traditional knowledge. It is important to distinguish two types of informed consent in this regard. First, there is the informed consent which needs to be given by a *national government*, signatory to various relevant treaties. This type of prior informed

---

67 See Article 1 of the Protocol: 'Parties shall protect the dignity and identity of all human beings and guarantee everyone, without discrimination, respect for their integrity and other rights and fundamental freedoms with regard to any research involving interventions on human beings in the field of biomedicine'. See the preamble of Recommendation 2006(4): 'Biomedical research that is contrary to human dignity and human rights should never be carried out'. For more, see Trouet, C. (2004), 'New European guidelines for the use of stored human biological materials in biomedical research', *Journal of Medical Ethics*, 99–103.

68 See Article 13.2.vii of the Protocol, which stipulates: '2. The information [for research participants] shall cover the purpose, the overall plan and the possible risks and benefits of the research project, and include the opinion of the ethics committee. Before being asked to consent to participate in a research project, the persons concerned shall be specifically informed, according to the nature and purpose of the research: . . . *vii. of any foreseen potential further uses, including commercial uses, of the research results, data or biological materials*'. (My italics.) Also Article 13, Nr. 74 of the Memorandum of the Protocol, stipulating that: 'indent vii [of Article 13 § 2] requires the researcher to disclose to the potential participant any foreseen commercial use of data, research results or biological materials to be obtained from the potential participant during, or prior to, the research. The requirement in this indent does not reflect any endorsement or condemnation of research conducted with commercial applications in mind. Rather, it acknowledges the fact that the motivation for participation in biomedical research for many persons may be out of solidarity, and information on foreseen commercial uses of their contribution to the research may be important to them in making a decision on whether to take part or not. Additionally, *recital 26 of Directive 98/44/EC of the European Parliament and of the Council of 6 July 1998 on the legal protection of biotechnological inventions states* that whereas if an invention is based on biological material of human origin or if it uses such material, where a patent application is filed, the person from whose body the material is taken must have had an opportunity of expressing free and informed consent thereto, in accordance with national law.' (My italics.)

69 From the 17 countries which signed the Protocol, four countries ratified the Protocol so far, more in particular Slovakia, Bulgaria, Hungary and Slovenia (http://conventions.coe.int/Treaty/Commun/ChercheSig.asp?NT=195&CM=8&DF=11/11/2005&CL=ENG, last visited 27 January 2007). Five ratifications are needed to come into effect.

consent requirement is articulated in the Convention on Biological Diversity (CBD),[70] more in particular Article 15(5), which stipulates that 'access to genetic resources shall be subject to prior informed consent of the Contracting Party providing such resources, unless otherwise determined by that Party'. The prior informed consent requirement is also implemented in the Bonn Guidelines.[71] Prior informed consent in the context of genetic resources is defined by the International Union for Conservation of Nature and Natural Resources' (IUCN) guide to the CBD as 'consent of the contracting party which is the genetic resource provider, based on full and complete information provided by the potential genetic resource user prior to consent for access being granted . . .'.[72] Similarly, the European Union has underlined its desire to take into account the principles embedded in CBD. The European Commission recently stated that it welcomes the Bonn Guidelines on Access to Genetic Resources and Benefit-sharing, agreed by the Conference of the Parties (COP) in the Hague on 19 April 2002.[73] [74]

Second, there is informed consent which needs to be obtained from an *individual holder* or a *local community*. This is the type of informed consent which is relevant in a human rights discourse. It is argued that a right to informed consent has to be adopted in adapting patent law to fit the needs of indigenous peoples in the framework of bioprospecting.[75] Does the principle, laid down in Article 15(5) CBD and elaborated in the Bonn Guidelines, imply that every patent applicant has to show evidence that he received consent from the government, the local community and/or every single holder? The European Commission did not make any reference to the prior informed consent requirement for the use of biological material of plant or animal origin: the EU Biotechnology Directive does not mention informed consent for the use of biological material in recital 27.[76]

---

[70] Convention on Biological Diversity (CBD), 5 June 1992. See http://www.cbd.int/convention/convention.shtml (last visited June 2009).

[71] Bonn Guidelines on Access to Genetic Resources and Benefit-sharing, agreed by the Conference of the Parties (COP) in the Hague on 19 April 2002 (COP 6 Decision VI/24, see http://www.biodiv.org/decisions/default.asp?lg=0&dec=VI/24, last visited June 2009).

[72] Glowka, L.F., Burhenne-Guilmin, et al. (1994), *A guide to the Convention on Biological Diversity* (Gland, Switzerland: IUCN).

[73] COP 6 Decision VI/24, see http://www.biodiv.org/decisions/default.asp?lg=0&dec= VI/24, last visited June 2009.

[74] Communication by the European Communities, Brussels, 12 September 2002 (see previous footnote). Also see the Submission by the European Community and its Member States on Traditional and Intellectual Property Rights, Brussels, 14 June 2002.

[75] General Comment no. 17, 2005, para. 32 (see footnote 41).

[76] See reference footnote 3a.

3.2 Right to Protection

For quite some time, mechanisms have also been suggested to offer legal protection as proclaimed in Article 27(2) UDHR and Article 15(1)(c) ICESCR (see Section 1.2), to holders of biodiversity and related traditional knowledge.[77] A new *sui generis* IP tool has been put forward in this regard, referred to as 'Collective Community Intellectual Property Rights (CCIPRs)'[78] or 'Traditional Intellectual Property Right (TIP right)'.[79] Consensus still has to be achieved on a wide range of issues, before it will be possible to elaborate a blueprint of an adequate and widely acceptable *sui generis* regime.

An alternative approach to factor in the right of protection and remuneration of holders of biodiversity and related traditional knowledge, is to develop measures to share the benefits resulting from the use and exploitation of biodiversity and traditional knowledge. More in particular, to oblige patent holders on innovations resulting from these genetic resources and associated knowledge, to share the benefits. The introduction of a disclosure of origin requirement in the patent law application procedure is a possibility for production of evidence in respect of benefit sharing rules. In Europe, the origin requirement was dealt with in the EU Biotechnology Directive, in particular in recital 27.[80] Recital 27 requires that 'whereas if an invention is based on biological material of plant or animal origin or if it uses such material, the patent application should, where appropriate, include information on the geographical origin of such material, if known; whereas this is without prejudice to the processing of patent applications or the validity of rights arising from granted patents'. Although recital 27 contains a praiseworthy principle, the wording of recital

---

77 For an extensive overview, see Van Overwalle, G. (2005b), 'Protecting and Sharing Biodiversity and Traditional Knowledge: Holder and User Tools', *Ecological Economics*, Volume 53, Issue 4, 1 June, 585–607.

78 Leistner (2004), 'Traditional Knowledge', in S. Von Lewinski (ed.), *Indigenous Heritage and Intellectual Property* (The Hague–London–New York: Kluwer Law), 141.

79 Cottier, T. and M. Panizzon (2004), 'Legal Perspectives on Traditional Knowledge', 7 *Journal of International Economic Law*, 2, (371), 387–388; Cottier, T. (1998), 'The Protection of Genetic Resources and Traditional Knowledge: Towards More Specific Rights and Obligations in World Trade Law', *Journal of International Economic Law*, (555), 555.

80 For more information on the history of the development of recital 27, see Blakeney, M. (1999), 'Biotechnology, TRIPs and the Convention on Biological Diversity', *Bio-Science Law Review*, (144), 148; Straus, J. (1998), 'Biodiversity and Intellectual Property', *AIPPI Yearbook* 1998/IX, (99), 99: 'Genetic resources have become an issue of high priority to scientists, industry, politicians and even the public at large. . . . they form a warehouse of enormous use potentials for plant – and animal breeding, food, chemical and environmental industries, pharmaceuticals and medicine'.

27 is so noncommittal, that one can wonder if the recital will have any effect at all. Notwithstanding the noncommittal language of the Biotechnology Directive, Belgium and Denmark took serious action to integrate the principle in their respective patent legislation.[81]

4. HUMAN RIGHTS LIMITING THE EXERCISE OF PATENT RIGHTS

A third way in which human rights may have an effect in patent law, is by limiting the exercise of the monopoly rights of the patent holder, once the patent right is granted.

4.1 Right of Access to Public Health

The right of access to public health is proclaimed in the UDHR, which stipulates that 'Everyone has the right to a standard of living adequate for the health and well-being of himself and of his family, including food, clothing, housing and medical care' (Article 25(1) UDHR). The right is equally guaranteed in the ICESCR, which claims that '1. The States Parties to the present Covenant recognize the right of everyone to the enjoyment of the highest attainable standard of physical and mental health' (Article 12 ICESCR). States are therefore required to strike an adequate balance between the effective protection of the moral and material interests of authors and States parties' obligations in relation to the right to health.[82] Similarly, the Oviedo Convention takes the right to health to heart in putting forward that 'Parties, taking into account health needs and available resources, shall take appropriate measures with a view to providing, within their jurisdiction, equitable access to health care of appropriate quality' (Article 3).

The relationship between the right of access to human health and patent law has been formally recognized in the TRIPs Agreement. The TRIPs Agreement clearly stipulates in Article 8(1) that Members may, in formulating or amending their laws and regulations, adopt measures necessary to protect public health and nutrition, and to promote the public interest in sectors of vital importance to their socio-economic and technological development, provided that such measures are consistent with the provisions of the Agreement. One

---

[81] For more details, see Van Overwalle, footnote 77. Also see Van Overwalle, G. (2006), 'The implementation of the Biotechnology Directive in Belgium and its after effects, the introduction of a New Research Exemption and a Compulsory License for Public Health', 37 *IIC*, 889–920.

[82] General Comment no. 17, 2005, para. 39 (e) (see footnote 41).

measure to safeguard public health from the potential hindering effects of patents, is a compulsory license. In case a patent holder refuses to grant licenses, a court or government could grant a compulsory license to a third party without the authorization of the right holder. The establishment of such compulsory licensing mechanism for public health reasons can further be based on Article 30 of the TRIPs Agreement, which allows limited exceptions to the exclusive rights conferred by a patent in the interest of public health. Furthermore, reference can be made to the Doha Ministerial Declaration of 14 November 2001, which explicitly stipulates that the TRIPs Agreement can be implemented and interpreted in a manner supportive of public health, by promoting both access to existing medicines and research and development into new medicines.[83] Last but not least, references can be made to the Declaration on the TRIPs Agreement and public health of the same date, which specifically states that each Member has the right to grant compulsory licenses and the freedom to determine the grounds upon which such licenses are granted.[84]

For countries with no or insufficient manufacturing capacities the condition in Article 31(f) of the TRIPs Agreement, that products made under a compulsory license must be 'predominantly for the supply of the domestic market', proved to be a stumbling block. However, at the Ministerial Conference in Doha in November 2001, the WTO Members were not able to reach an agreement on the way to create extra flexibilities enabling those countries to profit from the compulsory licensing system. The negotiations on this issue remained deadlocked during almost two years. On 30 August 2003 the General Council then agreed on a Decision allowing a waiver from the obligations set out in paragraphs (f) and (h) of Article 31 of the TRIPs Agreement with respect to pharmaceutical products in the interest of the above-mentioned countries.[85] The Decision also comprised safeguards to prevent that the products were diverted from the markets for which they were intended. A separate Chairman's Statement, although not a text approved by the WTO Members, provided comfort to those who feared that the decision might be abused to undermine patent protection. More than two years later, the General Council

---

[83] Ministerial declaration, adopted on 14 November 2001 (WT/MIN(01)/DEC/1), more in particular Point 17 (available at http://www.wto.org/english/thewto_e/minist_e/min01_e/mindecl_e.htm, last visited June 2009).

[84] Declaration on the TRIPS agreement and public health, adopted on 14 November 2001 (WT/MIN(01)/DEC/2), more in particular Point 5(b) (available at http://www.wto.org/english/thewto_e/minist_e/min01_e/mindecl_trips_e.htm, last visited June 2009).

[85] WT/L/540 and Corr. 1 (available at http://www.wto.org, last visited June 2009).

finally agreed to permanently amend the TRIPs Agreement[86] by inserting a new Article 31bis and an Annex to the TRIPs Agreement, containing definitions, required notifications and details on the other safeguarding measures.[87]

In the same vein, a recent initiative has been taken by the European Commission to introduce compulsory licenses for public health reasons. Indeed, a regulation of the European Parliament and of the Council on compulsory licensing of patents relating to the manufacture of pharmaceutical products for *export* to countries with public health problems is accepted on 17 May 2006.[88] This regulation obliges the Member States to grant a compulsory license for the manufacture and sale of patented pharmaceutical products for the export to countries without or with insufficient production facilities in the pharmaceutical sector, where a number of conditions is fulfilled.

Concerns about potential access problems in the field of health care were also the subject of many debates in EU Member States. Fresh in various Member States' memories, was the behaviour of the company Myriad Genetics. As is sufficiently well known, Myriad Genetics obtained several European and US patents for the screening of breast cancer genes,[89] but licensed the test exclusively to a limited number of commercial genetic laboratories within specific geographical regions.[90] This highly restrictive licensing policy gave rise to a strong reaction[91] and triggered the contemplation of

---

86 Decision of 6 December 2005, WT/L/641.

87 Article 31bis will be formally built into the TRIPS Agreement when two thirds of the WTO's members have accepted the change. They have set themselves until 1 December 2007 to do this, but the deadline may be extended if necessary. At present, only five member states have accepted, namely the United States, Switzerland, El Salvador, Rep. of Korea and Norway.

88 Regulation No. 816/2006 of the European Parliament and of the Council of 17 May 2006 on compulsory licensing of patents relating to the manufacture of pharmaceutical products for export to countries with public health problems, O.J. L, 157 of 9 June 2006 (available at http://eur-lex.europa.eu/en/index.htm, last visited February 2007).

89 The so-called BRCA1 and BRCA2 genes (BRCA1: WO 96/05306, WO 96/05307 and WO 96/05308; and BRCA2: WO 97/22689). For more details, see Verbeure, B., G. Matthijs and G. Van Overwalle (2006), 'Analysing DNA patents in relation with diagnostic genetic testing', *European Journal of Human Genetics* (EJHG), 26–33.

90 For more details, see Walpole, Dawkins, Sinden and O'Leary (2003), 'Human gene patents: the possible impacts on genetic services healthcare', *Medical Journal of Australia*, 256–283. Also see Van Overwalle, G., E. Van Zimmeren, B. Verbeure and G. Matthijs (2006), 'Models for facilitating access to patents on genetic inventions', 7 *Nature Review Genetics*, February, 143–148.

91 See Herrlinger, K. (2005), *Die Patentierung von Krankheitsgenen* (Köln, Carl Heymanns Verlag); Matthijs and Halley (2002), 'European-wide opposition against the

measures preventing highly restrictive exercise of patent rights. As a tool to remedy potential harmful effects of bio-patents and unreasonable behaviour of patent holders, and inspired by the Doha Declaration, some EU countries such as Belgium and France, have added a compulsory license 'for public health' to their catalogue of compulsory licenses, to supply the *domestic* market in case of refusal to license.[92] Other EU countries, such as the Netherlands, can resort to their universal, catch all 'public interest' compulsory license clause in case of public health need.[93] Also non-EU Member States, such as Switzerland, currently debate the introduction of a compulsory license system for public health. Legislation to introduce the possibility of granting compulsory licenses for public health reasons to *export* pharmaceuticals to developing countries with no or insufficient manufacturing capacities, is under way as well. As the relevant European regulation is promulgated, EC Member States are able to grant such licences immediately, as regulations have direct effect in EC law. In principle, it will not be necessary to include specific provisions in the national patent acts. However, it remains to be seen to which extent these measures will really meet the needs of the sick and – especially – the poor.

4.2 Right to Education and Research

The right to education is recognized in the UDHR, which proclaims that 'Everyone has the right to education' (Article 26(1)) and in the ICESCR, which stipulates that 'The States Parties to the present Covenant recognize the right of everyone to education' (Article 13(1)). Closely linked with the right to education, is the right to freedom of research, proclaimed in Article 15(3) ICESCR: 'The States Parties to the present Covenant undertake to respect the freedom indispensable for scientific research and creative activity'.

The implications of the right to education and especially the right to research in patent law, have been the subject of debate for a long time. The right to freedom of research is of utmost importance in a knowledge based

---

breast cancer gene patents', *European Journal of Human Genetics*, 783–784; National Research Council, *Reaping the Benefits of Genomic and Proteomic Research: Intellectual Property Rights, Innovation, and Public Health* (Washington D.C.: National Academies Press), Prepublication Copy, December 2005, pp. 51–53 (http://www.nap.edu/catalog/11487.html, last visited April 2006).

[92] For more details, see Van Overwalle, G. (2006), 'The Implementation of the Biotechnology Directive in Belgium and its Aftereffects. The Introduction of a New Research Exemption and a Compulsory License for Public Health', 37 *International Review of Intellectual Property and Competition Law* (IIC), 889–920.

[93] See Article 57(1) of the current Dutch Patent Act (available at http://www.wipo.int/clea/docs_new/en/nl/nl020en.html).

economy. It has been argued repeatedly that the right to research can be jeopardized by patents. Some States have established safeguards for research against the overwhelming effect of patents by enacting a research exemption. However, current research exemptions often suffer from legal uncertainty as opposing interpretations exist as to its scope, both in Europe and in the US.[94] The situation could be improved by resorting to human rights discourse and claiming that the right to research is a fundamental human right also in an IP context, which justifies the introduction of a mandatory, wide and clear-cut experimental use exception in patent law on the international level.

4.3 Right of Access to Information

Putting Articles 27(2) UDHR and Article 15(1)(c) ICESCR in context (see Section 1.2), clearly demonstrates that the right to protection, recognized in those articles, is inextricably linked with two other rights, the right of access to cultural life and the right to the benefits of scientific progress. The right to benefit indeed seeks to encourage the active contribution of creators to the arts and sciences and to the progress of society as a whole.[95] Both the UDHR and the ICESCR clearly place a discernible emphasis on the interests humans have in the access to knowledge. Indeed, the right recognized in Article 27(2) UDHR can be read in connection with Article 27(1), which provides that 'Everyone has the right freely to participate in the cultural life of the community, to enjoy the arts and to share in scientific advancement and its benefits'. Likewise, the right laid down in Article 15(1)(c) ICESCR can be interpreted in relation to some other rights, more in particular the right of everyone 'to take part in cultural life' (Article 15(1)(a)) 'to enjoy the benefits of scientific progress and its applications' (Article 15(1)(b)) and 'the freedom indispensable for scientific research and creative activity' (Article 15(3)). The relationship between Article 15(1)(c) ICESCR and these rights is at the same time mutually reinforcing and reciprocally limitative.

How is the right of access being reflected in patent law? The explosion of patents has raised serious concerns with regard to the access to and use of patents. Especially in the field of genetics and ICT, many patents have been granted in recent years. In genetics, for example, up to the end of 2004, the European Patent Office (EPO) granted 2,913 patents containing the term 'nucleic acid' in the claims, and 549 of these were granted in 2004 alone. In the ICT field, a same tendency can be witnessed. The omnipresence of such

94 See Van Overwalle et al., footnote 90.
95 General Comment no. 17, 2005, para. 4 (see footnote 41).

high volumes of patents has raised serious concerns about access to and use of ICT- and genome-related inventions, as the expansion of patents might result in a patent thicket and generate an anti-commons effect.[96]

At first sight, human rights discourse might offer a valuable legal basis to remedy the access problem in patent law. However, applying principles of access to knowledge in a patent context calls for caution, as access to information is an ambivalent concept in patent law. Patent law requires that the patented invention is disclosed in a manner sufficiently clear and complete for the invention to be carried out by a person skilled in the art.[97] The technical knowledge about the invention, disclosed in the patent description, is published and thus widely accessible: anyone can consult the technical description of the patented invention at the patent-issuing authorities. Some patent offices have enforced accessibility standards by establishing freely accessible patent databases.[98] Overlooking the legal prescription and the actual practice, patent law indisputably contributes to the realization of the right to *access* to information. Despite the fact that access to information is guaranteed under patent law, restrictions emerge with regard to the *use* of that information. Employing the patented information for further development and commercialization, requires the consent of the patent holder. The ambiguity within patent law is not that patent law bluntly hinders access to and diffusion of information,[99] but rather that it restricts use of information. Patent law thus is very ambivalent with regard to the right of access. Having said this, it is quite clear that patent law contributes to, rather then hinders, access to knowledge. Subsequently, the debate on open access and the proposal for a Treaty on Access to Knowledge (commonly referred to as the A2K Treaty),[100] calls for some caution.

---

[96] See Van Overwalle et al., footnote 90. Also see Van Zimmeren, E., B. Verbeure, G. Matthijs and G. Van Overwalle (2006), 'A Clearinghouse for Diagnostic Testing: the Solution to Ensure Access to and Use of Patented Genetic Inventions?', *Bulletin of the World Health Organization*, 352–359; Verbeure, B., E. Van Zimmeren, G. Matthijs and G. Van Overwalle (2006),'Patent pools and diagnostic testing', 24 *Trends in Biotechnology* (*TIB*), vol. 3, March, 115–120.

[97] Cf. Article 29 (1) TRIPs, Article 83 EPC and Article 112 Utility Patent Act (35 USC 112).

[98] Freely accessible patent search sites are www.espacenet.com from the European Patent Office (EPO), or http://www.uspto.gov/patft/index.html the database of the US Patent and Trademark Office (USPTO).

[99] Admittedly, recent research has demonstrated that patent law indirectly slows down the publication of scientific papers. See Van Overwalle, G. (2006), 'Reconciling Patent Policies and University Mission', 13 *Ethical Perspectives*, 231–247; Van Overwalle, G. (2006), 'Octrooien op maat? Naar een evenwicht tussen publieke opdracht en privaat goed', in B. Pattyn and G. Van Overwalle (eds), *Tussen Markt en Agora. Over het statuut van universitaire kennis* (Leuven: Peeters), 181–214.

[100] Treaty on Access to Knowledge, Draft 9 May 2005 (available at

5. CONCLUSION

Human rights and IP, two bodies of law that were once strangers, have now become increasingly intimate bedfellows.[101] The 'intimate' relationship between human rights and IP can be assessed and appreciated in different ways. Some scholars argue that human rights have *absolute* priority over patent rights, that human rights have primacy over economic policies and agreements, that human rights have normative predominance. They claim that patent rights are instrumental rights, which serve the interests and needs that citizens identify, through the lens of human rights, as being fundamental. Human rights are pressed into service on behalf of human rights. Property rights come to serve human rights.[102] The present paper agrees that human rights law has normative primacy over IP law. It is imperative to take into account human rights discourse in a patent law context. Patent law should be assessed from a human rights' perspective. However, human rights should feed into patent law in a more *moderate*, complementary manner. Patent law is an autonomous legal system of its own kind, with an intrinsic *raison d'être*. It is an instrument, a legal tool, aiming to serve both private and public objectives, both reward for innovation and societal well being through the production of new goods and services. Human rights are valuable and necessary complements of the patent system. They feed into the objective of public interest in patent law. They serve as a counter balance of patent rights centering too one-sidedly on trade, access to markets and economic calculus. For patent law to be widely accepted and generally recognized as a tool fostering both private and public interest, it is vital that current patent law regimes are inextricably linked with human rights discourse, and that human rights assist in defining the utter limits of patent rights.

As has become clear from the exploration in the present chapter, the respect for human dignity introduces certain limits on patentable subject matter in patent law, in order to safeguard the rights of human beings and human

---

http://www.cptech.org/a2k/consolidatedtext-may9.pdf, last visited February 2007). The initial proposal for the formation of an A2K Treaty was launched by Argentina and Brazil at the 31st Session of the WIPO General Assembly, Geneva, 27 September to 5 October 2004 (see point V in particular: '[. . .] we note with particular interest the idea of establishing an international regime that would promote access by the developing countries to the results of publicly funded research in the developed countries. Such a regime could take the form of a Treaty on Access to Knowledge and Technology'). An initiative which is equally important in this regard is the Berlin Declaration on Open Access to Knowledge in the Sciences and Humanities, 23 October 2003 (available at http://oa.mpg.de/openaccess-berlin/berlindeclaration.html, last visited February 2007).

[101] Helfer, L., see footnote 1.

[102] An exponent of this school of thought can be found in Drahos, see footnote 5.

embryos. The right to food opens an avenue to impose restrictions in patent law in the interest of consumers. The right of informed consent invites patent law to be cautious in respect of the rights of donors of human biological material, testees and patients, and the rights of traditional knowledge holders. The human right to access to public health safeguards the rights of patients, by limiting the rights of patentees through the introduction of a compulsory license system, whereas the right to research is safeguarded for researchers entering well defined areas of exploration. Finally, the right of access provides adequate trajectories for innovators or users, to have efficient access to technological innovations and improvements through the disclosure requirement.

When assessing patent law through the lens of human rights law, some issues remain unresolved. First, some unclarities as to concepts and scope live on. Secondly, the lack of enforceability of various human rights is problematic. Thirdly, factoring human rights into patent law, might give rise to increasing legal uncertainty. Given the expanding nature of human rights and applying a universal and holistic approach of human rights[103] in a patent law context might run counter to legal certainty. Legal certainty might require a more distinct approach, where a clear and limited catalogue of human rights, which have to be taken into account in a patent context, is provided. However, designing a closed list of human rights seems inadequate, as patent rights may be limited and restricted for a multitude of reasons (see Article 4 ICESCR). Fourthly, the relationship between human rights and human values remains unclear and controversial. This might also create problems of legal (un)certainty as well. Last but not least, it is not yet fully clear what the exact relationship is between the well know twin concept in patent law of *ordre public* and morality, and human rights.

Notwithstanding some remaining unsettled issues, great effort should be put into taking full account of human rights considerations in patent law and into making a human rights approach in patent law even more explicit and exacting. For patent law to be widely accepted and generally recognized as a tool fostering both private and public interest, it is vital that current patent law regimes are inextricably linked with human rights discourse, and that human rights assist in defining the utter limits of patent rights.

103 See the contribution of Cees Flinterman Chapter 2 in the present volume.

BIBLIOGRAPHY

Legal Doctrine

Alston, P. (1987), 'Out of the Abyss: the Challenges Confronting the New U.N. Committee on Economic, Social and Cultural Rights', *Human Rights Quarterly*, 332–384.

Alston, P. (1984), 'Conjuring up New Human Rights: a Proposal for Quality Control', *AJIL*, 607–623.

Benkard, G. (1993), *Patentgesetz*, in *Beck'sches Kurz Kommentare*, 4 (München: Beck).

Bernhardt, W. and R. Krasser (1986), *Lehrbuch des Patentrechts* (München: Beck).

Blakeney, M. (1999), 'Biotechnology, TRIPs and the Convention on Biological Diversity', *Bio-Science Law Review*, 144–149.

Brinkhof, J. (2000), 'Clinical trials. De situatie in Nederland', in G. Van Overwalle (ed.), *Octrooirecht en geneesmiddelen* (Brussels: Bruylant) 93–103.

Brody, B.A. (2006), 'Protecting Human Dignity and the Patenting of Human Genes', in *Perspectives on Gene Patenting: Science, Religion, Industry, and Law in Dialogue* (Washington: AAAS).

Chapman, A.R. (1996), 'A "Violations Approach" for Monitoring the International Covenant on Economic, Social and Cultural Rights', *Human Rights Quarterly*, 23–66.

Commission on Intellectual Property Rights (COIPR) (2002) established by the Secretary of State for International Development of the British Government, *Integrating Intellectual Property Rights and Development Policy*, May 2001, London, September 2002.

Cottier, T. (1998), 'The Protection of Genetic Resources and Traditional Knowledge: Towards More Specific Rights and Obligations in World Trade Law', *Journal of International Economic Law*, 555–571.

Cottier, T. and M. Panizzon (2004), 'Legal Perspectives on Traditional Knowledge', 7 *Journal of International Economic Law*, 2 (371), 387–388.

Crawford, J. (ed.) (1988), *The Rights of Peoples* (Oxford: Clarendon Press).

Drahos, P. (1999), 'The Universality of Intellectual Property Rights: Origins and Development', *Intellectual Property and Human Rights*, Conference organised by the WIPO in collaboration with the Office of the UN High Commissioner for Human Rights to commemorate the 50th Anniversary of the Universal Declaration of Human Rights, Geneva, 9 November 1998. The paper presented at the WIPO Conference was later published as 'Intellectual Property Rights and Human Rights', *I.P.Q.*, 1999, 349–371.

Eide, A. (1996), 'Human Rights Requirements to Social and Economic Development', *Food Policy*, 23–39.

Eide, A. (1989), *The Right to Adequate Food as a Human Right*, Study Series No. 1 (Geneva and New York: United Nations Center for Human Rights).

Eide, A., W.B. Eide, S. Goonatilake, S. Gussow and J. Omawale (eds) (1984), *Food as a Human Right* (Tokyo: United Nations University).

Eide, A. (1989),'The human right to adequate food and freedom from hunger', FAO.

Eide, A., A. Oshaung and W.B. Eide (1991), 'Food Security and the Right to Food in International Law and Development', *Transnational Law and Contemporary Problems*, 1(2), 416–467.

Fierens, J. (2002), 'La dignité humaine comme concept juridique', *J.T.*, 577–582.

Geiger, C. (2006), 'Constitutionalising Intellectual Property Law? The Influence of Fundamental Rights on Intellectual Property in the European Union', 37 *IIC*, 371–500.

Gervais, D. (2003), *The TRIPs Agreement. Drafting History and Analysis* (London: Sweet & Maxwell).

Glowka, L.F. and Burhenne-Guilmin et al. (1994), *A Guide to the Convention on Biological Diversity* (Gland (Switzerland): IUCN).

Gotzen, F. (1989), 'Industriële eigendomsrechten' in R. Dillemans and W. van Gerven (eds), *Beginselen van Belgisch Privaatrecht, XIII, Handels- en economisch recht, Deel I, Ondernemingsrecht*, volume A (Brussels: Story), 287–309.

Helfer, L.R. (2006), 'Toward a Human Rights Framework for Intellectual Property', *Vanderbilt University Law School Public Law and Legal Theory. Working Paper 06-03* (available at http://ssrn.com/abstract=891303, last visited July 2006).

Helfer, L.R. (2003), 'Human Rights and Intellectual Property: Conflict or Coexistence?', *Minnesota Intellectual Property Review*.

Hermeren, G. (2006), 'European Values, Ethics and Law. Present Policies and Future Challenges', in *Jahrbuch für Wissenschaft und Ethik*, 5–30.

Herrlinger, K. (2005), *Die Patentierung von Krankheitsgenen* (Köln: Carl Heymanns Verlag).

Leistner (2004), 'Traditional Knowledge', in S. Von Lewinski (ed.) *Indigenous Heritage and Intellectual Property*, The Hague–London–New York, Kluwer Law, 141–163.

Lesser, W. (1987), 'International Patent Agreements for Protecting Biotechnology Products and Processes Worldwide', *Agribusiness*, vol. 3, 351–363.

Marx, W. (1952), 'Zur Patentierung von Pflanzenzüchtungen', *GRUR*, 456–458.

Matthijs and Halley (2002), 'European-wide Opposition Against the Breast Cancer Gene Patents', *European Journal of Human Genetics*, 783–784.

National Research Council (NRC) (2006), *Reaping the Benefits of Genomic and Proteomic Research: Intellectual Property Rights, Innovation, and Public Health* (National Academies Press, Washington D.C.) Prepublication Copy, December 2005.

Remouchamps, L. (1969), *Octrooien*, in *Algemene Praktische Rechtsverzameling* (Brussels: Larcier).

Schermers, H.G. (1988), 'The International Protection of the Right of Property', in F. Matscher and H. Petzold (eds), *Protecting Human Rights: the European Dimension* (Köln: Carl Heymanns), 565–580.

Schutjens, M.H.D.B. (1993), *Octrooirecht en geneesmiddelen. Een rechtsvergelijkende studie naar de juridische aspecten van medisch-farmaceutische uitvindingen in het octrooirecht* (Apeldoorn: Maklu).

Sterckx, S. (2005), 'The Ethics of Patenting – Uneasy Justifications', in P. Drahos (ed.), *Death of Patents* (Oxon: Lawtext Publishing), 175–211.

Straus, J. (1998), 'Biodiversity and Intellectual Property', *AIPPI Yearbook 1998/IX*, (99), 99.

Trouet, C. (2004), 'New European Guidelines for the Use of Stored Human Biological Materials in Biomedical Research', *Journal of Medical Ethics*, 99–103.

Trouet, C. (2003a), *Van lichaam naar lichaamsmateriaal. Recht en het nader gebruik van cellen en weefsels* (Intersentia), p. 503.

Trouet, C. (2003b), 'Informed Consent for the Research Use of Human Biological Materials', *Med Law*. 22(3), 411–9.

Van Leeuwen, J.C. (1951), Tussenkomst op het *Symposium betreffende gebieden waarover de bescherming door octrooien zich behoort uit te strekken, BIE*, 1951, 106–112.

Van Overwalle, G. (2008), 'L'intérêt général, le domaine public, les commons et le droit des brevets d'invention', in M. Buydens and S. Dussolier (eds), *L'intérêt général et l'accès à l'information en propriété intellectuelle* (Brussels: Bruylant), 149–175.

Van Overwalle, G. (2008), 'Biotechnology and Patents: Global Standards, European Approaches and National Accents', in D. Wüger and T. Cottier (eds), *Genetic Engineering and the World Trade System* (Cambridge: Cambridge University Press), 77–108.

Van Overwalle, G. (2006), 'The Implementation of the Biotechnology Directive in Belgium and its Aftereffects. The Introduction of a New Research Exemption and a Compulsory License for Public Health', 37 *International Review of Intellectual Property and Competition Law (IIC)*, 889–920.

Van Overwalle, G. (2006), 'Reconciling Patent Policies and University Mission', 13 *Ethical Perspectives*, 231–247.

Van Overwalle, G. (2006), 'Octrooien op maat? Naar een evenwicht tussen publieke opdracht en privaat goed', in B. Pattyn and G. van Overwalle (eds), *Tussen Markt en Agora. Over het statuut van universitaire kennis* (Leuven: Peeters), 181–214.

Van Overwalle, G. (2005), 'Legal and Ethical Aspects of Bio-Patenting: Critical Analysis of the EU Biotechnology Directive', in P. Drahos (ed.), *Death of Patents* (Oxon: Lawtext Publishing), 212–227.

Van Overwalle, G. (2005), 'Protecting and Sharing Biodiversity and Traditional Knowledge: Holder and User Tools', *Ecological Economics*, Volume 53, Issue 4, June, 585–607.

Van Overwalle, G. (2000), 'Klinische proeven en volksgezondheid. Naar een herijking van het algemeen belang in het octrooirecht', *Tijdschrift voor Privaatrecht (TPR)*, 899–968.

Van Overwalle, G. (1999), 'Patent Protection for Plants: a Comparison of American and European Approaches', 39 *IDEA-Journal of Law and Technology* (US), 143–194.

Van Overwalle, G. (1997), *The Legal Protection of Biotechnological Inventions in Europe and in the United States. Current Framework and Future Developments* (Leuven: Universitaire Pers), p. 78.

Van Overwalle, G. (1996), *Octrooieerbaarheid van plantenbiotechnologische uitvindingen. Een rechtsvergelijkend onderzoek naar een rechtvaardiging van een uitbreiding van het octrooirecht tot planten. – Patentability of Plant Biotechnological Inventions. A Comparative Study towards a Justification of Extending Patent Law to Plants (Substantive Summary)* (Brussels: Bruylant), p. 739.

Van Overwalle, G. (1993), 'Protecting Innovations in Plant Biotechnology: Patents or Plant Breeders' Rights?', *Mededelingen van de Faculteit Landbouwwetenschappen Universiteit Gent (Proceedings of the Sixth Forum for Applied Biotechnology, Brugge)*, vol. 57, 1521–1536.

Van Overwalle, G., E. van Zimmeren, B. Verbeure and G. Matthijs (2006), 'Models for facilitating access to patents on genetic inventions', 7 *Nature Review Genetics*, February, 143–148.

Van Zimmeren, E., B. Verbeure, G. Matthijs and G. van Overwalle (2006), 'A Clearinghouse for Diagnostic Testing: the Solution to Ensure Access to and Use of Patented Genetic Inventions?', *Bulletin of the World Health Organization*, 352–359.

Vasak, K. (1990), 'Les différentes catégories des droits de l'homme', in A. Lapeyre, F. de Tignuy and K. Vasak (eds), *Les dimensions universelles des droits de l'homme* (Brussels: Bruylant), vol. I, 297–316.
Vasak, K. (1984), 'Pour une troisième génération des droits de l'homme', in C. Swinarski (ed.), *Studies and Essays on International Humanitarian Law and Red Cross Principles in Honour of Jean Pictet* (The Hague: Martinus Nijhoff), 837–845.
Verbeure, B., E. Van Zimmeren, G. Matthijs and G. van Overwalle,'Patent Pools and Diagnostic Testing', 24 *Trends in Biotechnology (TIB)*, vol. 3, March, 115–120.
Verbeure, B., G. Matthijs and G. van Overwalle (2006), 'Analysing DNA Patents in Relation with Diagnostic Genetic Testing', *European Journal of Human Genetics (EJHG)*, 26–33.
Walpole, Dawkins, Sinden and O'Leary (2003), 'Human Gene Patents: the Possible Impacts on Genetic Services Healthcare', *Medical Journal of Australia*, 256–283.

Legislation

Council of Europe, Recommendation Rec(2006)4 of the Committee of Ministers to member states on research on biological materials of human origin, 15 March 2006 (available at https://wcd.coe.int/ViewDoc.jsp?id=977859&BackColorInternet=9999CC&BackColorIntranet=FFBB55&BackColorLogged=FFAC75, last visited February 2007).
Council of Europe, Additional Protocol to the Convention on Human Rights and Biomedicine Concerning Biomedical Research, Strasbourg, 25 January 2005, *European Treaties Series*, no. 195 (available at http://www.coe.int/T/E/Legal_Affairs/Legal_co-operation/Bioethics/Activities/Biomedical_research/195%20Protocole%20recherche%20biomedicale%20e.pdf, last visited April 2006).
Council of Europe, Steering Committee on Bioethics, Explanatory report to the Additional Protocol to the Convention on Human Rights and Biomedecine Concerning Biomedical Research, Strasbourg, 25 January 2005 (available at http://www.coe.int/T/E/Legal_Affairs/Legal_co-operation/Bioethics/Activities/Biomedical_research/195%20ER%20recherche%20biomedicale%20e.pdf, last visited April 2006).
Convention for the Protection of Human Rights and Dignity of the Human Being with regard to the Application of Biology and Medicine – Convention on Human Rights and Biomedicine, Oviedo, April 1997.
EU, Regulation of the European Parliament and of the Council, No. 816/2006 of 17 May 2006 on compulsory licensing of patents relating to the manufacture of pharmaceutical products for export to countries with public health problems, *O.J. L*, 157 of 9 June 2006 (available at http://eur-lex.europa.eu/en/index.htm, last visited February 2007).
Treaty on European Union, *Official Journal of the European Communities C* 325/11, 24 December 2002 (available at http://europa.eu.int/eur-lex/lex/en/treaties/index.htm, last visited June 2006).
Submission by the European Community and its Member States on Traditional and Intellectual Property Rights, Brussels, 14 June 2002 Charter of Fundamental Rights of the European Union, (2000/C 364/01).
Official Journal of the European Communities C, 364/1, 18 December 2000.
Directive 98/44/EC of 6 July 1998 of the European Parliament and of the Council on the legal protection of biotechnological inventions, *Official Journal EC L* 213/13 of 30/07/1998 13 (available at http://europa.eu.int, last visited April 2006).

Proposal for a Council Directive on the legal protection of biotechnological inventions, October 1988, *Official Journal EC C*, 13 January 1989, 10/3. The proposal was eventually rejected by the European Parliament on 1 March 1995 (see *Official Journal EC C*, 20 March 1995, 68/26).

Unesco, Universal Declaration on the Human Genome and Human Rights was adopted unanimously and by acclamation at UNESCO's 29th General Conference on 11 November 1997. The following year, the United Nations General Assembly endorsed the Declaration (available at http://portal.unesco.org/shs/en/ev.php-URL_ID=1881&URL_DO=DO_ TOPIC&URL_SECTION=201.html, last visited June 2006).

United Nations – Committee on Economic Social and Cultural Rights, General Comment on Article 15(1)(c) of the Covenant (General Comment no. 17), Geneva, 7–25 November 2005, para. 32 [E/C.12/GC/17 12 January 2006] (available at www.unhchr.ch, last visited June 2006).

United Nations – Sub-Commission on the Promotion and Protection of Human Rights, Resolution 2000/7, 'Intellectual property rights and human rights', 17 August 2000 (available at http://www.unhchr.ch/Huridocda/Huridoca.nsf/0/c462b62cf8a07b13c 12569700046704e?Opendocument, last visited July 2006).

International Covenant on Economic, Social and Cultural Rights, adopted by the General Assembly, resolution 2200A (XXI) of 16 December 1966, and entered into force on 3 January 1976 (available at http://www.ohchr.org, last visited June 2006).

World Trade Organisation (WTO), Amendment of the TRIPS Agreement, Decision of 6 December 2005, WT/L/641 (available at http://www.wto.org/english/tratop_e/trips_e/wtl641_e.htm, last visited February 2007).

WTO Ministerial declaration, adopted on 14 November 2001 (WT/MIN(01)/DEC/1) (available at http://www.wto.org/english/thewto_e/minist_e/min01_e/mindecl_e.htm, last visited April 2006).

WTO Declaration on the TRIPS agreement and public health, adopted on 14 November 2001 (WT/MIN(01)/DEC/2) (available at http://www.wto.org/english/thewto_e/minist_e/min01_e/mindecl_trips_e.htm, last visited April 2006).

Agreement on Trade-Related Aspects of Intellectual Property Rights (TRIPS Agreement), contained in an Annex to the Marrakesh Agreement Establishing the World Trade Organization, signed in Marrakesh, Morocco on 15 April 1994 (WTO Agreement) (available at http://www.wto.org/english/tratop_e/trips_e/t_agm0_e.htm, last visited November 2008).

Treaty on Access to Knowledge, Draft 9 May 2005 (available at http://www.cptech.org/a2k/consolidatedtext-may9.pdf, last visited February 2007).

Berlin Declaration on Open Access to Knowledge in the Sciences and Humanities, 23 October 2003 (available at http://oa.mpg.de/openaccess-berlin/berlindeclaration.html, last visited February 2007).

Bonn Guidelines on Access to Genetic Resources and Fair and Equitable Sharing of the Benefits Arising out of their Utilization, Conference on the Parties (COP) 6 Decision VI/24, 19 April 2002 (available at http://www.biodiv.org/decisions/default.asp?lg=0&dec=VI/24, last visited November 2008).

Convention on Biological Diversity (CBD), 5 June 1992 (available at http://www.unep.ch/bio/conv-e.html).

Andean Communities – Subregional Integration Agreement of the Andean Community (Cartagena Agreement), Decision 486 – Common Provisions on Industrial Property, 14 September 2000 (available at http://www.wipo.int/clea/docs_new/en/ac/ac005en.html, last visited June 2006).

Belgium – Belgian Patent Act [Wet op de uitvindingsoctrooien], 24 May 1854, *Offical Gazette [Belgisch Staatsblad]*, 25 May 1854.
Belgium – Belgian Patent Act, 24 May 1854, Parliamentary Proceedings [*Handelingen*], 1853–54, 8 December 1853, 181.
Denmark – Order no. 1086 of 11 December 2000, entering into force 20 December 2000, amending Order no. 374 of 19 June 1998 on patents and supplementary protection certificates (available at http://www.wipo.int/clea/en/details.jsp?id=1144, last visited November 2008).
European Patent Organisation (EPO) – European Patent Convention of 5 October 1973 (EPC) (available at http://www.european-patent-office.org/epc/pdf_e.htm, last visited April 2006).
The Netherlands – Dutch Patent Act 13 December 1994 (available at http://www.wipo.int/clea/docs_new/en/nl/nl020en.html).
USA – Utility Patent Act of 18 July 1952 (UPA), laid down in Title 35 of the *United States Code (35 USC)* (available at http://www.uspto.gov/web/offices/pac/mpep/consolidated_laws.pdf, last visited November 2008).

Case Law

European Commission of Human Rights (ECHR), Grand Chamber, 11 January 2007, Case of *Anheuser-Busch Inc. v. Portugal* (Application no. 73049/01) (available at http://cmiskp.echr.coe.int/tkp197/view.asp?item=2&portal=hbkm&action=html&highlight=ANHEUSER-BUSCH%20%7C%20PORTUGAL&sessionid=11307840&skin=hudoc-en, last visited February 2007).
ECHR, 22 November 1995, *S.W. v U.K., Publ. Cont., Series A*, vol. 335-B, § 44 (available at http://cmiskp.echr.coe.int/tkp197/view.asp?item=1&portal=hbkm&action=html&highlight=S.W.%20%7C%20%22THE%20UNITED%20KINGDOM%22&sessionid=11307033&skin=hudoc-en, last visited February 2007).
ECHR, in *Smith Kline and French Laboratories Ltd v the Netherlands*, from 4 October 1990 (Application no. 12633/87) (available at http://cmiskp.echr.coe.int, last visited February 2007).
European Patent Office (EPO), Technical Board of Appeal, 21 February 1995 (T 356/93) (Appeal on the decision of the Opposition Division, 15 December 1992), *Plant Genetic Systems* case.
EPO, Opposition Division, 15 December 1992, concerning European patent application bearing publication number 242.236, *IIC*, 1993, 618.
EPO, Opposition Division, 31 March 1992, (concerning European patent application bearing publication number 122.791, *Lubrizol (Plant Gene Expression).*
USA – *John Moore v The Regents of the University of California*, Supreme Court of California, decided 9 July 1990, 793, *P2d*, 479.

Opinions

Group of advisers to the European Commission on the ethical implications of biotechnology (GAEIB), Opinion no. 8, 25 September 1996, Ethical aspects of patenting inventions involving elements of human origin (available at http://ec.europa.eu/european_group_ethics/docs/opinion8_en.pdf, last visited November 2008).
GAEIB, Opinion no. 3, 30 September 1993, Ethical questions arising from the Commission Proposal for a Council Directive on Legal Protection for

Biotechnological Inventions (available at http://ec.europa.eu/european_group_ethics/docs/opinion3_en.pdf, last visited June 2006).

European Group on Ethics in Science and New Technologies (EGE), Opinion no. 16, Ethical Aspects of Patenting Inventions Involving Human Stem Cells (available at http://ec.europa.eu/european_group_ethics/docs/avis16_en.pdf, last visited November 2008).

EGE, Opinion no. 8, *Ethical aspects of patenting inventions involving elements of human origin*, 25/09/1996. (available at http://europa.eu.int/comm/european_group_ethics/gaieb/en/opinion8.pdf, last visited April 2006).

13. Human rights as a constraint on intellectual property rights: the case of patent and plant variety protection rights, genetic resources and traditional knowledge

Charles R. McManis*

One of the great questions of our time is how to promote global economic development, while at the same time preserving the local biological and cultural diversity of 'this fragile earth, our island home.'[1] The international debate over how to reconcile these two seemingly conflicting goals has increasingly focused on the interplay among three international agreements that have entered into force during the past 15 years.[2]

---

* Thomas & Karole Green Professor of Law and Director, Intellectual Property & Technology Law Program, Washington University School of Law.

1 Book of Common Prayer 370 (1977).

2 The international agreements relevant to the legal protection of TK, which is the principal focus of this chapter, range from those that are essentially aspirational in character to those that impose concrete legal obligations backed by international enforcement mechanisms. In the former category are such agreements as the UN International Covenant on Economic, Social, and Cultural Rights, which entered into force in 1976, the International Labor Organization's Convention (No. 169) concerning Indigenous and Tribal Peoples in Independent Countries, which entered into force in 1991, and the Convention on Biological Diversity (CBD), which entered into force in 1993, and is the first international agreement to make explicit reference to the protection of traditional knowledge. For a discussion of the first two treaties, see below note 24 and accompanying text. For a discussion of the CBD, see below notes 3, 16–17, and accompanying text.

At the opposite end of the spectrum is the World Trade Organization (WTO) Agreement on Trade-Related Aspects of Intellectual Property Rights (TRIPS), which entered into force in 1995 and requires its members to adhere to specific minimum standards for the protection and enforcement of IPRs and establishes an international dispute settlement process to resolve disputes between members and to impose sanctions on members who fail to carry out their obligations under TRIPS. For a discussion of the TRIPS Agreement, see below notes 5–8, 13–15, and accompanying text.

The Convention on Biological Diversity (CBD), which was opened for signature at the Earth Summit in Rio de Janeiro in 1992, seeks to promote the conservation, sustainable use, facilitated access to, and equitable sharing of benefits arising out of the utilization of genetic resources. As a part of this larger objective, Article 8(j) of the CBD specifically calls upon its members to 'respect, preserve and maintain knowledge, innovations and practices of indigenous and local communities embodying traditional lifestyles relevant for the conservation and sustainable use of biological diversity, and to promote their wider application with the approval and involvement of the holders of such knowledge, innovations and practices and encourage the sharing of benefits arising from the utilization of such knowledge, innovations and practices'.[3] To date, over 190 countries (with the notable exception of the USA) have ratified the CBD.[4]

The Agreement on Trade-Related Aspects of Intellectual Property Rights (the TRIPS Agreement) is one of a bundle of agreements embodied in the larger 1994 Agreement Establishing the World Trade Organization (WTO), which currently has 150 members.[5] The TRIPS Agreement seeks to stimulate international trade and economic development by setting international minimum standards for the protection and enforcement of intellectual property rights.[6] As of 1 January 2005, all but the least-developed members of the WTO

Falling between these two extremes is the Food and Agriculture Organization (FAO) International Treaty on Plant Genetic Resources for Food and Agriculture, which entered into force in 2004 and creates a formal 'Multilateral System' – that is, a system of 'common-pool goods' – in 36 genera of crops and 29 genera of forages, guaranteeing both 'facilitated' (that is, free or low cost) access to these genetic resources and a system for equitable sharing of the benefits derived from any commercialized products that incorporate materials from the Multilateral System. See below notes 9–12 and accompanying text.

[3] Available at http://www.cbd.int/convention.shtml?lg-0&a-cbd-08 (last visited 10 July 2009).

[4] Available at http://www.cbd.int/information/parties.asp (last visited 10 July 2009).

[5] For the Agreement Establishing the World Trade Organization and related agreements to be administered by the WTO, see http://www.wto.org/english/docs_e/legal_e/legal_e.htm (last visited 10 July 2009). This agreement, together with the TRIPS Agreement and other results of the Uruguay Round of Multilateral Trade Negotiations, are included as annexes attached to the Final Act embodying the results of the Uruguay Round of Multilateral Trade Negotiations [hereinafter Final Act]. For the complete bundle of agreements, see http://www.wto.org/english/docs_e/legal_e/03-fa_e.htm (last visited 10 July 2009). For the current membership of the WTO, see http://www.wto.org/english/thewto_e/whatis_e/tif_e/org6_e.htm (last visited 10 July 2009).

[6] Agreement on Trade-Related Aspects of Intellectual Property Rights, Including Trade in Counterfeit Goods [hereinafter TRIPS Agreement], available at http://www.wto.org/english/docs_e/legal_e/legal_e.htm (last visited 10 July 2009).

were obligated to be into full compliance with TRIPS, including its controversial requirements governing patent and plant variety protection.[7] Disputes over compliance with TRIPS obligations are subject to resolution through the larger WTO dispute settlement process, and multilateral trade sanctions may be authorized to enforce compliance.[8]

Finally, in 2001, the Conference of the Food and Agricultural Organization (FAO), adopted the new International Treaty on Plant Genetic Resources for Food and Agriculture (FAO International Treaty),[9] which was negotiated with the understanding that it would be in harmony with the Convention on Biological Diversity, and is similar to the CBD in its overall objectives to promote the conservation, sustainable use, and equitable sharing of benefits arising out of the use of plant genetic resources for food and agriculture, as well as associated traditional agricultural knowledge, for sustainable use and food security. However, the FAO International Treaty also goes well beyond the CBD, in that it builds on an existing national and international system of *ex situ* germplasm collections of genetic resources for food and agriculture, namely the Consultative Group on International Agricultural Research (CGIAR),[10] and creates a formal 'Multilateral System' – that is, a system of 'common-pool goods' – in 36 genera of crops and 29 genera of forages, guaranteeing both 'facilitated' (that is, free or low cost) access to these genetic resources, and a system for equitable sharing of the benefits derived from any commercialized product that incorporates materials from the Multilateral System.[11] Having obtained the required number of adoptions, approvals, and ratifications, the International Treaty entered into force on 29 June 2004 and currently has 120 members.[12]

An important TRIPS-related development with respect to the protection of TK was announced in the WTO's 2001 Doha Ministerial Declaration, which

---

7 For the transitional provisions of TRIPS, see TRIPS Agreement, above note 6, Articles 65 and 66. For the international minimum standards for patent protection, see id., Articles 27–34. For the international standard for plant variety protection, see id., Article 27.3(b).

8 For the dispute settlement and enforcement provisions of the TRIPS Agreement, see TRIPS Agreement, above note 6, Article 64, and the Final Act, above note 5, Annex 2, Dispute Settlement Understanding, available at http://www.wto.org/english/docs_e/legal_e/28-dsu_e.htm (last visited 10 July 2009).

9 International Treaty on Plant Genetic Resources for Food and Agriculture [hereinafter FAO International Treaty], available at http://www.planttreaty.org/texts_en.htm (last visited 10 July 2009).

10 See http://www.cgiar.org (last visited 10 July 2009).

11 See Brush, Stephen B. (2005), 'Protecting Traditional Agricultural Knowledge', 17 *Washington U.J.L.& Pol'y* 59, available at http://law.wustl.edu/journal/17/index.html (last visited 10 July 2009).

12 See FAO International Treaty, above note 9.

instructed the WTO's Council for TRIPS to examine, *inter alia*, 'the relationship between the TRIPS Agreement and the Convention on Biological Diversity, [and] the protection of traditional knowledge and folklore'.[13] A separate WTO Declaration on the TRIPS Agreement and Public Health affirmed that TRIPS does not and should not prevent members from taking measures to protect public health, recognized that WTO members with insufficient or no manufacturing capacities in the pharmaceutical sector could face difficulties in making effective use of compulsory licensing under the TRIPS Agreement, and instructed the Council for TRIPS to find an expeditious solution to this problem.[14] This Declaration led to the Decision of 30 August 2003, and a proposed revision of TRIPS, allowing countries with manufacturing capacity to make and export pharmaceutical products to countries with public health needs, notwithstanding Article 31(f) of TRIPS, which limits compulsory licensing predominantly to the supply of the domestic market.[15]

An important development in the implementation of the CBD was the 2003 promulgation of the Bonn Guidelines on Access to Genetic Resources and Benefit Sharing.[16] These Guidelines are designed to assist Parties, Governments, and other stakeholders in developing an overall access and benefit-sharing (ABS) strategy, and in identifying the steps involved in the process of obtaining access to genetic resources and benefit-sharing.[17]

Finally, an important development in the implementation of the FAO International Treaty was the 2006 First Session and Report of the Governing Body of the International Treaty on Plant Genetic Resources for Food and Agriculture.[18] In this session, the Governing Body adopted a Standard Material Transfer Agreement, as required by Article 12.4 of the Treaty, which contains the benefit-sharing obligations specified in Article 13.2(d) of the Treaty, and fixed the rate and modalities for sharing of benefits arising out of the commercialization of a product that incorporates material accessed from the Multilateral System, as required by Article 13.2(d)(ii) of the Treaty.[19]

The often fractious North–South debate leading up to and generated by the adoption of these three treaties has produced a cascade of 'thinking globally and acting locally' to reconcile the goals of global economic development and

---

13 See http://www.wto.org/English/thewto_e/minist_e/min01_e/mindecl_e.htm (last visited 10 June 2009).

14 See http://www.wto.org/english/thewto_e/minist_e/min01_e/mindecl_trips_e.htm (last visited 10 July 2009).

15 See generally, http://www.wto.org/english/tratop_e/trips_e/pharmpatent_e.htm (last visited 10 July 2009).

16 See http://www.cbd.int/abs/bonn.shtml (last visited 10 July 2009).

17 Ibid.

18 See http://www.planttreaty.org/meetings/gbi_en.htm (last visited 10 July 2009).

19 Ibid.

the conservation, sustainable use, access to and an equitable sharing of the benefits arising from the use of biodiversity and associated traditional knowledge.[20] In this debate one frequently hears the view expressed that the protection of genetic resources and traditional knowledge of indigenous peoples and local communities do not readily fit into the existing intellectual property regimes of the industrialized world, and that because these regimes basically promote the interests of the industrialized world and encourage what has come to be called (and vilified as) 'biopiracy',[21] an entirely new, *sui generis* system of legal protection for traditional knowledge, together with an international obligation on the part of innovators to equitably share benefits arising out of the use of biodiversity and associated traditional knowledge, is urgently required.[22]

Generally overlooked in this fractious North–South debate, however, is that claims to intellectual property rights and claims to an equitable sharing of benefits arising from the use of genetic resources and associated traditional knowledge are based on common moral foundations. This paper will examine these common moral foundations in an effort to stimulate dialogue about, and elicit a moral and spiritual commitment to, what has been called 'the way of all the earth'.[23] In particular, the paper will argue that, assuming there to be an

---

[20] See, for example, McManis, Charles R. (2003), 'Intellectual Property, Genetic Resources and Traditional Knowledge Protection: Thinking Globally, Acting Locally', 11 *Cardozo J. Int'l & Comp. L.* 547 [hereinafter McManis, Thinking Globally, Acting Locally]; McManis, Charles R. (1998), 'The Interface Between International Intellectual Property and Environmental Protection: Biodiversity and Biotechnology', 76 *Wash. U. L. Q.* 255 [hereinafter McManis, Biodiversity & Biotechnology].

[21] See, for example, http://www.etcgroup.org/documents/Biopiracy+10Com.pdf (last visited 28 May 2007): 'Biopiracy refers to the appropriation of the knowledge and genetic resources of farming and indigenous communities by individuals or institutions seeking exclusive monopoly control (usually patents or plant breeders' rights) over these resources and knowledge.'

[22] See, for example, Posey, Darrell A. and Graham Dutfield (1996), *Beyond Intellectual Property: Toward Traditional Resource Rights for Indigenous Peoples and Local Communities*, Ottawa: IDRC Publications, 92, 94–100 (discussing traditional resource rights, community IPRs, and community intellectual rights as alternatives to IPRs, that 'accommodate more adequately the concern of traditional communities to prevent others from privatizing their knowledge and resources'. Id. at 100). For a counterargument that existing intellectual property regimes (inclusive of the closely related law of unfair competition) and associated contractual mechanisms, can provide far more comprehensive legal protection for traditional knowledge holders than critics generally acknowledge, see McManis, Charles R. (2004), 'Fitting Traditional Knowledge Protection and Biopiracy Claims into the Existing Intellectual Property and Unfair Competition Framework', in Ong, Burton (ed.), *Intellectual Property and Biological Resources* (Singapore: Marshall Cavendish Academic), 425–510.

[23] See Dunne, John (1972), 'The Way of All the Earth', quoted in Fasching,

emerging human right on the part of individual holders of traditional knowledge and/or genetic resources to have the opportunity to give prior informed consent and receive an equitable share of any benefits arising from the use of such knowledge and/or resources by others,[24] the most effective way to

---

Darrell J. and Dell deChant (2001), *Comparative Religious Ethics: A Narrative Approach* 4 (Wiley Blackwell).

[24] The legal basis for this rather large assumption can be found in a variety of international agreements articulating basic human rights, as well as those specifically addressing the rights of indigenous peoples. For example, Article 15 of the International Covenant on Economic, Social and Cultural Rights, adopted and opened for signature, ratification and accession by General Assembly resolution 2200A (XXI) of 16 December 1966 (entry into force 3 January 1976), in accordance with Article 27 of the Covenant, available at http://www.unhchr.ch/html/menu3/b/a_cescr.htm (last visited 10 July 2009), states that:

> 1. The States Parties to the present Covenant recognize the right of everyone:
> (a) To take part in cultural life;
> (b) To enjoy the benefits of scientific progress and its applications;
> (c) To benefit from the protection of the moral and material interests resulting from any scientific, literary or artistic production of which he is the author.
> 2. The steps to be taken by the States Parties to the present Covenant to achieve the full realization of this right shall include those necessary for the conservation, the development and the diffusion of science and culture.
> 3. The States Parties to the present Covenant undertake to respect the freedom indispensable for scientific research and creative activity.
> 4. The States Parties to the present Covenant recognize the benefits to be derived from the encouragement and development of international contacts and co-operation in the scientific and cultural fields.

Likewise, Article 12 of the Convention (No. 169) concerning Indigenous and Tribal Peoples in Independent Countries, adopted on 27 June 1989 by the General Conference of the International Labour Organisation at its seventy-sixth session, entry into force 5 September 1991, available at http://www.unhchr.ch/html/menu3/b/62.htm, last visited 10 July 2009, states that:

> Governments shall have the responsibility for developing, with the participation of the peoples concerned, co-ordinated and systematic action to protect the rights of these peoples and to guarantee respect for their integrity.

Article 5 of the Convention states that:

> In applying the provisions of this Convention:
> (a) The social, cultural, religious and spiritual values and practices of these peoples shall be recognised and protected, and due account shall be taken of the nature of the problems which face them both as groups and as individuals;
> (b) The integrity of the values, practices and institutions of these peoples shall be respected;
> (c) Policies aimed at mitigating the difficulties experienced by these peoples in facing new conditions of life and work shall be adopted, with the participation and co-operation of the peoples affected.

Finally, in 2006, the UN Human Rights Council adopted an important Declaration on the Rights of Indigenous Peoples, see http://www.un.org/esa/socdev/unpfii/en/declaration.html (last visited 10 July 2009), but the adoption process came to a halt in

enforce that right would be to modify the TRIPS Agreement to require the disclosure of source and evidence of prior informed consent to use such traditional knowledge and/or genetic resources as a condition for enforcing an otherwise valid patent or plant variety protection certificate that is derived from such knowledge and/or resources.

I. THE MORAL FOUNDATIONS OF INTELLECTUAL PROPERTY LAW AND POLICY

The moral justification most often given for intellectual property protection is strictly utilitarian, or instrumental, and illustrates what the classical rhetorical tradition would call an argument from consequences. Indeed, this utilitarian moral foundation for intellectual property rights is enshrined in Article I, section 8, clause 8 of the United States Constitution, which states that 'The Congress shall have Power [. . .] To promote Progress of Science and useful Arts, by securing for limited Times to Authors and Inventors the exclusive Right to their respective Writings and Discoveries'.[25]

In Western legal and philosophic terms, traditional knowledge and human knowledge generally can be divided into what the United States Constitution speaks of as 'Science' and 'the useful Arts'. These terms are not to be understood in their modern sense, however, but as a distinctly eighteenth century effort on the part of the framers of the US Constitution to capture the Greek philosophic distinction between *theoria* (those things worthy of being known for their own sake) and *praxis* (those things worthy of being known as a useful means to some other end). It is in this eighteenth century sense that the US Constitution is to be understood when it states that the constitutionally mandated purpose of statutory copyright and patent law in the United States is to 'promote the Progress of Science and the Useful Arts'.[26] Thus understood, this constitutional clause appears sufficiently capacious to encompass essentially all types of traditional knowledge, be it traditional cultural expressions (TCEs) or 'folklore' (that is, expressions of the traditional beliefs, legends, and customs of a people, all of which are presumptively valuable for their own sake), handicrafts (which are capable of being valued both for their own sake

November 2006 when the UN General Assembly's Third Committee, apparently at the behest of a number of African states, see http://www.iwgia.org/sw18043.asp (last visited 10 July 2009), adopted a non-action resolution, meaning that there would be no voting on the Declaration during the sixty-first plenary session of the General Assembly. Id.

[25] See U.S. Const. art. 1 § 8 cl. 8.

[26] Id.

and as useful means to other ends), or traditional medicinal or agricultural knowledge (the two main categories of traditional *praxis*, or useful knowledge).

This fundamental division of human knowledge into utilitarian 'arts', or *praxis*, and philosophically valuable 'Science', or *theoria*, respectively, is also reflected in the titles of the two 'Great Conventions' adopted in the late nineteenth century for the more effective international protection of intellectual property – namely the 1883 Paris Convention for the Protection of Industrial Property[27] and the 1886 Berne Convention for the Protection of Literary and Artistic Works.[28] Industrial property includes any work of the human intellect that might serve a useful function, while literary and artistic works include virtually any expression of those things worthy to be known for their own sake.

The Paris Convention declares that the protection of 'industrial property' has as its object patents, utility models, industrial designs, trademarks, services marks, trade names, indications of source or appellations of origin and the repression of unfair competition.[29] It goes on to state that 'industrial property' shall be understood in the broadest sense and shall apply not only to industry and commerce proper but likewise to agricultural and extractive industries and to all manufactured or natural products.[30] Likewise, the Berne Convention states that the term 'literary and artistic works' shall include every production in the literary, scientific and artistic domain, whatever may be the mode or form of its expression.[31] Echoing this same broad division of human knowledge, the 1967 Convention Establishing the World Intellectual Property Organization (WIPO) – the United Nations agency that is today responsible for promoting the protection of intellectual property worldwide as well as administering the Paris and Berne Conventions – states that intellectual property includes not only the forms of intellectual property protection recognized in the two Great Conventions, but also 'all other rights resulting from intellectual activity in the industrial, scientific, literary or artistic fields'.[32]

---

27 Available at http://www.wipo.int/treaties/en/ip/paris/trtdocs_wo020.htm (last visited 10 July 2009) [hereinafter Paris Convention].

28 Available at http://www.wipo.int/treaties/en/ip/berne/trtdocs_wo001.htm (last visited 10 July 2009) [hereinafter Berne Convention].

29 Paris Convention, art. 1 cl. 2, available at http://www.wipo.int/ (last visited 28 May 2009).

30 Paris Convention, art. 1 cl. 3, available at http://www.wipo.int/treaties/en/ip/paris/trtdocs_wo020.htm#P71_4054 (last visited 10 July 2009).

31 Berne Convention, art. 2 cl. 1, available at http://www.wipo.int/treaties/en/ip/berne/trtdocs_wo001.htm (last visited 10 July 2009).

32 See http://www.wipo.int/tk/en/glossary/index.html (last visited 10 July 2009).

The capaciousness of the foregoing constitutional and treaty terms makes it evident that they are designed to cover the entire spectrum of innovative human activity, inclusive of any innovative human activity that might be defined as 'traditional knowledge'. At the same time, the US Constitution makes it equally clear that the intellectual property protection authorized must serve an essentially utilitarian public purpose – that is, promoting 'the Progress of Science and the useful Arts' – and must be limited not only in time but also in respect of the subject matter and persons eligible for protection – that is, the 'Writings' of 'Authors' and 'Discoveries' of 'Inventors' (from which a constitutional copyright standard of originality and a constitutional patent standard of inventiveness have respectively been deduced). These features of intellectual property law make it clear that intellectual property rights are the product of bargained for exchange among members of a given generation, wherein society at large grants an individual a limited term of carefully qualified and limited exclusive rights in return for the individual's disclosure of the results of innovation or creativity. Granting such exclusive rights stimulates innovation and creativity, results in public disclosure of such innovation and creativity, and provides an incentive to commercialize such innovations and creativity.

While the Paris Convention contains no analogous broad language, that is only because the goals of the Paris Convention are more modest, as it merely obliges its members to offer 'national [that is, non-discriminatory] treatment' to the nationals of other member countries with respect to any industrial property protection that the member country chooses to provide for its citizens, and establishes an international priority system for the registration of industrial property.[33] While the Berne Convention goes a step further, establishing certain minimum standards for copyright protection in addition to obliging its members to accord national treatment to the nationals of other member countries, and specifying that the exercise of these rights shall not be subject to any formality, it is only in the TRIPS Agreement that international minimum standards for the protection and enforcement of intellectual property rights in general are prescribed, and in so doing the TRIPS Agreement states that the 'protection and enforcement of intellectual property rights should contribute to the promotion of technological innovation and to the transfer and dissemination of technology, to the mutual advantage of producers and users of technological knowledge and in a manner conducive to social and economic welfare, and to a balance of rights and obligations'.[34]

---

33 See Paris Convention, art. 3, available at http://www.wipo.int/treaties/en/ip/paris/trtdocs_wo020.htm#p81_6245 (last visited 10 July 2009).

34 TRIPS Agreement, art. 7, above note 6.

If the objective of intellectual property law is to provide a limited form of affirmative protection for industrial property and literary and artistic works, Article 10bis (2) of the Paris Convention makes it clear that the objective of the associated field of unfair competition law is to provide defensive protection against 'any act of competition contrary to honest practices in industrial or commercial matters'.[35] While Article 10bis (3) of the Paris Convention states that various forms of deceptive commercial conduct injurious to competitors – that is, passing off, trade disparagement, and deceptive advertising – are 'in particular' to be prohibited, both the broad language of Article 10bis (2) and the complementary language of Article 39 of the TRIPS Agreement make it clear that all natural and legal persons, and not simply commercial competitors, are to be the beneficiaries of this protection.[36] Likewise, Article 40 of TRIPS recognizes that because some contractual licensing practices or conditions pertaining to intellectual property rights which restrain competition may have adverse effects on trade and may impede the transfer and dissemination of technology, nothing in TRIPS prevents member countries from specifying licensing practices or conditions that constitute an abuse of intellectual property rights having an adverse effect on competition.[37]

In addition to the foregoing utilitarian justification for intellectual property rights, however, theorists have also sought to justify intellectual property rights on the basis of non-instrumental arguments from antecedents, or philosophic first principles. The two most commonly invoked philosophical justifications for intellectual property rights include the Lockean labor theory of property and the Hegelian justification for property rights as a necessary extension of personal autonomy.[38]

In Book II, Chapter V of his *Two Treatises on Government*, John Locke states that '*Labour* being the unquestionable Property of the Labourer, no Man but he can have a right to what that is once joined to, at least where there is enough, and as good left in common for others.'[39] In addition to the foregoing (and oft-overlooked) proviso by which Locke qualifies his labor theory of

---

35 Available at http://www.wipo.int/treaties/en/ip/paris/trtdocs_wo020.html P 213_35515 (last visited 10 July 2009).

36 Available at http://www.wto.org/english/docs_e/legal_e/27-trips_04d_e.htm#8 (last visited 10 July 2009).

37 Id.

38 See generally Merges, Robert P., Peter S. Menell and Mark A. Lemley (2006), *Intellectual Property in the New Technological Age* 2–10 (4th edn) New York: Aspen Publishers; Cohen, Julie E., Lydia Pallas Loren, Ruth L. Okediji and Maureen A. O'Rourke (2006), *Copyright in a Global Information Economy*, New York: Aspen Publishers, 11–13 (2nd edn).

39 Locke, John (1690), *Two Treatises of Government*, Book II, Chap. V.

property with a requirement that 'enough and as good' be left in common for others, he also specifies that:

> The same Law of Nature, that does by this means give us Property, does also *bound* that *Property* too . . . As much as any one can make use of to any advantage of life before it spoils; so much he may by his labour fix a property in. Whatever is beyond this, is more than his share, and belongs to others. Nothing was made by God for Man to spoil or destroy.[40]

Although Locke does not specifically discuss (or even envision) intellectual property, which was, after all, only beginning to emerge as a discrete concept in seventeenth century England, his labor theory nevertheless seems to have particular salience with respect to the ownership of products of intellectual labor. At the same time, as the twentieth century philosopher, Robert Nozick, cautions in his *Anarchy, State and Utopia*, this labor theory does not mean that the owner of a can of tomato juice who dumps it into the ocean can claim ownership of all of the high seas.[41] Not only would such a claim seek to encompass more than the owner's labor produced, thus exceeding the implicit limits a labor-based theory of property, but it would also fail to leave enough and as good in common for others, thus violating the Lockean proviso as well.

An alternative philosophical justification for intellectual property can be found in a perspective developed by G.W.F. Hegel in his *Philosophy of Right*.[42] The premise underlying this perspective is said to be that 'to achieve proper self-development – to be *a person* – an individual needs some control over resources in the external environment. The necessary assurances of control take the form of property rights'.[43] But under this theory, not all property or loss of same is equally important:

> Some objects may approach the fungible end of the continuum so that the justification for protecting them as specially related to persons disappears. They might just as well be treated by whatever general moral rules govern wealth-loss at the hands of the government . . . On the other hand, a few objects may be so close to the personal end of the continuum that no compensation [for loss] would be 'just'. . . . If my kidney may be called my property, it is not property subject to condemnation for the general public welfare.[44]

---

40 Id.

41 Nozick, Robert (1984), *Anarchy, State and Utopia* 175, cited in Merges, Menell and Lemley, above note 38.

42 See Radin, Margaret Jane (1982), 'Property and Personhood', 34 *Stan. L. Rev.* 957.

43 Id.

44 Id.

Instrumental and non-instrumental justifications converge in various 'democratic' justifications of intellectual property rights as necessary to ensure a robust public domain and an uncensored marketplace for ideas. Professor Jessica Litman, for example, notes that 'The most important part of the public domain is a part we usually speak of only obliquely: the realm comprising aspects of copyrighted works that copyright does not protect.'[45] As Litman points out, a central limitation on the scope of copyrights is that these rights extend only to the author's original expression, and not to the underlying facts or ideas expressed. A second limitation on these exclusive rights is that others may make fair use even of an author's original expression for such purposes as criticism, comment, news reporting, teaching, scholarship, or research. Professor Neil Weinstock Netanel adds that copyright law fulfills both a production function and a structural function, by encouraging creative expression on a wide array of political, social, and aesthetic issues – activities constituting vital components of a democratic civil society – and doing so, moreover, through the creation of copyright industries that are independent of direct government control.[46] Indeed, this is precisely the significance of the Berne Convention's requirement that the exercise of copyrights shall not be subject to any formality.

In addition to these instrumental and non-instrumental justifications for intellectual property rights, however, is another as yet largely overlooked justification, which can be extrapolated from a peculiar feature of intellectual property rights – namely that, of all species of property, only intellectual property is subject by law to a limited term of protection. This limited term of protection has profound moral implications, as it functions to transform one generation's intellectual property into a gift to subsequent generations.[47] This justification will be discussed in more detail in Part III of this chapter. First, however, it is important to identify the moral foundations of claims on the part of traditional knowledge and genetic resource holders to a right to prior

---

45 Litman, Jessica (1990), 'The Public Domain', 39 *Emory L. J.* 965, quoted in Cohen et al., above note 38, at 14–15.

46 Netanel, Neil Weinstock (1996), 'Copyright and a Democratic Civil Society', 106 *Yale L. J.* 283, quoted in Cohen et al., above note 38, at 16.

47 My thanks to Martin J. Adelman, Theodore and Jame Pedas Family Professor of Intellectual Property & Technology Law and Co-Director of the Intellectual Property Program at the George Washington University Law School for initially calling my attention to this fundamental insight. For a cultural introduction to the relationship between property and giftgiving, see Hyde, Lewis (1979), *The Gift: Imagination and the Erotic Life of Property*, London: Vintage Publishers. See also Godelier, Maurice (1996), *The Enigma of the Gift*, Chicago: University of Chicago Press; and Mauss, Marcel (1990), *The Gift: The Form and Reasons for Exchange in Archaic Societies*, New York: W.W. Norton & Co.

informed consent and an equitable sharing of benefits arising out of the use of that knowledge and/or those resources.

All of the foregoing moral foundations can also be said to underlie the emerging legal obligation to conserve genetic resources through facilitated access and benefit sharing, as well as the more specific legal obligation to 'respect, preserve and maintain knowledge, innovations and practices of indigenous and local communities embodying traditional lifestyles relevant for the conservation and sustainable use of biological diversity, and to promote their wider application with the approval and involvement of the holders of such knowledge, innovations and practices and encourage the sharing of benefits arising from the utilization of such knowledge, innovations and practices'.[48] Thus, we must next examine various fundamental concepts and distinctions relevant to the conservation of genetic resources through facilitated access, benefit sharing, and the legal protection of traditional knowledge.

II. FUNDAMENTAL CONCEPTS AND DISTINCTIONS RELEVANT TO CONSERVATION OF GENETIC RESOURCES THROUGH FACILITATED ACCESS, BENEFIT SHARING, AND THE LEGAL PROTECTION OF TRADITIONAL KNOWLEDGE

As we have seen, the Convention on Biological Diversity calls for the conservation of genetic resources through facilitated access to these resources and equitable sharing of benefits arising from the use of these resources. As a part of that general obligation is a more specific obligation to provide legal protection for traditional knowledge.

Traditional knowledge (TK) has been defined as 'a body of knowledge built by a group of people through generations living in close contact with nature'.[49] TK typically includes 'a system of classification, a set of empirical observations about the local environment, and a system of self-management that governs resources use'.[50] Contrary to popular belief, TK is not static and

---

[48] CBD Article 8(j), above note 3 and accompanying text.

[49] Executive Secretary, UNEP/CBD Ad Hoc Open-Ended Working Group on Access and Benefit Sharing, Report on the Role of Intellectual Property Rights in the Implementation of Access and Benefit Sharing Arrangements 5 at ¶ 21, available at http://www.biodiv.org/doc/meetings/abs/abswg-01/official/abswg-01-04-en.pdf (last visited 10 July 2007) [hereinafter UNEP/CBD Report].

[50] Id.

unchanging, but rather develops and changes over time, albeit by means of traditional or customary practices.[51]

Whether TK is understood in the strict sense as encompassing only knowledge and ideas as such or in a broader sense as extending to expressions of knowledge and ideas as well (that is, traditional cultural expressions, or TCEs), TK in any event serves as a means of cultural identification, and thus must be understood holistically, as both its spiritual and practical elements serve to integrate a community with its environment.[52] Likewise, while the WIPO's Intergovernmental Committee (IGC) on Genetic Resources, Traditional Knowledge and Traditional Cultural Expressions has developed two sets of draft provisions, one for TK as such and one for TCEs, the IGC nevertheless recognizes that 'for many communities these are closely related, even integral, aspects of respect for and protection of their cultural and intellectual heritage'.[53]

The IGC also points out that while it might not be possible to develop a singular and exclusive definition of TK, it also might not be necessary for purposes of extending legal protection to TK, as neither of the two basic intellectual property conventions administered by the WIPO – namely the Paris Convention for the Protection of Industrial Property and the Berne Convention for the Protection of Literary and Artistic Works – contains exclusive definitions of what constitute 'inventions', 'industrial designs', or 'literary and artistic works', respectively.[54] Moreover, national intellectual property (IP) systems likewise function perfectly satisfactorily without ironclad definitions,

---

[51] See Balick, Michael J. (2007), 'Traditional Knowledge: Lessons from the Past, Lessons for the Future', in Charles R. McManis (ed.), *Biodiversity and the Law: Intellectual Property, Biotechnology and Traditional Knowledge*, London: Earthscan Publishers, 280 [hereinafter McManis, *Biodiversity and the Law*], also available at http://law.wustl.edu/centeris/Papers/Biodiversity/PDFWrdDoc/Balick.pdf (last visited 10 July 2009). Tradition is simply 'a filter through which innovation occurs'. UNEP/CBD Report, above note 1. Consequently, it is 'traditional methods of research and application and not always particular pieces of knowledge that persist'. Id.

[52] de Carvalho, Nuno Pires (2007), 'From the Shaman's Hut to the Patent Office: A Road Under Construction' [hereinafter Carvalho], in McManis, *Biodiversity and the Law*, above note 51, 241, 243–244, also available at http://www.law.wustl.edu/centeris/Papers/Biodiversity/PDFWrdDoc/Fromshaman2.doc (last visited 10 July 2009).

[53] See WIPO/IGC Draft Provisions on Traditional Cultural Expressions/Folklore and Traditional Knowledge, available at http://www.wipo.int/tk/en/consultations/draft_provisions/draft_provisions.html (last visited 10 July 2009).

[54] WIPO/IGC, Matters Concerning Intellectual Property and Genetic Resources, Traditional Knowledge and Folklore – An Overview, ¶ 65, available at http://www.wipo.int/edocs/mobcs/+K/en/wipo–grtkf_ic_1/wipo_grtkf_ic_1_3.doc (last visited 10 July 2009).

as the more important definitional and conceptual issues have to do with the substantive and procedural standards affecting the availability, acquisition, scope, maintenance and enforcement of intellectual property rights.[55]

Finally, the IGC recognizes that two IP-related concerns have been articulated in the field of TK: first, with respect to the availability of intellectual property protection for TK holders (that is, the need for affirmative legal protection), and secondly, with respect to the acquisition by parties other than TK holders of intellectual property rights (IPRs) over traditional knowledge-based creations and innovations (that is, the need for defensive legal protection).[56] The IGC also notes that 'many traditional societies have developed highly sophisticated and effective customary intellectual property systems . . . [that] have, until now, remained invisible from the point of view of the formal intellectual property system . . .' and that there is 'a need to further study the relationship between customary protection of traditional knowledge and the intellectual property system'.[57]

The need to address the foregoing concerns is urgent, as TK is currently threatened by the larger phenomenon of biodiversity loss, which includes biocultural loss – that is, the 'extinction of experience'[58] – as well as genetic resource loss as such.[59] Traditional knowledge is also threatened by a number of other forces, including the loss of indigenous land rights, poverty, and the standardizing effects of globalization.[60]

---

55 Id.

56 Id. ¶ 63.

57 Id. ¶ 68.

58 Maffi, Luisa (ed.) (2001), *On Biocultural Diversity: Linking Language, Knowledge, and the Environment*, Washington: Smithsonian Institution Press. See also Maffi, Luisa, 'Linguistic and Biological Diversity: The Inextricable Link', available at http://www.terralingua.org/DiscPapers/DiscPaper3.html (last visited 4 June 2007).

59 For a discussion of the impending 'sixth great extinction' – due to the impact of human activity on the natural world – see Pimm, Stuart L. and Thomas M. Brooks (1997), 'The Sixth Extinction: How Large, Where, and When?', in Raven, Peter H. (ed.), *Nature and Human Society: The Quest for a Sustainable World*, Washington: National Academy Press.

60 See generally Wood, Alexander, Pamela Stedman-Edwards and Johann Mang (eds) (2000), *The Root Causes of Biodiversity Loss*, London: Earthscan.

III. THE COMMON MORAL FOUNDATIONS OF INTELLECTUAL PROPERTY LAW AND THE CONSERVATION OF GENETIC RESOURCES THROUGH ACCESS AND BENEFIT SHARING

As we have seen, a largely overlooked justification for intellectual property rights, which also underlies the emerging obligation to grant access to and equitably share the benefits arising from the conservation and sustainable use of genetic resources, is that intellectual property rights and the access and benefit sharing obligation alike create incentives to members of a given generation to disclose innovation and creativity and to conserve and sustainably use genetic resources not only for the benefit of that generation itself, but also in order to make a gift of that generation's innovations, creativity and conserved biodiversity for the benefit of future generations. This intergenerational gift justification finds its roots not only in widely held religious beliefs and a study of comparative religious ethics, but is also embodied in a perspective called 'religious naturalism', which takes the view that human beings, as a part of creation, have an obligation to preserve and sustainably use both the natural world and their own human creativity and innovativeness for the benefit of future generations as well as for their own personal benefit and that of their immediate offspring.

The authors of an important recent comparative study of religious ethics seek to persuade their readers of the importance of what they call 'the way of all the earth' – a biblical phrase that could also be translated as 'the way of all flesh', or 'the way of all mortal beings'.[61] In this study, the authors identify and distinguish two tendencies at war in every person and in every community or religious faith – namely competing tendencies that they label the 'sacred' and the 'holy'.

> The experience of the sacred encourages us to divide the world into sacred and profane, such that we see ourselves as human and all strangers as profane and less (or less than) human. The experience of the holy encourages us to break down that division and discover the humanity of the stranger. The first creates sacred societies, the second holy communities. The first tends to ethnocentricity; the second is anti-ethnocentric. A sacred society sees the Ultimate (God, or Brahman, or however the Ultimate is named) in its own image and rejects all others (strangers) as less than human. A holy community, by contrast, sees all persons as created in the image of a holy that is without image (God, or Emptiness, or however named) and believes that to welcome the stranger or outcast is to welcome the holy. The task of an ethic of the holy is not to eliminate the morality of a society, but to transform it by breaking down the divisions between the sacred and the profane through narratives of

---

61 Fasching and deChant, above note 23, at 4.

> hospitality to the stranger, which affirm the human dignity of precisely those who do not share one's identity and one's stories.[62]

But how can this transformation, or way of all the earth, take root in a world that seems increasingly inflamed with religious divisions and hatred for those who do not share one's identity and one's stories? One response is that of *religious naturalism*, 'wherein our scientific understandings of who we are and how we got here – the Epic of Evolution – serves as the unifying story or Myth'.[63] In the end, each of the world's great religions is said to address two fundamental human concerns: How Things Are and Which Things Matter. How Things Are becomes formulated as a Cosmology or Cosmos; Which Things Matter becomes codified as a Morality or Ethos.[64] The role of religion 'is to integrate the Cosmology and the Morality, to render the cosmological narrative so rich and compelling that it elicits our allegiance and our commitment to its emergent moral understandings'.[65]

> That we need a planetary ethic is so obvious that [one] need but list a few key words: climate, ethnic cleansing, fossil fuels, habitat preservation, human rights, hunger, infectious diseases, nuclear weapons, oceans, ozone layer, pollution, population. Our global conversations on these topics are, by definition, cacophonies of national, cultural, and religious self-interest. Without a common religious orientation, we basically don't know where to begin, nor do we know what to say or how to listen, nor are we motivated to respond.[66]

The role of religious naturalism is thus to lay the foundations for such a planetary ethic – 'an ethic that would make no claim to supplant existing traditions but would seek to coexist with them, informing our global concerns while we continue to orient our daily lives in our cultural and religious contexts'.[67] In a recent study, Professor Ursula Goodenough explains how the Epic of Evolution provides humanity with a unifying story or myth, from which can be extrapolated six moral capacities – namely: strategic reciprocity and the virtues of humaneness, fair-mindedness, courage, reverence, and mindfulness – that Goodenough argues have arisen during our evolutionary history and undergird our ability to flourish in community.[68] These moral

---

62 Id. at 18, Figure 1.1.

63 Goodenough, Ursula (2007), 'Naturalizing Morality', in McManis, *Biodiversity and the Law*, London: Earthscan, above note 51, 35–41.

64 Goodenough, Ursula (1998), *The Sacred Depths of Nature*, Oxford: Oxford University Press, xiv.

65 Id.

66 Id. at xv.

67 Id. at xvi.

68 Goodenough, above note 63, 37–49.

capacities stand in tension with our susceptibilities to greed, hubris, self-absorption, fearfulness, xenophobia, and prejudice – 'behaviours that overwhelm us in the face of prolonged stress when we hunker down and engage not in community but in self-interested survival patterns, the default behaviour of all creatures'.[69]

As Professor Jim Chen notes, the academic community bears a singularly immense responsibility to educate the public with respect to the coming ecological apocalypse, brought on by the 'Evil Quartet' of deadly horsemen: habitat destruction, overkill, introduced species and secondary extinctions.[70] At the same time, says Chen, realigning law with the scientific understanding of biodiversity loss 'produces it own epiphany, its own spiritually satisfying path toward detecting an "echo of the infinite, a glimpse of its unfathomable process, a hint of universal law". . .' .[71]

IV. TOWARD THE LEGAL PROTECTION OF TRADITIONAL KNOWLEDGE

Given the common moral foundations of intellectual property law and the conservation of genetic resources through facilitated access, benefit sharing, and the legal protection of traditional knowledge, what specific options exist for the protection of traditional knowledge? Based on current trends in the protection of TK, three overlapping scenarios for the future protection of TK can be projected – namely (1) continued reliance on existing means of legal protection for TK;[72] (2) development of non-uniform, country-specific (or region-specific) means for protecting TK;[73] and (3) development of internationally harmonized approaches to the protection of TK.[74] For each of these

---

69 Id. at 37.

70 Chen, Jim (2007), 'Across the Apocalypse on Horseback: Biodiversity Loss and the Law', in McManis, *Biodiversity and the Law*, above note 51, 42–57.

71 Id. at 52, quoting Holmes, Oliver Wendell (1897), 'The Path of the Law', 10 *Harv. L. Rev.* 457.

72 See generally McManis, Charles R. (2004), 'Fitting Traditional Knowledge Protection and Biopiracy Claims into the Existing Intellectual Property and Unfair Competition Framework' [hereinafter McManis, *Fitting TK into Existing IP Regimes*], in Burton Ong (ed.), *Intellectual Property and Biological Resources*, Singapore: Marshall Cavendish Academic, 425–510.

73 See generally Barber, Charles V., Lyle Glowka and Antonio G.M. La Vina (2002), 'Developing and implementing national measures for genetic resources access and benefit-sharing' [hereinafter Barber et al.], in Laird, Sarah A. (ed.), *Biodiversity and Traditional Knowledge: Equitable Partnerships in Practice*, London: Earthscan, 363–414.

74 See generally Carvalho, above note 4.

scenarios, the relevant trends and projections on which they are based will be identified and both affirmative and defensive means for protecting TK will be evaluated. Of these three scenarios, this chapter concludes that the most effective way to legally protect traditional knowledge is through existing systems of IPRs and the 'hybrid' FAO system of facilitated access to and sharing of benefits arising out of the commercial use of plant genetic resources for food and agriculture, supplemented by adoption of a requirement (to be embodied in a revision of the TRIPS Agreement) that patent and plant variety protection certificate holders disclose the origin and provide evidence of prior informed consent to use relevant traditional knowledge and/or genetic resources as a condition for enforcing an otherwise valid patent or certificate that is derived from such knowledge and/or resources.

A. Existing Means for Extending Legal Protection to TK

The TRIPS Agreement establishes minimum standards of affirmative legal protection for seven categories of intellectual property,[75] of which six are relevant to the protection of TK and TCEs.[76] Of the six categories, two (that is, copyrights and related rights and industrial design protection) are primarily relevant to the protection of TCEs, two (that is, patents and undisclosed information) are primarily relevant to the protection of TK, and two (that is, trademarks and geographical indications) are relevant to the protection of both TK and TCEs. TRIPS also recognizes (but does not specify explicit minimum standards for) an additional form of IP protection for plant varieties,[77] which is relevant to the protection of traditional agricultural knowledge (TAK). Two important supplementary (and independent) legal means of protecting both TK and TCEs are through the law of unfair competition and through the mechanism of contracts.

---

[75] See generally *UNCTAD-ICTSD Resource Book on TRIPS and Development* (2005), Cambridge: Cambridge University Press.

[76] See generally McManis, Fitting TK into Existing IP Regimes, above note 72, 434–447.

[77] See TRIPS Agreement, above note 17, Article 27.3(b). Although the TRIPS Agreement does not expressly incorporate the minimum standards for plant variety protection (PVP) that are established in the International Convention for the Protection of New Varieties of Plants (commonly known by its French acronym, UPOV) of 2 December 1961, as revised at Geneva on 10 November 1972, on 23 October 1978, and on 19 March 1991, available at http://www.upov.int/en/about/upov_convention.htm (last visited 10 July 2009), it does require that such protection be 'effective,' and this is generally understood to mean that compliance with the minimum standards of UPOV would be sufficient to satisfy the obligations imposed by Article 27.3(b) of the TRIPS Agreement. See generally below notes 83–85, 98 and accompanying text.

Any TK or TCE that is not widely known or readily accessible to humanity generally may (and indeed must) be protected as undisclosed information.[78] This protection is not limited to those who are engaged in a trade or business, but extends to any natural person or legal entity possessed of information that is valuable because it is not generally known.[79] Any TK or TCE that is or might become widely known, thus losing any claim to protection as undisclosed information, may nevertheless qualify for one or more of the other forms of intellectual property protection required by the TRIPS Agreement.

For example, certain aspects of TK and TCEs may be protected as literary or artistic works under copyright law or as industrial designs under *sui generis* industrial design law. A very low level of originality or creativity will suffice to meet the copyright requirement for protection, and the relatively lengthy term of protection specified for literary and artistic works is another attractive feature of copyright protection.[80] Where TK or TCEs are embodied in useful articles, they may qualify for industrial design protection, whether or not they qualify for copyright protection.[81]

TK may also be protected under patent law. While critics tend to dismiss the relevance of patent law for TK protection on the ground that patent protection is limited to protection of individual inventors whose inventions meet the exacting standards of novelty, utility (or 'industrial application'), and non-obviousness (or 'inventive step'), it is important to note that novelty in patent law means little more than that the claimed invention is not disclosed in the 'prior art'.[82] What counts as prior art and how novelty and non-obviousness are defined in various patent systems around the world is highly variable.

Even TK that does not meet these patent standards is nevertheless protectible through the mechanism of contracts, including contracts assigning patent ownership, if TK provides the starting point for the development of a patentable invention. Plant variety protection (PVP) is a particularly attractive alternative means for protecting TAK, as it dispenses with any non-obviousness requirement, and generally requires only that new plant varieties be distinct, uniform, and stable (DUS).[83] While the novelty and DUS standards

---

[78] See McManis, *Fitting TK into Existing IP Regimes*, above note 72, 436–438.
[79] Id. See above note 36 and accompanying text.
[80] Id. at 438–440.
[81] Id. at 440.
[82] Id. at 443.
[83] See McManis, Charles (2005), 'Are There TRIPS-Compliant Measures for a Balanced Co-existence of Patents and Plant Breeders' Rights? Some Lessons from the United States of America' [hereinafter McManis, *Balanced Co-existence of Patent and Plant Breeders' Rights*], *Compilation of the 2002 and 2003 Joint Symposia Documents of the World Intellectual Property Organization (WIPO) and the International Union for the Protection of New Varieties of Plants (UPOV)* 64 [hereinafter Joint WIPO/UPOV Symposia Documents].

may discriminate against some traditional landraces, PVP nevertheless offers significant protection for innovative TAK holders. At the same time, PVP systems generally explicitly permit protected varieties to be used to develop other new varieties, as long as the latter are not 'essentially derived' from the protected variety,[84] and some PVP systems also permit farmers to save and replant seeds of a protected variety, either at no cost or at a discount.[85] Patent protection can likewise be made subject to reasonable experimental use limitations.

Finally, trademarks, geographical indications, and legal prohibitions against unfair competition can be used to protect the identity of TK and TCE holders against the likelihood of confusion in the marketplace or the dilution of famous identifying symbols.[86]

The principal means by which TK holders can prevent the assertion of IPRs by others is by making relevant disqualifying information available to patent and trademark examiners, either directly or through the development of publicly available and searchable databases.[87] An additional means of both affirmatively protecting the identity of TK holders and preventing the unauthorized commercial use of that identity is through the mechanism of certification and collective marks and protected geographical indications.[88] Finally, TK holders can invoke the legal remedies afforded by the law of unfair competition to prevent any act of competition contrary to honest practices in industrial or commercial matters, including the creation of misleading associations between TK holders and a particular commercial product.

The principal limitations on the foregoing approaches to providing affirmative protection for TK and TCEs are (1) fragmentation of protection and a failure to address the protection of TK and TCEs holistically;[89] (2) the high transaction costs that are often entailed in securing or enforcing these forms of protection;[90] (3) the unavailability of competent and affordable legal counsel to represent the interests of TK holders in securing or enforcing such protection;[91] and (4) TK is often shared widely among communities, making it difficult, if

---

[84] See Jördens, Rolf (2005), 'UPOV's Perspective', Joint WIPO/UPOV Symposia Documents, above note 83, at 19.

[85] See McManis, *Biodiversity and Biotechnology* (1998), above note 20, at 278.

[86] See McManis, *Fitting TK into Existing IP Regimes* (2004), above note 72, 441–442.

[87] See Carvalho (2007), above note 52, 247–248.

[88] See McManis, *Fitting TK into Existing IP Regimes* (2004), above note 72, 441–442.

[89] See Carvalho (2007), above note 52, at 259–261.

[90] See Van Overwalle, Geertrui (2007), 'Holder and User Perspectives in the Traditional Knowledge Debate: A European View', in McManis, *Biodiversity and the Law*, above note 51, 355, 360–361.

[91] Id. For examples of possible solutions to this problem, see below note 119.

not impossible, to identify (or even define) true or legitimate owners or to obtain prior informed consent from same.[92] While the first three limitations can to some extent be overcome by various types of capacity building,[93] the fourth constitutes an inherent limitation in the use of IP tools as the primary or sole means of protecting TK.[94]

B. Non-uniform Country(or Region)-specific Means of Protecting TK

The CBD's affirmation of the 'sovereign right' of states to exploit their own genetic resources pursuant to their own environmental policies has stimulated a variety of national and regional measures for regulating access to genetic resources and promoting benefit sharing.[95] These measures may promote, tolerate, or discourage the practice of 'bioprospecting'.[96] If a country (or region) wishes to encourage bioprospecting, it would do well to follow the example of Costa Rica, and put in place a system that is (1) relatively simple and attractive to the private sector and research institutions; and (2) adds value to its stock of genetic resources, which involves investing in building scientific capacity.[97] Other good examples of how this approach can be used to provide affirmative legal protection for TK are to be found among the International Cooperative Biodiversity Group (ICBG) projects sponsored by the US National Institutes of Health.[98]

More common, however, are national and regional systems that give greater weight to protecting against 'biopiracy' and safeguarding other interests and values, such as the prior informed consent of local and indigenous communities.[99] Such ABS legislation is problematic for two reasons: first, it

---

92 For suggested solutions to the problem of identifying TK holders, see below notes 116–118 and accompanying text.

93 For examples of the sort of capacity building that might be required, see above note 57, and below notes 97 and 119 and accompanying text.

94 For a suggested 'hybrid' solution to this problem, see below notes 116–118 and accompanying text.

95 See generally Barber et al. (2002), above note 73.

96 Id. An outright prohibition against access to genetic resources, however, would appear to violate the CBD requirement that members facilitate access to genetic resources.

97 Id. As a practical matter, such a system will largely rely on private contracting, with minimal state regulation and intervention.

98 See generally Rosenthal, Joshua P. (1999), 'Drug Discovery, Economic Development and Conservation: The International Cooperative Biodiversity Groups', 37 *Pharmaceutical Biology* 5 (Supplement 1999). See also McManis (2003), *Thinking Globally, Acting Locally*, above note 20, 553–554, 565–576.

99 Two examples are the Philippines Executive Order 247 on Access to Genetic Resources (EO 247), and Decision 391 of the Andean Pact. See Barber et al. (2002), above note 73.

may actually thwart the CBD goal of facilitating access (particularly academic research access) to genetic resources, if the access and benefit sharing provisions are not transparent or are too burdensome. Secondly, such legislation may simply trigger an international 'race to the bottom','as bioprospecting activities will tend to shift to those countries with the least restrictive legislation.[100] Regional agreements may ameliorate the latter problem, but only if coherent regional benefit-sharing arrangements are included and such agreements are widely adopted throughout the various regions of the world.

Similar problems have arisen with respect to national and regional legislative attempts to recognize the role of farmers as keepers of genetic resources and sustainers of crop evolution by recognizing a broad farmers' privilege to save and replant seeds of protected plant varieties, while at the same time attempting to accomplish benefit sharing through a centralized funding mechanism imposing a licensing fee on commercialization of protected plant varieties, which will be paid into a fund to promote traditional farming techniques.[101] Taxing certified crop varieties in this manner is likely to offer

---

[100] Id. Although Philippines Executive Order 247 (EO 247), above note 99, represents the first comprehensive access and benefit-sharing (ABS) regime, for the first four years of EO 247's operation, only 15 applications were received – most of them from local universities seeking academic research agreements – and only one commercial research agreement was approved. Moreover, Bristol-Myers Squibb announced that it will not pursue natural products research in countries that impose requirements similar to those contained in EO 247. See Barber et al. (2002), above note 73, 408–409. While regional agreements, such as Decision 391 of the Andean Pact, may deter competition among countries and promote regional benefit-sharing, Decision 391 itself does not establish specific mechanisms through which benefits may be shared among member states. Id. at 381 (Box 12.5). Indeed, some critics argue that nothing short of a 'biodiversity cartel' will effectively combat biodiversity loss and promote equitable benefit sharing. See, for example, Vogel, Joseph Henry (2007), 'From the "Tragedy of the Commons" to the "Tragedy of the Commonplace": Analysis and Synthesis through the Lens of Economic Theory', in McManis, *Biodiversity and the Law*, above note 51, at 115.

[101] See generally Brush, Stephen B. (2007), 'The Demise of "Common Heritage" and Protection of Traditional Agricultural Knowledge' [hereinafter Brush], in McManis, *Biodiversity and the Law*, above note 51, at 297, 309–311, discussing the shortcomings of India's Act No. 123, 1999 for the Protection of Plant Varieties and Farmers' Rights, and the Organization of African Unity's African Model Legislation for the Protection of the Rights of Local Communities, Farmers and Breeders and for the Regulation of Access to Biological Resources. This shortcoming is avoided in the FAO International Treaty, above note 9, as Article 9 of the FAO International Treaty implicitly seems to recognize the UPOV minimum standards for the protection of plant varieties, see above notes 77, 83–85 and accompanying text, even it explicitly states that 'Nothing in this Article shall be interpreted to limit any rights that farmers have to save, use, exchange and sell farm-saved seed/propagating material, subject to national law and as appropriate.' See generally Brush, above, at 305–309.

meager financial resources, for two reasons. First, even in industrialized countries PVP certificates have relatively low or negligible economic value, depending on the scope of the statutory privilege of farmers to save and replant seeds of protected varieties.[102] Secondly, modern breeding programs are increasingly dependent on the use of 'elite' breeding lines that are several generations removed from farmers' varieties, thus making it difficult to estimate the contribution that a single landrace or collection makes to the value of a modern variety.[103]

C. Development of Harmonized International Approaches to the Legal Protection of TK

Suggestions for developing a harmonized international approach to the legal protection of TK have taken three forms. First, are a variety of suggestions for modifying international patent and/or plant variety standards to require, as a condition of acquiring or enforcing patents or PVP rights, that the applicant or rights holder disclose the source of any genetic resources and/or TK relied upon in developing the relevant invention or plant variety and provide evidence of prior informed consent (PIC) of the relevant source countries, communities and/or individuals.[104] Secondly, are a variety of more ambitious suggestions for creating an entirely new, *sui generis* form of IP protection for TK, somewhat analogous to the 1996 EU decision to create a new, *sui generis* form of IP protection for databases.[105] Thirdly, are suggestions modeled on the recently adopted hybrid form of facilitated access to plant genetic resources

---

[102] Id. at 310–311.

[103] Id. at 311. An international system requiring documentation of the origin of genetic resources used in plant breeding and in developing patented plant varieties would ameliorate this problem. Articles 12 and 13 of the FAO International Treaty, above note 9, seek to promote the establishment of such an international system by requiring that all plant genetic resources to which the FAO International Treaty applies be transferred subject to a material transfer agreement that recognizes an obligation to share monetary and other benefits of commercialization of products that incorporate materials accessed through the Multilateral System established by the FAO International Treaty. A disclosure of origin and prior informed consent requirement, discussed below notes 101–108 and accompanying text, would also promote the establishment of such a system.

[104] See generally Sarnoff, Joshua D. and Carlos M. Correa (2006), *Analysis of Options for Implementing Disclosure of Origin Requirements in Intellectual Property Applications*, New York: United Nations Publications. See also McManis (2004), *Fitting TK into Existing IP Regimes*, above note 72, 469–474; Carvalho (2007), above note 52, 249–257.

[105] See generally McManis (2004), *Fitting TK into Existing IP Regimes*, above note 72, 474–478; Carvalho (2007), above note 52, 258–261.

for food and agriculture, proprietary protection for improved plant varieties (including at least some landraces embodying TAK), and mandatory benefit-sharing, embodied in the FAO International Treaty for Plant Genetic Resources for Food and Agriculture (ITPGRFA).

The principal difficulty with the first approach is that requiring disclosure of source and evidence of PIC as a condition for *acquiring* patent protection is arguably inconsistent with the TRIPS Agreement and would thus require a revision of TRIPS.[106] Notwithstanding the recent success in revising the TRIPS compulsory licensing requirements,[107] it is highly unlikely that the industrialized world will agree to the incorporation into TRIPS of such a condition for acquiring patent rights, for two reasons. First, such a requirement would impose on patent offices a crushing burden to evaluate the sufficiency of disclosures on potentially large numbers of patent applications with respect to matters about which patent offices have no particular expertise.[108] Secondly, a majority of issued patents ultimately turn out to be worthless, and would thus not generate any economic benefits in any event.[109]

A more nuanced version of the disclosure of source and PIC requirement is to make it a condition for the *enforcement* of an otherwise valid patent or PVP certificate, by analogy to the well-established equitable patent defense of unclean hands, which would thus avoid any conflict with the requirements of the TRIPS Agreement.[110] While the appropriate disclosures could be required as a part of the application process, the sufficiency of those disclosures would be evaluated by courts, not patent offices, and only upon issuance of an otherwise valid patent or certificate having sufficient value that the right holder is seeking to enforce it through infringement proceedings. The de facto penalty for inadequate initial disclosure of source and/or PIC would be that, as a condition for enforcing an otherwise valid and clearly valuable IP right, the right holder would first be required to retroactively negotiate a benefit sharing agreement with any relevant source country, communities, and/or individuals from whom PIC originally should have been obtained.[111] The primary limita-

---

106 See de Carvalho, Nuno Pires (2000), 'Requiring Disclosure of the Origin of Genetic Resources and Prior Informed Consent in Patent Applications Without Infringing the TRIPS Agreement: The Problem and the Solution', 2 *Wash. U. J. L & Pol'y* 371. See also Carvalho (2007), above note 52, 251–255.

107 See above notes 14–15 and accompanying text.

108 See McManis (2004), *Fitting TK into Existing IP Regimes*, above note 72, 471.

109 Id. To transform this disclosure of origin and PIC requirement into a binding universal legal norm, however, it should eventually be incorporated into the TRIPS Agreement.

110 See Carvalho (2007), above note 52, 255–257.

111 See McManis (2004), *Fitting TK into Existing IP Regimes*, above note 72, 471–472,

tion on this form of TK protection is that it assumes the ability to define and identify those TK or genetic resource holders from whom PIC must be obtained.

While much international attention has been given to proposals to create a new, *sui generis* form of IP protection for TK, the history of efforts to develop *sui generis* forms of IP protection, including the recent experience of the EU in creating *sui generis* database protection, does not bode well for the success of this effort, for two reasons. First, *sui generis* proposals tend to unleash intense political lobbying on the part of a narrow class of interested stakeholders, and the outcome is thus likely to be more a product of the relative political clout of the various stakeholders than on what is actually in the public interest.[112] Secondly, even where political clout does not wholly determine the outcome, cobbling together hybrid IP systems by randomly combining elements of patent and copyright protection may well fail to calibrate the cost of acquiring protection with the resulting value of the rights bestowed.[113] Either the cost is too high, and the rights turn out to be worthless,[114] or the cost is too low in light of the private benefits bestowed, and the public winds up paying a subsidy to rightholders without any commensurate benefit to the public.[115]

A third international approach to TK protection is illustrated by the recently adopted FAO ITPGRFA, which envisions a hybrid system, ensuring 'facilitated access' to (that is, no IP protection on) plant genetic resources in the precise form received into the Multilateral System, but also ensuring the development of both public and proprietary improved plant varieties based on plant genetic resources from the Multilateral System, and mandatory benefit sharing with respect to commercially developed plant varieties.[116] These benefits are to be deposited

112 McManis (2004), *Fitting TK into Existing IP Regimes*, above note 72, at 474–475.

113 Id. at 475–476.

114 This is the case with respect to US plant variety protection. See McManis (2005), *Balanced Co-existence of Patent and Plant Breeders' Rights*, above note 83, 71–72.

115 This is arguably the case with respect to the EU's new *sui generis* form of protection for databases, discussed above note 57 and accompanying text. See generally 'DG Internal Market and Services Working Paper: First evaluation of Directive 96/9/EC on the legal protection of databases' (12 December 2005), available at http://ec.europa.eu/internal_market/copyright/docs/databases/evaluation_report_en.pdf (last visited 10 July 2009). Based on ten years of experience under Directive 96/9/EC, this Working Paper concludes that the evidence thus far casts doubt on the necessity of providing 'sui generis' protection for databases to ensure a thriving database industry and discusses four possible options: (1) Repeal the whole Directive; (2) withdraw the 'sui generis' right; (3) amend the 'sui generis' right; and (4) maintain the status quo.

116 See generally Brush, above note 101.

into an appropriate mechanism, such as a Trust Account, which the Governing Body can utilize for purposes of implementing the ITPGRFA,[117] which presumably includes not only compensating identifiable TAK holders but also subsidizing traditional farming practices that contribute genetic resources to the Multilateral System, thus ameliorating the problem of defining and identifying specific TAK holders.[118]

D. Conclusions

Given the foregoing difficulties attending the various non-uniform country (or region)-specific approaches to TK and TCE protection, and similar difficulties attending two of the three suggested harmonized international approaches to TK and TCE protection, it would appear that the most effective way to legally protect TK and TCEs is through existing systems of IPRs and the 'hybrid' FAO system of facilitated access to and sharing of benefits arising out of the commercial use of plant genetic resources for food and agriculture, supplemented by a modification of the TRIPS Agreement to require the disclosure of origin and evidence of prior informed consent to use such traditional knowledge and/or genetic resources as a condition for enforcing an otherwise valid patent that is derived from such knowledge and/or resources. Such a requirement would help ensure that the grant of IP protection will promote, rather than thwart, the equitable sharing of benefits arising out of the use of genetic resources and associated traditional knowledge. While this approach admittedly fails to protect TK and TCEs holistically, may involve substantial transaction costs in securing and enforcing such rights, and may thus require the development of a corps of *pro bono* IP lawyers in order to be effective,[119] it nevertheless avoids the most intractable aspects of the other suggested scenarios for securing legal protection for TK and TCEs.

If a *sui generis* solution to TK and TCE protection is pursued, it should be formulated with an awareness of the practical definitional and conceptual problems that will inevitably arise with respect to (1) the subject matter to be protected; (2) the scope of exclusive rights to be granted for that subject matter

---

117 FAO ITPGRFA, above note 2, Articles 13.2(d)ii) and 19.3(f).

118 See generally Guerin-McManus, Marianne, Kent C. Nnadozie and Sarah A. Laird (2002), 'Sharing financial benefits: trust funds for biodiversity prospecting', in Laird, above note 73, 333–359.

119 See, for example, Gollin, Michael A (2007), 'Answering the Call: Public Interest Intellectual Property Advisors (PIIPA)' and McManis, Charles R. (2007), 'Answering the Call: The Intellectual Property and Business Formation Legal Clinic at Washington University' in McManis, *Biodiversity and the Law*, above note 51, 441, 468, who respectively discuss an existing network of *pro bono* IP lawyers and an existing IP legal clinic.

and the limitations on same; (3) the standards for claiming ownership; and (4) the rules governing co-ownership and resolution of disputes among co-owners. Before international agencies and national governments embark on such an ambitious and controversial project, however, it might well be preferable to attempt a more modest, yet theoretically well-founded revision of the existing IP system, such as requiring the disclosure of origin of genetic resources and/or traditional knowledge relied on and evidence of prior informed consent as a condition of enforcing an otherwise valid patent or plant variety certificate. Such a modification has the virtue of being relatively easy to implement and administer, to say nothing of holding the potential for actually generating economic benefits to be equitably shared with traditional knowledge holders.

14. A comment on 'Human rights as a constraint on intellectual property rights: the case of patent and plant variety protection rights, genetic resources and traditional knowledge'

Martin J. Adelman*

In a thoughtful analysis of various issues, both legal and moral, relating to traditional knowledge and genetic resources (Chapter 13), Professor McManis has proposed a major change to patent systems of the world, 'requiring the disclosure of origin of genetic resources and/or traditional knowledge relied on and evidence of prior informed consent as a condition of enforcing an otherwise valid patent or plant variety certificate'. He does this even though he seems to recognize that it is fundamentally unfair for nations that have not enforced patent rights in the past to benefit from the extremely valuable information which the patent system has placed in the public domain through expired patents while at the same time seeking to be compensated for the use of its genetic resources which in the eyes of the patent system are also in the public domain. The same may be said for traditional knowledge to the extent that it is not maintained secret in the conventional trade secret law sense.

It should also be remembered that everyone benefits from patented technology as it is technology that embodies an inventive leap over the prior art. It may be used for a fee during the life of the patents covering it and then it passes completely into the public domain. Further, Professor McManis recognizes in his text at footnote 47 of his chapter that the patent system is a morally sound system which presents future generations with patented technology free of charge with the understanding that they will do the same for their future

* Martin J Adelman is Theodore and James Pedas Family Professor of Intellectual Property and Technology Law; Co-Director of the Intellectual Property Law Program; Co-Director of the Dean Dinwoodey Center for Intellectual Property Studies, George Washington University Law School.

generations. His proposal is thus fundamentally unfair and burdensome, but as I shall point out it is also unworkable.

In the United States an applicant for a patent must, either in the specification or in a separate paper filed with the USPTO, disclose the closest prior art to his claimed invention unless the examiner indicates that he is aware of that art. Hence if an applicant is informed of certain traditional knowledge that is the closest prior art, it must be disclosed. Similarly, if the genetic resources constitute the closest prior art, the technical details of those resources must be disclosed as they are prior art. The failure to disclose the closest prior art or even prior art which a reasonable examiner would consider important can lead to the inability to enforce the patent under the equitable doctrine known as 'inequitable conduct'.

Now if Professor McManis's proposal were adopted, were there any question about whether some traditional knowledge or genetic resources constituted the closest prior art, litigation would center on first determining what is the closest prior art and then, if it is traditional knowledge or genetic resources, the acquisition of them would have to be examined. Hence any attempt to enforce the resulting patent would require the court to examine the circumstances under which the applicant learned of the traditional knowledge or acquired the genetic resources even though the court rules that the applicant made an invention that was not obvious over that art and otherwise satisfied the utility and enablement requirements. This rule would impose substantial litigation costs on the patentee, but it would be limited in the end to additional disclosure regarding prior art that must be reviewed by the USPTO although not for the information that would now be required.

However, I doubt if this rule would satisfy advocates of a disclosure rule such as proposed by Professor McManis because there are many inventions that flow from other inventions that themselves could flow from genetic resources or traditional knowledge. After all a cascade of inventions might be based in whole or in part on the original use of genetic resources or traditional knowledge, but from a patent law point of view the first inventor creates prior art that is likely to be the closest prior art to an invention stimulated by the first invention. Let us take for example a quasi-fictional example from the field of steroid chemistry, the most heavily patented field in the early post-war period. The facts of the steroid story are modified so as to better bring out the legal implications of the McManis disclosure proposal.

A number of natural steroids were available at the end of the Second World War at very high cost. These included cortisone, progesterone and testosterone. The need was great for low cost steroids and the economic potential for anyone who could find a way to make such steroids cheaper was very large. Chemists knew that if someone could find a cheap source of a known natural steroid such as diosgenin, it was likely that an inventive chemist could develop a process for converting it into progesterone. Around this time a leading chemist, Dr Russell Marker, was spending a summer in Mexico in the state of Veracruz near Orizaba amonst the native peoples of Veracruz. These people were very muscular and Dr. Marker asked why this was so. The Veracruz people explained to him that they believed that it was their diet, a diet that considered primarily of wild yams unique to the state of Veracruz. Dr Marker speculated that these wild yams must contain a large quantity of a steroid such as diosgenin, known to exist but only in small quantities in plants and known to have anabolic properties. At the end of his vacation he rushed home to his laboratory in Pennsylvania and ran a number of chemical tests of the large wild yam that he took from Veracruz. Sure enough this yam was about 10 per cent diosgenin. Moreover, he realized that now he could use this yam to seed a field of yams. After some investigation he determined that the soil and climate in southeastern Texas was similar to that of Veracruz. He made a deal with a large landowner in that area to develop a crop of Mexican yams. This was successful beyond his wildest dreams so now he had a cheap source of diosgenin. He then went to work in his laboratory and within four months developed a landmark process for converting diosgenin to progesterone. This process is now known as the 'Marker degradation'.

Dr Marker promptly filed for patents around the world on his process for making progesterone. He then widely publicized his process and the key fact that Mexican yams were the key to cheap diosgenin which his process would make into cheap progesterone. After he filed his patent applications he learned that a Japanese chemist in the 1930s had stumbled on Mexican yams and published a short article in an obscure Japanese chemical journal disclosing that Mexican yams contained a large amount of diosgenin. Immediately after learning of this Japanese publication, he informed all the relevant patent offices of this close prior art. Shortly thereafter Syntex Inc. was formed in Houston, Texas to exploit the diosgenin in wild Mexican yams which were now grown in Texas. Syntex promptly purchased all of Dr Marker's patent rights and began to experiment with ways to make use of the cheap progesterone it could produce with the Marker degradation process. It particularly was interested in making cortisone, which the Mayo Clinic had found was very useful in the treatment of rheumatoid arthritis, but was practically unavailable to patients because of the cost. Cortisone has an oxygen atom at the 11th carbon, an absolute requirement for biological activity. Unfortunately there were then and still today no known natural sources for starting materials that contain that feature. In 1952 two Upjohn biochemists, Peterson and Murray, discovered how to introduce this crucial oxygen atom by fermentation of progesterone with the mold Aspergillus nigercans, a microorganism which is unique to the soil of northern Italy. The biology of the mold Aspergillus nigercans was described by an Italian microbiologist around 1905 in his published doctoral dissertation, a dissertation that Peterson and Murray had never read. At Upjohn Peterson and Murray were working with this mold to see if it would produce a useful antibiotic. Alas, it did not, but when fed progesterone for dinner, surprisingly it converted the progesterone into cortisone. Naturally Upjohn promptly filed for patent protection throughout the world on this important discovery and when combined with Synthex's progesterone provided the world with inexpensive cortisone.

It doesn't stop at this point. After the discovery of the advantage of deleting the 19th carbon to create 19-norprogesterone because it produced a stronger effect, Djerassi and Rosenkranz working for Syntex invented norethisterone (norethindrone or 19-nor-17α-ethynyltestosterone). Norethisterone is the primary ingredient in the most popular version of the pill that stormed the world in 1961 and made Djerassi world famous and very rich and Rosenkranz very rich as well. Of course the story of the pill doesn't stop with Djerassi and Rosenkranz. Dr Herchel Smith, the chemist who endowed the patent law chairs at the University of Cambridge and Queen Mary, took norethisterone and with great difficulty put an ethyl group rather than the usual methyl group provided by nature at the 13th carbon to dramatically improve norethisterone. This compound is known as norgestrel, the most common form of modified progesterone used in the pill even today.

At the end of the day all of these important inventions described above were enabled by the discovery of large amounts of diosgenin in Mexican yams by Dr Marker and the work of the mold Aspergillus nigercans in inserting an oxygen atom on the 11th carbon of the steroid ring. Yet none of this amounted to the closest prior art with respect to any patent. Hence, no disclosure of origin would be needed under the McManis disclosure rule. The above shows that limiting the McManis disclosure rule to the closest prior art would not provide the protection for genetic resources and traditional knowledge which its proponents seek. Of course any other rule is unworkable.

It is quite obvious that all the proposals for altering the patent system to provide help to enforce claims based on genetic resources or traditional knowledge are unworkable and misguided. Proponents of such disclosure should be told that when they agree to pay for all of the once patented knowledge that is in the public domain and will provide patents for such knowledge, then a payment can be arranged for the Mexican yam or the mold Aspergillus nigercans.

Index